MW01506111

Democracy's Resilience to Populism's Threat

The recent global wave of populist governments, which culminated in Donald Trump's victory in 2016, has convinced many observers that populism is a grave threat to democracy. In his new book, Kurt Weyland critiques recent scholarship for focusing too closely on cases where populist leaders have crushed democracy, and instead turns to the many cases where would-be populist authoritarians have failed to overthrow democracy. Through a systematic comparative analysis of thirty populist chief executives in Latin America and Europe over the last four decades, Weyland reveals that populist leaders can only destroy democracy under special, restrictive conditions. Left-wing populists suffocate democracy only when benefiting from huge revenue windfalls, whereas right-wing populists must perform the heroic feat of resolving acute, severe crises to achieve this. Because many populist chief executives do not face these propitious conditions, Weyland proves that despite populism's threat, democracy remains resilient.

Kurt Weyland is the Mike Hogg Professor in Liberal Arts in the Department of Government at the University of Texas, Austin. He has studied populism across Latin America over the last thirty-five years. He is the author of *The Politics of Market Reform in Fragile Democracies* (2002), *Making Waves* (2014), and *Assault on Democracy* (2021).

Democracy's Resilience to Populism's Threat

Countering Global Alarmism

KURT WEYLAND

University of Texas, Austin

CAMBRIDGE
UNIVERSITY PRESS

Shaftesbury Road, Cambridge CB2 8EA, United Kingdom

One Liberty Plaza, 20th Floor, New York, NY 10006, USA

477 Williamstown Road, Port Melbourne, VIC 3207, Australia

314–321, 3rd Floor, Plot 3, Splendor Forum, Jasola District Centre, New Delhi – 110025, India

103 Penang Road, #05–06/07, Visioncrest Commercial, Singapore 238467

Cambridge University Press is part of Cambridge University Press & Assessment, a department of the University of Cambridge.

We share the University's mission to contribute to society through the pursuit of education, learning and research at the highest international levels of excellence.

www.cambridge.org
Information on this title: www.cambridge.org/9781009432467

DOI: 10.1017/9781009432504

© Kurt Weyland 2024

This publication is in copyright. Subject to statutory exception and to the provisions of relevant collective licensing agreements, no reproduction of any part may take place without the written permission of Cambridge University Press & Assessment.

First published 2024

Printed in the United Kingdom by TJ Books Limited, Padstow, Cornwall

A catalogue record for this publication is available from the British Library

Library of Congress Cataloging-in-Publication Data
NAMES: Weyland, Kurt, author.
TITLE: Democracy's resilience to populism's threat : countering global alarmism / Kurt Weyland, University of Texas, Austin.
DESCRIPTION: New York, NY : Cambridge University Press, 2024. | Includes bibliographical references and index.
IDENTIFIERS: LCCN 2023025035 (print) | LCCN 2023025036 (ebook) | ISBN 9781009432467 (hardback) | ISBN 9781009432504 (ebook)
SUBJECTS: LCSH: Populism. | Democracy. | Right-wing extremists – Latin America. | Left-wing extremists – Latin America. | Right-wing extremists – Europe. | Right-wing extremists – United States. | Comparative government.
CLASSIFICATION: LCC JC423 .W447 2024 (print) | LCC JC423 (ebook) | DDC 320.56/62–dc23/eng/20230712
LC record available at https://lccn.loc.gov/2023025035
LC ebook record available at https://lccn.loc.gov/2023025036

ISBN 978-1-009-43246-7 Hardback

Cambridge University Press & Assessment has no responsibility for the persistence or accuracy of URLs for external or third-party internet websites referred to in this publication and does not guarantee that any content on such websites is, or will remain, accurate or appropriate.

Contents

List of Tables		*page* vii
Acknowledgments		ix
1	The Populist Threat to Democracy	1
2	How Institutional Constraints and Conjunctural Opportunities Condition Populism's Threat to Democracy	30
3	Neoliberal and Right-Wing Populism in Latin America	74
4	"Bolivarian" and Left-Wing Populism in Latin America	117
5	Right-Wing and Traditionalist Populism in Europe	159
6	Right-Wing Populism in the USA: Trump in Comparative Perspective	196
7	Conclusion: Theoretical and Comparative Implications	227
References		261
Index		301

Tables

1 Conditions for the suffocation of democracy
  by populist leaders   *page* 63
2 Listing of populist governments (and location of case studies)   65

Acknowledgments

While advancing an argument that I have gradually developed over the last few years, this book draws on the ample research about populism that I have conducted over more than three decades, since witnessing the meteoric rise and quick fall of neoliberal populist Fernando Collor de Mello in Brazil from 1989 to 1992 (the subject of my very first publication: Weyland 1993). Off and on during this long time period, I collected enormous heaps of documents, gathered tons of survey data, and interviewed innumerable high-level people involved in the politics of populism, including Collor himself. Moreover, I presented bits and pieces of this research at so many talks, workshops, and conferences – and in subsequent publications – that I cannot possibly remember all the commentators and discussants.

A probably incomplete list of informants and colleagues to whom I owe gratitude include the following people – and please forgive me if my aging brain inadvertently omitted your name: Barry Ames, Zoltan Barany, David Bartlett, Michael Bernhard, Daniel Brinks, Jason Brownlee, Thomas Burt Wolf, Maxwell Cameron, David and Ruth Collier, Michael Conniff, Michael Coppedge, Eduardo Dargent, Carlos de la Torre, Zachary Elkins, Steve Ellner, Venelin Ganev, Marco Garrido, François Gelineau, John Gerring, Gary Goertz, Carol Graham, Kenneth Greene, Stephan Haggard, Frances Hagopian, Jonathan Hartlyn, Kirk Hawkins, Bert Hoffmann, Evelyne Huber, Bonn Juego, Robert Kaufman, Frances Lee, Fabrice Lehoucq, Jonatán Lemus, Steve Levitsky, Juan Pablo Luna, Patricia Maclachlan, Raúl Madrid, Thais Maingon, Scott Mainwaring, Isabela Mares, Hiroshi Matsushita, Rose McDermott, Marcelo Vianna Estevão de Moraes, Gerardo Munck, Yusuke Murakami, María Victoria Murillo, Marcos Novaro, Ziya Öniş, the late María Matilde Ollier, Philip Oxhorn, Vicente Palermo, Aldo Panfichi, Aníbal Pérez-Liñán, German Petersen Cortés, John Polga-Hecimovich, Timothy Power, Karen Remmer, Matthew Rhodes-Purdy, Fernando Rosenblatt, Cristóbal Rovira

Kaltwasser, Peter Rudolf, Wojciech Sadurski, Cynthia Sanborn, Daron Shaw, William Smith, Richard Snyder, Marcel Domingos Solimeo, Zeynep Somer-Topcu, Bartholomew Sparrow, Ben Stanley, Martín Tanaka, Mark Thompson, Daniel Treisman, Diego Vega, the late Francisco Weffort, Friedrich Welsch, Carol Wise, and Christopher Wlezien.

I thank Rachel Blaifeder and the Cambridge team, especially Claire Sissen, Jadyn Fauconier-Herry, Sunantha Ramamoorthy, and copy-editor Dan Harding, for their great professionalism and efficiency in shepherding this book through the review and production process. Moreover, I am very grateful to the two expert reviewers, who provided a wealth of critical comments and constructive suggestions. I tried very hard to address all of this feedback and use it to improve the volume.

Three people deserve special thanks: Andrew Stein, who over so many years has generously supplied me with a wealth of comments and insights, documents and materials, data and surveys; Kenneth Roberts, my former Stanford classmate, with whom I have discussed the politics of populism on innumerable occasions in many different settings over the decades, and whose important work on the topic has been highly influential on my own thinking; and Wendy Hunter, my essential writing coach, most attentive sounding board, toughest critic, greatest support – and much, much more – *¡Muchas gracias por acompañárme en esta larga aventura!*

This book is dedicated to my mother, Else Weyland, whose fundamental life maxims have guided me in so many important ways.

I

The Populist Threat to Democracy

Populism has disturbed and disrupted democracies for decades, in various areas of the world. But for much of this time, it was seen as a transitional or residual problem that would soon pass. In the region most affected by populism – Latin America – various personalistic plebiscitarian leaders had won government power since the 1930s and had enacted substantial socioeconomic and political transformations.[1] Yet observers regarded this upsurge of populism in the mid-twentieth century as a transitional stage of development. Newly mobilized mass groupings were falling for charismatic *caudillos*, but these irresponsible, unaccountable presidents would soon disappoint people's excessive hopes. As the citizenry learned from these bad experiences, populism would quickly lose appeal; advancing modernization would bring democratic maturation (Germani 1978).

By contrast to Latin America, where personalistic plebiscitarian leaders managed to win majority support, in Europe populism emerged as a fringe phenomenon. Diehard movements hailing from the radical right long remained marginal and looked like a moribund remnant of resentful nostalgia tinged with paleo-fascism, which generational replacement, ongoing post-modernization, and liberal value change would surely eliminate. For these reasons, early observers saw the different regional versions of populism as a temporary problem or a limited nuisance, rather than a serious threat to democracy. Developmental progress, political learning, and democratic institution building would sooner or later contain and overcome its political fallout and forestall or limit any damage to liberal pluralism.

---

[1] For stylistic reasons, I use "personalistic plebiscitarian leadership" interchangeably with the term populism. Later, I explain this notion, which is central to my political-strategic definition of populism.

Against all expectations, however, populism refused to disappear. In Latin America, one wave of populism followed upon the other. After the military regimes of the 1960s and 1970s had suppressed classical populism à la Juan Perón (1946–55) and Getúlio Vargas (1951–54), a new type of populism arose in the restored democracies of the 1980s and 1990s. Interestingly, several of these leaders proved populism's typical adaptability by promoting market-oriented adjustment programs, which reversed the protectionist state interventionism spearheaded by their classical forebears (Roberts 1995; Weyland 1996). Soon thereafter, personalistic plebiscitarian leadership took another surprising twist: Left-wing populists came to contest this turn to neoliberalism and won massive support with a return to state interventionism in the early 2000s (Weyland, Madrid, and Hunter 2010; Levitsky and Roberts 2011). Continuing this dizzying slalom, in recent years a new, culturally conservative type of right-wing populist emerged (Kestler 2022), most prominently Jair Bolsonaro in Brazil (2019–22) (Hunter and Power 2019).

Thus, while each version of populism did remain a temporary phenomenon, populism as a political strategy proved irrepressible and recurring; and through its rapid mutations, it demonstrated its adaptability, which boosted its chances of electoral success. With their skill in taking advantage of any opportunity and win power under variegated circumstances, personalistic plebiscitarian leaders became a frequent threat to democracy in Latin America. Just like Argentina's Perón had done in the 1940s and 1950s, neoliberal populist Alberto Fujimori in Peru (1990–2000) as well as anti-neoliberal populist Hugo Chávez in Venezuela (1999–2013) suffocated democracy and imposed competitive-authoritarian regimes; and right-winger Nayib Bukele in El Salvador (2019–present) is pushing as hard for "eternal" self-perpetuation as left-winger Evo Morales (2006–19) did in Bolivia. In fact, with the normative delegitimation and international prohibition of military coups in Latin America, populism now constitutes the most serious danger to liberal pluralism in the region.

As populism defied expectations by continuing to haunt much of Latin America, it achieved an even more surprising feat in Europe by starting to win greater support and emerging from its extremist ghetto (Akkerman, De Lange, and Rooduijn 2016; more skeptical recently: Bartels 2023: chap. 6). Indeed, rejuvenated right-wingers or personalistic plebiscitarian leaders of a conservative orientation eventually managed to capture government power even in the highly developed, solidly democratic western half of the Old Continent, as in Italy after 1994 (Newell 2019) and Austria in 1999. In more and more countries, populism turned into a serious competitor, for instance by advancing to presidential runoff elections in France in 2002, 2017, and 2022. And in Eastern Europe, many new democracies that had embraced political liberalism with such enthusiasm in 1989 experienced a backlash that brought growing numbers of populists to power (Krastev and Holmes 2019: chap. 1). Shockingly, some of them squeezed or even suffocated democracy, most strikingly and consequentially in the poster children of the post-communist transition: Poland and especially Hungary.

To achieve this increasing electoral success, Europe's populist movements and parties tried hard to leave their paleo- or neofascist origins behind. They recruited fresh, young leaders and employed more attractive appeals by raising new issues that mainstream parties did not want to touch, such as mass immigration, seen as a problem by substantial segments of the citizenry. In these ways, personalistic plebiscitarian leaders left marginality behind and put mainstream parties on the defensive, challenging their dominance of the electoral arena. By invoking and normalizing widespread fears and resentments, populist challengers induced some establishment formations to modify their own message, while drawing voters away from those parties that refused to undertake such opportunistic moves. With their unsavory yet savvy campaigns, illiberal, anti-pluralist leaders turned into effective contenders for chief executive office, threatening to undermine the quality of democracy, if not jeopardize its survival.

These risks became highly acute and salient in 2016 with the shocking Brexit referendum and the stunning electoral triumph of Donald Trump. If populist movements could achieve such unexpected success in two of the oldest, strongest democracies in the world, whose unshakable consolidation nobody had hitherto doubted, then a fundamental reassessment seemed to be in order. Had observers seriously underestimated the danger posed by populism? Democracy suddenly looked fragile and precarious.

After all, populist election victories raised the urgent question whether the "really existing" regimes of liberal pluralism were being weakened by oligarchic ossification, technocratic detachment, and the resulting representational deficits (Mounk 2018). How grave was their vulnerability to attack? Indeed, liberal democracy has an inherent weakness and potentially fatal flaw: Populist leaders who win government power can, in principle, exploit their electoral mandate and institutional attributions and resolutely concentrate power, distorting and perhaps asphyxiating democracy (Levitsky and Ziblatt 2018). Would headstrong Trump, for instance, bend or even break the USA's corroded checks and balances, impose his will while disrespecting judicial constraints, and use all kinds of tricks to engineer a reelection victory? Would US democracy, already hollowed out by deepening political and affective polarization, totter or even crumble under the brash populist's energetic assault (Ginsburg and Huq 2018b; Graber, Levinson, and Tushnet 2018; Mounk 2018; Sunstein 2018; Mettler and Lieberman 2020; Lieberman, Mettler, and Roberts 2022)?

POPULISM'S INHERENT THREAT TO DEMOCRACY

The advance of populism in Latin America and Europe during the early twenty-first century, which helped to feed a global wave of populism that reached Asia as well (Mizuno and Phongpaichit 2009; Kenny 2018), was problematic and worrisome because populism by nature stands in tension with liberal pluralism and democracy (Urbinati 2019; Sadurski 2022; Issacharoff 2023). This danger arises from the core of populism, namely personalistic plebiscitarian leadership, which is anti-institutional, polarizing, and confrontational. This book adopts a political-strategic definition, which is best suited for assessing populism's effective impact by examining the political and institutional repercussions of populist governance; the section on "Central Concepts" later in this chapter comprehensively discusses and justifies this definitional approach.

The political-strategic definition conceives of populism as revolving around personalistic, usually charismatic leadership that is sustained by direct, unmediated, uninstitutionalized connections to a heterogeneous, amorphous, and largely unorganized mass of followers (Weyland 2001, 2017, 2021b; Carrión 2022: 9–14; Kenny 2023, forthcoming). Personalistic leaders are dominant and domineering, surround themselves with personal loyalists, and run their movements at will. They attract their main support from followers who fervently believe in their redemptive mission – a direct emotional connection that avoids intermediation and organization and is averse to institutionalization, which would supplant total dedication to the charismatic savior with a "mechanical" relationship (Andrews-Lee 2021). Consequently, personalistic plebiscitarian leadership constitutes the main axis of populism.

Both of these principal features – personalism and plebiscitarianism – stand at cross-purposes with liberal pluralism. Personalistic leaders are strong-willed and constantly seek to boost their own autonomy and power. No wonder that they see liberal institutions, especially checks and balances, as obstacles to overcome. They try to undermine or suspend the separation of powers by imposing their unchallengeable dominance and hegemony. They try to capture all independent institutions and suffocate oppositional forces. Where they succeed, they erode political liberty, skew electoral competition, and engineer their own self-perpetuation, for years if not decades. With its anti-institutional bent, populism is pushing democracy toward backsliding; if it manages to operate unchecked, it moves toward competitive authoritarianism.

Plebiscitarianism reinforces and exacerbates these deleterious tendencies. By basing their quest for and exercise of power on direct, unmediated, and uninstitutionalized connections to amorphous, heterogeneous, not very well-organized masses of followers, personalistic leaders lack a solid base of political sustenance. Because their support is potentially fickle, they try to strengthen it through deliberate confrontation and polarization. By turning politics into a war against supposedly craven and dangerous enemies, they want to induce their followers to rally around the leader and develop fervent emotional attachments. This conflictual strategy, however, entails disrespect for tolerance and pluralism. It turns democratic competitors, who have legitimate rights to win elections and then govern, into total foes that must be combated with all means and definitely blocked from gaining control of the state. Claiming the monopolistic representation of "the will of the people," while denouncing their opponents as corrupt, selfish elites, populist leaders employ an ample set of machinations and tricks to preclude any alternation in power – suppressing political competitiveness, a core principle of democracy (Schmitter 1983: 887–91).

With these pernicious tactics, populism poses serious threats to democracy. What makes this risk especially acute is the cunning strategy of personalistic plebiscitarian leaders, who seek to exploit a congenital vulnerability of liberal pluralism: Political freedom protects even those who intend to undermine or abolish this freedom. Accordingly, where populist leaders triumph in democratic elections, they can use their legitimately won attributions to dismantle democracy from the inside; and they can employ formally legal mechanisms for this illegitimate purpose. In institutional settings that are particularly open to change, power-hungry populists have strangled liberal pluralism without violating any laws or constitutional provisions, as Viktor Orbán (2010–present) managed to do in Hungary (Scheppele 2018, 549–52; Körösényi, Illés, and Gyulai 2020: 79–90). Where the institutional framework is firmer, populist presidents can appeal to popular sovereignty and invoke their electoral mandate to push aside legal obstacles and engineer power concentration in para-legal ways (Brewer-Carías 2010; Weyland 2020: 392–99).

Because populism inherently challenges democracy, its wave-like advance in the early third millennium seemed to endanger liberal pluralism in a wide range of countries. In fact, personalistic plebiscitarian leaders have asphyxiated a number of Latin American democracies over the decades; more recently, they have done increasing damage in Europe, particularly the post-communist East; and in 2016, Donald Trump won office in the paragon of liberal democracy, whose institutions had been designed to forestall the rise of demagogic outsiders. If even this "least likely case" fell to populism, where was liberal pluralism still safe? Would democracy crumble under the pressures of personalistic plebiscitarian leaders?

HOW SEVERE IS THE POPULIST THREAT?

The shock of Trump's election, the most striking instance of populism's worldwide spread, unleashed an outpouring of concern and fear about democracy's fate, indicated in the black cover, scary title, and bestselling success of Levitsky and Ziblatt's (2018) *How Democracies Die*. Many other volumes painted dire pictures as well (Ginsburg and Huq 2018b; Graber, Levinson, and Tushnet 2018; Mounk 2018; Sunstein 2018; Mettler and Lieberman 2020). Indeed, some commentators went so far as to raise the specter of "tyranny" (Snyder 2017) and even "fascism" (Connolly 2017; Stanley 2018).

Arguably, however, these initial observers were overly impressed by the fearsome possibilities that populist agency can, in principle, hold; shell-shocked, they did not examine how likely such a deleterious outcome was. They highlighted "*how* democracies die," but did not analyze under what conditions democracies actually die, and how easy or difficult it is to kill them. Indeed, the focus on the possibilities of democratic death made observers overestimate the probabilities of democracy's downfall. By outlining all the potential ways in which democracies *can* die, scholars suggested that democracy can die rather easily.

This book presents a more balanced picture by systematically assessing the probabilities of democracy's death. The exact risk depends on the conditions under which populist leaders actually manage to impose their hegemony and dismantle liberal pluralism from the inside. For this purpose, I not only examine cases in which this outcome has occurred, as initial observers tended to do (Ginsburg and Huq 2018b; Levitsky and Ziblatt 2018; Kaufman and Haggard 2019), but consider a comprehensive set of populist governments and probe their regime impact:[2] Why did democracy fall in some settings and situations, yet not in many others? This analytical procedure, which avoids the methodological problem of "selection on the dependent variable" (King, Keohane, and Verba 1994: 129–37, 141–49), immediately yields a clear result: Not all populist chief executives managed to sate their power hunger – far from it; instead, democracy survived populist governments in many cases.

In fact, wide-ranging statistical studies find that only in about one-third of cases have populist chief executives done substantial damage to democracy; and they have truly suffocated liberal pluralism only in approximately one-quarter of all instances (Kyle and Mounk 2018: 17; Ruth-Lovell, Lührmann, and Grahn 2019: 9–10).[3] My earlier investigation of thirty cases of personalistic plebiscitarian governance in contemporary Latin America and Europe, the two regions with particularly large numbers of populist governments, yielded an even lower death rate, namely 20 percent (Weyland 2020: 397–99; see also Weyland 2022a: 12–14). Thus, the probability of democracy's downfall, not to speak of its lasting replacement by competitive authoritarianism, has actually not been very high. Instead, liberal pluralism has demonstrated considerable robustness.

Populism's danger has been limited because sustained efforts to asphyxiate democracy have succeeded only under fairly restrictive conditions: The coincidence and intersection of distinctive institutional weaknesses and unusual conjunctural opportunities were necessary prerequisites for the populist strangulation of democracy in Latin America and Europe after the end of the Cold

---

[2] All the populist chief executives examined in this book are men, with one exception, Argentina's Cristina Fernández de Kirchner. With apologies to her, this book therefore uses male pronouns to avoid cumbersome expressions such as "s/he" or the grammatically problematic neosingular "they." See similarly Matovski (2021: 4, n. 3).

[3] Focusing on average effects at the level of statistical aggregates, Kenny (2020: 268–70) finds that populist governments reduce press freedom – but only to a limited extent. In a brand new study, Cole and Schofer (2023: 19, 23, 25) report "substantial" effects, but do not clarify their exact magnitude.

War (Weyland 2020: 399–402). Thus, assaults by personalistic plebiscitarian leaders do not advance easily; populists cannot dismantle democracy at will but depend on favorable preconditions to realize their nefarious designs. This important finding can alleviate recent fears. Populism is far from universally lethal.

Instead, a differentiated picture emerges. Democracy is very safe in advanced industrialized countries such as the USA, where institutional strength and high levels of socioeconomic development cushion against the severe, acute crises that populist leaders can use to win overwhelming mass support. In less consolidated democracies, personalistic plebiscitarian chief executives have greater room for maneuver. But even in systems of middling institutional strength, they still face substantial constraints, which they can shove aside only under unusual circumstances, when they benefit from extraordinary windfalls or – paradoxically – confront exceptional challenges. Overall, then, liberal pluralism displays considerable, albeit differential resilience in facing the threat that populism undoubtedly poses.

MAIN ARGUMENTS

Populism's Threat: Institutions and Conjunctural Factors as Crucial Conditions

This book offers a realistic assessment of the danger arising from populism by systematically analyzing the specific conditions under which personalistic plebiscitarian leaders actually manage to dismantle democracy and install competitive authoritarianism. By demonstrating that this deleterious outcome prevails only under certain restrictive circumstances, the investigation overcomes earlier observers' preoccupation with deleterious *possibilities* and provides an empirically based estimate of real *probabilities*. While possibilities appear open-ended and can therefore look scary, an assessment of probabilities yields much more relevant information about effective risks, which are significantly lower than often feared.

My analysis starts from the political-strategic definition of populism, which revolves around personalistic plebiscitarian leadership. Accordingly, democracy faces the most acute danger where headstrong, overbearing leaders find the greatest room of maneuver, and where unusually strong and broad mass support boosts their political clout and enables them to push through their undemocratic aspirations. By contrast, where populist chief executives encounter firm and resilient constraints, especially an entrenched institutional framework, or where they lack the chance to garner overwhelming popular backing, liberal pluralism has a great deal of immunity against their machinations and depredations.

Heuristically, the political-strategic definition thus suggests two types of factors as crucial preconditions for the populist destruction of democracy. First, some type of institutional weakness is a necessary prerequisite for power-hungry chief executives to establish and cement their hegemony, undermine the partisan opposition, squeeze civil society, and seriously skew the electoral arena: Only brittle fortresses can be breached. Second, because even weak or medium-strong institutions hinder or impede populist assaults, there is a second necessary condition for these power grabs to succeed: Only if personalistic leaders encounter unusual conjunctural opportunities for boosting their plebiscitarian support to sky-high levels can they achieve their undemocratic goals. Under normal circumstances, they may do some damage, but do not command the clout to smother liberal pluralism definitively.

As Chapter 2 explains in depth, institutional weakness in contemporary Europe and Latin America can take three forms. First, the Old Continent's parliamentary systems, with their attenuated separation of powers, are relatively open to legal transformation; consequently, populist prime ministers may manage to disfigure democracy from the inside. Second, many of Latin America's presidential systems have been habituated to para-legal infringements: Transgressive presidents go beyond formal rules, arrogate attributions, and impose changes with impunity, trying hard to push aside objections and opposition from the legislative and judicial branch (Levitsky and Murillo 2009, 2013; Brinks, Levitsky, and Murillo 2019). Third, some Latin American countries have suffered from high instability, with institutional frameworks rocked and battered by serious conflicts, as evident in irregular evictions of presidents or violent coup attempts. Such precarious institutional settings have especially low resilience.

These three types of institutional weakness provide different openings for populist leaders, and they diverge in their degree of institutional debility. High instability makes a democracy particularly fragile, whereas more stable presidential systems constitute the least propitious settings for personalistic plebiscitarian leaders; after all, para-legal impositions provoke considerable resistance and friction. With their attenuated separation of powers, which facilitates the legal asphyxiation of democracy, parliamentary systems are intermediate in this ranking of institutional weakness.

The conjunctural opportunities for boosting plebiscitarian mass support also come in three different types. First, populist chief executives who reap enormous resource windfalls, primarily from voluminous hydrocarbon exports, obtain a flood of revenues that allows for the widespread distribution of enormous benefits; the grateful citizenry reciprocates with intense backing. Thus, exceptionally good times play into the hands of personalistic plebiscitarian leaders. Interestingly, exceptionally bad times *can* have even higher political payoffs. Deep, pressing crises give bold chief executives the chance to avert a catastrophe, lift the population out of worsening misery, and earn especially profound and widespread appreciation. By frontally combating and miraculously overcoming huge problems, the courageous leader glaringly proves his charisma and turns into the heroic savior of the people. Therefore, as the second and third type of conjunctural opportunities, acute, severe economic crises or massive threats to public security can also be crucial for personalistic plebiscitarian chief executives to demonstrate their unique prowess and vault to unchallengeable predominance.

Democracy's fate then depends on the ways in which these three types of institutional weakness and three forms of conjunctural opportunities come together and interact. Interestingly, my study finds three distinctive alignments and patterns, as the next section explains.

Three Narrow Paths toward the Populist Strangulation of Democracy

The limited number of instances in which populist chief executives have in fact destroyed democracy have depended on three distinctive coincidences in which one type of institutional weakness has interacted with a specific combination of conjunctural opportunities. Thus, the necessary conditions for the actual downfall of liberal pluralism have aligned in three different bundles. Accordingly, there have been three different paths along which personalistic plebiscitarian leaders have managed to impose competitive authoritarianism. Interestingly, these different processes of undemocratic involution have largely corresponded to three different types of populism that the expert literature has long distinguished, namely neoliberal populism in Latin America, the subsequent wave of Chávez-style, "Bolivarian" populism in the region, and conservative, traditionalist populism in Europe. As this striking correspondence suggests, my empirically based analysis yields results that are conceptually valid and theoretically meaningful.

What are these three paths and their underlying combinations of necessary conditions? First, populist prime ministers in Europe have managed to take advantage of parliamentarism's openness, with its limited number of institutional veto players, under one condition: If an antecedent economic collapse has discredited the political establishment, partisan veto players have been decimated (cf. Tsebelis 2002), and personalistic leaders have won lopsided parliamentary majorities, which have given them free rein for pursuing their autocratic designs. This process played out quickly in Hungary under Viktor Orbán (2010–present), and along a more sinuous and rockier road in Turkey under Recep Tayyip Erdoğan (2003–present).[4]

Second, populist presidents in Latin American countries subject to paralegal impositions have faced greater constraints, given the separation of powers enshrined in presidentialism. Consequently, they have succeeded in asphyxiating democracy only when encountering a truly unique constellation of conjunctural opportunities, namely a simultaneous double crisis: a devastating economic downturn and a fearsome challenge to public safety.

---

[4] As explained in Chapter 5, Erdoğan faced an additional, extraconstitutional veto player, namely Turkey's historically powerful and coup-prone military.

This extraordinary coincidence of disasters paved the road toward competitive authoritarianism in Peru under Alberto Fujimori (1990–2000) and recently, in a somewhat less drastic manifestation, in El Salvador under Nayib Bukele (2019–present).

Third, high instability facilitates populist assaults on democracy; after all, a tottering house is easier to overthrow. Consequently, the enormous popularity boost emerging from the successful resolution of crises is not required for completing the wrecking job. Instead, in these precarious settings, the massive distribution of benefits enabled by a huge hydrocarbon windfall played the crucial role. Thus, in these battered presidential systems of Latin America, this exogenous factor provided the necessary conjunctural opportunity for personalistic plebiscitarian leaders to promote undemocratic power concentration, as Hugo Chávez did in Venezuela (1999–2013), Evo Morales in Bolivia (2006–19), and Rafael Correa in Ecuador (2007–17).

In sum, my theory emphasizes the crucial importance of combinations of distinct institutional weaknesses and specific conjunctural opportunities as necessary preconditions for the populist asphyxiation of democracy. These causal factors are derived from the political-strategic definition of populism: Institutional weakness provides room for maneuver to personalistic leaders, who incessantly seek to concentrate power. Yet only if conjunctural opportunities appear as well can these leaders garner overwhelming support, push aside the remaining institutional obstacles, attack the opposition, cement their hegemony, and thus destroy democracy.

This book's assessment of the actual danger emanating from contemporary populism builds on, updates, and expands my earlier study of the current challenges facing liberal pluralism in Latin America and Europe (Weyland 2020). The broader and far more in-depth analysis presented in the following chapters confirms the prior empirical findings and theoretical arguments. At the same time, it includes a number of new high-profile cases, such as the left-winger Andrés Manuel López Obrador in Mexico (AMLO, 2018–present), the ideologically shifty Nayib Bukele in El Salvador (2019–present), and the right-winger Jair Bolsonaro in Brazil (2018–22).

The extended time frame also covers the trajectories of populist governance and the corresponding fate of liberal pluralism at greater length. In some instances, there has been a further descent into competitive authoritarianism, as in Hungary and Turkey. But there have also been encouraging developments: Several personalistic plebiscitarian leaders have suffered electoral defeats, such as Boyko Borisov in Bulgaria (2021), Andrej Babiš in the Czech Republic (2021), "Janez" Janša in Slovenia (2022), and most prominently Donald Trump in the USA (2020) and Jair Bolsonaro in Brazil (2022). Moreover, Igor Matovič felt compelled to resign in Slovakia (2021), and Pedro Castillo's rule collapsed after an unrealistic self-coup attempt in Peru (2022). For the time being, these ousters ended populist threats to democracy (although some leaders, especially Trump, may seek a comeback).

As a result, there is no indication that, during the 2018–2023 period, personalistic plebiscitarian leadership has turned more lethal and endangered liberal pluralism even more severely. The relatively sanguine findings of my earlier study (Weyland 2020; see also Weyland 2022a, 2022b) stand.

The Role of Populism's Haphazard Agency

There is a noteworthy, theoretically important aspect of populist politics that this book's case studies reveal, but that my succinct prior analysis (Weyland 2020) had not highlighted: Personalistic plebiscitarian leadership has its own weaknesses and frailties. Many populist chief executives fail in their governance and even their "political survival"; indeed, they sometimes fail very quickly and irreversibly. Consequently, it is not only democracy that can "die" (Levitsky and Ziblatt 2018); populism can die as well – and the political downfall of a populist chief executive usually helps democracy survive (Weyland 2022a).

After all, populism inherently constitutes a risky political strategy. Personalistic plebiscitarian leaders are by nature headstrong and overbearing, transgressive and confrontational; they are political incarnations of "toxic masculinity," which commonly provokes powerful reactions. This hostility, in turn, can endanger the tenure of populist chief executives. After all, their clout depends on direct, uninstitutionalized connections to their followers, which makes their support base precarious. Failure to prove their charisma can leave them denuded of backing and exposed to counterattacks from the establishment forces that they relentlessly antagonized. For these reasons, populist incumbents live dangerously. They skid on ice and march through battle zones and minefields. The risks of political failure and ignominious eviction run high.

In general, populist agency is inherently haphazard and unpredictable in its performance and success. After all, personalistic plebiscitarian leaders diverge fundamentally from mainstream politicians, who tend to rise gradually, acquire a great deal of experience along the way, and learn to refrain from very bold and innovative – yet risky – initiatives. Consequently, establishment politicians often do a satisfactory job; while not performing miracles, they do not turn into disasters either.

By contrast, many personalistic plebiscitarian leaders are untested outsiders without any track record in electoral politics and governance (see, in general, Serra 2018); they appear out of political obscurity (like Fujimori), ideological marginality (like Bolsonaro), or a different sphere of life (like Trump). Moreover, they rise unexpectedly and meteorically because they use unconventional means, employ transgressive tactics, and raise controversial issues that the political establishment did not dare to touch. All of these maneuvers can bring unexpected, stunning success – but also dramatic failure. Many a populist has followed the trajectory of antiquity's Icarus, ambitiously ascending toward the sun, yet sooner or later falling to his death.

For these reasons, populist agency has an extraordinarily broad probability distribution of performance and outcomes, ranging from miraculous heroism to unmitigated disaster. Some of the new chief executives, such as Peru's Fujimori (see Chapter 3), courageously confront longstanding problems and show a surefootedness and grasp that can reverse catastrophic decline and bring enormous relief to the suffering population. Others, by contrast, such as Ecuador's Abdalá Bucaram (1996–97; see Chapter 3) and the Philippines' Joseph Estrada (1998–2001; see Chapter 7), are "totally out of their depth," fail to get a handle on the challenges facing them, adopt unpromising measures, or do not chart a coherent course of action. While striking success boosts the clout of populist chief executives and thus aggravates their threat to democracy, failure can bring the quick downfall of potential autocrats and thus safeguard liberal pluralism. As Weber (1976: 140–42, 655–57) emphasized, charismatic leaders must perform impressive feats; if they clearly fail, their disappointed followers may abandon and even turn on them.

For these reasons, political agency is an additional factor that affects the fate of populism and its threat to democracy in significant ways. In the edifice of my theory, however, this agency is nested in the institutional structures and exogenous conjunctural opportunities that my approach highlights. These objective factors set the parameters in which agency can make a difference. Thus, the room for populist leadership is distinctly limited. Personalistic plebiscitarian politicians cannot simply create and "construct" their own chances of success; instead, to achieve their undemocratic goals, they depend on institutional weaknesses and conjunctural opportunities that are largely given. Only inside this constellation of conditions can they employ their opportunistic tactics and try to make the best of the situation they face.

Whereas the institutional and conjunctural factors of my theory can be ascertained objectively and thus give rise to a systematic explanatory framework, agency is much harder to pin down. But because of the personalistic nature of populist leadership, which revolves around a single dominant individual, this factor plays an important role as well. The case studies of Chapters 3–7 therefore pay attention to the quality of leadership.

The error-proneness and frequent failings of personalistic plebiscitarian chief executives constitute an additional reason why populism does not imperil democracy as much as recent observers have feared. Even when the necessary conditions for the populist strangulation of liberal pluralism are given, this constellation is not sufficient for turning imminent danger into a deleterious outcome. After all, power-hungry leaders may squander a golden opportunity provided by institutional weakness and a conjunctural opening through incompetence and mistakes. As the case of Trump exemplifies (Woodward 2018, 2020; Woodward and Costa 2021), the defenders of liberal pluralism benefit from all the flaws in their tormentors' agency.

In sum, the inherent debilities of personalistic plebiscitarian leadership favor the survival of democracy. While liberal pluralism does have important weaknesses, especially a worrisome vulnerability to "executive aggrandizement" (Bermeo 2016: 10–13) and to "incumbent takeover" by popularly elected leaders (Svolik 2015: 730–34), populism has its own weaknesses, which arise from its core characteristics. After all, personalistic leaders' penchant for supremacy and dominance antagonizes many other powerful players, while reliance on charismatic performance and quasi-direct appeals gives these contentious populists a fickle political base. In combination, these distinctive features create a considerable probability of early downfall. And where populism falls, democracy most often remains standing.

CENTRAL CONCEPTS

Democracy and Its Destruction: A Procedural, Institutional Approach

Democracy: The Combination of Popular Sovereignty and Liberal Safeguards

This book conceives of democracy in conventional, procedural terms (Dahl 1971).[5] For definitional purposes, therefore, I consider neither inputs (e.g., active citizen participation) nor outputs (e.g., equity-enhancing policies). Accordingly, democracy – in its modern, necessarily representative form – is a political regime in which the rulers are selected via free, fair, competitive elections and exercise government power inside limits set by guarantees of human and civil rights and by institutional checks and balances; yet they are free of imposition by actors without domestic democratic legitimation, such as the military or a foreign hegemonic power. I thus embrace the standard definition employed in the democratization literature since the 1980s (O'Donnell and Schmitter 1986; Przeworski 1991; Schmitter and Karl 1991), which the burgeoning writings on democratic backsliding have adopted as well (Ginsburg and Huq 2018b; Levitsky and Ziblatt 2018; Waldner and Lust 2018; Haggard and Kaufman 2021).

As this definition and its theoretical provenance suggest, modern representative democracy combines political liberalism and popular sovereignty. The latter principle means that political rule ultimately emanates from the people; therefore, it rests on the consent of the common citizenry and allows for their meaningful participation. Popular sovereignty thus excludes other sources of authorization and legitimation, such as the traditional idea of the divine right of kings (including theocracy as in Iran's Islamic Republic), yet also modern notions such as the Communist Party vanguard (McAdams 2017) or expert rule and technocracy. In a democracy, by contrast, political rule is accountable and responsive to the people, and only the people.

Representative democracy combines this foundational principle with the basic liberal goal of safeguarding the maximum of individual freedom without infringing on the freedom of others. For this purpose, liberalism needs a state

---

[5] For stylistic reasons, however, I use the term democracy interchangeably with "liberal pluralism."

that is strong enough to protect people from their fellow citizens, but not so strong that it can abuse its power and oppress people for the benefit of selfish, power-hungry rulers (Held 2006: chap. 3). Liberalism therefore insists on firm institutional limitations on political rule, especially a well-rooted constitution with iron guarantees of civil and political liberties and a clear separation of powers. These limitations confine even the political rule emanating from the people, in order to forestall a tyranny of the majority. Thus, while embracing popular sovereignty as the ultimate base of democracy, liberalism deliberately constrains its exercise.

This prudential limitation seeks to avoid the paradox of sovereignty, namely that in one last act of sovereign choice, the people abdicate their political rights and delegate them to a nondemocratic ruler. After all, popular sovereignty could in principle allow the citizenry to give up their right to rule. It is precisely this opening that populist leaders try to exploit in their relentless efforts to concentrate power, skew democratic competition, and prepare their incumbent takeover. For this purpose, they systematically push to weaken or eliminate liberal safeguards. In light of populism's global advance in recent years, liberal constraints on political rule therefore carry special importance for protecting liberty and democracy.

Given the populist threat, it is crucial to highlight that liberal principles and the corresponding restrictions on the exercise of political rule are core components of modern representative democracy, which by design does not rest on popular sovereignty alone but on its combination with political liberalism. Because popular sovereignty holds the paradoxical risk of allowing for its own abolition, it urgently needs liberal complements and limitations to ensure its own endurance and persistence. Only through this fusion with liberalism can popular sovereignty guarantee the survival of freedom-enhancing democracy.

Accordingly, liberal constraints are not constraints on democracy but constraints *for* democracy; they are not alien limitations but constitutive components of this regime type. By contrast, nonliberal, majoritarian notions of democracy are fundamentally flawed, and they carry huge risks: They allow a temporary, circumstantial majority to reshape the institutional framework and empower rulers who then marginalize, if not suppress, new majorities that could and most likely would form in the future. Thus, a "tyranny of the majority" soon turns into the tyranny of a minority that effectively disregards any current and future majorities. The combination of political liberalism and popular sovereignty avoids this contradiction and inversion.

To assess populism's threat to democracy, this conceptual clarification is decisive. After all, populist leaders skillfully invoke popular sovereignty in their efforts to strip away liberal constraints on their personalistic plebiscitarian rule. For this purpose, they depict liberal principles and institutions as the bastions of selfish elites that "the people" need to take by assault. But any elimination of checks and balances and takeover of independent institutions would primarily boost their own personal power and predominance – and thus undermine and eventually strangle democracy. To forestall such a creeping destruction of democracy, it is crucial to resist populists' one-sided appeals to popular sovereignty and insist on maintaining the combination and balance of the majoritarian and liberal components of democracy that are decisive for its modern representative version.

Democracy's Destruction: Subverting Competitiveness

Populism's sneaky efforts to suffocate democracy gradually from the inside create the analytical problem of determining the point when democratic backsliding passes the boundary to competitive authoritarianism. After all, personalistic plebiscitarian leaders use the institutional attributions won through elections to dismantle checks and balances and concentrate power step by step. When does this sequence of infringements and arrogations add up to a regime change? Because representative democracy rests fundamentally on free and fair elections, the essential criterion is the serious abridgment of political competitiveness (Schmitter 1983: 887–91). Where opposition forces have a real opportunity of winning and electoral outcomes are subject to effective uncertainty (Przeworski 1991: 10–14, 40–50), democracy prevails. By contrast, governmental determination to skew electoral procedures starkly, seriously hinder and harass the opposition, or decisively manipulate the vote count crosses the threshold to authoritarianism.[6]

While the focus on political competitiveness provides a clear criterion for ascertaining democracy's death, assessing the seriousness of incumbents' infractions is difficult. Indeed, undemocratic populists who command genuine popularity may sometimes see no need to deploy the authoritarian instruments that they have systematically acquired; only when their electoral prowess diminishes may they feel compelled to show their true colors and resort to manipulation, as in Bolivia in late 2019 (see later in this chapter and Chapter 4). For these reasons, the populist destruction of democracy is not easy to certify. As a result, the proliferating projects that cross-nationally assess and measure democracy and its quality, such as Freedom House, Polity, and Varieties of Democracy, differ substantially in their scoring of specific cases and of changes over time (Huber and Schimpf 2017: 337–39; Elff and Ziaja 2018: 99–102; Ginsburg and Huq 2018a: 19–21; Paldam 2021: 18–28; Pelke and Croissant 2021: 440–43).

Despite these difficulties, however, there is virtual consensus among democracy indices and country experts about the populist termination of democracy in

---

[6] To capture populists' gradual dismantling of democracy, this book commonly uses metaphors of asphyxiation. Yet while strangled individuals' resurrection must wait until the Day of Last Judgment, the revival of democracy can happen quickly after its populist assassin has lost government power. With the elimination of personalistic plebiscitarian hegemony, the formal institutions of democracy can resume their unimpeded functioning and guarantee open competitiveness again, as happened in Peru and Ecuador after the exit of competitive authoritarians Fujimori in 2000 and Correa in 2017.

five cases examined in this book, namely Fujimori's Peru, Chávez's Venezuela, Bukele's El Salvador, Orbán's Hungary, and Erdoğan's Turkey. There is more uncertainty on Morales' Bolivia and Correa's Ecuador, both among rating projects and regional specialists (e.g., Levitsky and Loxton 2019: 344–47 vs. Cameron 2018). Democracy indices, however, are skewed by the left-of-center orientations of many scholars, who tend to judge ideologically proximate governments such as those two cases with disproportionate leniency (Gerring and Weitzel 2023: 24–26).

To correct for this problem, my book relies on the most careful, thorough, and comprehensive assessments that are available in the recent literature (Sánchez-Sibony 2017, 2018, 2021). These systematic, in-depth evaluations convincingly establish that Correa and Morales pushed beyond democratic backsliding and installed competitive authoritarianism by greatly skewing political competition through discriminatory electoral rules, the governmental takeover of the judiciary and of electoral management, constant attacks on the partisan and societal opposition, heavy pressure on the media in Ecuador, and the corralling of rural voters in Bolivia (Sánchez-Sibony 2017: 131–34, 2018: 101–18, 2021: 121–38). These undemocratic machinations were revealed in the Bolivian crisis of late 2019, when his unconstitutional push for continuous self-perpetuation induced Morales to resort to substantial electoral fraud, as painstakingly documented by the international organization that the incumbent himself asked to adjudicate the post-electoral controversy (OAS 2019a, 2019b; see discussion in Chapter 4). For these reasons, Correa's Ecuador and Morales' Bolivia also count as instances in which populist leaders strangled democracy to death.

In conclusion, in seven of the forty cases investigated in this book and scored in Table 1 (see Chapter 2), governing populists destroyed democracy with their power concentration and their corresponding efforts to disable checks and balances and muzzle the opposition. By deforming the electoral arena and violating liberal rights and safeguards, Fujimori, Chávez, Morales, Correa, Bukele, Orbán, and Erdoğan imposed majoritarian hegemony under their own predominant command and thus asphyxiated democracy.

Populism: A Political-Strategic Approach

The Problems of Other Definitions

As already indicated, this book depicts personalistic plebiscitarian leadership as the main axis of populism. To explain and justify this political-strategic definition (see prior attempts in Weyland 2001, 2017, 2021b), a brief look at the conceptual history of populism is unavoidable. As every commentator highlights, populism has long been a highly contested concept; definitional consensus has remained elusive. There has been conceptual progress, however. Some old controversies have faded. For instance, most experts nowadays agree that populism was not specific to one historical time period, such as early import-substitution industrialization in Latin America. Instead, populism has clearly been a recurring phenomenon and has appeared in many regions of the world. Consequently, populism is not by nature confined to any specific historical, structural, institutional, or cultural context.

Moreover, most political scientists avoid economic notions of populism (Sachs 1989; Dornbusch and Edwards 1991), which associate the concept with politically driven irresponsibility in economic policy-making, such as pre-electoral spending sprees and inflationary programs responding to demands for alleviating social inequality. But such fiscally unsustainable measures have been adopted not only by populists but by a great variety of governments, which have differed in partisan sustenance and ideological orientation (Sachs 1989; Dornbusch and Edwards 1991). For political analysis, therefore, the label of economic populism, applied indiscriminately despite these important political differences, is of little use (see criticism in Weyland 2001: 11).

Given this helpful narrowing of definitional options, the continuing conceptual disagreements involve the three main approaches featured in recent handbooks on populism (Rovira Kaltwasser, Taggart, et al. 2017; similarly De la Torre 2019), namely ideational, political-strategic, and cultural-performative definitions. Cultural and performative approaches define populism via its distinctive style, which in Ostiguy's (2017) terminology is ostentatiously "low": Populist movements and leaders deliberately employ plebeian, counter-elitist diction, especially coarse language spiced up with curse words; they dress and act like lower-class people; and they claim to enjoy the pastimes of the "little man" by playing soccer and ogling sexy fashion models.

But while cultural and performative approaches are descriptively quite accurate in highlighting populism's "low" style, they go too far in their constructivism. By concentrating on the cultural framing and meaning of populism, they neglect the crucial question of what populist leaders and movements do in politics: How they seek to win government power, how they govern when they hold power, and how this exercise of power affects politics and institutions, especially democracy. Thus, cultural-performative scholars concentrate on populism's outward appearance at the expense of its inner core – which concerns the accumulation and wielding of political power.

Relatedly, cultural and performative approaches overestimate the latitude and capacities for "framing" by populist leaders. In particular, they highlight how populist leaders can "perform" and discursively create crises (Moffitt 2016: 121–32); but they underestimate that such performances are only convincing, effective, and impactful if real problems exist that are acute and severe. Thus, populist crisis discourse "works" only if it has an observable, objective base. Populist leaders certainly have some room for maneuver by dramatizing existing difficulties, but this framing can only be successful within limits set by the actually prevailing conditions.

In other words, populist problem identification and crisis rhetoric can boost leaders' support to some extent, but within clear and fairly narrow margins.

No leader can conjure up a crisis if serious, pressing problems do not exist and deeply affect large numbers of people. And only when a true catastrophe afflicts a country, such as hyperinflation or a massive public security challenge, do populist leaders get a chance to exploit the situation for obtaining huge, overwhelming mass support.

Whereas cultural and performative approaches overestimate the latitude and agency of populist leaders, ideational approaches surprisingly neglect leadership and highlight only the role of the masses – as if populism's followers acted on their own, rather than primarily through their leader.[7] Ideational scholars define populism via its main discourse and the "thin" ideology it embodies. This oratory conjures up the virtuous, pure people and demonizes the selfish, corrupt elites that populists accuse of disregarding and betraying the common citizenry. To remedy this alleged perversion of democracy, populism promises to empower the "common man" and woman and to use political rule for executing "the will of the people," interpreted like Rousseau's *volonté générale* (Hawkins and Rovira Kaltwasser 2017a; Mudde 2017).

With this definition, however, ideational approaches misunderstand the very nature of populism, which fundamentally differs from true bottom-up approaches such as Marxian class struggle or social movement contention: Populism blatantly fails to empower the people. Instead, this discursive promise uniformly remains unfulfilled, for an unavoidable reason: "The people" is a highly heterogeneous, amorphous agglomerate that, on its own, lacks the capacity to act, or even to arrive at a clear common interest. The *volonté générale* is a fiction (Arrow [1951] 1963). While an industrial working class may have the relative cohesion, and a social movement the organization, to take specific political initiatives, the broad, disparate welter of individuals, families, networks, and groupings that makes up "the people" does not.

Instead, it is constitutive of populism that "the people" delegate their much-proclaimed agency to a leader who claims to embody the *volonté générale* and even to incarnate the people. As Venezuela's Bolivarian leader used to announce, "Chávez is the people, and the people is Chávez"; similarly, his Bolivian disciple Evo Morales' twitter handle is "@EvoEsPueblo." Urbinati (2019) captures this substitution of representation by organic identification in her book title, *Me the People*. Thus, the leader, as the authentic, organic mouthpiece, unquestionably and monopolistically speaks for the people and *as* the people; the people can only speak through this leader (Rosanvallon 2020: 15, 49–53, 99–103).

Interestingly, this collective ventriloquism means that the leader is authorized to say and do whatever he wants: All his words and deeds automatically *are* the voice and agency of the people. Thus, this idea of political incarnation effectively assigns all power to the leader; conversely, it disempowers the

---

[7] Mudde and Rovira Kaltwasser (2017), for instance, focus on "the populist leader" only in chapter 4, halfway through their book.

people, who "cannot" disagree with their organic mouthpiece. In particular, individuals and specific groups are left completely powerless because their interests and will necessarily have to cede before "the people" – as interpreted by the leader (Urbinati 2019).

By missing this essential populist twist (Weyland 2017: 53–55), namely followers' automatic delegation of their political agency to the leader and populism's corresponding failure effectively to empower "the people," ideational approaches paint a distorted picture of populism. With their focus on the discursive contrast between the good people vs. the bad elites, they fail to draw the proper distinction between true bottom-up approaches, such as Marxian class mobilization and social movements, versus populism, which deceptively claims to be a bottom-up approach but effectively operates from the top down via personalistic plebiscitarian leadership. Definitions need to capture the core meaning of a phenomenon (Gerring 2012: 117–19). By focusing on "the people" as the main actor confronting "the elite," ideational approaches do not fulfill this crucial requirement: They miss the decisive importance of populist leadership.[8]

In political reality, no populist movement has effectively vested power in its followers, not to speak of "the people" in general. Left-wing formations advance bottom-up claims most insistently; Spain's PODEMOS has elicited particularly high expectations for spearheading a participatory transformation of politics. Strikingly, however, in-depth research shows that even inside this movement, which was inspired by the most progressive, Laclauian notions of populism, personalistic leadership quickly asserted itself, imposed its dominance, and purged the top leader's main rival (De Nadal 2021; Mazzolini and Borriello 2022: 295–96; see also Villacañas 2017: 158–64, 253–57, 265, 273). Thus, even this "least likely case" suffered the populist twist. Supposedly horizontal, bottom-up decision-making predictably gave way to vertical, predominantly top-down populism.

More broadly, a recent investigation demonstrates that populist parties are overwhelmingly leader-centered, rather than practicing the internal democracy that the claim of popular empowerment would imply. Thus, these self-proclaimed forces for participatory change and democratic rejuvenation drastically diverge from their main promise. As Böhmelt, Ezrow, and Lehrer (2022: 1147–50) highlight, this empirical finding supports the political-strategic definition of populism and casts doubt on the conceptual validity and analytical value of ideational approaches.

In general, populists are notorious for their insincere performances and deceptive appeals; how can billionaire Trump, for instance, claim to be the authentic voice of his "deplorable" core followers? Therefore, a focus on populist discourse and its ideational scaffolding is not the most valid approach

---

[8] On the essential role of personalistic, charismatic leadership in populism, see also Pappas (2019: 93–106).

for capturing the meaning of populism. In fact, ideational approaches have serious problems of conceptual validity, misclassifying populist leaders especially in Latin America. The most rigorous measurement procedure, designed by Hawkins (2010: chap. 3; see also Hawkins, Carlin, et al. 2019), yields numerous false negatives:[9] It misses many important leaders who regional experts almost uniformly regard as populists, such as Argentina's Carlos Menem and Néstor and Cristina Fernández de Kirchner, Colombia's Álvaro Uribe, Paraguay's Fernando Lugo, and Peru's Alejandro Toledo (Hawkins and Rovira Kaltwasser 2017a: 519; Ruth and Hawkins 2017: 269–70).

What is much more indicative and important than what populists say is what they do: how they act in politics, especially how they seek and exercise political power. This is the central focus of the political-strategic definition.

The Political-Strategic Approach to Populism

My definition elucidates the political core of populism as a distinctive strategy for winning and wielding political power. Accordingly, populism revolves around personalistic, usually charismatic leadership sustained by (quasi-) direct, unmediated, uninstitutionalized connections to a heterogeneous, amorphous, and largely unorganized mass of followers (Weyland 2017: 55–59). Populism rests on the supreme predominance of a personal leader who is unconstrained by rules and organizations and who makes decisions with unquestionable discretion as he sees fit. This unbounded agency uses institutions only as instruments, avoiding and evading their constraints. Personalistic leaders have unchallengeable command and unfettered disposition over their support movements or parties, whose organizational structures lack solidity and are inherently provisional and subject to tactical transformation or arbitrary intervention from the top, driven by the self-interests, if not whims of the supreme leader (Kostadinova and Levitt 2014: 500–4; Rhodes-Purdy and Madrid 2020: 321–25, 329; Frantz et al. 2022: 919–21). Personalism prevails especially where the leader created his own party and manages to use it at will as his electoral vehicle (Frantz et al. 2022: 921), or where he captured complete command over an uninstitutionalized, personalistic party formed by a charismatic movement founder, as in the unusual case of Argentine Peronism (Andrews-Lee 2021: 164–95).

Populism combines such personalistic leadership with plebiscitarianism as the principal strategy for winning and exercising political power. Whereas other types of personalistic leaders use particularistic deals, massive patronage, and widespread clientelism as their main base of political sustenance (Weyland 2001: 14; see also Mouzelis 1985), those personalistic leaders who

---

[9] Developed for European radical-right parties that were stuck in opposition, the ideational definition also has a fundamental problem dealing with populist parties that achieve government power – and thus look more and more like "the establishment" and "the elite," the targets of their earlier attacks (Jungkunz, Fahey, and Hino 2021).

turn populist make direct, personal, and emotional appeals to broad masses of people, via rallies or via radio, TV, or nowadays social media. They connect to citizens as directly, closely, and comprehensively as possible, as Chávez did with hours and hours of live TV shows and Trump with incessant tweeting. By establishing a constant presence in their followers' lives and by feeding off of the adulation they receive in return, such charismatic leaders act like the embodiment of the people (Weber 1976: 140–42, 654–64; Urbinati 2019).

This intimate identification, reminiscent of the Holy Communion, is designed to forge and maintain particularly intense bonds, as revealed by the outpouring of public crying after Chávez's untimely death. This super-charged emotion is designed to compensate for the weakness of institutional linkages and the absence of organizational discipline. After all, the tremendous heterogeneity of the people, especially in post-industrial, highly pluralistic societies, hinders organization building. Instead, the effort to encompass the full breadth of "the people" gives populist movements an amorphous structure; they rely on emotional affinity rather than institutional solidity.

With this definition, the political-strategic approach highlights charismatic leadership that rests on a mass following (Weyland 2001: 12–14). This combination of personalism and plebiscitarianism is essential for understanding populism (see also Carrión 2022: 9–14; Kenny 2023, forthcoming). While historically obvious and widely recognized for Latin America, the central role of personalistic leaders in populist movements also prevails in other regions, such as Europe (e.g., England's Nigel Farage, Holland's Pim Fortuyn and Geert Wilders, France's Jean-Marie and Marine Le Pen, Italy's Silvio Berlusconi and Matteo Salvini, Austria's Jörg Haider, Poland's Jarosław Kaczyński, Slovakia's Vladimír Mečiar, Hungary's Viktor Orbán, Bulgaria's Boyko Borisov, and Turkey's Recep Erdoğan). Populism in Asia is leader-centric as well (India's Narendra Modi, the Philippines' Rodrigo Duterte, Thailand's Thaksin Shinawatra, Japan's Junichiro Koizumi).

Certainly, Europe's parliamentary systems, in which chief executives need constant majority acquiescence from the legislature, create incentives for somewhat stronger party structures and organizational networks than under Latin America's presidentialism, where most populist leaders command flimsy electoral vehicles (Rhodes-Purdy and Madrid 2020). But even under parliamentarism, populist leaders exercise personalistic predominance over their movements. They can override organizational rules, arrogate any decision, and handpick candidates for offices, as Hungary's Orbán has done inside his party, which he co-founded and has dominated for many years. Similarly, Polish populist Jarosław Kaczyński, who for tactical reasons has foregone the premiership since 2015,[10] has promoted a cult of personality focused on his tragically

---

[10] By not exposing his extremism to the public limelight (see Pytlas 2021: 341–42, 348; Bartels 2023: 204), Kaczyński has sought to avoid discrediting his party's government and turning into a lightning rod for Poland's energetic and contentious opponents to populism.

deceased twin brother,[11] has commanded charismatic authority inside his own movement, has exercised complete, "absolutist" control over his party (Pytlas 2021: 340, 342, 347–50), and has selected and removed prime ministers at will. Thus, although the institutional requirements of parliamentarism have induced some populist parties in Europe to build firmer organizations, populism in the region is characterized by the uncontested preeminence of personalistic leaders.

By highlighting the combination and intersection of pronounced personalism and largely unmediated plebiscitarianism, the political-strategic definition allows for delimiting populism's extension. Many cases are clear-cut. For instance, while Chávez was a prototypical populist, his handpicked successor Nicolás Maduro (2013–present) does not qualify because he is distinctly uncharismatic (Andrews-Lee 2021: 141–42). Even where the tremendous complexity of politics yields some impure, if not ambiguous cases, the political-strategic definition proves its discriminatory value. For instance, although his movement rested on an unusual degree of bottom-up mobilization via energetic social movements (Harten 2011: 75–91; Anria 2018), Bolivia's Evo Morales (2006–19) counts as a populist because he boosted his personal supremacy and political indispensability as the unifying bond, which enabled his obstinate and increasingly controversial push for one reelection after the other (Brockmann Quiroga 2020: 33–46; McNelly 2021: 87). By contrast, Nicaragua's Daniel Ortega does not qualify because his return to the presidency in 2006 was not based on fervent popular appeal but on "one of the most disciplined parties in Latin America" and its patronage machine (Feinberg and Kurtz-Phelan 2006: 79). Indeed, Ortega has governed as an increasingly patrimonial, even dynastic ruler – a nonpopulist type of personalism (Weyland 2001: 13). For empirical research, the political-strategic approach thus draws fairly clear conceptual boundaries and avoids the accumulation of false negatives that plague ideational measurements.

In theoretical terms, the political-strategic approach builds primarily on Max Weber's (1976: 140–42, 654–64) seminal analysis of charisma, by contrast to other sources of legitimation and the corresponding organizational and programmatic linkages (see also Mouzelis 1985; Kitschelt 2000; Kenny forthcoming). As charismatic politicians, populists do not base their quest for power on solid networks or organizational structures, but seek mass support by invoking a providential mission to redeem the people and save them from dangerous enemies. Because they proclaim a visionary project that they themselves define, they can adduce this nebulous goal to justify any step along the way.

---

[11] Sadurski 2022: 144–45, 161. In Warsaw's most central basilika, St. John's Archcathedral, where important national heroes such as Marshal Józef Piłsudski (1867–1935) are prominently commemorated with large sculpted plaques, a blank space is left right next to Kaczyński's dead twin brother – for Poland's current populist leader (personal observation, Warsaw, July 7, 2022).

Effectively, thus, populist leaders often use their heroic legitimation as power-seeking operators with weak, fickle ideological commitments. Because they end up making specific political decisions and policy choices primarily for instrumental purposes, they are always willing to shift course and suspend, if not abandon, their prior positions. This flexibility allows populists to take advantage of a great variety of opportunities and even turn adversity into advantage, especially through bold efforts to combat crises and thus demonstrate their charismatic prowess. This adaptability, which enables populists to exploit any weakness and vulnerability of liberal democracy, exacerbates the political risks inherent in personalistic plebiscitarian leadership.

The political-strategic definition, which is crucial for elucidating the politics of populism, has had even greater analytical payoffs in recent years, given populism's global advance. Now that populist leaders have won elections and become chief executives in so many countries, a focus on the actual behavior of personalistic plebiscitarian leaders has become even more important for understanding populist policy and politics.

When populist movements and parties began to rise in the electorate, ideational approaches, which concentrate on the input side of politics and on popular "demand" for populism, held some analytical leverage by examining how and why populist preferences formed among voters and how these attitudes – though only together with other sentiments and resentments – gave birth to new parties and allowed them to build support. But these approaches do not elucidate how populist leaders govern and how they use their new institutional attributions to undermine democracy.

By contrast, the political-strategic approach concentrates precisely on these crucial issues of political rule and governance, which now take center-stage and constitute the current research frontier in the exploding literature on populism. My definition has great heuristic value by inspiring many interesting hypotheses. The emphasis on personalistic leadership suggests, for instance, that populist chief executives surround themselves with inexperienced family members, loyalists, and cronies, rather than experts or party politicians; that they weaken government institutions and bureaucracies through incessant "political" interference; that they constantly try to bend or break institutional checks and balances; that they energetically concentrate and extend their power; that they enact bold, high-profile measures that lack careful preparation and fiscal sustainability and carry a high risk of failure; that they shun alliances with independent power brokers; that coalitions that are unavoidable (especially in Europe's parliamentary systems) remain precarious and prone to breakdown; that their inherent penchant for confrontation and conflict creates grave risks of political collapse and irregular removal from office; that where they do win in these confrontations, they gradually strangle democracy; that to garner support for this authoritarian involution, they act in constant campaign mode; etc.

Thus, the political-strategic approach promises considerable analytical payoffs by suggesting a wealth of conjectures and insights into populist politics and by alerting scholars to their problematic regime effects. In contrast, ideational approaches have – by their own admission (Hawkins and Rovira 2017b: 533–34) – little to say about leaders' strategic actions and the resulting political and institutional repercussions. Indeed, the political-strategic approach has the distinctive advantage of yielding several counter-intuitive insights. For instance, whereas mainstream researchers depict crises as problematic challenges (e.g., Nelson 2018: 1, 31), my theory highlights the opportunities that crises can potentially offer to populist leaders: In principle, bold agency can quickly resolve certain types of crises such as hyperinflation, and thus elicit an enormous outpouring of support, which then facilitates assaults on democracy, as under Peru's Fujimori (see Chapter 3).

The political-strategic approach can also explain the puzzle of dramatic turnarounds in populists' fate: Relying on uninstitutionalized and therefore precarious mass support, long-dominant leaders can quickly fall. For instance, still highlighting his success against hyperinflation and guerrilla insurgency, Fujimori won a second reelection in mid-2000; yet shortly thereafter, his totally personalistic rule collapsed like a house of cards under the shock of an unprecedented corruption scandal. Similarly, Bolivia's Evo Morales seemed headed toward continuous reelection in late 2019, but was surprisingly evicted through massive citizen protests over electoral fraud (Lehoucq 2020; Wolff 2020).

Moreover, the political-strategic approach helps explain why irregular evictions of populist leaders in presidential systems of government, which are accompanied by mass protest and enormous controversy, forestall comebacks: In recent decades in Latin America, no personalistic plebiscitarian leaders who suffered interruptions of their tenure in office have managed ever to return to the presidency. By contrast, parliamentary systems as in Europe allow for the easier, less conflictual removal of populist leaders through votes of no confidence. Less damaging to prime ministers' political standing, such ousters have allowed for comebacks. Accordingly, Silvio Berlusconi in Italy, Vladimír Mečiar in Slovakia, Boris Borisov in Bulgaria, and Janez Janša in Slovenia recaptured the premiership on two later occasions (Weyland 2022a: 14–15).

All these interesting insights about populist politics emerge from the political-strategic definition; alternative approaches have less heuristic value. In politics, actions are decisive, not "discourse" (Kenny forthcoming). With the emergence of so many populist governments around the world, the focus of the political-strategic approach on the quest for power, the exercise of power, and the resulting regime effects has become ever more important and valuable. The present book therefore employs this conceptualization of populism.

RESEARCH DESIGN

To assess the real threat that populism poses to liberal democracy, this book investigates the regime impact of personalistic plebiscitarian leadership in Europe and Latin America since about 1980 and draws inferences for the USA as well. By considering a wide range of cases, this study avoids the selection on the dependent variable of prior analyses (e.g., Levitsky and Ziblatt 2018; Kaufman and Haggard 2019). Rather than concentrating on chief executives who did succeed in imposing their hegemony and who thus strangled democracy, I also include the large number of instances in which liberal pluralism survived personalistic plebiscitarian leadership.[12] Only such a comprehensive analysis allows for assessing the likelihood of democracy's asphyxiation and for ascertaining the real risk posed by populism. With this breadth, my investigation clearly shows that populist leaders often fail in their power-concentrating efforts. Because the necessary conditions for pushing through their undemocratic projects, institutional weakness *and* conjunctural opportunities, are often missing, liberal democracy has good chances of enduring and persisting.

In regional terms, the study focuses on Latin America and Europe, where populist governments have been most frequent. Each of these regions also shares a number of common background factors, which make it easier to identify the specific factors accounting for the main difference of outcome, namely the populist strangulation of democracy in some cases, yet its survival in numerous others. In other regions, by contrast, such as Asia, populism has been infrequent (Hellmann 2017: 164, 171–74). And while populist leaders have in recent years started to capture chief executive office in Southeast Asia (Mizuno and Phongpaichit 2009; Kenny 2018), those countries are heterogeneous in historical, socioeconomic, cultural, institutional, and political terms; this multiplicity of differences makes it more difficult to identify the crucial causal factors. For this inferential purpose, the basic logic of Mill's "method of difference" and Przeworski and Teune's ([1970] 1982: 32–34) "most similar systems" design is better suited. Therefore, this study investigates primarily regions that encompass many "similar systems," namely Latin America and Europe, especially Eastern Europe (see recently Connelly 2020).

There are three additional reasons for this regional focus. First, Latin America and Europe are relatively similar to the USA, where the dearth of experiences with populists in power has created great uncertainty and intense fears. Trump's election and his transgressive presidency, which culminated in an unprecedented mob invasion of Congress, have instilled grave doubts in liberal pluralism's resilience. Whereas Americans used to take democracy for granted, the sudden shock has prompted observers to (over)emphasize its weaknesses and highlight the danger emanating from populism. As belief in American exceptionalism has collapsed, learning from foreign experiences has become imperative. To derive instructive lessons, it is particularly useful to investigate populism's impact on democracy in settings that share important characteristics with the USA. The resulting insights will turn especially relevant

---

[12] For a similar effort to examine both "positive" and "negative" cases, focused on the emergence of populist leaders, see Pappas (2019: chap. 4). See also De la Torre and Srisa-nga (2022) for an up-to-date global overview.

if the resentful ex-president, still smarting from his narrow Electoral College defeat in 2020, makes a comeback in 2024 and then redoubles his attack on liberal pluralism.

Second, there is an important pragmatic reason for focusing on Latin America and Europe. Both regions have had decades of experiences with populist governments, which have motivated a great deal of scholarship. This wealth of extant studies is crucial for a wide-ranging investigation, which necessarily has to rely to a good extent on secondary literature. Third, my own work has long concentrated on Latin America, and increasingly on Europe as well. This background knowledge, together with language competence, facilitates an understanding of populist experiences, which often invoke historical grievances, as in Hungary (Treaty of Trianon 1920). Moreover, I have conducted primary research on populism in Argentina, Bolivia, Brazil, Peru, and Venezuela over the course of the last thirty-five years. Therefore, I have a treasure trove of materials to draw on. While I can cite only a small part of these documents and interview notes, they have informed my understanding of populist politics across Latin America.

ORGANIZATION OF THE STUDY

After the present introduction, Chapter 2 explains the book's theoretical arguments. Based on the political-strategic approach, I highlight the inherent threats that populism poses to democracy, which arise from the domineering, hegemonic tendencies and autocratic impulses of personalistic leaders and the political clout provided by potentially "overwhelming" plebiscitarian mass appeal. But as the frequent survival of liberal pluralism shows, populist chief executives are not automatically and uniformly able to smother democracy. Instead, they can resolutely concentrate power only under certain conditions, which provide special room for their undemocratic machinations. Two necessary conditions are required: Institutional weakness gives personalistic leadership considerable latitude, and conjunctural opportunities allow plebiscitarian chief executives to boost their popular support to unusual breadth and strength. Thus, largely exogenous preconditions limit the destructive potential of populism.

Indeed, even in favorable circumstances, populist leaders do not necessarily succeed. Instead, personalism is error-prone, and its penchant for boldness carries great risks. Populist leaders may therefore fail to take advantage of institutional weaknesses or conjunctural opportunities. Where they have committed serious miscalculations and mistakes,[13] establishment sectors aggrieved by populists' confrontational approach have managed to strike back. Thus, in several cases, democracy has not died because populist leaders have (politically) "died," suffering irregular evictions from office.

---

[13] On the important repercussions of political mistakes, see recently Treisman (2020).

Chapters 3–5 substantiate these theoretical arguments through in-depth examinations of the main types of populism prevailing in Latin American and Europe during the last few decades. Attention first turns to neoliberal populism in Latin America, where presidential systems with their checks and balances mostly command middling degrees of institutional strength but are open to para-legal machinations, especially chief executives' self-serving bending of the rules. Even these plastic institutional settings, however, create constraints on presidents' power hunger, which populist chief executives can overcome only under exceptional circumstances, namely when acute, severe, yet resolvable crises affect both the economy *and* public security. Consequently, only Alberto Fujimori in Peru, who faced both devastating hyperinflation and a massive guerrilla assault, and Nayib Bukele in El Salvador, who confronted sky-high crime and the economic shock of the COVID-19 pandemic, garnered such widespread popular backing that they managed to destroy democracy and install competitive-authoritarian regimes. Chapter 3 shows through systematic comparisons that populist leaders who confronted only one of these crises were unable to strangle liberal pluralism. Presidents who failed to resolve a serious crisis, or who took bold, risky measures without facing a looming catastrophe proved even less successful and often ruined their political careers.

As Chapter 4 explains, Latin America's recent crop of left-wing populists, especially the "Bolivarian" grouping inspired and led by Venezuela's Hugo Chávez, had an easier path to imposing their predominance and asphyxiating democracy. Chávez and his main disciples, Bolivia's Evo Morales and Ecuador's Rafael Correa, won elections in countries that during the preceding years had been plagued by high instability, as evident in dangerous coup attempts and irregular ousters of presidents. Facing only weak institutional obstacles to their autocratic aspirations, these Bolivarian populists benefited from the enormous revenue windfalls produced by the global commodities boom, specifically sky-high prices for their countries' voluminous hydrocarbon exports. This huge gift allowed for expansionary economic policies and generous social benefit programs, which boosted the presidents' clout and facilitated their unfair, undemocratic self-perpetuation in power. By contrast, left-wing populists who did not benefit from large hydrocarbon windfalls, and those who governed in more stable settings with stronger institutions – such as Mexico with its fairly independent courts and electoral body, its federalism, and its strict presidential term limit – proved unable to accumulate preponderant power and move to competitive authoritarianism.

Chapter 5 turns to Europe. By contrast to the constitutional design of Latin American presidentialism, the Old Continent's parliamentarism embodies much greater openness to change because of its lower number of institutional veto players; after all, a parliamentary majority grants a populist prime minister the capacity to pass power-concentrating laws, dominate judicial appointments, and thus undermine any counter-balance. As regards conjunctural opportunities, a serious economic crisis that discredits the previously governing parties and gives a populist challenger a decisive electoral victory reduces the number of partisan veto players and thus provides great latitude for power concentration. These conditions enabled right-wing populists Viktor Orbán in Hungary and Recep Erdoğan in Turkey to establish political hegemony and suffocate democracy. By contrast, the absence of economic crisis tends to foreclose an electoral sweep and forces reliance on unreliable governing coalitions; and greater institutional strength, such as judicial independence in Italy and semi-presidentialism in Poland, hinders power concentration by personalistic plebiscitarian leaders and thus allows liberal pluralism to survive, however precariously, as in contemporary Poland.

Chapter 6 then examines the most prominent and arguably most important case of contemporary populist governance, namely the Trump presidency. The comparative analysis of Latin America and Europe suggests sanguine lessons for democracy's fate under this strong-willed leader. After all, the USA ranks high on institutional strength and low on conjunctural opportunities; thus, none of the necessary conditions for the populist strangulation of democracy is fulfilled. My in-depth investigation indeed finds that the institutional checks and balances enshrined in the long-lasting, virtually unchangeable constitution have held firm. Moreover, America's advanced economy and complex society have proven largely immune to sudden crises, nor susceptible to huge windfalls; even the economic shock caused by the COVID-19 pandemic was quickly mitigated by enormous compensatory spending and a speedy recovery.

In line with my theory, therefore, Trump did not manage to impose his political hegemony, curtail the role of Congress and the judiciary, undermine the partisan opposition, subdue civil society, or muzzle the media. While the transgressive president did considerable damage to liberal norms, he did not abridge democratic institutions. Indeed, his incessant defiance provoked a pro-democratic backlash and stimulated an upsurge of political participation, which contributed to Trump's midterm setback in 2018, his presidential loss in 2020, and the defeat of many of his most dangerous disciples in the midterms of 2022. Notably, Trump ended up as one of the rare populist presidents to lose a reelection bid.

Chapter 6's analysis of Trump's failure to do serious damage to US democracy corroborates the main arguments of my theory: Institutional strength and the absence of conjunctural opportunities for boosting populist leadership protected liberal pluralism. Indeed, America's democracy demonstrated its continued vibrancy through its mobilizational and participatory response to the challenge clearly posed by this personalistic plebiscitarian president.

Chapter 7 concludes by summarizing the study's main findings and theoretical arguments. Subsequent sections draw out important broader implications. First, formal institutions prove surprisingly important; even frameworks of middling strength pose substantial obstacles to populist power grabs, which only the coincidence of unusual conjunctural opportunities enable these leaders to overcome. Second, the important insights arising from my wide-ranging investigation demonstrate the value of the political-strategic definition of populism. While alternative definitions focus on discourse, ideology, or performative style, my emphasis on actual political behavior and its institutional repercussions is crucial for the most urgent task that the burgeoning literature on populism currently faces, namely to elucidate populism's threat to liberal democracy.

Chapter 7 also examines some additional factors and extensions of my arguments. First, influences across cases can make some, though limited, difference. Personalistic plebiscitarian leaders can turn into role models and inspire disciples in other countries to follow in their footsteps. But with their transgressive and confrontational behavior, populist leaders can also serve as deterrents, hurting the political chances of similar politicians elsewhere. Moreover, one populist experience, especially through its corrosive effect on the party system, can open the door for populist candidates in the future; thus, countries can fall into "serial populism" (Roberts 2014: 58–63, 126–28). Interestingly, however, populist successors tend to do less damage to democracy than the initial front-runner.

Second, I examine the most outstanding instances of populist governance in contemporary Asia, namely Thaksin Shinawatra in Thailand (2001–6), Joseph Estrada (1998–2001) and Rodrigo Duterte (2016–22) in the Philippines, and Narendra Modi in India (2014–present). By and large, the main factors of my theory – the degree of institutional strength and the availability of conjunctural opportunities – can account for the impact of these personalistic plebiscitarian chief executives on democracy. Regional specificities, however, also mattered in some cases. In particular, the military and the king played a decisive role in Thailand, and an unrestrained, harsh crackdown on crime in the Philippines yielded unusual political rewards.

The book ends by emphasizing the fairly sanguine lessons of this comprehensive investigation. While populism clearly constitutes a serious threat to democracy, liberal pluralism commands a great deal of resilience, which personalistic plebiscitarian leaders can overpower only under special, limited conditions. This core finding can allay the grave concerns that many observers have expressed in recent years. Democracy's fate is not nearly as dire as often feared.

2

How Institutional Constraints and Conjunctural Opportunities Condition Populism's Threat to Democracy

As many scholars and other commentators have stressed in recent years, populist command of the government creates significant risks for democracy. Indeed, my political-strategic approach highlights that personalistic plebiscitarian leadership stands in inherent tension with liberal pluralism. Headstrong charismatic politicians constantly challenge and seek to undermine institutional checks and balances; and they tend to launch frontal attacks on opposition forces, whom they do not respect as legitimate competitors, but try to vanquish as "enemies of the people." All of these illiberal machinations are designed to concentrate power and establish political hegemony; the more successful they are, the more they move the polity toward competitive authoritarianism. For these reasons, populism seriously jeopardizes democracy. The fears of so many important authors certainly have valid foundations (Ginsburg and Huq 2018b; Levitsky and Ziblatt 2018; Mounk 2018; Kaufman and Haggard 2019; Mettler and Lieberman 2020; especially shrill: Snyder 2017; Stanley 2018).

But this book's main message is that the perilous potential of populism is far from always becoming reality; instead, the danger is often averted. Although populist chief executives incessantly *try* to skew political competitiveness and expand their power, many of these efforts to asphyxiate democracy do not succeed. Personalistic plebiscitarian leaders eagerly push and shove, but they often encounter manifold obstacles and do not get their way. Liberal democracy commands significantly greater resilience than recent observers have feared. While in principle, it can be dismantled from the inside by democratically elected populists, such sneaky demolition attempts usually face considerable, often resourceful resistance. Liberal checks and balances are difficult to overcome because they form an interlocking syndrome that draws substantial support from important stakeholders. Therefore, populist chief executives have managed to disassemble these institutional constraints only under fairly restrictive conditions and special circumstances. Only a few charismatic leaders have succeeded in strangling democracy; in a majority of cases, liberal pluralism has survived personalistic plebiscitarian governance.

Sustained populist pressure has steamrolled democracy only when two distinctive conditions have coincided, namely preexisting institutional weakness and conjunctural opportunities for boosting the chief executive's plebiscitarian mass base. First, charismatic leaders find the best chances for their personalistic power concentration project where the established institutional framework is particularly open to transformation or suffers from fragilities and debilities already. A brittle fortress, not to speak of a sandcastle, is easier to conquer. By contrast, institutional strength condemns transgressive leaders to hitting their head on firm walls and finding their quest for dominance blocked.

Second, to overcome the remaining constraints that even weak or middling institutions impose, personalistic leaders need enormous clout, which depends on lopsided backing from a massive majority of the people – the plebiscitarian aspect of populism. By invoking popular sovereignty, a supremely popular chief executive can overpower most opposition. While savvy political tactics, rhetorical gifts, and skillful performances can certainly help charismatic politicians boost their followership (cf. Moffitt 2016), there are crucial objective factors that strongly condition successful support generation. Without real bases, populist leaders cannot vault to a position of supremacy that allows them to vanquish the remaining veto players.

What is crucial for boosting populist mass support are two types of conjunctural opportunities that allow leaders to prove their charisma – either by averting catastrophic losses or by providing massive benefits. Paradoxically, certain kinds of acute, severe crises give populists a unique opportunity to perform magic by resolving the problem with bold, drastic countermeasures. Because people have a strong aversion to losses, such relief – even if it requires temporary sacrifice – earns a successful crisis manager an outpouring of backing. The best example of such a serious conjunctural challenge is runaway inflation, which threatens the livelihood of most people, but which a drastic adjustment program can, in principle, quickly stop (Weyland 2002: chaps. 3, 5). When encountering such a costly, yet resolvable threat, personalistic leaders can potentially perform the alchemistic trick of turning adversity into advantage: If they manage to demonstrate their credentials as saviors of the people, they receive widespread gratitude and intense admiration. The miraculous feat of averting a looming catastrophe strengthens the charismatic bond and multiplies the leader's mass following.

In a more straightforward way, a major bonanza and revenue windfall also enable populist leaders to engineer great improvements in popular well-being. By administering a substantial increase in prosperity, they can "miraculously" boost life chances, especially for poorer people. By turning into the nation's benefactor, they demonstrate how their political predominance finally fulfills the long-neglected needs of the suffering people, previously marginalized by selfish, corrupt elites that had long maintained a stranglehold over the government.

Both types of conjunctural opportunities are largely exogenous to populist leadership, as explained later. Thus, my theory highlights given parameters that strongly condition how far the power concentration drive of personalistic plebiscitarian politicians can advance. Even charismatic chief executives do not encounter a degree of political plasticity that gives them free rein for their autocratic designs. Instead, they face preexisting institutional barriers of differential strength, and they depend on conjunctural developments to get the chance to overcome these barriers and achieve undemocratic hegemony.

Consequently, the objective constellation is crucial for explaining why only a minority of populist chief executives manages to strangle democracy – whereas many others fail in this effort. The necessary conditions for asphyxiating liberal pluralism are stringent: Only the coincidence of institutional weakness *and* a special conjunctural opportunity allows charismatic politicians to push through their autocratic project. For these reasons, populism is far from always overpowering democracy; liberal pluralism often survives the serious inherent risks that personalistic plebiscitarian leadership certainly poses.

This predominantly objectivist account does attribute some role to political agency, however. While given parameters provide necessary conditions for the populist destruction of democracy, they are not sufficient causes. The skill and success with which personalistic plebiscitarian chief executives take advantage of conjunctural opportunities for boosting their support are also important. For instance, do presidents distribute the benefits of resource windfalls in politically visible and strategic ways? Do populist leaders manage to combat urgent crises resolutely and effectively? After all, a crisis primarily poses a challenge. Turning this adversity into advantage by averting an imminent catastrophe and thus bringing enormous relief to the desperate population is a difficult task. Only leaders with aptitude can pass this demanding test and thus boost their charisma to the stratospheric levels required for entrenching their political hegemony in undemocratic ways. This additional condition – skillful political agency – makes the populist destruction of democracy even less likely.

For all of these reasons, populist leaders' capacity to do severe damage to democracy is distinctly limited. My analysis thus yields the encouraging conclusion that the grave concerns and dire warnings voiced in recent years have gone too far. Democracy enjoys much greater resilience than scholars shocked by the Brexit vote and Trump's election victory have feared. Strong institutions reliably safeguard liberal pluralism against succumbing to populist machinations, as the US experience corroborated. Even institutions that are weaker provide a good deal of protection, which personalistic plebiscitarian leaders can sweep aside only under unusual circumstances. The prospects of liberal pluralism are not as dark as many contemporary observers have painted them.

POPULISM: INHERENT TENDENCIES TOWARD AUTHORITARIANISM

There certainly are strong, valid reasons for the widespread concerns about populism's threat to democracy: The risk is real. This danger arises directly from personalistic plebiscitarian leadership, the central axis of populism according to my political-strategic approach. Specifically, personalism inspires the quest for political supremacy and unchallengeable authority, a preponderance of power that opens the door to abuse and jeopardizes liberal democracy. Indeed, personalism naturally has an anti-institutional impetus and combats checks and balances, which constitute essential safeguards for democratic freedom. Moreover, plebiscitarianism with its reliance on direct, largely unorganized mass support constitutes a fairly precarious, volatile base of populist rule. To compensate, leaders try to elicit particularly intense commitment from their followers by stoking constant confrontation against "enemies of the people." To supercharge the charismatic bond, they turn politics into a war. By fiercely attacking the opposition and abridging its rights, they skew the political and electoral arena and undermine democracy. Thus, both of populism's definitional features seriously endanger liberal pluralism.

As regards personalism, strong-willed, overbearing leaders are determined to stretch their own autonomy and clout and achieve the largest room for maneuver. Convinced of their quasi-divine mission, they seek full political hegemony. Consequently, they want to overcome the separation of powers, a cornerstone of liberal democracy. Moreover, they eagerly try to perpetuate their own rule, shredding term limits and preventing electoral alternation with tricks. In all of these ways, they try to abolish the institutionalized uncertainty that is foundational for democracy (Przeworski 1991: 10–14, 40–50).

By contrast to populism, liberal democracy is fundamentally anti-personalistic. It relies on strong, firm institutions to prevent the abuse of government power and protect individual liberty. Resting on Weber's (1976: 124–30) rational-legal type of legitimacy, democracy establishes an institutional framework that treats everybody as equal before the law. But personalistic leaders, convinced of their own exceptional importance, claim to be above the law; charisma entails inherent aversion to rules (*Regelfremdheit*, Weber 1976: 141). No wonder that populist politicians see liberal democracy as an enormous obstacle to their political strategy. They seek to strip away institutional constraints in order to enhance their own preeminence.

Thus, whereas liberal democracy is sustained by carefully designed and calibrated institutional configurations (Lijphart 1999), personalism acts like acid that corrodes and seeks to dissolve these hindrances to political arbitrariness. As Weber emphasized, charisma with its expansive momentum has an inherently anti-institutional bent. The anointed leader claims providential legitimacy for overriding and transforming the existing norms. As Jesus Christ declared: "It stands written [in the official rule books] – but I say unto you" (Weber 1976: 141, 657). Accordingly, personalistic politicians incessantly try to erode, bend, or break the checks and balances that are essential for maintaining political freedom and democratic competitiveness.

Like personalism, the plebiscitarian side of populism also causes serious, and interrelated, risks for democracy. Based on direct, unmediated appeals and uninstitutionalized connections to the followers, populist leadership rests on a flimsy, unreliable foundation (Weber 1976: 655–56). Whereas programmatic parties instill organizational discipline and clientelistic networks forge lasting bonds of personal reciprocity (Kitschelt 2000: 847–53), populist leaders do not command such firm, dependable support. Instead, through mass rallies, TV, or social media such as Twitter and WhatsApp, they convoke their backers with episodic face-to-face communications that seek to establish quasi-personal ties. But of course, by encompassing thousands, if not millions of people, these plebiscitarian appeals differ fundamentally from the "strong ties" of true personal relations (Granovetter 1973). While the leader seeks to establish a permanent presence in followers' lives, for instance through Hugo Chávez's hours and hours of TV shows and Donald Trump's avalanche of tweetstorms, this presence is by nature ethereal and lacks the close familiarity and reciprocity that undergird direct, firm personal bonds. Consequently, this fictional, performative personalism does not guarantee a solid base for plebiscitarian, populist rule. Instead, charismatic authority is by nature subject to lability (Weber 1976: 656).

To compensate for this congenital weakness and forestall a meltdown in their mass support, charismatic politicians seek to make the outreach to their followers particularly intense and fervent. In the absence of organizational discipline and clientelistic linkages, they maximize the emotional energy of bonding with their followers and try to elicit total, unconditional commitment and devotion (Weber 1976: 140, 142, 655–58; see recently Andrews-Lee 2021: 30–37, 54–59). For this purpose, they discard regular, respectful political competition and instead frame their democratic opponents as dangerous foes and "enemies of the people." By provoking all-out conflict, they try to induce their supporters to rally around them in this war. They incite fierce political battles in order to turn into indispensable protectors of the people who are forced to take their side. These deliberately confrontational tactics destroy political tolerance and liberal pluralism and replace rule-bound competition with a fight to the political death. In particular, determined to avert defeat by their supposedly nefarious adversaries, populist leaders are always tempted to (mis)use any means at their disposal in order to block or undo opposition victories. Liberal democracy cannot thrive in this conflict zone, and risks getting trampled to death.

This penchant for polarization reflects not only the power hunger of personalistic leaders but also the inherent weaknesses of their plebiscitarian approach. After all, the precarious base provided by quasi-personal, unorganized mass support entails a great deal of political vulnerability. Performance fluctuations or embarrassing scandals can quickly deflate the popularity and followership of populist leaders and jeopardize their political fate. Striking failures have in several cases culminated in ignominious evictions from office (Weyland 2022a).

To preempt these risks to their own tenure, populist chief executives follow the motto that offense is the best defense and eagerly attack their declared enemies and potential adversaries (Weyland 2019: 325–26). For this purpose, they seek to undermine all opposition forces and take over their institutional bastions, especially the other branches of government and independent agencies such as the election administration. The aggressive approach and expansive drive of populist politicians, which threatens liberal pluralism, thus stem in part from the urge to avert the risks arising from the precarious nature of plebiscitarianism. Populist leaders do not only want to concentrate power; they feel the need to do so in order to protect themselves against counterattacks from the political forces whom they themselves antagonized.

For all of these reasons, the confrontation that charismatic politicians systematically promote is self-perpetuating and self-reinforcing. Polarization feeds on polarization, exacerbating the damage to liberal pluralism that scholars bemoan (McCoy and Somer 2019, 2022; Svolik 2019; Mettler and Lieberman 2020). Because adversaries are tempted to respond in kind to populists' relentless forays, a vicious circle begins to swirl. This whirlpool risks destroying democracy, either by inducing populist incumbents to smother liberal pluralism or, contrariwise, by provoking coups against the autocratic pushiness of personalistic plebiscitarian rulers (Helmke 2017; Kuehn and Trinkunas 2017; Levitsky and Murillo 2020).

In sum, populism by nature poses serious threats to democracy. Personalistic plebiscitarian leadership is inherently antagonistic to liberal checks and balances and jeopardizes the preservation of individual freedom and of competitiveness, which is democracy's core (Schmitter 1983: 887–91). In recent decades, several populist leaders – Fujimori, Chávez, Morales, Correa, Bukele, Orbán, and Erdoğan – have in fact asphyxiated liberal pluralism and installed authoritarian rule. Thus, recent observers are certainly justified in expressing concern that populism imperils liberal pluralism.

But the crucial question is, how severe is this peril? How likely is it that personalistic plebiscitarian leaders can actually achieve their illiberal, autocratic goals and strangle democracy? As my theory argues, the effective threat of populism depends on the coincidence of institutional weakness, which opens room for personalistic power concentration, and on conjunctural opportunities for boosting plebiscitarian mass support, which can give populist chief executives the overwhelming clout for installing competitive authoritarianism. The following sections examine these two types of necessary conditions in turn.

POPULIST AGENCY VS. INSTITUTIONAL CONSTRAINTS

With its transgressive, expansive impetus, personalistic plebiscitarian leadership inherently stands in tension with institutional constraints.[1] Where checks and balances are tight and firm, populist chief executives are hobbled and cannot do lasting damage to democracy. Yet where institutions leave room for discretion, where they are easy to disrespect with impunity, or where they can be dismantled or transformed at will, there is a real potential for democratic involution. Thus, institutional weakness is a crucial permissive cause for democratic backsliding promoted by populists; conversely, institutional strength and stickiness reliably protect liberal pluralism.[2]

Interestingly, the openings that institutional structures leave for sneaky populists depend not only on their formal design and configuration, such as parliamentarism vs. presidentialism (see in general Linz 1990; Tsebelis 1995, 2002; Lijphart 1999) but also on the underlying strength of the institutional framework. As institutionalists have long emphasized (Huntington 1968; Mainwaring and Scully 1995; Elkins, Ginsburg, and Melton 2009; Mainwaring 2018; Brinks, Levitsky, and Murillo 2019), political systems vary greatly on this fundamental factor. Two dimensions of institutionalization hold special importance, namely the degree of compliance that institutions command, and their stickiness and endurance (Levitsky and Murillo 2009, 2013; Brinks, Levitsky, and Murillo 2019: 16–28; see in general Mahoney and Thelen 2010: 7–14).

Accordingly, institutions are weak, first, if they cannot reliably guide and shape political behavior, but are commonly disregarded and lack effective sanctions for deterring such shirking. If enforcement is lax and actors frequently get away with disrespecting the rules on the books, formal institutions lack relevance and bite. The second source of weakness arises if institutions can be changed with ease. In that case, the framework of rules fails to impose constraints on current power holders, who can simply strip away the existing fetters. Even worse, institutions of high plasticity can turn into instruments for incumbents to pursue their goals; easy to reforge, they provide

---

[1] The following paragraphs draw heavily on Weyland (2020: 392).

[2] The institutional and constitutional framework creates much firmer constraints on populist agency than the party system, whose strength is subject to fluctuations in political support. Indeed, in their initial electoral upsurge, populist leaders can quickly dislodge and destroy existing parties, especially if they benefit from the conjunctural opportunities discussed later. Therefore, party strength does not constitute a significant independent variable beyond the two main factors highlighted in this book. For instance, opposition parties that can electorally defeat populist presidents survive in countries not afflicted by acute, massive crises, as in Bolsonaro's Brazil and the USA under Trump, but not in crisis-wrecked Peru under Fujimori, recession-plagued Venezuela during Chávez's first term, and crime-ridden El Salvador under Bukele. As regards the relative strength of governing populist formations (Rhodes-Purdy and Madrid 2020: 326–27), this factor shapes democracy's fate in contradictory ways: For instance, it hindered Menem's quest for continuing self-perpetuation in 1998–99 in Argentina, but facilitated Orbán's resolute drive for illiberal hegemony in Hungary.

tailor-made tools for pursuing power concentration and curtailing the opposition. With such opportunistic usage, the law serves not as the essential scaffolding of democracy but as a building block for authoritarianism (Corrales 2015; Scheppele 2018).

These two dimensions yield a simple typology with – in principle – three forms of institutional weakness, resulting from the possible combinations of easy changeability and weak compliance. Accordingly, political regimes suffer from institutional weakness if they are highly susceptible to legal changes of formal rules; if there is widespread, unsanctioned disrespect of formal rules; or – in intersection – if powerful actors can employ para-legal or illegal means *and* push through transformations of formal rules.

First, some institutional frameworks facilitate their own fully legal transformation through electoral rules that produce disproportionate majorities, and through regime institutions that create weak checks and balances and set low thresholds for changing the constitution.[3] Such weakness via comparatively easy changeability creates the principal risk for democracy in advanced countries because it allows a populist leader gradually to dismantle and suffocate liberal pluralism through a series of perfectly legal measures, which are more difficult to oppose than open violations and forceful impositions. Domestic and international defenders of democracy find it difficult to draw a clear line in the sand and mobilize for safeguarding democracy's core principles. Even educated mass publics, which tend to be particularly committed to liberal values, and vibrant, resourceful societies may be at a loss about when and how to resist a populist's savvy usage of "autocratic legalism" (Corrales 2015; Scheppele 2018).

A second type of institutional weakness prevails where "creative reinterpretations," flexible extensions, or simple infringements of formal rules are feasible, if not common, and do not carry effective sanctions. In these settings, chief executives can arrogate attributions that they officially do not possess, overstep formal boundaries unimpeded, and use strong informal pressures to take control of supposedly independent agencies.[4] In Argentina, for instance, Carlos Menem (1989–99) unilaterally decided to use decree powers far beyond the emergency situations for which the constitution foresaw them and for which they had consistently been used before (Ferreira Rubio and Goretti 1998); and Cristina Fernández de Kirchner (2007–15) para-legally removed the Central Bank president, ultimately by having the police block access to his office (Rebossio 2010).

If the official rules lack stringency and bite, and if political actors get away with these kinds of deviant behavior, they can potentially concentrate power

---

[3] Indeed, great ease of constitutional amendment is "associated with an increased risk of [constitutional] death" (Elkins, Ginsburg, and Melton 2009: 140).

[4] The book employs the term "para-legal" for these kinds of institutional changes that happen in the gray zone between fully legal and clearly illegal.

and surreptitiously move toward authoritarianism while leaving a pristine set of democratic rules on the books. But such a fairly open and growing gulf between the legal framework and actual political practice is problematic and risky by offering a wedge for domestic opposition and international criticism. Relying only on para-legal imposition provokes resistance and conflict, especially in world regions with dense linkages to Western countries, the global protagonists of liberal values and democratic principles (cf. Levitsky and Way 2010). The contention stirred up by para-legal machinations creates substantial friction and slows down the advance of populists' autocratic projects, which may therefore run up against presidential term limits. Indeed, opposition mobilization may expose the personalistic transgressors to forceful counterattacks, which can jeopardize their own tenure in office and thus abort their strangulation of democracy (Weyland 2022a; see also Kuehn and Trinkunas 2017; Sato and Arce 2022).

Consequently, what is more dangerous for democratic survival is the third, combined pattern, unfolding in sequence: With an opening burst of para-legal measures, populist aggressors remove institutional obstacles to the wholesale transformation of the constitutional framework; then they take advantage of this plasticity to tailor-make a new set of rules. Often, the initial breach forces through the convocation of a constituent assembly, which – under populist hegemony – pliantly redesigns major regime institutions by augmenting the attributions of the chief executive, weakening mechanisms of horizontal accountability, and introducing direct-democratic procedures designed to engineer plebiscitarian acclamation (for the paradigmatic Venezuelan case, see Brewer-Carías 2010 and Corrales 2022: chap. 2; for additional cases, see Corrales 2018).

Thus, where pushy populists can forcefully transform the existing rules with impunity, they often – in a seemingly paradoxical but entirely logical and strategic fashion – use initial violations to impose a new institutional framework that fortifies their own power and cements their preeminence. Then they rigorously enforce their new tailor-made rules against the opposition, often in a politicized way that resorts to "discriminatory legalism," in line with the old motto: "For my friends, anything and everything; yet for my enemies, the law" (Weyland 2013: 23–25; Müller 2016: 44–47).

This crafty sequence, in which an initial para-legal push shatters the whole institutional framework and ushers in a profound, comprehensive transformation, is especially likely where the established order has already been shaken by drastic challenges. In presidential systems, forceful efforts to remove chief executives through irregular means and rudely interrupt their supposedly fixed terms of office can have a particularly destabilizing impact. Where such attempts succeed, they set a deleterious precedent and further undermine institutional resilience. In such situations of high instability, the sequence of para-legal imposition and constitutional overhaul has the highest likelihood of unfolding. Compared to the middling degrees of institutional strength associated with easy changeability and para-legal change alone, the combination of these two types that can unfold under high instability makes the constitutional order extraordinarily brittle and fluid.

What threats to democracy arise from these types of institutional weakness, which give populist chief executives substantial, even increasing room for maneuver? The following three sections demonstrate how personalistic plebiscitarian leaders can pursue their illiberal and authoritarian goals by taking advantage of easy legal changeability, the para-legal imposition of institutional transformations, and their sequential combination under high instability.

RELATIVE OPENNESS TO INSTITUTIONAL CHANGE: THE RISK
INHERENT IN PARLIAMENTARY SYSTEMS

In their formal design, some institutional frameworks, especially the majoritarian "Westminster model" (Lijphart 1999: chap. 2), are open to legal transformation because they facilitate the formation of lopsided parliamentary majorities and stipulate low requirements for constitutional amendments. By contrast, other systems make such alterations prohibitively difficult or proclaim basic principles as unalterable. The US constitution, for instance, is extraordinarily hard to reform because in addition to supermajorities in both houses of Congress, three-quarters of the states have to approve any amendment (on the importance of constitutional rigidity, see recently Tsebelis 2022).

In general, the smaller the number of independent "veto players" that an institutional configuration features, the more open to transformation it tends to be, and the lower is its stickiness and likely persistence. According to the author of this theory, "veto players are individual or collective actors whose agreement is necessary for a change of the status quo" (Tsebelis 2002: 19). Constitutional frameworks that concentrate authority and promote the political alignment of different branches of government have few veto players and therefore allow for easy transformations. By contrast, a far-reaching and strict separation of powers and the imposition of supermajority thresholds for approving alterations, such as constitutional amendments, foster institutional stasis. The complexity of institutional configurations, which combine a variety of components ranging from the number, attributions, and selection rules of legislative chambers to the presence and stringency of judicial review, give rise to multifaceted edifices that shape the elasticity and resilience of the overarching framework (see especially Lijphart 1999; Tsebelis 2002).

Among these variegated institutional features, the single most important structure, which has therefore drawn the greatest interest from political scientists (ranging from the seminal analysis by Linz 1990 to Mainwaring and Shugart 1997 and Cheibub 2007), is the system of government, especially the difference between parliamentarism and presidentialism. In terms of the preceding discussion of institutional weaknesses, parliamentary systems embody relatively easy changeability. Their formal design facilitates legal rule changes because they enshrine comparatively few checks and balances in their institutional set-up. After all, prime ministers depend on parliamentary toleration and usually command majority support in the legislature, with which they can pursue the overhaul of infraconstitutional rules, including electoral laws. By exacerbating disproportionality, these changes in turn can help engineer an overwhelming parliamentary majority, which then allows for approving constitutional amendments or summoning a constituent assembly.

The number of veto players is especially low in parliamentary systems with a unicameral legislature (Tsebelis 2002: 78–79). If, in addition, the electoral system has a strong majoritarian bent, fully democratic, free, and fair elections can produce supermajorities that can overhaul the constitution and thus have free rein for pursuing any goal they embrace – a golden opportunity for power-hungry populists. With this combination of institutional features, which created unusually weak checks and balances, Hungary constituted Eastern Europe's "most majoritarian" democracy (Bogaards 2018: 1490). No wonder that the easy changeability of this parliamentary system – together with a special opportunity discussed later – enabled populist prime minister Viktor Orbán to asphyxiate liberal democracy in perfectly legal ways. Typically, this personalistic leader started with a quick redesign of the constitution and then cemented his predominance by further skewing electoral rules.[5] In Turkey, Recep Tayyip Erdoğan similarly took advantage of the openings provided by a parliamentary system and a fairly flexible constitution to push systematically toward competitive authoritarianism; yet because he confronted an extra-official veto player, namely the military, he was compelled to proceed in more gradual and winding ways, as Chapter 5 explains (Esen and Gumuscu 2016; Cagaptay 2017; Somer 2019; Yavuz 2021).

As these two experiences of democracy's self-destruction show, parliamentarism with its attenuated separation of powers – especially when combined with unicameralism and high constitutional flexibility, as in Hungary (Lorenz 2005: 358–59) – imposes comparatively weak formal-institutional constraints on populist rulers. The low number of veto players allows, in principle, for constitutional transformations that strangle political liberalism without violating a single official rule (Scheppele 2018). Due to its formal legality, such a sneaky suppression of democracy is particularly difficult to oppose, both for domestic anti-populists and for international guardians of liberal pluralism, such as the European Union (Pirro and Stanley 2022: 92–94).

Fortunately, however, the potential danger inherent in the easy changeability of parliamentarism does not automatically become reality – it only transpires under special conditions, which do not occur frequently, as discussed later. Often, partisan fragmentation prevents the government from marshaling

---

[5] See especially Scheppele 2018; and Körösényi, Illés, and Gyulai 2020; see also Krasztev and Van Til 2015; Lendvai 2017; Pirro and Stanley 2022: 91–95, 97.

the necessary cohesion and clout for passing institutional changes, especially transformations of the constitution.

After all, most parliamentary systems use proportional representation for elections, which fosters multiparty systems. In Europe's ever more complex and heterogeneous societies, parties have proliferated as the old catch-all parties have lost support to new contenders. Yet while diminished, the formerly predominant parties have not collapsed; instead, they continue to limit the space available for newcomers, including populists (on the interesting case of Spain, e.g., see Mazzolini and Borriello 2022: 290–93). For these reasons, it is rare for one party, including a charismatic leader, to win a clear majority, not to speak of a supermajority that can unilaterally approve constitutional amendments or promulgate a whole new charter. Thus, parliamentary systems usually compensate for their low number of institutional veto players by featuring a comparatively high number of partisan veto players (Tsebelis 2002: 19–20, 79).

The political obstacles arising from party fragmentation have hobbled populist leaders in several of Europe's parliamentary systems. Headstrong Vladimír Mečiar in Slovakia (1990–91, 1992–94, 1994–98), for instance, pursued similar illiberal goals as Hungary's Orbán in a polity that allowed for easy constitutional change (Fish 1999: 53–54). But because Mečiar's party lacked a parliamentary majority, his push for political hegemony was hindered by his unreliable coalition partners (Haughton 2002). Similarly, party fragmentation helped Italian democracy survive Silvio Berlusconi's populist governments (1994, 2001–6, 2008–11; Taggart and Rovira Kaltwasser 2016: 351–52). As his party *Forza Italia* never won a majority, he had to form alliances with obstreperous right-wing parties. Therefore, the *Cavaliere*'s governments were always tension-ridden and lacked the clout to transform the institutional order; in particular, a major effort at constitutional reform failed in 2006 (Körösényi and Patkós 2017: 319).

Thus, parliamentary systems have few institutional veto players, but they often make up for this weakness through electoral rules that give rise to a number of partisan veto players (Tsebelis 2002: 78–80). The political friction and governmental lability that result from party fragmentation create obstacles for populist leaders. If they depend on heterogeneous, fractious support coalitions, they cannot easily take advantage of the institutional openness arising from the attenuated separation of powers. Thus, due to other institutional safeguards, especially proportional representation, parliamentarism's easy susceptibility to rule changes usually does not have serious, truly deleterious repercussions for democracy.

There is a basic difference between institutional and partisan veto players, however, which makes parliamentary systems more susceptible to change – and therefore to populist strangulation efforts – than presidential systems in principle are: Whereas the configuration of institutional veto players is firmly enshrined in the constitution, the constellation of partisan veto players is less solid because it emerges from the interaction of infraconstitutional electoral rules and the distribution of political preferences. In particular, the legislative strength of parties depends on their electoral performance, which can change drastically due to scandals or crises. Accordingly, an electoral earthquake can replace a multiparty legislature with the dominance of one political force. Because partisan veto players can suffer a meltdown, parliamentary systems with their low numbers of institutional veto players have an Achilles' heel that populist leaders can exploit. In sum, parliamentarism's reliance on partisan veto players provides lower safeguards than presidentialism with its larger number of institutional veto players.

Parliamentarism's weak flank has important implications for democracy's resilience to populist strangulation efforts. As I argue in the section on "The Importance of Exogenous Opportunities" later in this chapter, the capacity of power-hungry leaders to overcome party fragmentation, reduce the number of partisan players, and push through their undemocratic projects depends on crises that discredit establishment parties and facilitate populist triumphs in elections. First, however, our attention turns to other kinds of institutional weakness.

PARA-LEGAL IMPOSITION OF CHANGE: WEAKNESSES IN PRESIDENTIAL SYSTEMS

Due to their formal configuration, constitutional frameworks that foresee larger numbers of institutional veto players are more difficult to change and therefore pose substantial obstacles to the transformative impulses of populist chief executives. A presidential system of government embodies a strict separation of powers, and bicameralism creates further constraints. These safeguards only exert effective force, however, if institutional rules command reliable compliance. But this condition is not uniformly guaranteed. Instead, chief executives often control great de facto power, based on their party leadership, command over patronage, and authority over the forces of organized coercion (see especially Mainwaring and Shugart 1997).

Where the rule of law suffers from weaknesses, as in much of Latin America and the rest of the developing world, formal institutions are more or less porous and cannot firmly constrain political actors. Instead, strong-willed presidents can bend or override official rules – and may get away with their transgressions and infringements.[6] Thus, they can chip away at checks and balances, corrode the constitutional framework, and gradually enlarge their room for maneuver. Where the institutional configuration suffers from such a lack of bite, populist leaders can, in principle, try to strangle liberal democracy by imposing a whole series of power-concentrating transformations in para-legal ways.

---

[6] Huntington 1968; Mainwaring and Scully 1995; Levitsky and Murillo 2009, 2013; Brinks, Levitsky, and Murillo 2019.

Yet despite this possibility of para-legal change, many of Latin America's presidential systems command a reasonable degree of institutional strength – more than European parliamentarism. After all, official checks and balances hinder the fully legal overhaul of the constitutional order that is feasible on the Old Continent. Compared to this smooth process, para-legal alterations provoke resistance and conflict. The bending or breach of formal rules carries political costs and risks. Pressure on existing laws and the forceful imposition of change provoke opposition, which has in recent decades increased with domestic modernization and the cross-national diffusion of liberal principles and democratic norms, especially in the Americas. This gradual legalization of politics has increasingly inhibited para-legal transformations, which used to be common in Latin America.

All of this friction makes it difficult for personalistic plebiscitarian leaders to push through their projects of power concentration via a comprehensive series of para-legal changes. Due to their own confrontational strategy, new populist presidents often face strong, if not majoritarian opposition in Congress and encounter courts full of judges appointed by the old "political class." These adversaries commonly use – and even stretch – their own attributions in trying to impede the illiberal and undemocratic designs promoted by the chief executive.[7]

As a result, personalistic plebiscitarian leaders can usually make only limited headway with their efforts at para-legal imposition. Active opposition and passive resistance slow down their advance. Above all, a forceful push for a constituent assembly is very difficult, if not impossible, under normal conditions. For this reason, the chance for a comprehensive, overarching revamping of the constitutional order that could really jeopardize democracy is low. Because in the face of political obstacles, para-legal change can proceed only at a glacial pace, term limits sooner or later foreclose further populist machinations. Consequently, despite an infringement here and an infraction there, democracy normally survives.

It is only under exceptional conditions – discussed later – that para-legal, if not illegal change enables a personalistic plebiscitarian president to undo the established constitutional framework and abolish democracy. A unique cumulation of severe crises provided such a conjunctural opportunity for Alberto Fujimori in Peru, and El Salvador's Nayib Bukele has recently benefited from a similar coincidence. But the fact that these para-legal assaults on liberal pluralism were feasible only under such extraordinary conditions shows that many presidential systems in Latin America with their middling levels of institutionalization create considerable protection for liberal pluralism.

---

[7] An emblematic recent case is the political activism of Brazil's Supreme Court judge Alexandre de Moraes, who combated Bolsonaro's pressures on liberal pluralism with unilateral expansions of judicial authority that raised serious concerns about violations of democracy (Nicas 2023).

Consequently, a number of Latin American populists did not succeed with their para-legal pressures on the institutional framework; others ceded to opposition and reluctantly abandoned such efforts, including the attempt to lift or disregard existing term limits – a crucial goal of personalistic plebiscitarian rulers. For instance, Argentina's Carlos Menem had his crass overuse of decree powers reined in by a constitutional convention in 1994 and was compelled to step down at the end of his second term in 1999. Álvaro Uribe (2002–10) in Colombia accepted the results of a plebiscite defeat in 2003 and shelved an ambitious constitutional reform; moreover, he reluctantly complied with a Supreme Court ruling that barred his plan of another reelection in 2010 (Ginsburg and Huq 2018a: 24–26). Also, when the entourage of Argentina's Cristina Fernández de Kirchner (2007–15) floated the idea of abolishing term limits in 2012, massive opposition protests and low popularity ratings blocked this move. Thus, several populist presidents in Latin America have not managed to force through power-concentrating and tenure-extending institutional reforms that could have paved the way toward authoritarianism.

Thus, the medium levels of institutionalization that prevail in much of Latin America create substantial obstacles for personalistic plebiscitarian leaders to promote their illiberal goals and destroy democracy. While para-legal change is feasible, it usually prompts resistance; the resulting political costs often impede its proliferation. In many countries, pushy presidents can take one step at a time, but they cannot impose a whole series of transformations that could squeeze and eventually squash liberal pluralism. Consequently, para-legal change can open the door to authoritarianism only under very special circumstances, as discussed later.

HIGH INSTABILITY: BRITTLE INSTITUTIONAL FRAMEWORKS

Political liberalism faces much greater risks where the institutional order is truly weak and the obstacles to para-legal, if not illegal change are low. In a brittle framework of rules, high instability can emerge. Such precariousness prevails where striking precedents of irregular political maneuver have occurred and achieved their goals or not drawn prohibitive sanctions. In particular, have forceful pressures and extraprocedural machinations pushed out presidents prematurely, a hugely conflictual move? Have these political shocks happened in countries whose constitutions have lacked durability and undergone serial replacement (cf. Lutz 1994; Lorenz 2005)? While the third wave of democratization (1970s–1980s) has enhanced institutional strength in Latin America, especially through strong international efforts to prevent military coups, some countries have experienced distinctive phases of high instability after their institutional order has been battered by serious challenges.

In presidential systems as in Latin America, the main causes and clearest indicators of high instability are unconventional, procedurally problematic removals of chief executives: Incumbents see their officially fixed terms of office interrupted and are forced out through spiraling contentious protests, discriminatory parliamentary scheming, or, even worse, military coercion. Where disruptive events such as popular insurgencies, severely politicized impeachments, or attempted or successful coups recur and topple more than one president in short order, the institutional framework becomes truly precarious. This degree of institutional debility undermines the resilience of liberal pluralism and gives new personalistic plebiscitarian leaders particular latitude for pursuing their political projects, especially the undemocratic concentration of power.

High instability is the third and most severe type of institutional weakness considered in my theory. Like the other types, I treat this permissive cause as an antecedent condition for populist power grabs. By assessing the level of institutional strength before a personalistic plebiscitarian leader takes office, I avoid inferential problems such as endogeneity. After all, populist chief executives themselves energetically try to dismantle institutional constraints; where they are successful, they may create or exacerbate political instability. To avoid mistaking this effect as a cause, my analysis ascertains whether high instability precedes the rise of a personalistic plebiscitarian leader. In this way, my study treats high instability as a factor exogenous to episodes of populist governance.

Interestingly, such high instability prevailed in the years *before* the election of three of Latin America's left-wing, Bolivarian populists who ended up suffocating democracy (Levitsky and Loxton 2013; Weyland 2013; Carrión 2022: 57–60, 64–73). During the decade preceding the governments of Evo Morales and Rafael Correa, contentious mass demonstrations, sometimes combined with questionable congressional maneuvers, had driven two presidents from power in Bolivia (2003, 2005) and in Ecuador (1997, 2005); the latter country had lost another president in a civil-military coup (2000; see Pachano 2005; Mejía Acosta and Polga-Hecimovich 2011: 100–4). Similarly, the years before Hugo Chávez's election in 1998 had been rocked by two dangerous coup attempts in 1992, which helped to trigger a politicized presidential impeachment in 1993. Thus, these conflictual events had already pounded democracy's institutional scaffolding before these personalistic plebiscitarian leaders took the helm.

Indeed, this high instability erupted on a historical background of institutional fluidity. All three countries had over the decades experienced a great deal of constitutional churn. Ecuador had replaced its 1978 charter by adopting a new constitution in 1998, only ten years before Correa pushed through a complete replacement – which would become the twentieth constitution in the country's fewer than 200 years of independent history. Bolivia had enacted a major constitutional reform in 1994, twelve years before Morales started pushing through his own overhaul, which yielded the nation's seventeenth charter. Venezuela, in turn, had since the early nineteenth century cycled through twenty-six constitutions, the third-highest number in the world (Elkins, Ginsburg, and Melton 2009: 23, 26). With such legacies of serial replacement (Levitsky and Murillo

2013: 95–100), constitutional frameworks lacked solidity and the strength to anchor the political order.

Built on such shifty ground, these battered democracies were especially vulnerable to the forceful initiation of institutional transformations and had little resilience against the hegemonic projects of populist leaders. High instability embodies a particularly low degree of institutional strength, which differs from the middling levels prevailing in countries subject to the occasional imposition of para-legal change. Where formal rules are precarious and cannot command reliable compliance because recent drastic challenges have established dangerous precedents, personalistic leaders enjoy great room for maneuver to pursue their power-concentrating and self-perpetuating projects. Previous sappers have already undermined the protective fortress of liberal pluralism. These breaches facilitate further assaults.

This institutional weakness can enable new populist presidents to employ para-legal pressure for ushering in a comprehensive project of power concentration and gradual suppression of liberal pluralism. For this purpose, they try to arrogate a right that they officially do not possess by pushing through the convocation of a constituent assembly, even against resistance from other branches of government. If – under the special conditions examined later – they manage to garner overwhelming mass support, they can turn the principle of popular sovereignty against the established liberal framework and forge ahead with their imposition. Predictably, the constitutional conventions summoned with these strong-arm tactics do the populists' bidding: They boost presidential powers, allow for reelection, and undermine checks and balances, for instance by abolishing the upper chamber of congress.[8] Thus, the initial breach of rules enables the creation of a new institutional framework with weak safeguards and predominant majoritarianism, tailor-made for populist authoritarianism (Levitsky and Loxton 2013; Weyland 2013).

Where these para-legal projects of illiberal institutional transformation went forward, the populist redesign of the constitution often turned into a continuous process as power-hungry leaders sought to fortify and further extend their hegemony. Typically, personalistic plebiscitarian presidents pursued first and foremost their own self-perpetuation in power. While the charters emerging from the initial overhaul forced by Chávez, Correa, and Morales allowed for one consecutive reelection, during their second terms these presidents pushed for lengthening their tenure through additional changes or various tricks (Carrión 2022: 190–206). For instance, Chávez called a plebiscite to lift presidential term limits in 2007; and after he lost, he simply organized another referendum in 2009 – and finally won. With one para-legal step after the other, these populists trampled democracy to death.

---

[8] For the emblematic case of Chávez, who established a roadmap later followed by left-wing populists in Bolivia, Ecuador, and Honduras (Weyland 2013), see Brewer-Carías (2010). For the "Bolivarian" cases more broadly, see Corrales (2018).

Thus, under conditions of high instability, para-legal change can open the door to comprehensive efforts to overhaul the constitutional framework and initiate a process that over time suppresses liberal pluralism. Yet this continuous pushing and shoving provokes resistance as well. Therefore, this path toward the strangulation of democracy is politically feasible only under special conditions that allow the populist assailant to win massive popular support. The essential conjunctural opportunity that undergirds this outpouring of plebiscitarian acclamation is discussed in the section on "The Importance of Exogenous Opportunities" later in this chapter.

CONCLUSIONS ON INSTITUTIONAL DEBILITY

As the preceding three sections show, there are different types of institutional weakness that facilitate populist efforts to smother democracy. In their formal structure, parliamentary systems with their limited numbers of institutional veto players are fairly open to illiberal transformations. Presidential systems with their checks and balances enshrine a stricter separation of powers, but their rules and procedures can be bent or overridden through forceful para-legal machinations where the rule of law is not reliably guaranteed. Even worse, highly unstable polities with fluid institutional frameworks pose weak obstacles to the power hunger of personalistic plebiscitarian presidents.

An interesting insight emerges from this discussion, which suggests an ordinal ranking of relative institutional weakness. Obviously, high instability carries special risks for democratic survival. Then, among less precarious frameworks, the easy changeability of parliamentarism tends to provide greater latitude for populist machinations than what para-legal change under presidentialism permits. Thus, divergent from Linz's claim about the particular "perils of presidentialism" (Linz 1990; Linz and Valenzuela 1994), parliamentary systems have inherent institutional weaknesses that carry their own serious risks. Their attenuated separation of powers leaves considerable leeway for chief executives' power concentration efforts, the biggest threat to democracy after the end of the Cold War (Ginsburg and Huq 2018b; Haggard and Kaufman 2021). Given this danger, parliamentarism does not provide any firmer safeguard against the populist strangulation of democracy than does presidentialism (considering both the highly unstable and the more solid presidential systems).

This approximate equivalence of risks across parliamentary and presidential systems prevails especially after the virtual preclusion of military coups in contemporary Europe and Latin America; after all, coups had since World War II toppled disproportionate numbers of presidential systems (Linz 1990; Cheibub 2007). Indeed, throughout history, parliamentarism had not enjoyed a greater degree of stability, as the frequent downfall of parliamentary democracies during the interwar years corroborates (Metcalf 1998: 346; Weyland 2021a: 46–47). Overall, as recent statistical investigations confirm (see especially

Cheibub 2007) and as Chapters 3–5 corroborate, the system of government does not condition democracy's fate nearly as much as important authors had argued: Death rates under parliamentarism and presidentialism seem fairly similar.

In general, the preceding sections yield the distressing conclusion that no kind of institutional design can reliably foreclose undemocratic machinations. Charismatic politicians with their expansive and transgressive impulses and their relentless quest for greater power can usually find some loophole or soft spot through which they can try to breach the protective armor of liberal pluralism. Institutional engineering cannot make democracy impregnable.

But fortunately, these variegated institutional openings provide only permissive causes for the strangulation of democracy by personalistic plebiscitarian leaders. While some type of institutional weakness constitutes a necessary condition, such debility is insufficient as a cause and does not automatically lead to populist authoritarianism. As the infrequency of this lamentable outcome shows (Kyle and Mounk 2018: 17; Ruth-Lovell, Lührmann, and Grahn 2019: 9), charismatic politicians do not find it easy to engineer and cement their hegemony. They succeed with their illiberal, autocratic projects only if, in addition to some type of institutional weakness, they benefit from unusual opportunities as well. Accordingly, different types of conditions – namely, institutional debilities *and* favorable exogenous conjunctures – have to coincide for liberal pluralism to fall to populist power grabs.

THE IMPORTANCE OF EXOGENOUS OPPORTUNITIES: ACUTE YET RESOLVABLE CRISES OR HUGE WINDFALLS

While institutional weakness constitutes a necessary precondition for the populist asphyxiation of democracy, even institutions of limited resilience still hinder the dismantling of checks and balances and the establishment of illiberal hegemony. To overcome these remaining obstacles, power-hungry chief executives need special clout. Before the third wave of democratization, they could use their command over military coercion, push away constraints, and simply impose autocratic rule. But in recent decades, democracy protection by the West has largely ruled out such forceful impositions via self-coups, especially in Europe and Latin America with their dense linkages to advanced industrialized democracies.[9]

Consequently, the main way for illiberal and autocratic rulers to push aside democracy's institutional safeguards in the contemporary era is to accumulate lopsided political support. For this purpose, it is decisive for populist leaders,

---

[9] Levitsky and Way 2010. The one exception, Fujimori's self-coup of 1992, was only politically sustainable because – in line with the argument of the next paragraph – the new autocrat received a massive outpouring of popular support with 80–82 percent approval (Conaghan 1995: 227, 236; Cameron 1998a: 224–25; Weyland 2002: 128–29, 171–72; Carrión 2006a: 131–34).

who rely on numbers as their primary power capability (Weyland 2001: 12–14), to achieve massive plebiscitarian acclamation. After all, it is hard for opposition forces to resist the steamroller provided by a broad groundswell of popular approval and charismatic followership. If populist leaders find backing from a large majority of the citizenry, they can invoke popular sovereignty to spearhead a profound transformation of the constitutional framework and overwhelm remaining resistance to their hegemonic project. In these ways, they can take advantage of the easy changeability of parliamentary systems or force through para-legal change under presidentialism, especially where high instability makes the established order brittle and precarious.

In complex societies with a variety of socioeconomic interests and diverse political cleavages, winning disproportionate support that bridges these divisions is not an easy task. Even many populists, who appeal to "the people" as a whole, do not manage to achieve this feat. Instead, it is only under extraordinary circumstances that personalistic plebiscitarian leaders succeed in garnering sky-high popularity and electoral invincibility. These crucial conditions emerge from exogenous opportunities for charismatic heroes to prove their "supernatural" prowess by making a huge difference in their followers' lives. Interestingly, they can do so in opposite ways, either by benefiting a wide range of people and sociopolitical forces with enormous benefits, or by averting an imminent catastrophe and protecting the population from massive looming losses. Thus, exceptional conjunctures that diverge from normal, regular situations in either direction – by allowing for the distribution of exceptional gains or for the avoidance of stark, imminent costs – give populist chief executives the chance to prove their charisma and elicit an irresistible groundswell of support. While citizens commonly reward governments that distribute gains with an outpouring of backing, gratitude for leaders who manage to forestall impending losses, the less obvious payoff, is even more intense and powerful; indeed, this mechanism plays an especially important role in the politics of populism because success in combating crises really boosts charisma.

The Role of Crisis and Loss Aversion

As Weber (1976: 654) highlighted, charismatic leadership that instills fervent mass enthusiasm and thus gains the capacity to vault over institutional constraints usually arises in severe, acute crises (see recently Andrews-Lee 2021: 31–34). To attain such transformative leadership (cf. Burns 1978; Skowronek 2020), politicians leverage grave challenges for demonstrating their unique prowess. After the political establishment has blatantly demonstrated its failings by presiding over the preceding deterioration, a new charismatic hero boldly confronts the crisis, enacts a striking solution, and brings tremendous relief to the despondent citizenry. By forestalling an incipient catastrophe and effecting a "miraculous" turnaround, this courageous, determined leader turns into a providential savior of the people and elicits wide-ranging backing. A politician who spearheads such a dramatic rescue operation can count on a boundless outpouring of support – and use it to overwhelm opponents, cement political supremacy, and push toward competitive authoritarianism (see recently Matovski 2021: chaps. 2–3).

Weber's classical crisis argument finds a theoretical micro-foundation in modern cognitive psychology. Innumerable experiments and field studies, including applications to political science, have shown that individuals display disproportionate, intense aversion to losses (Thaler 1992: 64–66; Kahneman 2011: 283, 295–97; Zamir 2014; in political science, see Weyland 2002: chaps. 3, 5; McDermott 2004: 139–40; Weyland 2021a: 67–68, 71–73). Specifically, a cost has a subjective weight and psychological impact of significantly greater magnitude than an objectively equivalent gain. For instance, people are much more upset after losing $20 than they are happy about winning that amount. Because losses hurt so badly, actors that manage to avert imminent costs or reverse recent setbacks are rewarded with enormous gratitude. The higher the stakes, the greater is this political payoff for a successful leader. In particular, when a looming catastrophe, such as hyperinflation or an incipient civil war, imperils the population's basic livelihood, an energetic politician can potentially perform heroic salvation and thus prove his Weberian charisma. Because the "established political class," which failed to forestall the crisis, is likely to suffer total discredit, such a providential savior then faces little opposition to, and massive support for, any plan he chooses to pursue, including the destruction of democracy.

The role of loss aversion in bolstering charismatic saviors undergirds the paradoxical politics of populism. After all, regular chief executives prefer governing in normal times and see crises as problematic challenges to their political projects and policy programs. But for personalistic plebiscitarian leaders, crises are decisive in discrediting the performance and puncturing the control of the established political class; in this way, crises create the necessary opening for the meteoric rise of populist outsiders. And if these newcomers win office, they face a great opportunity for boosting their leadership to stratospheric levels, as Weber highlighted. If they manage to resolve urgent problems, they can achieve a degree of political supremacy that a regular politician can only dream of.

Certainly, however, the opportunities provided by crises also come at great risk. Successful chief executives ascend to political heaven, at least temporarily; but leaders who fail to devise effective solutions and therefore do not bring relief suffer a quick descent in their political fortunes, which can easily culminate in their ignominious eviction from office and their banishment into the political wilderness (Weyland 2022a). Thus, populism is a high-risk strategy with an exceptionally wide range of possible outcomes. On the one hand, it holds out prospects of tremendous success; but on the other hand, quite a few leaders fall off the tightrope and end up "crashing and burning." Of course, by disabling the main assailant, populist leaders' self-destruction substantially improves the chances for democratic survival or recovery.

Specifically, what factors condition how crises affect the political fate of populist leaders? First, if the crisis appears under the preceding government or is clearly exogenous, a new personalistic incumbent can avoid blame and even attack the prior administration for its failures. Second, it is crucial whether a plebiscitarian chief executive can decisively mitigate or resolve the challenge and thus avert massive imminent losses. The chances for success depend both on the nature of the crisis and, of course, on the incumbent's skill in combating it.

Some crises that threaten terrible hardship can, in principle, be quickly resolved with bold countermeasures. A prime example is hyperinflation,[10] which disastrously melts away people's incomes and savings, but which a bold stabilization plan, if properly designed and credibly enacted, can stop in its tracks. This sudden success drastically alleviates the suffering of the population, which reciprocates with an outpouring of support. Such a severe and acute, yet quickly resolvable crisis can therefore constitute a golden opportunity for a personalistic plebiscitarian leader. Deep conjunctural recessions, defined as a drop in gross domestic product (GDP) of at least 5 percent per year, can also play into the hand of new populist chief executives, because determined counter-cyclical spending can bring quick and substantial relief.

Other problems, by contrast, are impossible to resolve with a determined strike of apparent magic. The paradigmatic recent case is the COVID-19 pandemic. The super-contagious virus was impossible to extinguish and eliminate, and its recurring spread inflicted exorbitant costs on public health and the economy. Whereas regular governments took the prudent yet painfully slow route of limiting the damage and waiting for vaccinations to permit a gradual return to normality, populist leaders with their urge to impose miraculous solutions were at a loss. There simply was no way to terminate the catastrophic problem outright.[11] Yet leaders' evident incapacity to "save the people" with a heroic feat called their charisma into serious question. As the self-proclaimed savior proved unable to save, the emperor was caught naked. In their flailing efforts to extricate themselves from this embarrassing, politically costly predicament, populist chief executives resorted to veritable magic by wishing away the problem, denying its seriousness, and promoting utterly ineffective, if not dangerous miracle cures. While their dedicated core followers fell for these rhetorical stratagems, broad segments of the citizenry were unimpressed. Consequently, the evident inability to fulfill the promise of national salvation

---

[10] In strict economic terms, hyperinflation is defined as price rises above 50 percent per month – a true catastrophe (Weyland 2002: 96).

[11] Even a strong-willed leader such as Brazil's Bolsonaro had to admit his helplessness: "What do you want me to do?!? I am Messias [his middle name], but I cannot do miracles" (Jornal do Brasil 2020). No such admission of impotence is reported from President Trump, however, who persistently denied the severity of the threat and often claimed to have it under control: "This is a very contagious virus. It's incredible. But it's something that we have tremendous control over" (reported in Woodward 2020: 281).

cost many populist chief executives a substantial depletion of their support (Bayerlein et al. 2021; Meyer 2021; Foa et al. 2022).

Similarly, in the field of public security, there are some huge challenges that are resolvable, whereas others are stubbornly entrenched. Because political insurgencies usually have a centralized command structure, the state has, in principle, a chance to put a quick end to these massive attacks – if it can capture or kill the rebel leadership and thus impose a strategic defeat. By contrast, common crime is decentralized, dispersed, and capillary; therefore, even iron fist approaches, such as Latin America's infamous *mano dura*, usually do not bring lasting relief, as the tragic experiences of Central America's Northern Triangle over the last three decades show (Penski 2018; Rosen 2021). Organized crime and drug trafficking are virtually impossible to eradicate as well, given their enormous profitability and the perpetrators' lack of attractive alternatives. Therefore, even successful decapitation via the capture of drug king-pins often brings no improvement; instead, as ambitious new leaders compete fiercely for grabbing the top spot, violence can spiral upward, as in Mexico after President Felipe Calderón's declaration of a war on drugs in 2006–7 (Flannery 2013; Trejo and Ley 2020).

In sum, the nature of the challenges that personalistic plebiscitarian leaders face shapes their political fate. Only crises that are resolvable provide unusual opportunities for populist chief executives to demonstrate their charisma and establish political predominance. Thus, objective, largely given factors – an aspect of "structure" – strongly condition their chances for achieving massive political success.

Agency, however, matters as well. After all, there is an obvious second condition – namely whether chief executives actually manage to take advantage of the opportunity provided by an acute and severe yet resolvable crisis. Such crises obviously pose difficult challenges, as evident in preceding governments' incapacity to forestall their eruption. Bold plans of economic stabilization, for instance, or targeted anti-guerrilla strategies are not easy to devise, and even harder to enact and steadily implement. Consequently, resolvable crises are far from sufficient causes for boosting charismatic leadership. Instead, personalistic plebiscitarian incumbents must successfully combat the challenge in order to reap major political payoffs.

This additional condition requires skillful, competent agency. Successful agency is impossible to characterize in general terms, however. Elaborating an effective solution for a huge problem is a question of practical reason, which is by nature context-dependent and must consider the concrete circumstances of each specific situation. Accordingly, success hinges on a great variety of aspects, including a clear understanding or intuitive grasp of the nature and severity of the crisis; the resources, expertise, and administrative capabilities available for combating it; executive leadership and team coordination; and aptitude in explaining the situation to the population, communicating firm commitment to the solution, instilling trust, and winning stakeholders' cooperation. This enormous complexity is virtually impossible to unravel. Consequently, this study must rely on simple outcome measures to determine success.

By acknowledging this additional condition for the fate of charismatic leadership, my crisis argument assigns a significant role to political agency, which is crucial for the difficult task of finding a successful response to severe problems. But this study sees the room for agency as limited and highlights the real characteristics and features of crises, which reflect objective problems. My analysis thus diverges from constructivist arguments that attribute to populist leaders a great capacity to "perform" crises (Moffitt 2016: 121–32). Those claims imply that leaders can "construct" crises by exaggerating problems and framing them as exceptionally severe and acute.

My theory, by contrast, argues that crises are largely given and have firm objective roots. For sure, politicians often disagree over the exact severity of problems; long-serving incumbents naturally downplay them, whereas the opposition highlights the danger. But this margin for rhetorical maneuver is limited. Crisis claims only find strong, widespread resonance if the citizenry actually feels the pain and sees a catastrophe approaching; the situation must be objectively dire for stark warnings to exert much effect. Only grave, extraordinary problems that are plainly visible and exact great cost provide opportunities for boosting charismatic leadership (see recently Matovski 2021: 45–47, 79–81; and for the USA, see Lowande and Rogowski 2021: 1421).

Moreover, it would be exceedingly risky for a populist chief executive to provoke or engineer a crisis, such as an international conflict, while in office; the question of responsibility would obviously arise, enabling opposition forces to attack. In general, any crisis that erupts during the tenure of personalistic plebiscitarian leaders risks calling into question their charismatic claims of miraculous performance: Why did they not manage to avoid the worsening problem in the first place? Instead, as mentioned earlier, crises must be antecedent and exogenous for a charismatic leader to have the chance of reaping political benefits.

In sum, this book's crisis argument sees the role of populist agency as distinctly limited and confined primarily to the issue of crisis resolution: Can incumbents effectively cope with urgent problems? Politically exploitable crises, however, have clear exogenous, objective roots and are not the products of strategic creation or rhetorical construction. Framing can make some difference, but actual losses, popular experiences with real pain, and the obvious imminence of stark further deterioration are crucial for giving populist appeals widespread resonance. Due to the objective bases of crises, this study employs clear, easily measurable indicators for ascertaining their presence.

The Interaction of Crises with Institutional Weaknesses

As the preceding section established, the exogenous eruption of crises and chief executives' success in combating them are crucial additional factors that condition the populist strangulation of democracy. The interactive theory of this book argues that institutional weaknesses and special conjunctural opportunities have to coincide for the march toward authoritarianism to proceed. Both of these types of factors are necessary; only when joined together can they produce this deleterious outcome.

This interactive theory postulates a multiplicative relationship: The more pronounced the degree of institutional weakness, the less massive is the conjunctural opportunity that enables a populist chief executive to smother liberal pluralism. Conversely, the higher a democracy's institutional resilience, the greater the force required for suppressing it, and the more extraordinary the conjunctural opportunity that is required for providing this impulse.

Accordingly, in polities that suffer from particular institutional debility due to high instability, special circumstances that do not even qualify as crises are sufficient for opening the door to competitive authoritarianism, as the section on "High Instability" later in this chapter discusses. By contrast, where the institutional framework commands intermediate strength, democracy displays greater robustness; therefore, only an exceptional coincidence of conjunctural opportunities allows for its destruction. And by implication, a high level of institutional strength, as it prevails in advanced industrialized countries, makes political liberalism virtually impregnable; it would be unlikely to fall even under the pressure of a true catastrophe.

According to this multiplicative argument, in institutional settings of middling strength, the resolution of serious, acute crises is a necessary condition for the asphyxiation of democracy. Only such "miraculous" success earns populist chief executives the intense backing of large majorities and thus gives them the clout for successfully promoting authoritarian involution. Based on this widespread support, power-hungry populists can then take advantage of the relative openings of parliamentarism or impose para-legal change under presidentialism. Thus, to overcome institutional constraints of medium resilience, charismatic politicians must achieve the outstanding feat of forestalling an approaching catastrophe and reversing grave recent losses.

My interactive theory yields specific arguments for each type of institutional weakness. Accordingly, in parliamentary systems with their comparatively easy changeability, which allows for democracy's dismantling through perfectly legal means, massive economic challenges have provided the opportunity for the emergence of supremely powerful charismatic leadership that can asphyxiate liberal pluralism. In presidential systems, by contrast, the reliance on para-legal change can provoke vociferous opposition and generate substantial friction. Therefore, a pushy populist needs even greater clout, which only the "magical" feat of simultaneously resolving two severe crises, in the economy *and* in public security, can provide.

Thus, the greater the relative strength and resilience of an institutional framework, the more unusual must be the conjunctural opportunities for overcoming these obstacles. Under parliamentarism with its limited number of institutional veto players, an economic crisis can be sufficient for giving a charismatic leader hegemony and decimating the number of partisan veto players, thus removing the remaining impediments to authoritarian involution. Yet in a presidential system with its stricter separation of powers, only an imminent catastrophe arising from a double crisis enables an ambitious leader to prove the extraordinary charisma required for dismantling checks and balances through para-legal change. Thus, in the paradoxical politics of populism, the stronger the fortress to which populist transgressors lay siege, the graver are the challenges that are necessary for enabling these attackers to win sufficient power and prevail.

The Role of Dual Crises in Presidential Systems Subject to Para-legal Change

In Latin America's presidential systems of middling institutional strength, populist chief executives have managed to bend and break existing rules and impose constitutional transformations only under truly exceptional conditions. These rare opportunities have stemmed from antecedent catastrophic crises in two different spheres at the same time, namely the economy and public safety; and a populist leader had to perform true magic by combating both of these grave challenges with full force and great effect. As this providential savior succeeded in averting a dual collapse and ending disastrous losses unleashed under the predecessor's government, he won sky-high approval ratings that precluded any efforts by the political opposition or the judiciary to block his autocratic concentration of power. Who could obstruct a national hero with legalistic formalities?

The paradigmatic case of such amazing success was Peru's Alberto Fujimori, who averted a total economic meltdown and simultaneously won an incipient civil war; he then leveraged this unusual double accomplishment to establish his political dominance. When the Andean Samurai took office, his unlucky country was suffering both from disastrous hyperinflation (6,300 percent in 1990) and from a dangerous guerrilla insurgency: The brutal Shining Path inflicted mass terror while the police and military responded with equal cruelty, causing a combined death toll of 69,000 citizens. No wonder that this populist leader won 80–82 percent approval when he illegally closed Congress and the courts with the claim that only unrestricted presidential power could effectively overcome these two grave challenges, as he managed to do (Weyland 2002: 171–72; Carrión 2006a: 126–33; Murakami 2012: 296–98). Thus, a severe double crisis allowed Fujimori to prove his bold agency, bring drastic relief, garner overwhelming popularity, and gain the political predominance required for imposing constitutional change. In a country of middling institutional strength, only an unusual cumulation of acute problems allowed for the destruction of democracy.

Comparative analysis confirms that Peru's descent into populist authoritarianism rested on exceptional conditions. Like Fujimori, Argentina's Carlos

Menem defeated hyperinflation, but did not manage to perpetuate himself in power and destroy democracy; and like Fujimori, Colombia's Álvaro Uribe faced large-scale guerrilla insurgencies, but saw his bid for further reelection blocked like Menem. In both of these cases, liberal constraints, namely the two-term limit for presidents, ended up holding. Thus, success in overcoming one grave crisis was not sufficient for producing the steamroller of support that allows a populist leader to push aside resistance and abolish democracy. Fujimori only gained this blank check because he made great headway in combating two severe crises: an economic crisis (inflation above 50 percent per month or a drop in GDP greater than 5 percent per year) and a security crisis (an armed challenge by more than 5,000 insurgents or a murder rate above 35 per 100,000 inhabitants).

Thus, despite their susceptibility to para-legal change, Latin America's presidential systems of middling institutional strength provide a good deal of resilience for liberal pluralism. Except for cases of high instability (discussed in the section on this topic later in this chapter), Fujimori remained the only populist terminator of democracy in Latin America for almost three decades.

Only in recent years has another personalistic plebiscitarian leader managed to embark on the same path, by exploiting an exceptional constellation of grave challenges as well (while also benefiting from the lower institutional constraints posed by a unicameral legislature). With exceptional skill, Nayib Bukele in El Salvador has taken advantage of the COVID-19 pandemic, which has stumped so many populist leaders across the world (see earlier in this chapter). Through the quick imposition of drastic restrictions, he contained the virus' spread while averting its catastrophic economic fallout with unusually generous subsidies. Moreover, he used stringent lockdowns justified by the pandemic to drive down El Salvador's massive crime problem and maintained this accomplishment with a savvy combination of secret negotiations and harsh crackdowns. By making great headway on both fronts, Bukele won a supermajority in Congress that allowed him to overpower liberal checks and balances and push aside presidential term limits. Thus, as in Fujimori's case, unusual success in a two-front war, namely in health and the economy as well as in public safety, was required for Bukele's apparently unstoppable strangulation of democracy.

In sum, while many presidential systems in Latin America are subject to para-legal change, they nevertheless boast a degree of institutional resilience that personalistic plebiscitarian leaders can overcome only with the overwhelming support arising from striking success in combating two simultaneous crises. Given the charismatic basis of populism, the intensity of popular loss aversion constitutes a necessary cause for breaching liberal fortresses of middling strength. Thus, this relative institutional debility and an exceptional double crisis have to coincide to allow for democracy's strangulation by populist chief executives.

The Role of Crises in Parliamentary Systems

In Europe's parliamentary systems, with their comparatively easy changeability, populist leaders also needed a crucial popularity boost in order to succeed in destroying liberal pluralism with formally legal means. Consequently, exogenous crises played a crucial facilitating role as well. But due to parliamentarism's higher degree of institutional weakness compared to many of Latin America's presidential systems, the conjunctural opportunities necessary for smothering democracy were less exceptional. Consequently, one antecedent crisis was sufficient for opening the door for populist power grabs – not the coincidence of two different catastrophes that was required in Latin America.

Specifically, democracy succumbed to populist assaults only where serious economic crises devastated the parties sustaining incumbent governments and enabled populist challengers to win elections with clear, sometimes lopsided majorities. The resulting elimination of partisan veto players then allowed the new prime ministers to strip away institutional and political constraints and energetically concentrate power. In this vein, Hungary's Orbán benefited politically from the global collapse of 2008, which hit his country particularly hard: The drop in GDP of 6.6 percent in 2009 delegitimated the then-governing socialists and allowed the Magyar populist to win a resounding election victory in 2010 (Lendvai 2017: 78–80; Bogaards 2018: 1490–91). Similarly, Turkey's Erdoğan was helped by "the worst economic and financial crisis in modern Turkish history," which caused GDP to drop 6 percent in 2001 (Özel 2003: 82; also Cagaptay 2017: 84–85, 91–93).

By contrast, in the absence of resolvable exogenous crises, Silvio Berlusconi in Italy and Vladimír Mečiar in Slovakia did not do grave, lasting damage to democracy. The Italian populist never faced a severe, acute challenge; and because he did not save his compatriots from impending doom, his party did not win a legislative majority but needed coalition partners, which pulled in different directions and thus precluded a determined push for power concentration. Mečiar did confront a massive economic downturn in the early 1990s. But because this crisis had profound structural roots in the implosion of communism, it was impossible to overcome with a bold adjustment plan – unlike hyperinflation in Peru. Consequently, the Slovak premier also failed to turn into a national hero who could triumph in elections. Dependent on ideologically divergent allies, his strikingly autocratic efforts to brush aside institutional and political constraints did not succeed. In both countries, therefore, democracy survived and recovered quickly.

These contrasting experiences show that even the comparatively easy changeability of parliamentarism does not give personalistic plebiscitarian leaders free rein for achieving their illiberal designs. Instead, the conjunctural opportunities arising from a serious, yet resolvable crisis are necessary for providing populist leaders with the clout to vanquish partisan veto players and achieve the substantial legislative majorities required for enacting undemocratic change. Interestingly, however, the relative weakness of parliamentarism means that success against one crisis is sufficient for empowering populist leaders – not the near-miracle of effectively combating crises both in the economy and in public security that presidents in Latin America's fairly stable polities needed.

High Instability: Hydrocarbon Windfalls and the Distribution of Massive Benefits

My theory argues that the populist strangulation of liberal pluralism hinges on a set of fundamental correspondences: The more resilient a democracy's institutional framework is, the greater is the clout that a personalistic plebiscitarian leader needs to dismantle it, and the more dramatic and exceptional is the conjunctural opportunity necessary for achieving this transgressive clout. While the preceding section showed how these correspondences play out at middling levels of institutional resilience, where crises are decisive for paving the way for populist assaults, high instability makes democracy particularly vulnerable. Such a battered castle can be razed without the powerful mechanism of loss aversion and the exogenous opportunity provided by resolvable crises; instead, the broad distribution of substantial gains, made possible by unusual resource windfalls, is sufficient for giving personalistic plebiscitarian leaders the strong, widespread support with which they can roll back political liberalism and cement their authoritarian hegemony.

Thus, while the political rewards for gains are lower than the intense gratitude bestowed on saviors who manage to avert imminent losses, they can be sufficient for toppling tottering institutions that suffer from high instability. Where the institutional framework was precarious to begin with, the widespread, strong backing that personalistic plebiscitarian leaders can win through the distribution of huge unexpected benefits enables them to overwhelm the opposition, dismantle the remaining checks and balances, and resolutely concentrate power.

Populist chief executives obtained the chance for such extraordinary gift-giving from another largely exogenous factor, namely the sudden revenue windfalls produced by the exorbitant price increases of the global commodities boom in the early 2000s. In line with the ample literature on the resource curse (summarized in Ross 2015: 243–48), the dramatic revenue boost in the hydrocarbon sectors was particularly decisive. Petroleum has long had special symbolic significance as the national patrimony of major oil exporters. Moreover, the advance of nationalization has established state control in many countries and given governments direct possession of voluminous export proceeds and rents (Ross 2012: 5–8, 33–34, 38–43; Andersen and Ross 2014). Consequently, the price rises from 1998 onward, boosted further after 2003, rapidly swelled public coffers and gave the chief executives of large hydrocarbon exporters unusual opportunities to distribute the national treasure and "give back to the people" through wide-ranging social programs and massive investment projects.[12]

Through deliberate political targeting, savvy presidents could practically "buy" support with new benefits for the broader population, juicy contracts for businesspeople, and the general bonanza that the hydrocarbon windfall (coded in line with Fernández and Villar 2014) created. Strong majoritarian backing allowed these populist presidents to override the already-enfeebled institutional constraints, establish unchallengeable hegemony, and suffocate liberal democracy.[13] The influx of petroleum rents was especially crucial for the authoritarian project of Hugo Chávez, who was projected to lose a recall referendum demanded by the opposition in 2003. But the Venezuelan populist managed to take advantage of drastic oil price rises that happened exactly at that time: With the new stream of resources, he rapidly rolled out major social programs and thus engineered a victory, after deliberately postponing the vote to 2004. By contrast, Chávez's Ecuadoran disciple Lucio Gutiérrez (2003–5) began his government right before the huge hydrocarbon windfall and ruined his popularity and political chances by turning to economic orthodoxy and adjustment; besieged from all sides, he lost office in 2005 without doing severe damage to democracy.

Hydrocarbon windfalls gifted by the global commodities boom also under-girded the populist march to competitive authoritarianism in Morales' Bolivia and Correa's Ecuador. Based on the revenue abundance they commanded, these charismatic leaders followed in Chávez's footsteps, undermined liberal plural-ism with tailor-made new constitutions, and used the strong backing boosted by their massive benefit distribution to concentrate power, attack and weaken all opponents, and engineer consecutive reelections. By severely skewing com-petitiveness and effectively abolishing democratic alternation, these personalis-tic plebiscitarian presidents capitalized on the exceptional bounty provided by sky-high hydrocarbon prices to cement their political predominance.

As hydrocarbon windfalls constituted necessary conditions for the stran-gulation of liberal pluralism in highly unstable polities, the international price collapse of 2014 then made it much harder to consolidate this autocratic proj-ect. The economic downturn created particular risks for Correa, who as a typical populist outsider lacked organizational sustenance. In an opportunistic move, the Ecuadoran strongman therefore decided to forego another reelection in 2017. Instead, he backed his former vice-president, who was supposed to cope with the tougher economic times and prepare Correa's triumphant return

---

[12] As the literature on resource nationalism predicts, the boom also enabled these leaders to raise tax rates and even nationalize remaining parts of the hydrocarbon industry, which boosted government revenues beyond the mostly exogenous price rise.

[13] Interestingly, Chávez won office when, due to an oil price bust, Venezuela suffered from serious economic problems. In line with the preceding section, this crisis helped him take the early steps toward suffocating democracy.

in 2021. But unexpectedly, this successor moved resolutely toward redemoc-ratization (De la Torre 2018: 78, 83–86). Standing on firmer ground because of his party's roots in a multitude of strong social movements (Anria 2018), Morales did run for another controversial reelection in 2019. But accumulated discontent and outrage over attempted electoral fraud forced him to resign (Lehoucq 2020; Wolff 2020) – a regime collapse that after a great deal of fur-ther political trouble allowed for a free, democratic election in 2020.

Thus, the long advance and eventual failure of Correa's and Morales' undemocratic plans tracked the drastic rise and fall of global hydrocarbon prices and of the corresponding rents that the two personalistic plebiscitar-ian leaders could exploit for their illiberal purposes. This variation over time proves the crucial role that revenue windfalls play for the populist suppression of democracy in countries afflicted by high instability. In these particularly weak institutional settings, hydrocarbon booms and busts can deeply shape the political fate of populist leaders, and of liberal pluralism.[14]

THREE PATHS TOWARD THE POPULIST SUFFOCATION OF DEMOCRACY

The preceding theoretical discussion has identified the necessary conditions and contextual factors under which personalistic plebiscitarian leadership can turn lethal to liberal pluralism. First of all, institutional weakness is crucial in facilitating populist attacks on democracy. But this factor constitutes a permis-sive cause and is not decisive and sufficient on its own. Instead, there is another necessary condition, namely an unusual conjunctural opportunity that enables populist leaders to push aside the remaining institutional constraints on their autocratic quest for unchallengeable preeminence. Such a conjunctural oppor-tunity can arise either from an acute and severe yet resolvable crisis, or from a major windfall of hydrocarbon rents.

As the last few sections showed, there is a specific alignment among these necessary conditions: The three types of institutional weakness distinguished earlier make polities vulnerable to populist assaults boosted by different kinds of conjunctural opportunities. While in their quest for power concentration, populist leaders take advantage of any opportunity they encounter, there is an interesting pattern of correspondences: The greater the institutional debil-ity, the lower the exogenous impetus that enables populist chief executives to destroy democracy. Accordingly, in polities of particular institutional

---

[14] In Eastern Europe, voluminous EU subsidies gift governments the equivalent of politically dis-posable windfall rents provided by hydrocarbon exports. But this revenue influx is substantially lower than the petrodollars flooding into Venezuela, Ecuador, and Bolivia during the height of the commodities boom. Moreover, Brussels' subventions benefit governments of all stripes; thus, they cannot easily account for the strangulation of liberal pluralism by the populist Orbán in Hungary, in contrast to its preservation in the remainder of the region.

weakness, namely in parliamentary systems or in presidential systems of high instability, a single shock – though of two different kinds – allowed populist leaders to move toward authoritarianism. By contrast, in polities of intermediate resilience, namely presidential systems susceptible to para-legal change (yet without high instability), only the unusual coincidence of two grave challenges permitted the suffocation of democracy.

In turn, because presidential systems afflicted by high instability have the lowest institutional resilience, an exogenous shock that facilitates the massive provision of gains is sufficient for opening the door to the populist asphyxiation of democracy. By contrast, because parliamentary systems and especially presidential systems that are susceptible to para-legal change (but that are fundamentally solid) boast relatively greater institutional strength, only the powerful mechanism of loss aversion can fuel "successful" populist assaults: In these settings, the capacity to bring miraculous relief from serious imminent crises is a necessary precondition for conquering the liberal-pluralist fortress.

In sum, only the interaction of specific institutional weaknesses and unusual exogenous conjunctures can turn lethal for liberal pluralism. In all other cases, when these conditions do not coincide, democracy can escape unscathed or deterioration is limited and transitory. As a result of these correspondences, there are three fairly narrow paths toward the populist destruction of democracy. The three deleterious combinations are:

1. Hydrocarbon windfalls (HWI) in presidential systems suffering from high instability (HIN),[15] as in Venezuela under Chávez, Bolivia under Morales, and Ecuador under Correa.
2. The coincidence of an antecedent economic crisis (ECR) and a security crisis (SCR) in a presidential system susceptible to the para-legal imposition of change (PCH), as in Peru under Fujimori and now in El Salvador under Bukele.
3. Economic crisis (ECR) in parliamentary systems of easy changeability (ECH), as in Hungary under Orbán and Turkey under Erdoğan.

Interestingly, these three paths are substantively meaningful and correspond to three subtypes of populism distinguished by specialists (Mudde and Rovira Kaltwasser 2013; De la Torre 2017b: 196–203; Rovira Kaltwasser 2019: 39–50). They describe Latin America's left-wing, "Bolivarian" populists (HWI in HIN); the region's right-wing, neoliberal populists (ECR *and* SCR in PCH); and Europe's right-wing, traditionalist populists (ECR in ECH). In terms of basic ideological orientation and issue ownership, it makes sense that crises are crucial for right-wing populists in Latin America and Europe, whereas left-wing populists in Latin America depend primarily on huge windfalls. After all, right-wing forces see as their most fundamental goal the preservation or

---

[15] High instability facilitates the para-legal imposition of change. In Table 1, therefore, where HIN = 1, PCH = 1 as well.

restoration of stability, order, and normality.[16] Consequently, crises as the most dramatic, dangerous, and painful departures from the status quo are tailor-made for right-wing leaders to fulfill their self-defined task.

By contrast, left-wing forces are determined to bring improvements, better the status quo, especially the life chances of poorer, hitherto neglected sectors, and ideally construct a new society of universal well-being. Given that disproportionate loss aversion makes true *re*distribution difficult, leftists depend on resource abundance to redress deprivation and inequality and to win broad-based political support for moving toward more drastic structural change. Consequently, massive revenue windfalls are crucial for fueling their ambitious socioeconomic projects and boosting their political fortunes. In sum, there is an inherent logic as to why right-wing populists depend on crises and their left-wing counterparts on resource bonanzas.

The three paths are also theoretically meaningful and intersect with the rich literature on democracy and regime change by capturing the deleterious impact of the resource curse and the long-noted effect of crises. Indeed, my theory contributes to these writings in interesting ways. As regards the resource curse, my argument about the interactive relationship between hydrocarbon windfalls and high instability conforms to the institutionalist turn of recent authors, who have moved away from postulating the deleterious impact of commodities rents alone; instead, institutional strength can contain and prevent this fallout, as the oft-mentioned case of oil-rich Norway shows (Mehlum, Moene, and Torvik 2006; Corrales, Hernández, and Salgado 2020).

As regards the role of crises, my theory clarifies the difference between problems such as hyperinflation that determined, bold action can in principle resolve (albeit with considerable difficulty and risk), and deep-seated, stubborn difficulties such as the collapse of communism's central command economy or sudden overwhelming challenges such as the COVID-19 pandemic, which even daring countermeasures cannot rapidly and definitively overcome. The first type of antecedent crises can offer golden opportunities to populist leaders, but the last two defy any quick fix, reveal charismatic claims as hollow, and thus threaten personalistic plebiscitarian leaders with embarrassing deflation, as analyses on the pandemic's political fallout have found (Bayerlein et al. 2021; Meyer 2021; Foa et al. 2022). Developing these insights into a systematic typology of crises and their potential political repercussions could enrich this body of literature.

To assess the explanatory power of my theory, Table 1 scores a comprehensive set of populist experiences in Latin America and Europe (listed in Table 2) in terms of the three types of institutional weakness (HIN, PCH, and ECH) and the different types of conjunctural opportunities (HWI, ECR, and SCR).

---

[16] According to this rightist vision, neoliberalism seeks the restoration of the market system, which – in the natural order of things – used to prevail before the distortions and problems introduced by ill-advised state interventionism and protectionism.

TABLE 1 *Conditions for the suffocation of democracy by populist leaders*

Institutional weakness			Antecedent exogenous conjuncture			Regime outcome	
High instability (HIN)	Para-legal change (PCH)	Easy change (ECH)	Economic crisis (ECR)	Security crisis (SCR)	Hydrocarbon windfall (HWI)	Suffocation of democracy	Populist leader
Neoliberal and right-wing populism in Latin America							
0	1	0	1	1	0	1	**Fujimori – PER**
0	1	0	1	0	0	0	Menem – ARG
0	1	0	0	1	0	0	Uribe – COL
0	1	0	1(o)	0	0	0	Collor – BRA*
0	1	0	0	0	0	0	Bucaram – ECU
0	1	0	0	0	0	0	Serrano – GUA
0	1	0	0	0	0	0	Morales – GUA
0	1	0	0	0	0	0	Toledo – PER
0	1	0	0	0	0	0	García II – PER
0	1	0	1(o)	0	0	0	Bolsonaro – BRA*
0	1	0	1	(o)1	0	1	**Bukele – SAL@**
Bolivarian and left-wing populism in Latin America							
1	1	0	1	0	1	1	**Chávez – VEN**
1	1	0	0	0	1	1	**Morales – BOL**
1	1	0	0	0	1	1	**Correa – ECU**
1	1	0	0	0	0	0	Gutiérrez – ECU
0	1	0	0	0	0	0	Zelaya – HON
1	1	0	0	0	0	0	Lugo – PAR
0	1	0	0	0	0	0	Humala – PER
1	1	0	1	0	0	0	Castillo – PER
0	1	0	0	0	0	0	N. Kirchner-ARG
0	1	0	1	0	0	0	C. Kirchner-ARG
0	1	0	1	0	0	0	García I – PER
0	1	0	0	0	0	0	AMLO – MEX

(*continued*)

TABLE 1 (*continued*)

High instability (HIN)	Para-legal change (PCH)	Easy change (ECH)	Economic crisis (ECR)	Security crisis (SCR)	Hydrocarbon windfall (HWI)	Suffocation of democracy	Populist leader
Right-wing, traditionalist populism in Europe							
0	0	(o)1	1	0	0	1	Erdoğan – TUR#
0	0	1	1	0	0	1	Orbán – HUN
0	0	0	0	0	0	0	Kaczyński – POL
0	0	0	1(o)	0	0	0	Wałęsa – POL
1	0	1	1(o)	0	0	0	Mečiar – SVK*
0	0	1	0	0	0	0	Fico – SVK
0	0	1	1(o)	0	0	0	Matovič – SVK*
0	0	1	0	0	0	0	Babiš – CZE
0	1	1	0	0	0	0	Janša – SLV*
0	1	1	0	0	0	0	Băsescu – ROM
0	1	0	0	0	0	0	Borisov – BUL
0	1	0	0	0	0	0	Simeon – BUL
0	0	1	0	0	0	0	Berlusconi – ITA
0	0	1	1(o)	0	0	0	Johnson – GBR
0	0	1	0	0	0	0	Papandreou – GRE$
0	0	1	1(o)	0	0	0	Tsipras – GRE*$
Right-wing, traditionalist populism in the USA							
0	0	0	0	0	0	0	Trump – USA

Notes:

Per my theory, antecedent exogenous conjunctures, especially crises, constitute opportunities that a populist leader can only take advantage of by resolving the challenge. While the table lists the objective challenge, it indicates in parenthesis whether a chief executive succeeded in combating the challenge – which is crucial for boosting support and achieving hegemony.

* Early in term, leader faced an acute, severe crisis (often the "unresolvable" COVID-19 pandemic), but failed to resolve it and use it as a conjunctural opportunity.

@ Leader took advantage of an unusual opportunity to bring great relief against a severe yet stubborn, otherwise hard-to-resolve problem.

Leader faced an extraconstitutional veto player and took extra time to outmaneuver it.

$ Left-wing leader.

TABLE 2 *Listing of populist governments (and location of case studies)*

Neoliberal and right-wing populism in Latin America	
Alberto Fujimori, Peru, 1990–2000	(pp. 77–83)
Carlos Menem, Argentina, 1989–99	(pp. 84–87)
Álvaro Uribe, Colombia, 2002–10	(pp. 87–92)
Fernando Collor de Mello, Brazil, 1990–92	(pp. 94–97)
Abdalá Bucaram, Ecuador, 1996–97	(pp. 97–99)
Jorge Serrano, Guatemala, 1991–93	(pp. 99–102)
Jimmy Morales, Guatemala, 2015–19	
Alejandro Toledo, Peru, 2001–6	
Alan García, Peru, 2006–11	
Jair Bolsonaro, Brazil, 2018–22	(pp. 103–107)
Nayib Bukele, El Salvador, 2019–present	(pp. 108–115)
Bolivarian and left-wing populism in Latin America	
Hugo Chávez, Venezuela, 1999–2013	(pp. 124–129)
Evo Morales, Bolivia, 2006–19	(pp. 130–131, 135–137)
Rafael Correa, Ecuador, 2007–17	(pp. 132–135)
Lucio Gutiérrez, Ecuador, 2003–5	(pp. 137–140)
Manuel Zelaya, Honduras, 2006–9	(pp. 140–143)
Fernando Lugo, Paraguay, 2008–12	(p. 145, n.22)
Ollanta Humala, Peru, 2011–16	(pp. 143–145)
Pedro Castillo, Peru, 2021–22	(pp. 145–148)
Néstor Kirchner, Argentina, 2003–7	(pp. 148–150)
Cristina Fernández de Kirchner, Argentina, 2007–15	(pp. 149–151)
Alan García, Peru, 1985–90	
Andrés Manuel López Obrador, 2018 – present	(pp. 151–156)
Right-wing, traditionalist populism in Europe	
Recep Tayyip Erdoğan, Turkey, 2003–present	(pp. 164–168)
Viktor Orbán, Hungary, 2010–present	(pp. 169–172)
Jarosław Kaczyński, Poland, 2015–present	(pp. 172–177)
Lech Wałęsa, Poland, 1990–95	(pp. 178–179)
Vladimír Mečiar, Slovakia, 1990–91, 1992–94, 1994–98	(pp. 177–183)
Robert Fico, Slovakia, 2006–10, 2012–18	(pp. 183–184)
Igor Matovič, Slovakia, 2020–21	(p. 184)
Andrej Babiš, Czech Republic, 2017–21	(pp. 185–189)
Ivan 'Janez' Janša, Slovenia, 2004–8, 2012–13, 2020–22	(pp. 185–189)
Traian Băsescu, Romania, 2004–7, 2007–12, 2012–14	(pp. 185–189)
Boyko Borisov, Bulgaria, 2009–13, 2014–17, 2017–21	(pp. 185–189)
Simeon Borisov von Saxe-Coburg-Gotha, Bulgaria, 2001–5	(p. 182, n.29)
Silvio Berlusconi, Italy, 1994–95, 2001–6, 2008–11	(pp. 189–193)
Boris Johnson, Great Britain, 2019–22	
Andreas Papandreou, Greece, 1981–89, 1993–96	
Alexis Tsipras, Greece, 2015–19	(pp. 163–164, n.5)

As this examination shows, only the three combinations of conditions that the preceding discussion highlights lead to the destruction of democracy. Under other permutations, liberal pluralism survived in many countries. In numerical terms, democracy fell to personalistic plebiscitarian leaders only in a minority of instances. Of the forty cases investigated, a mere seven succumbed and moved into authoritarian rule (these seven cases are highlighted in bold in Table 1).

The findings of this wide-ranging comparative analysis offer reassurance: The dire warnings about populism's threat to democracy overestimate the risk. While populist leaders certainly try to concentrate power and smother liberal pluralism, they often do not succeed with their nefarious tactics. Observers seem overly impressed by the emblematic cases in which populist chief executives managed to asphyxiate democracy; the many instances in which such efforts sooner or later failed to make headway draw much less attention. Thus, the disproportionate salience commonly attributed to negative news has skewed assessments of recent experiences. For understandable but methodologically problematic reasons, leaders who destroy democracy stand out much more than authoritarian projects that are abandoned, quickly defeated, or soon reversed. The antidemocratic triumphs of Fujimori, Chávez, and Orbán are cognitively "available," whereas the very similar, yet aborted efforts of Guatemala's Jorge Serrano (1991–93), Ecuador's Gutiérrez, and Slovakia's Mečiar are largely forgotten. This distorted focus of attention, a type of problematic "selection on the dependent variable" (King, Keohane, and Verba 1994: 129–37, 141–49), inspires excessive anxiety. Fortunately, the actual empirical record is significantly more sanguine.

THE INSTITUTIONAL STRENGTH AND CONJUNCTURAL SOLIDITY OF ADVANCED DEMOCRACIES

The preceding analysis shows that even in the comparatively weaker institutional settings of Latin America and Eastern Europe, personalistic plebiscitarian leaders manage to asphyxiate liberal pluralism only under special conjunctural conditions, in a minority of cases. By implication, therefore, this deleterious outcome is especially unlikely to occur in the consolidated democracies of advanced industrialized countries. Thus, my theory provides a great deal of reassurance for the citizens of Western Europe and North America. While even these regions have seen the disturbing emergence of populist forces that have propounded illiberal projects and fueled damaging polarization, the actual threat posed by these disruptive challengers is low. Indeed, they have rarely won chief executive office; and when they have taken this first important step, as happened most prominently and consequentially with Trump's election, they have failed to overturn democracy, even where they have taken their autocratic projects and manipulative efforts shockingly far, as the US populist did in late 2020 and early 2021 (chronicled by Woodward and Costa 2021).

By drawing inferences from the few cases of authoritarian involution that have actually occurred in Latin America and Eastern Europe, my theory highlights the main factors that protect Western democracies with great reliability: first, well-entrenched institutional solidity and strength; and second, advanced socioeconomic development and societal steering capacity, which largely forestall the conjunctural opportunities mentioned earlier. After all, the most modern economies and societies in the global system's center are fairly immune to drastic crises, and are not exposed to sudden revenue windfalls either. Consequently, both of the types of factors that constitute necessary conditions for the populist asphyxiation of democracy are unlikely to plague the post-industrial West; and their coincidence, a specific requirement for the emergence of acute danger, is particularly improbable.

First of all, Western democracies rest on a great deal of institutional strength, anchored in firm, widely accepted constitutions that are not easy to change. The very duration of these democracies, mostly instituted by 1949, has contributed to their consolidation. As statistical analyses suggest, incumbent takeovers, including populist assaults, become highly unlikely after a liberal constitution has persisted for several decades (Svolik 2015: 730–34). Habituation sets in, and broad swaths of the citizenry become deeply committed to liberty and pluralism. Over the years, electoral competition in an open polity also tends to cement the rule of law by creating strong incentives to contain and gradually eliminate personal and political discrimination and to forestall and combat any governmental abuse of power. With the increasing legalization of modern life, backed up by the frequent strengthening and increasing autonomy of constitutional courts (Lijphart 1999: chap. 12), the judiciary zealously upholds the official rules and protects the constitutional framework from infringements.

For these reasons, it becomes practically impossible for personalistic chief executives to promote power concentration by pushing through para-legal change. In presidential systems, the constitutionally enshrined separation of powers therefore tends to function reliably. The tricks and machinations with which many Latin American populists have sought to advance their hegemonic goals are infeasible in advanced democracies. Instead, an interlocking web of constraints hobbles personalistic plebiscitarian leaders under Western presidentialism. And of course, high instability, which has opened the door to incumbent takeovers in some South American countries, is unheard of in the contemporary West, where even the cataclysmic collapse of party systems, as in Italy during the early 1990s, does not expose the established regime to existential threats.

In parliamentary systems, where the attenuated separation of powers creates the institutional opening for potentially problematic transformations, partisan veto players mostly preclude this risk. After all, most party systems in advanced nations continue to have fairly solid organizational structures and popular roots. Therefore, the old social-democratic, Christian-democratic, liberal, and conservative parties retain considerable support and are very unlikely to suffer electoral meltdowns. While establishment forces have fragmented and lost backing at the edges, where new groupings have emerged and grown over the years, the longstanding parties still limit the space available for populist forces. Illiberal challengers therefore cannot win clear victories, not to speak of lopsided majorities.

Consequently, a sudden reduction in the number of partisan veto players, which has enabled triumphant populists in Hungary and Turkey to take advantage of parliamentarism's relatively easy changeability and push toward autocracy, is highly unlikely in Western countries. Instead, a sturdy, though somewhat thinned, phalanx of partisan veto players keeps compensating for the dearth of institutional veto players and protecting liberal pluralism from power-hungry chief executives. In sum, institutional solidity and organizational strength constitute crucial safeguards that impede the populist strangulation of liberal pluralism in advanced countries. According to my theory, this robustness alone should be sufficient for guaranteeing democracy's survival.

Moreover, advanced industrialized countries also face a low probability of experiencing the other type of necessary condition that my theory has unearthed, namely the unusual conjunctural opportunities for exploiting institutional weakness for undemocratic purposes. As explained earlier, populist assailants can win overwhelming clout only if they encounter, and successfully resolve, acute, severe crises or if they benefit from exceptional hydrocarbon windfalls. But both of these exogenous shocks, negative or positive, are highly unlikely to affect the developed West. The impressive prosperity of complex economies and societies with their multitude of different, variegated sectors precludes both drastic downturns and sudden revenue boosts.

To start with the latter factor – the absence of massive windfall rents – the economies of Western Europe and North America do not depend on a narrow set of export products, as many developing countries do. Therefore, even the global commodities boom, which gifted petro-states such as Venezuela with an enormous flood of extra revenues, was far from providing a similar bonanza to the West. For instance, the shale-fracking boom in the USA did not affect the overall economy very much. As a result, no populist chief executive in the developed world can count on the seemingly unlimited surplus funds that allowed Hugo Chávez to boost his support with huge spending programs and thus propel his authoritarian project.

For the same reasons, advanced industrialized countries face a much lower risk of economic collapse than the sectorally concentrated, economically weaker nations of Latin America and Eastern Europe. Even the Great Recession of 2008, which originated in the USA, hurt this country significantly less (–2.9 percent growth in 2009) than, for instance, Hungary (–6.6 percent), where this crisis opened the door for Viktor Orbán's project of "autocratic legalism" (Scheppele 2018; Pirro and Stanley 2022: 91–95, 97). Moreover, their high tax take and their greater borrowing capacity allow Western countries to smooth out any downturns that do occur with generous compensation measures (Wibbels 2006: 443–52), as they uniformly demonstrated during the COVID-19 pandemic.

Other grave challenges, such as large-scale attacks by foreign or domestic terrorists, are unlikely to recur in Western democracies as well. The 9/11 attack was the first strike on the US mainland in nearly 200 years and has not been followed by similar assaults. While West European countries have suffered high-profile attacks as well (e.g., Spain in 2004 and France in 2015), these assaults did not assume the magnitude and symbolic charge of 9/11 and have not been repeated either. Moreover, the specter of civil war and genocide raised by alarmist observers (Hinton 2021; Walter 2022) is utterly implausible. For these reasons, Western democracies are not at risk of descending into the massive security crises that were crucial for paving the way for the populist destruction of democracy in Peru and El Salvador.

As regards security threats by foreign nations, what country in the world would dare to declare war on the global superpower and its NATO allies? Even Vladimir Putin, who broke the virtual taboo against conventional warfare in the twenty-first century, has studiously avoided any attack outside the borders of the former USSR. Conversely, a war that the populist chief executive of a Western country would deliberately start as a political ploy would be unlikely to produce a significant, lasting "rally round the flag" effect. Instead, such an irresponsible trick would probably draw intense criticism and provoke an upsurge of opposition.

For all of these reasons, the chances are exceedingly low that a personalistic plebiscitarian leader in a Western nation would win the overwhelming mass support that allowed some populist chief executives in Latin America and Eastern Europe to sweep away liberal safeguards, concentrate power, and march toward authoritarianism. Thus, the second type of necessary condition specified in my theory will probably not appear in advanced industrialized countries. Given the absence of the first requirement – institutional weakness – the lack of opportunities for taking advantage of such weakness provides extra guarantees for the survival of liberal pluralism. In the exceptional cases in which populist leaders have won chief executive office in the West at all – not an easy task, given fairly consolidated party systems – they have not managed to do serious damage to democratic institutions, as the cases of Silvio Berlusconi in Italy (Taggart and Rovira Kaltwasser 2016; Newell 2019) and of Donald Trump in the USA confirm (see Chapter 6).

Both of these sources of protection – institutional strength and resilience against exogenous shocks – rest on the high level of socioeconomic modernization achieved by Western countries. Pluralistic interests, high educational levels, and advanced norms and values give a wide range of political groupings, partisan forces, and societal sectors a firm stake in democratic liberalism. While they are disgruntled with mainstream politicians and discontented with the increasing turn toward technocracy, many citizens distrust the simplistic and irresponsible promises of populist leaders and abhor their crudeness and deliberate lack of civility (cf. Ostiguy 2017).

In turn, the vigilance of well-organized, resource-endowed civil societies and the growing litigiousness of the citizenry sustain compliance with formal institutions and block or limit efforts to override constitutional rules. Populist attempts to grab power, weaken checks and balances, restrict freedom of the press, and squeeze the opposition run into a dense web of obstacles and incur substantial political costs. As shown in the contemporary USA, every one of President Trump's controversial measures that threatened to abridge some facet of liberal democracy immediately provoked a withering barrage of court challenges, initiated by a great variety of citizens, nongovernmental organizations (NGOs), city governments, and state-level agencies.

In sum, advanced modernization undergirds liberal pluralism's resilience to populist attacks in the West. Consolidated democracies in prosperous economies and complex societies are virtually impossible to dismantle. Even during the interwar years, wracked by an exceptional coincidence of crises and by apocalyptic battles between communism, fascism, liberalism, and conservatism, advanced socioeconomic development, well-endowed and organized civil societies, and reasonably solid party systems reliably protected liberal pluralism in Western Europe (Cornell, Møller, and Skaaning 2017, 2020). Democracy in the contemporary West is even less likely to crumble under the much less severe challenges of the early twenty-first century.

UNINTENDED CONSEQUENCES OF POPULISM'S THREAT
TO DEMOCRACY: DEMOCRATIC MOBILIZATION
AND REJUVENATION?

Rather than smothering democracy, populism in the advanced West may exert the paradoxical effect of reinvigorating and rejuvenating stodgy, increasingly bloodless polities. After all, the very emergence of personalistic plebiscitarian outsiders showed the exhaustion of liberal pluralism and the representational deficits plaguing many representative systems.[17] Thus, populism itself is a symptom of trouble. Of course, this political strategy does not bring democratic improvement because charismatic leaders uniformly fail to fulfill their promise of empowering "the people"; instead, they exploit citizen discontent to garner support for boosting their own power and for pursuing undemocratic hegemony. Thus, while personalistic plebiscitarian politicians thrive on the deficient quality of present-day democracies, their own machinations make the problem worse, not better.

Interestingly, however, the illiberal and autocratic moves of populist leaders provoke opposition and countermobilization, which may help revitalize democracy, especially in Western countries with large educated middle classes

---

[17] For the USA, see e.g. Oliver and Rahn (2016: 194–96).

and resourceful civil societies. Populism's shocking threat shakes people out of their complacency; citizens who long took liberal pluralism for granted increase their political engagement and participation. This revaluation of democracy and infusion of political energy, which the institutional strength of Western polities channels into conventional arenas, especially elections, can produce a "reequilibration" of challenged systems (Linz 1978: chap. 5) and prompt a recovery of democratic quality (Ginsburg and Huq 2018a). In this indirect, unintentional fashion – as a deterrent stirring up its adversaries – populism may indeed make liberal democracy better, not worse.

Personalistic plebiscitarian leadership produces its own antibodies, which do not only protect democracy but may facilitate its rejuvenation. Precisely because populism poses a threat to liberal pluralism, it commonly causes powerful allergic reactions, especially resistance from a wide range of liberal-democratic groupings. Charismatic leaders' flagrant violations of civic norms and their transgressive institutional efforts stimulate intense and widespread countermobilization. Consequently, the electoral victory and governance of strong-willed populists can dispel the political apathy that has gradually spread in representative systems. By mobilizing their own fervent mass base and by promoting determined power concentration, personalistic chief executives also mobilize ample opposition sectors in defense of liberal pluralism. Groupings that populists' uncouth utterances and "low" attacks disparage are especially fired up. Inadvertently, these disruptive leaders give a broad and strong boost to political participation and may even prompt a reassertion of democratic values.

In institutionally weak regimes, this upsurge of participation often spills into the streets and leads to contentious crowd protests (Sato and Arce 2022) – which plays into the hands of populist chief executives, who love accusing their opponents of illegitimate disruption.[18] But the institutional strength of Western democracies leads liberalism's defenders to employ regular modes of political involvement, especially electoral efforts, which then, in a virtuous circle, reinvigorate democratic institutions (Putnam and Skocpol 2018: 8, 11). More citizens come forth as candidates, engage in a variety of campaign activities, or vote, as happened most strikingly in the US midterms of 2018, when abstention fell to levels not witnessed in a century. Moreover, a multitude of legal challenges against populist infringements enhance the political profile of the independent judiciary, reaffirming the liberal separation of powers.

In sum, rather than killing democracy, populism may indirectly and unintentionally revitalize it, especially in Western countries with resilient institutional frameworks. Contrary to the fears of historical institutionalists, who in their linear way of thinking about "path dependency" (Pierson 2000) extrapolate

---

[18] This was the losing strategy (Gamboa 2017; Cleary and Öztürk 2022: 214–15) forced on the Venezuelan opposition after Chávez took over all independent institutions and effectively disabled the official channels for autonomous participation.

current trends into the future and therefore predict continuing deterioration, democratic pluralism can unleash powerful forces for recovery and regeneration (Madrid and Weyland 2019: 181–83; Weyland 2020: 402). Through its participatory opportunities and competitive mechanisms, liberal democracy in an institutionally strong setting may well mobilize and channel the energies of active citizens and civil society organizations into a pro-democratic upswing. Problems therefore do not necessarily persist and worsen; instead, they can propel efforts at remediation and renewal. Gradual decay and growing danger tend to stimulate counterforces, which prompt cyclical turnarounds in political development. Precisely by threatening to undermine liberal democracy, populist leaders may inadvertently – through their deterrent effects – end up strengthening this rusty system and fuel attempts to alleviate or eliminate its well-known problems.

CONCLUSION

As many scholars and other observers have stressed, populism inherently stands in tension with liberal democracy and harbors authoritarian tendencies. But as the political experiences of recent decades show, this fundamental threat often remains unrealized; many populist leaders fail with their nefarious designs (Weyland 2022a). After all, personalistic plebiscitarianism prompts substantial resistance and runs into obstacles that power-hungry chief executives can push aside only under special conditions. Focusing on Europe and Latin America, this chapter has developed a theory highlighting the two types of factors that are decisive, namely prior institutional weakness of the democratic framework that a populist seeks to dismantle, and unusual conjunctural opportunities for winning the overwhelming power that is required for this wrecking job. Fortunately, these conditions do not commonly prevail, especially in combination. Consequently, the danger currently facing liberal pluralism is less acute and severe than recent warnings suggest.

According to my theory, the effective risk that populism poses to democracy depends, first of all, on a polity's institutional strength. The danger is therefore distinctly limited in advanced industrialized countries, where presidential systems enshrine firm checks and balances, while parliamentary systems tend to have several partisan veto players, which rein in illiberal and autocratic projects advanced by personalistic plebiscitarian leaders. Consequently, charismatic chief executives cannot do serious damage to liberal democracy, as corroborated by the failed efforts of Italy's Berlusconi; even Trump, who pushed unusually far, proved unsuccessful.

By contrast, the weaker institutional settings of Eastern Europe and Latin America leave personalistic plebiscitarian leaders greater room for maneuver. After all, many presidential systems are susceptible to para-legal change, and some slide into high instability, which creates particular vulnerability to populist power concentration efforts. And where party systems lack firm consolidation, electoral shocks can drastically reduce the number of partisan veto players and thus expose the Achilles' heel of parliamentary systems, whose attenuated separation of powers facilitates change, including populist machinations.

Interestingly, however, even these forms of institutional weakness do not give the illiberal aspirations of personalistic plebiscitarian chief executives free rein. Instead, efforts at authoritarian transformation provoke opposition that exploits the remaining institutional safeguards. Populist projects therefore make headway only under special circumstances – the second type of factors highlighted in my theory. Accordingly, democracy's asphyxiation depends on unusual conjunctural opportunities, namely when severe crises provide a chance for establishing heroic leadership, or when huge windfalls enable charismatic rulers to "buy" massive support. Where personalistic plebiscitarian leaders manage to take advantage of these opportunities, they gain such widespread, strong support that they can overwhelm any opposition and remove the remaining institutional constraints to their quest for unchallenged predominance.

My theory thus argues that two types of necessary conditions – institutional weakness and conjunctural opportunities – have to coincide for populist chief executives to undermine and suffocate democracy. These conditions are far from ubiquitous, and their coincidence, in particular, is quite uncommon. Therefore, populism's effective threat to liberal pluralism is not nearly as grave as many commentators have feared. As empirical analyses show (Kyle and Mounk 2018; Ruth-Lovell, Lührmann, and Grahn 2019; Weyland 2022a), incumbent takeovers are quite risky; numerous attempts have failed. The recent literature on democratic backsliding has not sufficiently considered this mixed record; its concerns are derived too much from the few outstanding cases of populist "success." Authors highlight deleterious possibilities. But the actual probability of undemocratic outcomes is not that high, and it is very low in institutionally strong polities.

Indeed, where institutional resilience prevails, as in advanced industrialized countries, populism may paradoxically stimulate a recovery and rejuvenation of democracy. The autocratic tendencies and uncouth, transgressive rhetoric of personalistic plebiscitarian leaders provokes aversion and revulsion, especially among the educated, urbane middle class, which comprises a large share of the citizenry in Western democracies. Vibrant, resourceful civil societies engage in sustained countermobilization, which in institutionally strong polities advances mainly through conventional channels, especially the electoral arena. As political interest and engagement rise, voting participation increases. Thus, by stimulating a powerful backlash, personalistic plebiscitarian leadership can inadvertently infuse exhausted representative systems with renewed democratic energy. Through its deterrent effects, populism can thus unleash positive impulses for tired, stale systems of liberal pluralism.

3

Neoliberal and Right-Wing Populism in Latin America

How severe is the actual threat that different types of populism pose to democracy? The following three chapters address this central question through in-depth analyses of large numbers of cases in which personalistic plebiscitarian leaders served as chief executives and sought incessantly to expand their powers. Each chapter examines one variant of populism and the corresponding path through which incumbent takeovers have occurred. I start in this chapter with neoliberal, right-wing populism in Latin America; Chapter 4 investigates the left-wing, "Bolivarian" variant that emerged in reaction to the regional wave of market reforms; and Chapter 5 probes right-wing, culturally conservative populism in Europe.

These analyses focus on the theoretical factors highlighted in Chapter 2, namely differences in institutional strength and conjunctural opportunities for boosting mass support. As regards the institutional framework, democracy in many Latin American countries commands middling levels of institutional robustness. Presidential systems, which often feature bicameral congresses and are sometimes combined with federalism, formally disperse power. Compared to the three-branch balance prevailing in the USA, however, a number of Latin American presidents have disproportionate attributions (Cox and Morgenstern 2001); moreover, their control over ample patronage and political appointments can "buy" support from legislators and state governors and thus give chief executives additional clout (Mainwaring and Shugart 1997). These power capabilities enable pushy populists to bend the rules and arrogate additional prerogatives. Because compliance with formal rules is spotty, para-legal change that further aggrandizes presidential authority is not uncommon (Levitsky and Murillo 2009, 2013; Brinks, Levitsky, and Murillo 2019).

Despite this plasticity of institutional rules, however, the presidential systems of many Latin American countries pose considerable obstacles to comprehensive power grabs and broad assaults on liberal pluralism. Due to their questionable legality, para-legal pressure tactics encounter resistance and cause a good deal of friction and conflict. As a result, such presidential arrogations of power usually do not cumulate and add up to a systematic suffocation of democracy. Chief executives can get away with the occasional infraction, but not with a full-scale dismantling of checks and balances. Trying to boost their clout, personalistic plebiscitarian leaders may test the limits; but under normal circumstances, they cannot break and erase these limits.

Therefore, even populist leaders with their energetic push for power concentration face fairly firm and resilient constraints. As my theory argues, they can impose political hegemony only under exceptional conditions, when two types of special conjunctural opportunities coincide, namely acute, severe, yet resolvable crises in the economy as well as in public security. These dramatic problems discredit the preceding government and shatter the grip of the whole political establishment. Conversely, they allow the new populist chief executive to prove his charisma through courageous, bold countermeasures, which – if successful – bring much-needed relief to the suffering population. Hyperinflation, in particular, can be quickly stopped with drastic adjustment programs, ending massive income losses for "the people." Despite the sacrifices imposed by tough stabilization measures, large numbers of citizens therefore support populist presidents who accomplish this seemingly miraculous feat and revere them as saviors. Organized violence, another terrible scourge, can also be defeated if the police or military manage to capture or kill the perpetrators' central leadership. Because citizens care enormously about their basic safety, such a striking victory also boosts presidential approval.

Only the groundswell of support unleashed by a combination of such striking achievements allows a personalistic plebiscitarian leader to steamroll the institutional obstacles arising from Latin American presidentialism and push through a major package of para-legal or even illegal change. Thus, under middling institutional strength, liberal pluralism dies and competitive authoritarianism arises only under truly extraordinary circumstances. Among Latin America's main crop of neoliberal populists (late 1980s to early 2000s), Peru's Fujimori was the sole president who managed to abolish democracy. When the Andean Samurai surprisingly won the 1990 election, he faced catastrophic hyperinflation, which devastated the economy, plus two dangerous guerrilla movements that had assailed the state for years, brutalized the population, and sowed deep fear across the far-flung country. To citizens' amazement, untested outsider Fujimori succeeded in ending skyrocketing price increases, and his police soon caught the top cadres of the largest terrorist group. These forceful efforts and their eventual success gave the president such overwhelming backing that he could spearhead a self-coup, engineer a power-concentrating constitution, install an authoritarian regime, and prolong his rule with additional para-legal measures.

Other neoliberal populists, by contrast, proved unable to impose similar political predominance and strangle democracy. Interestingly, a single crisis that new presidents effectively confronted did not boost their clout to a degree that allowed for the destruction of liberal pluralism. Although Argentina's Carlos Menem (1989–99) resolutely combated hyperinflation and Colombia's Álvaro Uribe (2002–10) energetically beat back violent guerrilla forces, neither one of them managed to push through institutional transformations that centralized power in the executive, subdued the opposition, and smothered democracy. While Menem and Uribe did achieve one reelection, they were compelled to step down at the end of their second term.

An additional set of neoliberal populists was even less successful; indeed, deficient performance, mistakes, and misdeeds led to their early eviction from office. Brazil's Fernando Collor de Mello (1990–92) also faced hyperinflation, but his inexperienced, heterogeneous economic team adopted an incoherent adjustment program that did not succeed in reestablishing price stability. This failure of crisis management weakened the brash president; therefore, he was vulnerable to a corruption scandal and suffered an ignominious impeachment halfway through his first term. Ecuador's Abdalá Bucaram (1996–97) fell even faster because he tried to copy Menem's drastic, initially painful adjustment plan although his country was *not* facing hyperinflation. This misguided borrowing "out of context," together with blatant corruption, provoked such a furious rejection that Congress removed the unpopular populist on the questionable charge of mental incompetence. An ill-considered emulation effort in Guatemala proved similarly disastrous: Although his country was experiencing neither an economic crisis nor an acute, massive security challenge, President Jorge Serrano (1991–93) decided to decree a self-coup à la Fujimori. But widespread domestic and international opposition quickly forced him to resign.

The present chapter systematically compares these variegated experiences and leverages their strikingly different fates to substantiate the theoretical reasoning of Chapter 2. Because exceptional conditions are required for personalistic plebiscitarian presidents to succeed with their undemocratic power grabs, democracy is safer from populism in its neoliberal variant than recent concerns suggest.

While Latin America's turn to the left ended the regional wave of neoliberal populism in the early 2000s (Weyland, Madrid, and Hunter 2010; Levitsky and Roberts 2011), there have been some recent cases of right-wing populism with neoliberal accents (Kestler 2022), which this chapter examines as well. First, El Salvador's Nayib Bukele (2019–present), who abandoned his left-wing roots and moved toward the right, is the only other personalistic plebiscitarian leader who managed to achieve a similar feat as Peru's Fujimori, namely "miraculous" success in combating two pressing, serious crises. By contrast to most other populist chief executives, who were stumped by the "unresolvable" COVID-19 pandemic, Bukele skillfully used his presidential attributions to contain the virus' spread through an ironclad lockdown. With this unilateral imposition, he averted considerable suffering and simultaneously forced down violent crime, a huge problem in El Salvador. To compensate for the lockdown's socioeconomic cost, the savvy president enacted generous financial subsidies and widespread food distribution. By achieving striking success on the health, economic, and security fronts, Bukele approximated Fujimori's accomplishments, boosted his charisma, and earned stratospheric popularity ratings. Consequently, his personalistic movement won a decisive victory in the congressional midterm elections of 2021, which enabled him to push through important para-legal changes and put his country on a rapid descent into competitive authoritarianism.

Whereas Bukele took advantage of an unprecedented challenge to chart the narrow path toward the populist suffocation of democracy, Jair Bolsonaro in Brazil (2019–22) failed to achieve this goal. This right-winger with hard-core authoritarian leanings was unable to overcome the institutional constraints enshrined in Brazilian presidentialism. In line with my theory, the absence of an antecedent economic and security crisis and his mishandling of the COVID-19 pandemic prevented Bolsonaro from winning majority support. The "Tropical Trump" attracted a fervent core of supporters with traditionalist cultural appeals and tough law-and-order measures of moderate success. Yet with popularity ratings hovering around 30 percent, he was in no position to force through para-legal change and impose his hegemony. Indeed, he lost his (constitutionally permitted) reelection bid in late 2022 – a rare failure for a populist president, and an important reprieve for Brazilian democracy.

These two recent experiences of right-wing populism in Latin America thus corroborate my theory: In presidential systems of middling institutional strength, only rare success in resolutely combating and largely containing or resolving two severe, acute crises, in the economy and in public security, enables populist leaders to asphyxiate liberal pluralism. Personalistic plebiscitarian presidents depend on an unusual coincidence of necessary conditions to achieve their hegemonic goal. For neoliberal populists, the path toward competitive authoritarianism is particularly narrow; democracy often survives their incessant pressures.

PERU'S DUAL CRISIS AND FUJIMORI'S DESTRUCTION OF DEMOCRACY

Among the many neoliberal populists of the late 1980s to early 2000s, only Peru's Fujimori managed to impose his anti-liberal domination. Under fairly robust presidentialism, truly exceptional conditions were required for suppressing democracy. Political outsider Fujimori simultaneously had to deal with an unprecedented double crisis, namely raging hyperinflation and the onslaught of powerful guerrilla movements, which frontally attacked the state and terrorized the population. By energetically combating and soon overcoming this unique dual challenge, the untested president super-charged his political capital and elicited overwhelming approval for his autocratic self-coup of April 1992. While external pressures forced Fujimori to abandon his initial project of an open dictatorship, the new constitution that he engineered in 1993 and his triumphant reelection in 1995 forged a competitive-authoritarian regime that harassed the opposition, disabled the judiciary, illicitly bought support, and imposed arbitrary measures through further para-legal change.

Peru was in unusually dire straits when this little-known agricultural engineer decided to run for president and unexpectedly won the contest in 1990 (Degregori and Grompone 1991; Schmidt 1996; Kenney 2004: 21–38; Carrión 2022: 53–57). A desperate adjustment plan that his predecessor had imposed to mitigate worsening economic problems had plunged the country into hyperinflation from September 1988 onward. Monthly price increases running in the double digits had exacerbated a severe economic contraction, a virtual catastrophe for Peru's innumerable lower-class and poor people (Weyland 2002: 86–89, 104). What contributed to the economic collapse was a second grave challenge, namely guerrilla insurgency. In a countrywide campaign that had caused at least 20,000 deaths by 1990 (Mauceri 1991: 97; see also 84–84, 96), the Shining Path killed not only state personnel but deliberately targeted civilian activists and reformers as well, in order to turn its own fundamentalist, Andean version of Maoism into the only alternative to the seemingly untenable, crumbling status quo. With their exemplary "punishments" and bombing attacks, these radical leftists made people fear for their lives.

Who would have wanted to become president of a country assailed by such extraordinary problems?[1] The surprise winner of the 1990 election looked particularly ill-equipped to cope with these hurricanes. After all, Fujimori was a complete newcomer who lacked political experience, anything resembling an organized political party, and connections to experts and administrators with whom he could forge an effective governing team (Degregori and Grompone 1991: 34–36, 125–28; Rospigliosi 1992: 353–55; Roberts 1995: 92–96; Schmidt 1996; Carrión 2022: 75–80). Against all odds, however, this quick learner and master calculator designed the strategies and developed the tools required for confronting the two main crises head-on.

First, because the uncertainty aggravated by the election of this untested novice fueled a further price explosion, he immediately jettisoned his gradualist approach to economic policy, betrayed his solemn campaign promises, and resolutely switched to orthodox neoliberalism (Stokes 2001: 47–53, 69–71). Consequently, he decreed a rigorous stabilization plan that, at the cost of huge short-term sacrifices, promised to stop hyperinflation in its tracks (Iguíñiz 1991; Hurtado Miller 1992; Velarde and Rodríguez 1992). Although this stunning turnaround left many of his initial supporters angry, it won support from around 55–60 percent of the population, eager to try any recipe to end their suffering (Stokes 2001: 130; Weyland 2002: 128–29; Kenney 2004: 130; Carrión 2006a: 135–37).

---

[1] Considering the massive problems assailing Peru, it is noteworthy that Fujimori's predecessor managed to serve out his full presidential term (McClintock 1989). This shows the resilience of the country's institutional framework at the time.

When this first adjustment plan proved insufficient for restoring economic stability, Fujimori redoubled the effort, enlisted a large team of neoliberal experts, and imposed their comprehensive program of profound market reform (Boloña 1993: 54–56; Velarde and Rodríguez 1994: 18–21; Weyland 2002: 117–18, 150–51; see also Mauceri 1995: 18–19). This fundamental overhaul of Peru's development model did forestall further price rises and end the fiscal hemorrhage of the state. The recovery of tax revenues and the proceeds generated by the privatization of public enterprises then allowed for a resumption of social spending and an expansion of benefit programs, which fueled a boom from 1993 onward (Roberts 1995: 102–7; Graham and Kane 1998: 85–99; Weyland 2002: 158, 175–76).

Second, to defeat the guerrilla insurgents, Fujimori developed a less bold but equally effective and less costly strategy. Notably, he did not unleash an all-out "dirty war" and refrained from using indiscriminate repression and large-scale torture, as several Latin American military regimes had done in the 1960s and 1970s.[2] Instead, the populist president designed a two-pronged approach: Additional support for peasant self-defense and vigilante groupings helped to drive armed radicals out of Peru's remote, mountainous rural regions; sophisticated intelligence and targeted police operations then caught their leadership in the cities. To push through this round-up, Fujimori claimed greater powers and attributions by decree (Mauceri 1995: 23–25; Cameron 1998a: 227; Kenney 2004: 165–66; Murakami 2012: 264–67).

The middling strength of Peru's institutional framework (cf. McClintock 1989) initially induced this personalistic plebiscitarian leader to work largely through official channels and procedures and seek approval for many of his initiatives in Congress. But opposition resistance to his ambitious projects and to the para-legal arrogations that he also employed eventually escalated to a constitutional conflict,[3] which the ever more autocratic president decisively broke by closing Congress and the courts with a military-supported self-coup in April 1992 (Kenney 2004: 203–7). Justified by the urgent need to spearhead a determined attack on the guerrilla fighters and to safeguard the recent restoration of economic stability (Fujimori 1992: 43–47), this daring power grab found support from 80 to 82 percent of respondents, who approved of the anti-insurgent struggle and rewarded Fujimori for his anti-inflation success as well.[4] When Peru's police succeeded in capturing most of the Shining Path leadership a few months later, citizen approval for the savior of the people solidified further (Mauceri 1995: 31).

---

[2] Off and on during the 1980s, the Peruvian military had employed such a highly repressive approach (Mauceri 1991: 91–93).

[3] Torres y Torres Lara 1992: 73–100; Mauceri 1995: 24, 28; Kenney 2004: 171–90, 196–98; Murakami 2012: 270–73, 279–95; Carrión 2022: 105–13.

[4] Conaghan 1995: 227, 236; Cameron 1998a: 224–25; Stokes 2001: 132, 142–46; Weyland 2002: 128–29, 171–74; Carrión 2006a: 131–34.

Strong international pressure against the blatant destruction of democracy, coming especially from Washington, forced Fujimori to convene a constituent assembly (Mauceri 1995: 29–31; Weyland 2002: 172; Kenney 2004: 243–46; Murakami 2012: 300–13). But this formal redemocratization merely covered a competitive-authoritarian regime with a threadbare façade. The new charter of 1993 strengthened and extended presidential powers and weakened the legislative branch by abolishing the upper house of Congress (Schmidt 1998: 113–14; Mauceri 2006: 45–52). Moreover, Fujimori drew on the political hegemony sustained by strong plebiscitarian support to pull the strings informally, get his congressional delegation to push through his initiatives with para-legal moves, and put heavy pressure on the courts, opposition parties, civil society, and the media. In all these ways, the autocratic president seriously skewed political competitiveness.

Indeed, after the successful populist won reelection by a landslide in 1995, he soon used his new mandate and continuing strong support to pave the ground for another candidacy in 2000. For this purpose, his loyal congressional delegation passed a controversial measure – under the Orwellian label, "law of authentic interpretation of the constitution" – that allowed him to disregard the two-term limit explicitly enshrined in his own 1993 charter; and when Peru's Constitutional Court objected, Fujimori's disciples purged and emasculated this counter-majoritarian body (Murakami 2012: 480–89; Carrión 2022: 185–90). Thus, after his blatantly unconstitutional self-coup, this personalistic leader drew on his strong plebiscitarian backing to entrench and extend his nondemocratic rule through continued para-legal change.

Fujimori held elections on schedule, employed only limited, targeted repression, even during the high point of the anti-guerrilla struggle in the early 1990s, and allowed for a good deal of liberal freedom throughout his reign. But his government used a growing tool box of tricks to contain and harass opposition forces and – literally – buy support from politicians, journalists, and civil society groupings (Murakami 2012: 495–97). Over time, the glow of his early accomplishments faded, and citizen concerns increasingly came to focus on other priorities.

Indeed, the populist president ended up facing a surprising "paradox of success" (Weyland 2000): By resolving a pair of acute, severe crises, he had restored normality – which many people sooner or later started to take for granted. As recovery from an illness brings initial relief, but not lasting happiness, so Fujimori's amazing feats produced an upsurge of support that allowed for the installation of competitive authoritarianism, but not sky-high backing for his autocratic rule over the long run. Precisely because he ended hyperinflation, for instance, people's economic needs and interests shifted to other, remaining problems, such as unemployment and low wages (Arce and Carrión 2010: 32–37, 43–47). But these rising demands were much harder to fulfill, especially for a convert to neoliberalism who could not endanger budget discipline by embarking on a huge spending spree.

Similarly, the strategic defeat of the Shining Path and the resulting drop in guerrilla violence initially gave Fujimori's backing a tremendous boost. But charismatic leaders cannot rest on their laurels for too long. Instead, they need to keep demonstrating their prowess through additional major achievements. Peru's populist president therefore searched for other urgent challenges that he could confront and that could justify the continued suppression of democracy. But his effort to turn his effective anti-guerrilla strategy against common crime made little headway: Whereas the police had managed to decapitate a centralized insurgency by catching the Shining Path leadership in one fell swoop, it was impossible to inflict the same knockout on the multiheaded hydra of regular criminals and violent gangs (Weyland 2002: 190–91). The meager payoffs of Fujimori's efforts to find and "create" new crises show again that constructivist arguments (Moffitt 2016: 121–32) are unpersuasive. Peru's successful populist failed to "perform" one crisis after the other. Instead, the objective features of actually existing problems matter enormously; the margin for agency and framing is narrow.

For these reasons, Fujimori's support started to erode after his unassailable reelection of 1995 (Murakami 2012: 441–44, 489, 506). Economic difficulties, partly the price for his pre-electoral expenditure boost, also fueled discontent, helping to draw popular attention away from the early anti-inflation success and toward other, more stubborn problems. The gradual decline in his plebiscitarian backing induced the personalistic incumbent to secure his predominance in more openly autocratic ways (overview in Carrión 2006b). These nefarious moves in turn antagonized Peruvians committed to liberal-democratic values, especially from the educated middle classes.

But although Fujimori's political fortunes trended downward, he retained considerable support among Peru's vast popular sectors, in the cities and the far-flung countryside (Carrión 2006a: 126–31). Indeed, in typical populist fashion, the chief executive frequently traveled across his nation far and wide, trying to demonstrate and strengthen his personal connection to "the little man" and woman. Setting foot in forgotten villages that no prior president had ever visited, donning local garb, and communing with poorer people in the streets, he used symbolic performances to maintain his plebiscitarian base (Murakami 2012: 376–79, 510). Moreover, he ceremoniously opened innumerable schools and health posts in long-neglected regions, as part of several high-profile social programs that extended significant benefits to Peru's ample marginalized groupings (Graham and Kane 1998; Schady 2000; Murakami 2012: 374–76). This masterful application of the populist playbook kept Fujimori electorally competitive and enabled him to claim another reelection victory in 2000. Based on his renewed mandate, he managed to disregard persistent domestic and international criticism, which highlighted a number of unfair manipulations that had induced the main opposition candidate to boycott the contest's second round (Conaghan 2005: 189–219).

Yet right after Fujimori seemed to have ensured his self-perpetuation in power, his rule unexpectedly collapsed like a house of cards (Cameron 2006: 270–83). This sudden downfall revealed the hollowness of his autocratic domination, a weakness resulting from the anti-institutional tendencies inherent in populism. As highlighted in Chapters 1 and 2, personalistic leadership is by nature wary of organizational entanglements. Accordingly, Fujimori had insisted on his unchallengeable autonomy, had based his regime on the plebiscitarian payoffs of his stunning initial successes against hyperinflation and the Shining Path, and had made virtually no effort at party building. Instead, for each major contest, the Andean Samurai had haphazardly created a new formation – and let it dissolve right thereafter (Roberts 2006: 137–41).

Without any semblance of a firm organization, Fujimori lacked a solid, reliable political base (Murakami 2012: 576–83). To compensate for the inexorable shrinkage of his plebiscitarian backing, he and his secretive spymaster relied ever more brazenly on simply buying support from a wide range of politicians, journalists, business people, and other important actors (Cameron 1998a: 236); and to make these corrupt deals enforceable, they recorded the transactions on video. When evidence of this unprecedented purchasing operation surfaced in public, the outcry was so massive that the legitimacy of Fujimori's rule evaporated virtually overnight (Conaghan 2005: 227–42; Cameron 2006: 270–83, Murakami 2012: 537–62, 576–85). After dominating Peruvian politics for a decade, the master manipulator was caught red-handed; he had no choice but to flee and resign from afar.

The stunning end of Fujimori's reign was as unexpected as the equally stunning success that this populist outsider achieved at the beginning of his unlikely tenure and that allowed him to destroy democracy and impose authoritarianism for many years. The Peruvian experience shows the full range of populism as a bold, high-risk strategy. If a personalistic plebiscitarian leader encounters an unusually propitious constellation of conjunctural opportunities, namely the coincidence of two massive, pressing crises, and if he succeeds in resolving these crises, the grateful citizenry rewards this "savior of the people" with an outpouring of overwhelming support. By invoking this political steamroller, the charismatic president can push aside institutional checks and balances, vanquish all opposition, and establish unchallengeable political predominance – though only temporarily.

As the following case studies confirm, it is only under these truly exceptional circumstances that right-wing populists have managed to suffocate liberal pluralism in contemporary Latin America. The middling institutional strength of the region's presidential systems is not easy to break. Astounding success in averting a double catastrophe is required for boosting plebiscitarian backing to a scope and intensity that allows for the abolition of democracy through a combination of para-legal and illegal change. Due to this stringent requirement, the threat arising from populism, examined here in its neoliberal variant, is less dire than commonly feared.

Moreover, the authoritarian rule that emerges under these unusual circumstances tends to be quite brittle. With its pronounced personalism and penchant for transgression, populist leadership is fundamentally averse to constructing the organizational scaffolding that could undergird regime consolidation and reliably sustain its persistence over the long run. Personalistic presidents who are "on top of the world" are reluctant to routinize their charisma and step back into the realm of regular mortals (see recently Andrews-Lee 2021: 27–28). Trusting in their extraordinary gifts and trying to maintain their unencumbered predominance, they refrain from encasing their leadership through organization building. As a result, their rule remains institutionally fragile; indeed, it turns precarious with the gradual corrosion resulting from the paradox of success mentioned earlier. To make up for this unstoppable ebbing of their plebiscitarian support, they resort to ever more dangerous expedients, including systematic bribery. In this way, they risk major scandals, which can rock their regime. Thus, by insisting they sit on their high horse, they may set themselves up for a sudden, drastic fall, which will break their political neck. Fujimori's meteoric rise and equally meteoric crash thus demonstrate the stunning volatility of populist experiences, which have a much wider range of potential outcomes than regular, institutionally confined politics.

Consequently, even where personalistic plebiscitarian leaders manage to take advantage of the exceptional opportunity provided by an acute double crisis, combat these challenges effectively, and leverage the resulting mass support for suppressing democracy, their rule is not secure over the long run. Instead, the authoritarian regimes imposed by right-wing populists are likely to fall as the population takes the restoration of normality for granted and the erstwhile hero's charisma fades. With that decline in their plebiscitarian base, the anti-organizational and anti-institutional tendencies of personalistic leaders can easily come to haunt them. Of course, their downfall can give democracy a new lease of life.

For both of these important reasons, namely the unusual, restrictive conditions for the installation of populist authoritarianism and this regime's inherent brittleness, the risk that neoliberal populism poses to liberal pluralism is limited. This version of populism has a low chance of destroying democracy in the first place; and where it does, democracy has a good chance of resurrection.

SINGLE CRISES AND THE SURVIVAL OF PRESIDENTIAL DEMOCRACY

Whereas Fujimori drew enormous political benefits from combating two profound crises, Argentina's Carlos Menem and Colombia's Álvaro Uribe faced – and faced down – only one of these challenges, namely hyperinflation or a guerrilla war, respectively. This success was substantial enough to provide them with great political clout and allow for one immediate reelection. But it did not give them the unchallengeable predominance to push aside liberal constraints and resolutely move to competitive authoritarianism. As a result, they were unable to achieve further self-perpetuation in power and had to comply with term limits, stepping down after two governing periods. Thus, although the conjunctural opportunity offered by one crisis boosted their political fortunes for years, their single achievement did not produce the massive, transgressive clout to trample on institutional checks and balances and enshrine the supremacy of their personalistic plebiscitarian leadership, as their Peruvian counterpart did.

Menem's Success against Hyperinflation – And the Persistence of Liberal Pluralism in Argentina

Carlos Menem (1989–99) took office at the height of an economic crisis that was so severe as to induce his predecessor Raúl Alfonsín (1983–89) to resign five months ahead of schedule (Palermo and Novaro 1996: 110–17). As hyperinflation raged, the new president felt compelled to betray his campaign promises of promoting economic expansion and a salary boost ("*salariazo*"). Instead, this ostentatious populist made a radical turnabout and imposed a neoliberal austerity plan.[5] To prepare his determined program of market reforms and credibly commit to this unexpected change of direction, Menem audaciously forged an alliance with traditional enemies of his nationalist, state-interventionist Peronist Party,[6] especially Argentina's major business conglomerate and a dogmatic neoliberal party (Alsogaray 1993: 161–71; Novaro 1998: 34–43). In this way, he drastically departed from decades of Peronist economic policy proposals and started to dismantle the protectionist development model of import-substitution industrialization that the much-revered party founder, Juan Domingo Perón (1946–55), had implanted with great fanfare (Schamis 2013: 166–70).

While rapidly interrupting the price explosion, Menem's stunning turnaround, initiated with the typical boldness of charismatic leadership, did not achieve lasting success, however. As inflation soon accelerated again, the new president dismissed his business allies and entrusted the adjustment efforts to a personal loyalist, rumored to be his half-brother (Smith 1991: 59–62; Teichman 2001: 114–18). But after another initial reduction of inflation, this strikingly personalistic move failed to guarantee stability as well. In despair, Menem finally made a concession that is difficult for a power-concentrating, control-oriented populist: He saw no other way but to delegate all of economic policy-making to a large, coherent team of neoliberal experts, namely Domingo Cavallo and his *Fundación Mediterránea* (Carrera 1994; Palermo

---

[5] Smith 1991: 52–55; Stokes 2001: 45–47, 71–72; Weyland 2002: 112–14; Mora y Araujo 2011: 61–64, 121–22; Roberts 2014: 209–13.

[6] For background on the foundation and trajectory of Peronism, see Waldmann (1974), Ranis (1995), McGuire (1997), Levitsky (2003), and recently Andrews-Lee (2021: chap. 6).

and Novaro 1996: 293–304; Corrales 1997: 62–69; Teichman 2001: 118–22; see also Corrales 2002: 173–74).

The new czar understood that success in overcoming the recurring crisis was decisive for Menem's political survival and therefore resorted to a last-ditch measure in order finally to defeat hyperinflation. Cavallo made Argentina's currency fully convertible and used the US dollar as an anchor to stop future price rises in their track. To give this emergency restraint credibility and sustainability, this bold stabilization plan combated the state's dangerous fiscal deficit with tough austerity and revenue-generating expedients, especially the hasty sell-off of public enterprises (Cavallo 1997: 174–81; see also Smith 1991: 63–65; Santoro 1994: 291–96, 302–4; Llach 1997: 135–39). With these daring moves, the powerful economy minister ushered in a comprehensive program of profound market reforms that greatly reduced state interventionism and opened Argentina to international trade and investment.

By frontally combating the scourge of runaway inflation, Menem's adjustment plans found a great deal of popular support, even from working-class people.[7] Although these tough measures caused substantial short-term hardships, and although the imposition of market reforms led to a worrisome increase in unemployment in later years, the defeat of hyperinflation brought tremendous relief to the population, especially poorer people, who were forced to rely on cash and therefore suffered daily losses. The end of this drain fueled a quick recovery that turned into a boom from 1991 to 1994. Renewed growth, price stability, and a crackdown on tax evasion also filled the state's fiscal coffers, allowing for a resumption and expansion of social spending (Palermo and Novaro 1996: 304–9; Weyland 2002: 150, 158).

With the economic turnaround finally engineered by Cavallo and his team, Menem became the savior of the people and achieved clear political predominance (Andrews-Lee 2021: 150–51). The president's striking accomplishments on the crucial economic front induced most of his Peronist Party to acquiesce – however reluctantly – in the high-profile abandonment of its longstanding commitment to protectionist state interventionism (Corrales 2002: chaps. 8–9). That the good economic times and Menem's high popularity gifted the party electoral victories in the congressional and gubernatorial elections of 1991 and 1993 clearly helped.

Based on his anti-inflation success, Menem's approval ratings ran at 50–60 percent during these years (Stokes 2001: 136–38; Weyland 2002: 126–27; Mora y Araujo 2011: 98, 122), a strong result in Argentina's traditionally divided polity. Yet the Peronist turned neoliberal never accumulated the overwhelming clout that Fujimori obtained by miraculously resolving two simultaneous crises. After all, Argentina was not facing a major security challenge

---

[7] Ranis 1995: xx–xxiv; Palermo and Novaro 1996: 230–31, 235–37; McGuire 1997: 226–38; Echegaray and Elordi 2001: 193–94, 202; Weyland 2002: 126–27; Mora y Araujo 2011: 98, 122.

when the populist leader won office. Because the country was not teetering on the brink of the abyss, as Peru did with its two catastrophic problems in 1990, Menem did not have the opportunity to bring the same massive relief that Fujimori provided to Peruvians. Overcoming only one severe challenge boosted the Peronist president's influence substantially, but not to the unchallengeable level that Fujimori reached with the exceptional feat of slaying two dangerous dragons.

Consequently, whereas Fujimori managed to impose authoritarianism with his self-coup of 1992, Menem could not dare to make such a blatantly illegal move, but had to proceed primarily inside the confines of the established institutional framework. While the Argentine president passed many specific measures with an unprecedented, procedurally problematic slew of "emergency" decrees (Palermo and Novaro 1996: 262–64, 480–81; Ferreira Rubio and Goretti 1998), he was compelled to rely for his major institutional and structural reforms on regular legislation, for which he had to find approval in both houses of Congress. Indeed, whereas Fujimori managed to undermine and pulverize the established parties in Peru, Argentina's opposition retained a good deal of defensive capacity.

To pursue the populist obsession with extending his tenure in office, Menem was therefore compelled to follow official procedures and employ democratic means. For this purpose, the Peronist president negotiated a deal – the *Pacto de Olivos* of 1993 – with the main opposition party that foresaw a major overhaul of the constitution but preserved the liberal-pluralist regime (Palermo and Novaro 1996: 414–16; Weyland 2002: 169–71). Through this balanced transaction, the incumbent won the right to run for one immediate reelection, but in exchange for several constraints on executive prerogatives, such as a limitation of the decree powers that he had para-legally arrogated (Negretto 2013: 145–65; Corrales 2018: 60–61).

The comparison with Peru is instructive for understanding the repercussions of right-wing populism for presidential democracy. As in Peru, Argentina's reformed charter permitted a consecutive second term, which Menem convincingly won – but he had to compete in a free and fair election. Contrary to Fujimori, Menem did not overturn democracy; he lacked the irresistible clout to break the liberal institutional framework or deform it in clearly undemocratic ways. While the Argentine president certainly made full use of his presidential powers and put some problematic pressure on liberal pluralism, for instance by packing the Supreme Court, he never managed to install competitive authoritarianism. Instead, democracy survived a decade of neoliberal populism, though with some black and blue spots (Levitsky and Murillo 2005: 31–35).

Indeed, the institutional framework modified in 1994 remained firm enough to preclude Menem's desire to run for a second consecutive reelection in 1999. The president, whose popularity ratings diminished with renewed economic problems and stubbornly growing unemployment, lacked the political clout to engineer another modification of the constitution – contrary to what Fujimori's loyalists did with para-legal means in Peru. Indeed, the sectors of the Peronist Party that had only begrudgingly supported Menem's drastic policy switch to neoliberalism now mobilized to foreclose his renewed candidacy; instead, they backed an intraparty rival who promised to put renewed emphasis on the social goals and nationalist proclivities of original Peronism (Palermo and Novaro 1996: 436–44; Levitsky and Murillo 2005: 34; Novaro 2009: 498–500, 540–41). Checkmated by limited control over his own populist movement and by the resilience of Argentina's institutional framework, Menem had no choice but to step down when his second term ended (Weyland 2002: 193–201).

The limitations of Menem's – certainly substantial – political success and the survival of liberal pluralism in Argentina shed additional light on the Peruvian case. Only the unusual coincidence of two acute, severe, yet resolvable crises gave Fujimori the extraordinary clout for overthrowing democracy and installing competitive authoritarianism. While success in combating one crisis boosted presidential influence and enabled both Menem and Fujimori to engineer presidential reelection and win a second term, it was only the exceptional opportunity provided by a second simultaneous crisis that gave the Peruvian populist substantially greater leeway, which allowed him to destroy democracy and push through another consecutive reelection as well.

Uribe's Success against Guerrilla Insurgencies – And the Persistence of Liberal Pluralism in Colombia

The political fate of Álvaro Uribe in Colombia (2002–10) corroborates this inference about the unique constellation of conjunctural opportunities that allowed for the asphyxiation of democracy in Peru. After all, Uribe's experience demonstrates that on its own, the other dangerous crisis that Fujimori had encountered and resolved, namely large-scale, brutal guerrilla attacks, also offered insufficient opportunities for an authoritarian power grab. While Colombia's populist president achieved high approval ratings and garnered impressive political support with his determined attack on violent left-wing militants (García-Sánchez and Rodríguez-Raga 2019: 93, 108–12), this success against one crisis alone did not provide enough of a political steamroller to push through his power-concentrating project fully. Instead, just like Menem, substantial progress in overcoming one major challenge enabled Uribe to amend the constitution, gain permission to run for one immediate reelection, and convincingly win a second term. But because he could not reshape the liberal institutional framework at will, he failed to plot his further self-perpetuation in power. Like his Argentine counterpart, he was therefore compelled to relinquish the presidential sash at the end of his second term.

Uribe turned populist in reaction to Colombia's worsening security crisis, which resulted from the cancerous growth of decades-old guerrilla challenges (Carrión 2002: 61–64; López Bayona 2016: 89–90, 99–101). From the 1960s onward, a peasant-based communist rebellion and a Castroite student-led movement had violently attacked the state. Military repression, combined with feeble reform efforts, drove the fighters into peripheral areas of the geographically fragmented country, but never managed to defeat and extinguish the festering insurgencies. Indeed, growing drug trafficking provided voluminous resources to the militants and enabled them to extend their armed challenges. As self-defense forces formed to compensate for the state's persistent weakness by battling the leftist fighters on their own, and as these right-wing paramilitaries started to participate in the narcotics trade as well, violence further increased, affecting various regions of the far-flung country.

After the Colombian state had long vacillated irresolutely between militarized counterattacks and peacemaking efforts, Uribe's predecessor Andrés Pastrana (1998–2002) tried to make negotiations work by granting the main guerrilla force huge concessions, especially control over a Switzerland-size swath of the country. Instead of bargaining in good faith, however, the insurgents-*cum*-drug traffickers seemed to use this suspension of military repression for further expanding their nefarious operations and acquiring additional armaments. Insecurity exploded as the virtual civil war afflicted large sections of the countryside and travel between Colombia's major cities turned hazardous (Pécaut 2003: chaps. 2–3).

A groundswell of revulsion against Pastrana's ineffective and counterproductive appeasement swept Uribe into office in the 2002 election.[8] After rising through one of Colombia's two traditional parties, Uribe had broken with the political establishment and embraced a populist strategy (Osorio 2012: 51–57, 67, 72–76). In particular, he systematically whipped up mass support by campaigning on a frontal attack against the insurgents. He promised finally to restore "law and order" and combat widespread common crime as well (Uribe 2002: 94–96). To boost his personalistic plebiscitarian leadership, charismatic Uribe appealed directly to "the people," both via the national media and through frequent personal appearances and meetings in neighborhoods and villages across the national territory. To connect to his followers without intermediaries, he refrained – in typical populist fashion – from forging a coherent party while in office (Kline 2009: 63–64, 172, 176–78, 183; Bermúdez 2010: 256).[9] Instead, Uribe governed with shifting groupings of supporters in Congress, whom he attracted with his resolute leadership (Pécaut 2003: 81–82).

To undergird his frontal assault on the guerrilla forces, the new president boosted the state's fiscal strength through major tax raises (Uribe 2012: 173–76; Flores-Macías 2022: chap. 4). The increased revenues funded a massive expansion and rearmament of Colombia's military and police (Kline 2009: 33–48, 167–71), which despite decades of lingering insurgencies had remained

---

[8] Kline 2009: 23–24; see Pécaut 2003: 79–80; Uribe 2012: 99, 123–24, 131; Carrión 2022: 86–89.
[9] Wills-Otero (2014: 200–3) seems to overestimate the role of the movement-party formed by Uribe's main political disciples, which lacked strong organization, left out important segments of the president's supporters, and never achieved a hegemonic position in Congress.

surprisingly small and weak. For his determined crusade to restore public safety at long last, Uribe also received billions of dollars and crucial military and intelligence assistance from the USA via Plan Colombia (Kline 2009: 45, 168–70; Uribe 2012: 182–185, 240–42).

With all of these efforts and his energetic take-charge approach (Galindo Hernández 2007: 151–52, 157), the bold populist, who faced defiant acts of left-wing terrorism on the very day of his presidential inauguration (Uribe 2012: 7, 141–45), managed to bring quick relief to the fearful population. His high-profile mobilization of military force put the insurgents on the defensive and made interregional travel and transport across the country safe again, lifting the virtual siege of Colombia's cities that the ascendant guerrilla forces had imposed in the early 2000s (Bejarano 2011: 233; Uribe 2012: 9, 149–52, 177–81, 191, 210). With the boost to military firepower and morale that resolute presidential leadership and US help fueled, the left-wing radicals also suffered substantial losses in battle and were forced to withdraw into remote areas. Although Uribe's security forces could not replicate Fujimori's early success in decapitating the main guerrilla movement,[10] determined counter-insurgency operations greatly reduced violent attacks, including the innumerable kidnappings that had cast a pall over the country (see data reported by Kline 2015: 67, 69–71; Colombia: Still Armed 2021: 35; see also Bejarano 2013: 337).

Because the daring populist was finally combating the escalating crisis head-on and was achieving fundamental improvements in public safety (Uribe 2012: 177–78, 191, 210), large numbers of citizens celebrated him as a hero and awarded him sky-high approval ratings (García-Sánchez and Rodríguez-Raga 2019: 93, 108–12). Moreover, in Colombia's rapidly fragmenting party system, a new, loose formation emerged that dedicated itself to supporting the savior of the people and that encompassed defectors from the two traditional parties as well (Vélez, Ossa, and Montes 2006: 16, 27; Kline 2009: 63–64, 72, 176–78, 183; Wills-Otero 2014: 200–3).

The Colombian president, however, never established the supreme predominance that Fujimori had enjoyed in Peru. Like Menem in Argentina, Uribe achieved great accomplishments in resolving one serious crisis – but not two simultaneous challenges, as Peru's chief executive had done. While the Argentine populist had not encountered a security crisis upon taking office, his Colombian counterpart did not face an economic crisis. Certainly, the North Andean country had suffered a sharp recession with a drop in GDP of 5 percent in 1998–99. But while the aftereffects lingered for years, the recovery started quickly and growth had resumed in 2000 already. Thus, by the time of Uribe's

---

[10] The Colombian military managed to kill crucial guerrilla leaders only in 2008, especially through a controversial strike in neighboring Ecuador, which yielded ample intelligence, including proof of the substantial support that Venezuela's left-wing populist Hugo Chávez had given the armed radicals (Kline 2015: 64, 72–74; see Uribe 2012: 40–41, 265–66, 274–75, 282–87, 291, 305, 314).

inauguration in mid-2002, the economy was clearly on the upswing. The new president therefore lacked the opportunity to confront another massive problem and further boost his charisma. As the contrast with Fujimori suggests, this absence of a second simultaneous crisis prevented Uribe from winning the overwhelming clout that had enabled the Andean Samurai to destroy democracy and install a competitive-authoritarian regime.

For these reasons, Uribe was compelled to promote his personalistic project through the official procedures of Colombia's institutional framework. From the outset, he pursued the typically populist goal of expanding his own power and weakening checks and balances. Trusting in the high popularity resulting from his anti-guerrilla success, he proposed an ambitious referendum on constitutional changes, which sought to debilitate Congress, undermine Colombia's parties, and augment presidential preeminence (Uribe 2002: 91–93; Bermúdez 2010: 198, 202). He initially went so far as to demand new congressional elections, which he expected to sweep, and pushed for a unicameral legislature, which would have eliminated an important veto player and facilitated executive dominance (Vélez, Ossa, and Montes 2006: 9, 11, 18–19).

Remarkably, these radical proposals, which critics decried as the core of an authoritarian project (Colectivo de Abogados José Alvear Restrepo 2003: 17–20; Amézquita Quintana 2008: 96), mirrored major changes that Uribe's ideological opposite Hugo Chávez had recently pushed through in Venezuela via a government-controlled constituent assembly (see Chapter 4). This striking coincidence demonstrates populist leaders' fundamental quest for power concentration, regardless of ideological differences. As in Venezuela, a victory in this plebiscitarian confrontation with the established "political class" would have paved the way for Uribe's populist hegemony and the corresponding democratic backsliding (Osorio 2012: 45–47).

But Colombia's charismatic president faced two significant obstacles. First, with only one major accomplishment, he could not follow Fujimori and simply override Colombia's institutional framework;[11] instead, he was compelled to seek legislative and judicial approval for holding his referendum. Predictable resistance in Congress led to the elimination of the most transformative and power-concentrating proposals, especially the installation of a unicameral Congress, the dissolution of the current legislature, and the convocation of new elections (Pécaut 2003: 84–87; Osorio 2012: 46; see also Bermúdez 2010: 200–2). Indeed, Colombia's two traditional parties responded to the threat posed by Uribe's referendum and his broader plebiscitarian strategy: They passed a political and electoral reform designed to strengthen their crumbling organizations and thus offer more effective opposition to the populist leader's pressures (Vélez, Ossa, and Montes 2006: 18–21, 29).

---

[11] Because Colombian democracy enjoyed middling institutional strength, Uribe could not follow Chávez either, who took advantage of Venezuela's high instability and forced through his own referendum on a constituent assembly with a quick burst of para-legal change.

Second, Uribe's popular support proved insufficiently broad and intense to guarantee approval for his watered-down referendum, which Constitutional Court rulings had complicated in procedural terms (Amézquita Quintana 2008: 79, 84; Bermúdez 2010: 205–6, 213, 226; referendum text reprinted in Osorio 2012: 105–12). While a strong majority of voters, grateful for the security improvements, backed their accomplished leader and wanted to grant him extended prerogatives, not enough citizens turned out, due in part to the opposition's vigorous abstention campaign (Amézquita Quintana 2008: 90–102). Because the referendum narrowly missed the required quorum, 25 percent of the citizenry (Kline 2009: 43–44), Uribe's ambitious initiative failed.

Thus, by contrast to Fujimori as well as Chávez, Uribe's popular backing lacked overwhelming strength. The Colombian populist was therefore unable to start dismantling liberal checks and balances. Because he suffered a stinging setback, which further limited his clout (Bermúdez 2010: 222, 225–26), the constitutional framework retained its firmness. With Uribe's referendum defeat, Colombian democracy avoided a descent toward competitive authoritarianism (Osorio 2012: 49–51, 61–62; see also Bejarano 2013: 341; Carrión 2022: 121–23, 142–43).

The ambitious populist did achieve his most immediate goal, however. Given Uribe's accomplishments in improving public safety and the promise to press ahead with the unfinished struggle against the guerrilla forces, his congressional supporters passed a constitutional amendment that allowed for one consecutive reelection. Based on his high popularity, the successful president won a lopsided victory in 2006, similar to Menem's triumph of 1995. Indeed, during his second term, the government managed to deal the armed militants the hardest blows by finally killing several top leaders and liberating high-profile kidnapping victims (Uribe 2012: 40–41, 265–66, 274–75, 282–87, 291, 305, 314). But while these military strikes sealed the strategic defeat of the long-lasting insurgency, they did not bring a great deal of additional relief to the population, after the turnaround in the security crisis that the Colombian government had achieved since 2002 already (see data reported in Kline 2015: 67, 69–71). Instead, Uribe was beginning to experience the paradox of success that had also weakened Fujimori and Menem during their second terms (Osorio 2012: 71–72).

Consequently, the Colombian populist did not command the steamroller of support to prolong his rule even further. When his confidants floated the idea of another consecutive reelection, the constellation of political forces in Congress made a new constitutional amendment infeasible; and Colombia's strong and independent Constitutional Court, which as the main bastion of political liberalism was by nature averse to power-hungry populism, struck down the project of a popular referendum and thus foreclosed Uribe's renewed candidacy in 2010 (Uribe 2012: 327–28; Kline 2015: 175–76, 189; Ginsburg and Huq 2018b: 187–89; Carrión 2022: 124–27; Issacharoff 2023: 107, 125–28). Like Menem in Argentina, the incumbent therefore had to vacate his office when his second term ended. While Uribe had stretched and disfigured liberal pluralism, for instance with human rights violations during the counter-insurgency struggle (Fierro 2014: 139–43), he had proven unable to impose total political dominance and abolish democracy.

In addition to Colombia's domestic institutional framework, which Uribe with his great but not overwhelming support could not override, this populist leader also faced external constraints that contributed to the survival of liberal pluralism. After all, his vigorous efforts to fight guerrilla violence depended on voluminous US aid via Plan Colombia. In exchange for these ample subsidies, the Colombian president had to refrain from open attacks on democracy, and congressional Democrats pushed for greater respect for human rights as well (Uribe 2012: 239–42, 245; see also Pécaut 2003: 169–71; Kline 2015: 74–79, 184).

Fujimori, however, had also relied on US support, both direct financial aid and backing for urgent renegotiations of Peru's external debt. Indeed, Washington's pressures after his 1992 self-coup had forced the Andean Samurai to relinquish his plan to impose an outright dictatorship. Yet while Fujimori was compelled to initiate steps toward formal redemocratization, he managed to maintain his competitive-authoritarian regime behind this façade, despite the Clinton government's official democracy-promotion agenda. In the same vein, Uribe had some room for maneuver as well, especially under the George W. Bush administration, which indicated its ideological affinity with Colombia's right-wing populist by extending US support to include the fight against left-wing guerrillas and not only drug traffickers (Uribe 2012: 183–84, 242). Given this latitude, Plan Colombia alone did not forestall surreptitious democratic backsliding and gradual authoritarian involution. Instead, Uribe's limited political clout, which prevented him from seriously undermining Colombia's checks and balances, was crucial as well.

In conclusion, Uribe's political fate corroborates my argument that Latin America's presidential systems of middling institutional strength have considerable resilience against the threat of populism. The separation of powers impedes incumbent takeovers not only under normal conditions but even when countries face a pressing, dangerous crisis, in the economy or in public security, and when a successful president can therefore win a great deal of support. Only under exceptional circumstances – when crises in both of these spheres coincide and when a new charismatic leader directly confronts these crises and soon manages to bring substantial relief to the afflicted population – can a populist win the massive, overwhelming clout to push aside institutional constraints and move to competitive authoritarianism. Facing only one of these conjunctural opportunities, Uribe – like Menem – achieved enough success to win a second term, but not enough to extend his tenure further and turn into an autocrat. By contrast to Peru, democracy therefore survived in Colombia, similar to Argentina; and under Uribe's successor, liberal pluralism recovered and gained greater vibrancy (Mayka 2016: 143–46).

CASES OF POPULIST FAILURE

Whereas Fujimori, Menem, and Uribe took advantage of acute crises to achieve great – albeit differential – political success, other neoliberal populists encountered much less propitious conditions or showed limited aptitude. Their failures, which culminated in premature evictions from office, resulted from a combination of different conjunctural opportunities and of political decisions and policy choices that were ill-adapted to the prevailing situation. As Chapter 2 discussed, objective conditions set the stage for neoliberal populists and deeply affected their political fate. Agency, however, can also play an important role. After all, it is a difficult task to design and enact effective countermeasures against major problems that push countries to the edge of the abyss.

Indeed, personalistic leaders are inherently ill-positioned to elaborate promising, realistic policy solutions. To guard their autonomy and enhance their predominance, these headstrong, domineering chieftains surround themselves with personal loyalists, weaklings, and sycophants. They are reluctant to enlist independent experts, whose professional planning, commitment to principles, and reliance on systematic procedures may rein in the leader's penchant for boldness. Convinced that they organically represent "the will of the people," populists act out of intuition rather than rationality. And to prove their charisma, they try to perform miracles with unconventional, daring masterstrokes and impose their will regardless of costs and risks. All these tendencies create tremendous uncertainty and a wide range of potential outcomes. While heroic deeds sometimes succeed and bring unexpected, even unimaginable payoffs, as in Peru under Fujimori, they can also end up in utter failure and make the situation worse.

Ironically, personalistic plebiscitarian leaders also have difficulty coping with noncrisis situations. After all, charismatic politicians have an innate proclivity to embark on bold stunts to demonstrate their prowess. But what if such risky moves do not fit the actual circumstances and therefore fail to achieve success and find political resonance? Imposing a disproportionate "solution" to a limited problem, especially at great cost, can provoke a great deal of opposition and turn an aspiring superhero into a villain, with disastrous political consequences.

The following sections examine populist chief executives who did not encounter propitious circumstances or who made serious mistakes in policy design or political judgment – and paid a heavy price by suffering early ousters. Of course, the downfall of personalistic plebiscitarian leaders tends to protect liberal pluralism from assault; where populism dies, democracy usually does not die. Conversely, this comparative analysis of populist self-destruction sheds further light on the political success of Fujimori, Menem, and Uribe. In particular, this contrast highlights how unusual the constellation of conditions, factors, and choices was that enabled the strangulation of democracy in Peru, the rare case in which neoliberal populism brought about this tragic outcome.

Failure to Resolve a Crisis: Collor's Downfall in Brazil

Upon taking office in March 1990, Fernando Collor de Mello (1990–92) faced a conjunctural opportunity for boosting his populist leadership; but contrary to Fujimori, Menem, and Uribe, he failed to take advantage of this opportunity. The Brazilian populist's inability to extinguish incipient hyperinflation undermined his claim to extraordinary leadership. The resulting political weakness made him vulnerable to the risks inherent in a populist strategy, which provokes incessant confrontation and frequent conflict. Therefore, striking denunciations of corruption in his entourage prompted his embarrassing impeachment in the middle of his first term. Collor's lack of success preserved democracy, sustained by a reassertion of Brazil's democratic parties.

For many years, Brazil had been plagued by high inflation, which spiraled upward from 228 percent in 1987 to 1,430 percent in 1989, the year of Collor's election. After several unsuccessful efforts to bring these accelerating price rises under control, the country slid into an acute crisis with the eruption of hyperinflation, which skyrocketed to 81.3 percent per month in February 1990. Immediately after his inauguration, a brash Collor therefore decreed a shock program of stabilization and adjustment (author interview with Collor 1995), just like Fujimori and Menem. Interestingly, Collor enjoyed a clearer mandate for these tough measures: After all, he had campaigned on a neoliberal platform, whereas his Argentine and Peruvian counterparts had lured voters with softer, less painful policy proposals, which they then blithely betrayed with their surprising conversions to the cause of marketization (Stokes 2001: 30, 45–53).

Yet although Collor started from a fairly strong political position, his government failed to extinguish inflation and chart a coherent, credible course of market reform. The inexperienced, heterogeneous set of economic aides assembled by the new president, an outsider to the national elite, hurriedly elaborated a daring adjustment plan (Silva 1993: 322–23), which went to the extreme of temporarily sequestering liquidity by freezing people's bank accounts above $1,100 (Bresser Pereira 1991: 8, 12–14, 17–30; Schneider 1991: 328, 330–31; see also De Faro 1990; Sabino 1991: 111–12, 126, 131–32). But this heavy-handed shock treatment, which contradicted Collor's broader program of economic liberalization (Bornhausen 1991; Weyland 2002: 122), did not manage to eradicate inflation. While the pre-inauguration surge into hyperinflation did not recur, price rises soon accelerated again and reached *monthly* rates above 10 percent in June 1990 and 18 percent in December (Schneider 1991: 330–33).

Thus, Collor, who had announced that he had "only a single bullet to kill the tiger of inflation" (cf. Weyland 2002: 109, 123; see also Bresser Pereira 1991: 30), clearly failed with his controversial and costly adjustment effort. Moreover, because the domineering president had claimed personal responsibility for economic policy-making (Sabino 1991: 114, 161), the blame fell squarely on him. A second, much less drastic stabilization plan did not work either (De Faro 1991; Schneider 1991: 334–35, 342). Yet the strong-willed leader refused to give up control over this crucial issue area by empowering a close-knit neoliberal team, as both Fujimori and Menem did. Thus, he did not enlist the technocratic expertise and organizational cohesion that under-girded economic adjustment and reform in other countries.[12] Furthermore, his weak political standing, including his feeble "party" with its small con-gressional delegation, hindered the imposition of a credible, effective pro-gram of orthodox adjustment as well (Schneider 1991: 322; Weyland 2002: 151–52, 163–64).

For these reasons, Collor's government never succeeded in stemming sub-stantial price rises and restoring economic stability. Instead, annual inflation ran at 433 percent in 1991 and 952 percent in 1992; these exorbitant rates were similar to the levels prevailing before his election. The Brazilian populist failed very clearly to bring the dramatic relief to the hard-pressed population that his Peruvian and Argentine counterparts achieved. As a result, his plebi-scitarian support quickly shrank and his popularity ratings dropped (Weyland 2002: 127–28).

Yet despite his weak political standing, Collor did not hesitate to employ the typical populist tactic of seeking constant confrontation with other power centers (author interview with Collor 1995; see also Schneider 1991: 338, 341; Weyland 1993: 10–13). He ostentatiously put Brazil's powerful military in its place and asserted civilian control over the institution that had dictatori-ally ruled from 1964 to 1985 (Hunter 1997). To push through his neoliberal opening of the economy to foreign competition, the president also fought with mighty business groupings that had taken advantage of decades of protection-ism to build up inefficient, overly costly industries (Bornhausen 1991; Weyland 2002: 143, 146); he ruffled feathers by contemptuously deriding Brazilian-made cars as clunkers. Last but not least, Collor attacked left-wing parties and their affiliated trade unions, which in turn offered stubborn opposition to his market reforms.

At the same time, Collor was reluctant to build a firm support coalition in Congress. To preserve his autonomy and personalistic clout,[13] he tried instead to base his populist rule on his plebiscitarian mass support, constantly invok-ing the 35 million votes of his electoral triumph (Bresser Pereira 1991: 12–14; Schneider 1991: 324–25; Silva 1993: 110, 385; Weyland 2002: 142, 146). But in prototypical populist fashion, he did not take any steps to solidify this support by transforming his flimsy electoral vehicle into anything resembling an orga-nized party (Schneider 1991: 336–37; Weyland 1993: 8–10). Consequently, the sustained decline of his approval ratings left him increasingly weak and

---

[12] Teichman (1997, 2001) and Van Gunten (2015) demonstrate the importance of technocratic elite cohesion for economic policy success, especially the resolution of crises.

[13] This is the main theme of the extensive memoir written by one of Collor's closest confidants (Silva 1993).

isolated (Lamounier 1993: 133–34), and he had difficulty winning parliamentary approval for his bills (Ames 2001: 191–95). Irresolutely in 1991 and with greater determination in 1992, Collor finally started to step down from his high horse and tried to forge a congressional alliance – but it was too little, too late (Ames 2001: 177–80). Parties that he had antagonized in prior years refused to join his limping government.

Collor's blatant failure to extirpate inflation, which deflated his charisma, and his lack of solid political sustenance made him vulnerable to the sensational corruption allegations voiced by his own jealous brother (Silva 1993: 210–13, 336–54; Kada 2003: 121; Pérez-Liñán 2007: 16);[14] such betrayal driven by longstanding private resentments constitutes a risk inherent in populist personalism. Yet whereas successful presidents such as Fujimori and Menem managed to ride out major corruption scandals,[15] the revelation of striking misdeeds can easily turn lethal for tottering leaders (Hochstetler 2006: 406–7; Pérez-Liñán 2007: 87–131). Attacked by the left and increasingly abandoned by his few friends and allies, the young populist – in despair – tried to mobilize his plebiscitarian base and called for mass demonstrations on his behalf. But due to his meager accomplishments and hollowed-out charisma, this typically populist tactic backfired and provoked an outpouring of countrywide protests *against* him (Weyland 1993: 23). Using this opportunity to checkmate the arrogant upstart who had sought to challenge its predominance, Brazil's party establishment, together with the anti-neoliberal left, impeached Collor in late 1992 (Kada 2003: 121–23; Pérez-Liñán 2007: 95–98, 125–26, 149–52; Roberts 2014: 205).

In sum, the Brazilian populist spoiled the opportunity that Argentina's Menem used for boosting his political standing and winning a second term in office. While hyperinflation alone does not enable personalistic plebiscitarian leaders to achieve unchallengeable hegemony and move to authoritarianism, as the comparison of Fujimori vs. Menem shows, it does give chief executives a good chance for demonstrating charisma. But by contrast to his Argentine counterpart, Collor failed to resolve the economic crisis and turn into the populace's savior. His experience corroborates that populist leaders are prone to errors; their insistence on personalistic predominance entails a reluctance to relinquish control via delegation to experts. The resulting difficulties in combating urgent problems can easily turn politically dangerous because populist leaders lack the organizational backing to endure stretches of low performance and survive major scandals (Weyland 1993).

---

[14] Allegedly, Collor's brother suspected that the president had "made a pass at" his attractive wife (Silva 1993: 342–46). This incident aggravated longstanding rivalries arising from (perceived) parental favoritism and the resulting intrafamilial conflicts (Silva 1993: 336–54).

[15] Especially instructive is the contrast with Fujimori, whose own wife publicly denounced corruption among the president's close relatives – but her husband survived the scandal (Conaghan 2005: 86).

Collor's ignominious ouster ushered in a reequilibration of Brazil's fledgling democracy (Weyland 1993: 25–27; cf. Linz 1978: chap. 5). The brash populist and his striking economic and political failure served as a deterrent that immunized the polity against the allures of personalistic plebiscitarian leadership. Instead, the political establishment closed ranks and in 1993–94 enacted a successful stabilization plan; the subsequent program of gradual market reform brought fifteen years of increasing prosperity and diminishing poverty and inequality, which undergirded democratic consolidation (Weyland 2002: 221–31).[16] As the party system gained greater firmness as well (Roberts 2014: 201, 206–7, 233–34), Brazil was long spared a reemergence of populism, by contrast to countries such as Peru, Ecuador, Italy, and Slovakia, where a personalistic plebiscitarian leader destructured the party system and thus paved the way for a whole series of populists (Roberts 2014: 58–63, 126–28, 276; Weyland 2022b: 37–38).

A Crisis Response to a Noncrisis: Bucaram's Downfall in Ecuador

Whereas Collor failed because his government did not find and enact an effective solution to a serious crisis, Abdalá Bucaram (1996–97) crashed even faster because he made the mistake of applying a prominent solution to an economic problem that was far from amounting to a crisis. This mismatch occurred because the Ecuadoran populist tried to prove his charisma and achieve striking policy success by emulating the convertibility plan with which Domingo Cavallo had finally ended hyperinflation in Menem's Argentina (see earlier in this chapter). Blinded by this stunning turnaround and apparent magic (Ibarra 1997: 24–25), Ecuador's personalistic plebiscitarian leader decided to emulate this drastic neoliberal approach and to hire the Argentine mastermind as well. In this way, Bucaram hoped to replicate Menem's political success, win strong, broad approval, and boost his clout in Ecuador's fragmented party system (Méndez Ortiz 2017: 32–34, 83; see also Roberts 2014: 158–59).

But Bucaram fell for Cavallo's famous policy approach without understanding the preconditions for the Argentine success. He adopted a high-profile solution although Ecuador was not suffering from the catastrophic problem for which Cavallo had developed his novel recipe: There was no hyperinflation. As a result, Bucaram's compatriots, ranging from business people to common citizens, were unprepared for this shock program and unwilling to accept its short-term costs, which would arise from austerity measures and tax increases (Ibarra 1997: 24, 28; Montúfar 1997: 24–26; Pérez-Liñán 2007: 26–27, 108; Freidenberg 2015: 115–16). Whereas by early 1991 Argentines had been desperate finally to extinguish recurring bouts of skyrocketing price rises by any means necessary, whatever the immediate cost, Ecuadorans were not facing this terrible predicament and therefore refused to swallow such bitter pills.

---

[16] For a comprehensive assessment from a policy-making perspective, see Alston et al. (2008).

Cavallo's big-bang program was attractive to Bucaram because as a populist leader, he was naturally eager to adopt daring, courageous measures rather than engaging in cautious tinkering. With this dramatic step, he sought to demonstrate his extraordinary prowess and perform miracles. But the Ecuadoran president, who enjoyed calling himself *"el loco"* (the crazy one) and who engaged in wild stunts to prove his nickname, missed the crucial issue of calibration: He made the fatal mistake of importing a bold yet costly solution for a crisis that did not exist. Without a proper diagnosis of the disease, however, even a miracle cure that healed another patient will likely fail.

For these reasons, Bucaram's imprudent replication of Argentina's adjustment plan elicited a great deal of criticism and rejection, which quickly erupted in mass protest. This economic discontent also helped inflame popular anger at rampant corruption and nepotism in the president's entourage;[17] his own son on his nineteenth birthday allegedly celebrated the first million dollars that he had skimmed off from the customs system. Indeed, graft tends to be particularly widespread in the governments of personalistic leaders: The lack of accountability allows not only for personal enrichment but also for persistent efforts to – literally – buy political support. As happened under Fujimori's rule (see earlier in this chapter), this bribery can be crucial for sustaining populist governments, given the weakness of party organization and programmatic commitments. Latin Americans often tolerate corruption when governments perform reasonably well. But when a president commits a huge policy mistake by enacting austerity measures that the economic situation does not justify, evidence of bribery provokes widespread revulsion.[18]

Within mere months of his inauguration, Bucaram's popularity therefore plummeted to a dismal 7 percent (CEDATOS 2012: 4). Denuded of plebiscitarian support, his presidency went up in flames. As mass demonstrations proliferated (Pachano 1997: 9–11; Méndez Ortiz 2017: 48–51), Congress looked for a way to oust this politically inviable personalistic leader so as to avert the "perils of presidentialism" à la Linz (1990). Because the opposition lacked the supermajority required for conducting a regular impeachment, it resorted to a para-legal expedient by removing the chief executive on charges of mental incapacity. Although Bucaram had declared himself crazy, this eviction, which the legislature rushed through with suspicious speed, was not based on any real proof or professional assessment and was therefore constitutionally questionable (Pérez-Liñán 2007: 26–28, 154–56; De la Torre 2015: 94–97, 126–27).

Bucaram's fate exemplifies the agency problems inherent in populism. Leaders are so insistent on their personalistic predominance that they forego thorough consultation and open debate. Because they, and they alone, run

---

[17] Ibarra 1997: 29; Pachano 1997: 9–11; Pérez-Liñán 2007: 26–28, 106–9, 129–30; Méndez Ortiz 2017: 42–46, 80, 85–86.
[18] As mentioned earlier, deficient economic policy performance made a bribery scandal lethal for Brazil's Collor as well.

the government, they are prone to making mistakes. Moreover, populist politicians have a strong predilection for embracing miracle cures in order to
turn into providential heroes and boost their charisma. Lured by Cavallo's
economic accomplishments and Menem's political success, Bucaram sought
to replicate the Argentine solution – yet overlooked the very different circumstances prevailing in Ecuador. Together with corruption, which mushrooms
under personalistic plebiscitarian leadership as well, this elementary policy
mistake quickly doomed Bucaram's presidency and prompted the quick-
est, most ignominious downfall of a populist chief executive in recent Latin
American history.

As the comparison with Collor shows, the agency problems of populism can
take different forms. Brazil's president encountered an objectively given crisis,
but his government failed to design and enact an effective solution. Conversely,
Ecuador's chief executive fell for a great solution, but did not face the crisis
for which this solution had been designed; therefore, he could not achieve the
success that this solution had produced in Argentina.

While representing "opposite" types of mismatch, Bucaram's mistake was,
of course, much more glaring than Collor's. After all, it is difficult to combat
acute, severe crises effectively; many governments fail in this endeavor, and
even Argentina's Menem needed three attempts to succeed. By contrast, the
misadapted policy choice in Ecuador was clearly avoidable and revealed a certain detachment from reality. This ill-considered reliance on a foreign import
thus shows how serious the agency problems inherent in populism can get.

In the short run, however, Bucaram's downfall protected Ecuadoran democracy against the danger of incumbent takeover, which is also inherent in populism. The institutional framework was spared a direct attack by this "crazy"
maverick. But the president's expulsion was constitutionally problematic and
helped undermine political stability. In subsequent years, two other evictions
of presidents by controversial means battered the constitutional order, so that
it turned into easy prey for left-wing, "Bolivarian" populist Rafael Correa
(2007–17), whose suffocation of liberal pluralism Chapter 4 examines.

A Self-coup Attempt without a Double Crisis: Serrano's Downfall in Guatemala

By contrast to the Ecuadoran case, Guatemalan democracy did suffer a frontal
assault by a populist leader. But because this daring executive takeover was
as misadapted to the prevailing conditions as Bucaram's adjustment plan, it
failed as decisively and provoked the protagonist's ouster as well. Interestingly,
like the Ecuadoran president, Jorge Serrano (1991–93) emulated a successful
foreign precedent, but also did so in the wrong place at the wrong time: He
decreed a self-coup modeled on Fujimori's blunt power grab of 1992 although
his country was not suffering from the coincidence of massive crises that
allowed his Peruvian role model to garner success. Consequently, rather than

destroying Guatemala's democracy, Serrano ended up destroying his own presidency and was quickly compelled to withdraw in disrepute.

From the beginning, Serrano shared many similarities with Fujimori in his political emergence and governing experience (Cameron 1998a: 219–24) – though definitively not in the conjunctural conditions he faced. As a fairly unknown outsider with messianic tendencies (Fernández Camacho 2004: 241–42, 245), the Guatemalan right-winger unexpectedly won the presidential election of 1990 in a crowded field (Bologna 1996: 5–6). Lacking an organized political party and a cohesive governing team, he relied on plebiscitarian appeals to obtain popular support, and on negotiations, patronage deals, and corruption to engineer backing in Congress (Cameron 1998a: 222–24; Fernández Camacho 2004: 244–45; Gálvez Borrell 2011: 56–57). Constant tensions with legislators made it difficult for the inexperienced president to enact and implement the neoliberal adjustment measures with which he sought to combat inflation. After all, in the year of his election, price rises had shot up to 41 percent. Confronting economic difficulties without a solid base of support and facing a good deal of political opposition and societal protest (Jonas 1995: 34–35), Serrano's governing performance was meager and his popularity suffered; by 1993, his approval ratings had dropped to approximately 20 percent (Cameron 1998a: 230; Kenney 2004: 287).

Given this political weakness, the chief executive started to face increasing challenges. His use of a secretive slush fund to literally buy support in Congress drew serious accusations of corruption. Moreover, audacious members of Guatemala's political establishment demanded greater payoffs for themselves, threatening otherwise to impeach Serrano, as had recently happened to Collor in Brazil (Cameron 1998b: 133–34; Kenney 2004: 287–89; Pérez-Liñán 2007: 183; see also Gálvez Borrell 2011: 59). In an immediate reaction to this dangerous blackmail, the cornered chief executive took a step that he had threatened before: He emulated Fujimori by closing Congress and the courts and announcing presidential government by decree (Helmke 2017: 117–19). Because he knew from his Peruvian role model's experience that open authoritarianism had become unviable in Latin America after the "third wave of democratization," he also followed Fujimori's exit plan by announcing new elections that would give rise to a constituent assembly.

Yet whereas Fujimori's self-coup had elicited an overwhelming outpouring of support, Serrano's copycat move found much less backing. While business groups and military sectors were hesitant, protests soon erupted and spread.[19] Moreover, the incumbent's blatant violation of the constitutional order prompted harsh international criticism, especially from the USA, the most powerful protector of Latin American democracy. Indeed, to forestall any further diffusion of the Peruvian precedent, foreign countries and international

---

[19] Villagrán de León 1993: 117, 120–21; Jonas 1995: 36; Bologna 1996: 9–11; Cameron 1998a: 225–29; Fernández Camacho 2004: 246–50, 254–59; Gálvez Borrell 2011: 70–77.

organizations employed all means at their disposal to foil Serrano's imitation attempt.[20] Facing an upsurge of domestic and foreign pressure, including the threat of serious sanctions, Guatemala's transgressive populist capitulated and resigned. This successful mass mobilization, elite opposition, and intense international involvement, which proved that undemocratic machinations had become illegitimate, gave Guatemalan democracy a refreshing boost and contributed greatly to its consolidation (Jonas 1995: 36; Cameron 1998a: 233).

The theory of Chapter 2 explains why Serrano's self-coup failed so quickly and decisively, whereas his role model Fujimori had succeeded with his power grab and then managed to install competitive authoritarianism behind a democratic façade. After all, the Peruvian populist took advantage of the exceptional coincidence of two severe, pressing crises to demonstrate amazing charisma and vault to unchallengeable predominance. Fear of a total collapse, namely a hyperinflationary meltdown *and* a full-scale civil war, induced a vast majority of Peruvians to back their providential savior and hand him the autocratic power he claimed to need.

Serrano, by contrast, made his desperate imitation effort although Guatemala was not facing even one of these terrible crises. First, there was no massive economic challenge. In particular, Guatemala was far from sinking into hyperinflation. The peak of 41 percent that price rises reached during the year of Serrano's election (1990) contrasted with Peru's 63 percent inflation during the *month* of Fujimori's inauguration (July 1990), and the staggering rate of 7,649 percent for that year. Indeed, by 1992, Serrano's austerity measures had forced inflation down to a mere 10 percent. Moreover, after a lengthy recession from 1981 to 1986 (Jonas 1995: 30), the economy had been growing steadily at annual rates of 3–4 percent thereafter. Thus, Guatemala was not suffering from an acute economic crisis that could have justified Serrano's power grab.

Second, the country's decades-old guerrilla insurgency, which had flared up into a full-scale civil war during the early 1980s, had been winding down from the mid-1980s onward. Essentially, the military had managed to defeat its enemies, with great brutality and remarkable cruelty. The Central American Peace Accord of 1987 eventually led to negotiations, which advanced only haltingly but forestalled another descent into open warfare (Jonas 1995: 30–31). Consequently, the "fear factor" (Cameron 1998a: 219–20, 227–28, 230), which was running so high during Fujimori's early presidency (1990–92), no longer played a huge role in Guatemala. The absence of an urgent security threat also foreclosed any chance for Serrano to turn into a charismatic savior who could win overwhelming support with courageous rescue efforts.

In sum, the Guatemalan populist clearly did not encounter the two conjunctural opportunities that – in combination – enabled Fujimori to succeed with his audacious self-coup, win massive support, and institute a nondemocratic

---

[20] Villagrán de León 1993: 119, 122, 124; Bologna 1996: 16–18; Cameron 1998a: 233; Fernández Camacho 2004: 248; Arceneaux and Pion-Berlin 2007: 15–16.

regime. Because Serrano lacked both of these necessary preconditions, his misguided emulation effort was doomed to failure. Cornered by his opponents, the Central American leader made a typically populist move by attempting a daring "flight forward" through the emulation of a strikingly successful foreign precedent. But Serrano misjudged by not considering the crucial conjunctural preconditions that had made Fujimori's power grab feasible. This contrast corroborates core elements of my theory and shows again how difficult and rare it is for neoliberal populists to destroy presidential democracies.

RIGHT-WING POPULISM IN CONTEMPORARY LATIN AMERICA

Neoliberal populism, which intersected with the regional wave of orthodox adjustment and determined market reform, reached its high point in Latin America during the late 1980s and 1990s; Colombia's Uribe was an important latecomer. In fact, during its initial bold and "heroic" phase, economic neoliberalism had strong affinities with charismatic political leadership (Roberts 1995; Weyland 1996). But once the new development model had achieved its breakthrough and the main task turned to implementation and consolidation, this synergy disappeared; brash transgressive leaders are not good at steady, predictable administration.

Interestingly, the subsequent wave of left-wing governments, Latin America's famous "pink tide," did not enact a drastic reversal of market reform in most cases; instead, it mainly brought a reequilibration by softening harsh orthodoxy, extending state regulation somewhat, and expanding social benefit programs substantially (Weyland, Madrid, and Hunter 2010; Levitsky and Roberts 2011). Due to this common moderation, the downfall of left-wing governments with the end of the commodities boom did not prompt a strong backlash and a return to determined neoliberalism. Moreover, because several leftist governments had been headed by populist leaders (Rovira Kaltwasser 2019: 45–50), aversion to this political strategy facilitated the rise of nonpopulists, such as Mauricio Macri in Argentina (2015–19) and Guillermo Lasso in Ecuador (2021–23).

In recent years, therefore, neoliberal populism has reappeared only in an attenuated version,[21] combined with strong elements of cultural conservatism (Kestler 2022). The most important case is Jair Bolsonaro (2019–22) in Brazil. There, leftist Dilma Rousseff (2011–16) had pushed economic policy in a statist, interventionist direction, causing a severe recession from 2014 to 2016. A resumption of market reform therefore rose on the political agenda.

---

[21] At the time of writing (March 2023), however, neoliberal, libertarian populist Javier Milei is rising rapidly in vote intentions for the upcoming presidential election in Argentina (Rivas Molina 2023), given the renewed economic crisis, with approximately 100 percent annual inflation, overseen by the left-wing Peronist incumbent and given the longstanding aversion to the country's political class among important segments of the citizenry.

Failure without Resolvable Crises: Bolsonaro in Brazil

After decades as an extremist, marginal maverick in Brazil's Congress, Bolsonaro unexpectedly captured the presidency in 2018. This shocking victory came in reaction to thirteen years of left-wing governance (2003–16), which in the 2010s had decayed and failed. As a notorious outsider, Bolsonaro also benefited from the incompetence and entrenched corruption of the fragmented welter of centrist and center-right parties that had governed after Rousseff's 2016 impeachment. Revulsion against the whole political class drove masses of voters into the arms of this cultural reactionary and law-and-order candidate (Meneguello 2021: 503–5). Typical of personalistic plebiscitarian leaders, Bolsonaro commanded no party to speak of and started his presidency with little support in Congress (Amaral 2021: 116–18; Melo 2021: 104–7). Notwithstanding this lack of solid political standing, he single-mindedly pursued an autocratic project by attacking a wide range of political enemies, fighting with independent institutions, and drawing the military into politics (Hunter and Vega 2022).

Bolsonaro shared with neoliberal populism an orthodox market orientation in economic policy (Dweck 2021). Accordingly, he recruited a team of experts led by one of Brazil's few "Chicago Boys," Paulo Guedes (Pereyra Doval 2021: 223, 227–29). The new economy minister sought to boost growth after the deep slump of 2014–16 with a bold, comprehensive program of privatizations, tax reform, and retrenchment of the costly pension system. Moreover, Bolsonaro announced a tough-on-crime approach and thus embraced a punitive, repressive stance in public security, as neoliberal populists Fujimori and Uribe had also done. Last but not least, he spearheaded a reactionary cultural crusade against "gender ideology," sexual tolerance, and advanced liberal values in general, with even more inflammatory and acrimonious language than Donald Trump used in the USA. To promote these causes, the Brazilian president attacked the press, civil society groupings, and the courts (yet begrudgingly respected adverse judicial rulings).[22]

But despite his obvious authoritarian leanings and openly announced nostalgia for Brazil's military dictatorship (1964–85), this right-wing populist managed to do little damage to the institutional framework of liberal pluralism. The fundamental reason was that Brazilian presidentialism commands middling institutional strength and enshrines a substantial dispersal of power, and that Bolsonaro did not encounter the kinds of conjunctural opportunities that enabled Fujimori to achieve striking political success, push aside institutional constraints, and overthrow democracy.

As regards institutional factors, Brazilian democracy has turned quite robust. After a rocky start in the late 1980s and early 1990s, including Fernando

---

[22] Amorim 2021: 467–76; Couto 2021: 42–45; Marona and Magalhães 2021: 121, 124–26; Ribeiro and Oliveira 2021: 332.

Collor's high-profile impeachment (see earlier in this chapter), consolidation advanced for almost two decades. The resulting stability was not shattered by protests starting in 2013 nor by the impeachment of Dilma Rousseff in 2016, which – while politicized, as most impeachments are – strictly followed constitutional procedures. As Congress demonstrated its independence and clout on that occasion as on many others, the courts have also guarded their autonomy and often stopped executive action; indeed, under Bolsonaro, they embarked on a striking expansion of judicial activism (Nicas 2023). Interacting with the clear separation of power at the national level, the political strength of state and local governments has created further constraints on the federal government. All of these checks and balances make para-legal change difficult and preclude any frontal assault on democracy. Bolsonaro's autocratic aspirations thus faced many institutional roadblocks.

At the same time, Brazil's hard-right populist lacked the conjunctural opportunities for removing these obstacles. Like Ecuador's Bucaram and Guatemala's Serrano, Bolsonaro won office when Brazil was neither in the throes of a deep economic crisis nor an acute and severe, yet resolvable security crisis. For sure, the country had recently suffered an unusually stubborn recession, which had seriously discredited the established parties and helped pave the way for Bolsonaro's improbable rise from isolated backbencher to victorious president. But by the time of his inauguration, the economy had already been in recovery for two years, achieving 1.9 percent growth in 2018.

Similarly, while Brazil's stubbornly high murder rate had risen by 20 percent during the two years from 2010 to 2012, this deterioration had merely restored the worrisome but not catastrophic levels of the early 2000s. Moreover, from 2012 to 2017, homicides had increased only slightly, by another 10 percent (Ribeiro and Oliveira 2021: 330, 335). With a drop of 11.2 percent in 2018 itself, crime thus did not amount to a surging, worsening crisis.

Furthermore, while Bolsonaro skillfully highlighted the country's serious public safety problems in an effort to boost his support, he actually lacked the means to effect major improvements. In Brazil's federal system, public security is the prerogative of state and municipal governments, not the national president. And despite his fierce autocratic proclivities, Bolsonaro could not unleash a "dirty war" by empowering vigilantes or promoting informal death squads to hunt down criminals in extralegal ways. The strength of human rights norms in Latin America and the scrutiny exerted by transnational NGOs and foreign governments, especially the powerful USA, made such an all-out, bloody anti-crime campaign, such as that spearheaded by Rodrigo Duterte in the Philippines (see Chapter 7), politically infeasible in Brazil. The only important change that Bolsonaro managed to effect was a substantial loosening of restrictions on gun ownership and usage (Ribeiro and Oliveira 2021: 333, 337, 340), which may not lower violence but actually increase it. For these reasons, the right-wing populist was unable to achieve massive progress in public safety, as Fujimori had done by decapitating the terrorist Shining Path.

While Bolsonaro's authoritarian project was impeded by the absence of resolvable crises when he became president, a real disaster irrupted during his second year in office: The COVID-19 pandemic threatened not only a medical catastrophe but also an economic collapse. Yet as explained in Chapter 2, this unexpected shock did not offer propitious opportunities for charismatic leaders. Most populist chief executives have therefore failed to leverage it to their political advantage and have instead drawn sustained criticism for their deficient, often strikingly incompetent performance (Bayerlein et al. 2021; Meyer 2021: 3, 13–14; Foa et al. 2022). After all, this health emergency was impossible to resolve in a decisive and speedy fashion. Whereas a bold adjustment package can quickly stop hyperinflation, there was no way to eliminate the highly contagious virus. This infeasibility risked revealing populists' claim to "save the people" as hollow and deflating their charisma. Caught in a massive bind, most personalistic plebiscitarian leaders resorted to the magic trick of denying the pandemic's severity – an unfailing recipe for making its fallout even worse. Bolsonaro was a prime example of this dysfunctional response, which ended up eroding his already limited approval ratings, undermining his political standing, and even fueling numerous public demands and congressional proposals for his impeachment.[23]

Thus, the Brazilian populist could not take advantage of the one catastrophic challenge that suddenly appeared, and he never encountered the kinds of urgent, deep, yet resolvable crises that had boosted Fujimori's political fortunes and enabled the Andean Samurai to destroy Peruvian democracy. Given these limitations, Bolsonaro did not frontally assault Brazilian democracy. In particular, the ultra-right president did not follow in Fujimori's footsteps by spearheading a self-coup, which his hard-core followers publicly advocated (Avritzer and Rennó 2021: 448, 451–54; Von Bülow and Abers 2022: 13). With this begrudging self-restraint, he avoided the fate of Guatemala's Serrano, who had spectacularly failed by undertaking such a power grab in a noncrisis situation. Bolsonaro thus had a sufficient grasp of prevailing circumstances to refrain from pursuing his autocratic aspirations in one fell swoop.

The absence of pressing yet resolvable crises also accounts for Bolsonaro's inability to boost his mass support and gradually achieve predominance in Brazilian politics. Although this far-right populist forcefully attacked his competitors and adversaries in politics and civil society, and although he put increasing pressure on Congress and the judiciary, he did not manage to engineer any constitutional change that significantly augmented presidential power and seriously damaged liberal pluralism. In particular, Bolsonaro did not skew voting rules nor capture the election administration;

---

[23] Ribeiro 2020; Avritzer and Rennó 2021: 447–48; Burni and Tamaki 2021: 114, 118, 123; Galarraga Cortázar 2021; Meneguello 2021: 500–1; Campello 2022: 211–12; Von Bülow and Abers 2022: 1–2, 6–11; Hunter and Power 2023: 128, 132–33.

competitiveness remained unharmed. Thus, Brazil's presidential democracy with its multidimensional dispersal of power withstood the challenges posed by strident populism. The variety of fetters created by the country's innumerable Lilliputians is not easy to tear apart (Mainwaring 1999; Ames 2001). Bolsonaro clearly lacked the political clout required to achieve his destructive goals.

Because the lack of propitious crisis conditions and his typically populist incompetence during the COVID-19 pandemic prevented Bolsonaro from winning broad mass support, he instead doubled down on intensifying his appeals and connections to his core supporters. For this purpose, he employed the main strategy of personalistic plebiscitarian leaders and promoted constant confrontation by stirring up deeply charged cultural and moral issues. In crude language, he insulted and ridiculed women, racial minorities, and the activist groupings advancing their causes. With this conservative fundamentalism, he cemented the loyalty of approximately 20–25 percent of the population, who stuck with their populist standard-bearer despite his meager and rocky government performance (Meneguello 2021: 501; Hunter and Power 2023: 134). This unusually solid base was the stepping stone for Bolsonaro's reelection bid in 2022.

But of course, the deep polarization that the ultra-right populist deliberately stoked also limited his support and turned him into the underdog for the presidential contest (Olsen 2022: 17). After all, large numbers of Brazilians despised and hated this uncouth brawler as intensely as his unconditional followers revered him. This widespread antipathy prevented the incumbent from winning strong majority approval. How could Bolsonaro invoke "the will of the people" if large segments of the population abhorred him and rejected him as their spokesman?

Thus, the profound divisions over basic moral and cultural issues that fundamentalist populists such as Bolsonaro and Trump energetically fueled restricted their popular appeal. As explained in Chapters 1 and 2, personalistic plebiscitarian leaders try to substitute for their movements' lack of organization by attracting particularly fervent backing and constantly marshal polarizing rhetoric for this purpose. Culturally reactionary populists, however, push this tactic to such an extreme that they inadvertently create a steep trade-off between the depth vs. breadth of their support: By attracting firmly committed followers with fire and brimstone slogans, they automatically antagonize many other sectors of society and drive those into the arms of the opposition. As they turn politics into a war over ultimate, nonnegotiable principles and values, they risk making too few friends, and too many enemies.

Interestingly, therefore, extreme polarization, which corrodes liberal civility and mutual toleration, counter-intuitively helps protect the institutions of democracy against populist assaults. The deep gulfs created by fundamental value conflicts constitute insurmountable boundaries to the resonance of hardcore populists' appeals and make it impossible for them to win approval from a large majority of citizens. Thus, by pushing similar cultural resentments and reactionary ideas as Trump, whose popularity ratings remained strikingly stagnant despite the booming economy of his first three years in office, Bolsonaro faced the same downside arising from the hardening of political front lines: His support was always hemmed in by a comparatively low ceiling. Like Trump, who paid for his norm violations with his reelection defeat, Bolsonaro maneuvered himself into a cul-de-sac and suffered the same fate as his American role model in 2022.

Although Bolsonaro had persistently sowed distrust in Brazil's electoral system, and although he lost by a surprisingly narrow margin (Olsen 2022: 15; Hunter and Power 2023), the Brazilian strongman did not spearhead the kind of post-electoral challenges that Trump relentlessly pursued in 2020–21. Because Brazil's electronic voting machines delivered a clear-cut result within three hours (Hunter and Power 2023: 126), and because many of his own political allies, including his vice-president, quickly recognized the outcome, the incumbent undertook only some meek efforts to contest his defeat. Therefore, the governmental transition and inauguration of his successor proceeded smoothly, demonstrating the strength of Brazilian institutions.

Thousands of discontented Bolsonaro supporters, however, took it upon themselves to protest. Militant truckers blocked highways right after the election, and patriotically clad crowds camped outside military barracks for weeks, calling for a (self-)coup. Finally, frustrated by Bolsonaro's inaction and by the celebratory start of the new left-wing administration, an enraged mob vandalized the seats of the three branches of government in January 2023, imitating the assault by Trump supporters on the US Capitol in January 2021 (Brazil's Democratic Institutions under Attack 2023). But with even less of a feasible plan, this destructive outburst backfired; condemned across the political spectrum, even by – quickly defecting – Bolsonaro allies, it ended up strengthening the successor government and bolstering its efforts to guarantee the full recovery of Brazilian democracy.

For all of these reasons, liberal pluralism in Brazil survived Bolsonaro's hard-right populism. The absence of antecedent crises that he could have resolved deprived the autocratic leader of opportunities to expand his popular support through striking accomplishments, as Fujimori had done; and his blatant failure to cope with COVID-19 further limited his following. Because he was unable to broaden his mass base, the Brazilian right-winger doubled down on his fundamentalist cultural appeals. This tactic ensured him a hard core of fervent supporters (Avritzer and Rennó 2021: 451), but also condemned his movement to minority status. With this meager plebiscitarian backing, Bolsonaro could not engineer any major constitutional change with official or para-legal means. Subject to the rules of free and fair competition, the incumbent suffered electoral defeat and lost office after a single term. As the personalistic threat to liberal pluralism was lifted, Brazilian democracy trumped reactionary populism – as happened in 2020–21 in the USA.

Striking Success against Unresolvable Crises: Bukele in El Salvador

Whereas Brazil's Bolsonaro found himself constrained by the absence of urgent, yet resolvable crises and flummoxed by the COVID-19 pandemic, Nayib Bukele in El Salvador (2019–present) demonstrated exceptional savvy by taking advantage of this health emergency to turn into a miraculous "savior of the people." With a strict and rigorously enforced lockdown (accompanied by generous economic assistance), he managed to contain the virus' spread and avert a medical catastrophe. And as the cunning populist realized as well, the tough mobility restrictions could also drive down crime, a huge problem that had been assailing the country for many years. Thus, Bukele noticed that COVID-19 offered an unusual opportunity for effecting a great (albeit short-term) improvement in public safety, a feat that under normal conditions is difficult to achieve, given the entrenched, widespread, and decentralized nature of common crime. Accordingly, the pandemic enabled him to impose a temporary solution to an otherwise unresolvable crisis.

With this uncommonly smart approach and the enormous relief it brought to the scared population, Bukele achieved sky-high popularity ratings, helped his party win a supermajority in the unicameral Congress, and thus gained free rein for the installation of competitive authoritarianism. By contrast to the serious problems that COVID-19 created for most other personalistic plebiscitarian leaders, Bukele's exceptionally adroit agency thus managed to turn adversity into advantage – yet to the grave detriment of Salvadoran democracy.[24]

Bukele's strangulation of liberal pluralism was facilitated by El Salvador's institutional framework, which enshrined significantly fewer veto points than Brazil's power-dispersing constitution. By contrast to the lusophone giant, the Central American midget is a unitary state. Bukele therefore had direct command throughout the national territory, which enabled him to force down crime and take all the credit for this accomplishment; in Brazil, by contrast, public security is primarily the responsibility of state governments. Whereas Bolsonaro always had to contend with powerful governors, Bukele did not face any counterweight. Moreover, El Salvador has a unicameral legislature of limited size, which is easier to control than Brazil's large bicameral Congress. Thus, El Salvador's streamlined institutional configuration created fewer obstacles to populist power concentration than personalistic plebiscitarian leaders encountered in most major Latin American countries. Bukele therefore had a much easier path toward realizing his autocratic aspirations than Bolsonaro.[25]

[24] I thank Jonatán Lemus for many interesting comments, observations, reflections, and newspaper articles on the Salvadoran case.
[25] I thank Jonatán Lemus for several of the arguments advanced in this paragraph.

Contrary to Bolsonaro's decades of hard-core rightism, Bukele's trajectory exemplifies the chameleonic nature of populism (Meléndez-Sánchez 2021b: 26–29), which had already been strikingly evident in the drastic policy switches of Latin America's early crop of neoliberal populists (Stokes 2001). Young and "cool" Bukele began his meteoric rise in the left-wing Frente Farabundo Martí para la Liberación Nacional (FMLN), which – after more than a decade of brutal civil war (1979–92) – had negotiated a peace agreement with the right-wing Alianza Republicana Nacionalista (ARENA) and thus prepared El Salvador's transition to democracy in the early 1990s (Lehoucq 2012: 81–86). After ARENA won four presidential elections in a row, the FMLN finally captured the chief executive office in 2009 and held it for two terms. Despite stiff party competition and alternation in power, however, the new democracy was plagued by deficient policy performance, weak state capacity, rampant crime, and endemic corruption; many citizen expectations remained sorely unfulfilled.[26] This discontent provided fertile ground for the rise of populism.

As an FMLN member, an ambitious Bukele won the mayoralty of the capital city in 2015 and skillfully used this prominent platform to prepare a presidential bid. Blocked by his party's old guard, he provoked his expulsion and ran on a minor party ticket (Roque Baldovinos 2021: 240–42). With a frontal attack on the discredited "political class" (IUDOP 2019), broadsides against the two main parties, fervent populist rhetoric, and religiously tinged appeals,[27] he captured a majority in 2019. In the chief executive office, the upstart turned to the right by embracing neoliberalism and by promoting a tough approach against the longstanding problem of crime and gang violence (Landeros 2021: 83–84). Employing *la mano dura* (the iron fist), he cracked down ostentatiously on suspected or real lawbreakers, forged a firm alliance with the police and military, and asserted his supreme charismatic authority (Masek and Aguasvivas 2021: 158, 161–63, 166; Stelmach 2021: 78–82).

In these ways, the new convert to right-wing populism energetically pursued the personalistic project of imposing his hegemony, which entailed asphyxiating Salvadoran democracy. For this goal, the opposition-controlled legislature, which was reluctant to approve Bukele's initiatives, constituted the frontline obstacle. In early 2020, the imperious president put unprecedented pressure on his stubborn adversaries by invading the unicameral Congress with a substantial military escort.[28] Strong international objections against a blatant regime overthrow forced him to back off from this drastic assault (Roque Baldovinos

---

[26] Lehoucq 2012: chap. 5; Moallic 2020; Meléndez-Sánchez 2021a: 24–30; Roque Baldovinos 2021: 233–38; Rosen, Cutrona, and Lindquist 2022: 6–8.

[27] Moallic 2020: 104–5; Nilsson 2022: 22–23; Siles, Guevara, et al. 2023: 148–55; see also Perelló and Navia 2022.

[28] Moallic 2020: 125; Hallock and Call 2021: 1592; Miranda 2021: 8–9; Stelmach 2021: 79; Wolf 2021: 67; Zemmouche 2021: 4–5.

2021: 246). Prevented from executing a self-coup like Fujimori (Tobar 2020: 74–76; Landeros 2021: 84–86; Miranda 2021: 8–9),[29] the aspiring autocrat sought to overcome this important setback by preparing for a takeover of Congress in the midterm elections of 2021.

This strategy was greatly furthered by the sudden irruption of the COVID-19 pandemic and by Bukele's exceptional skill in taking advantage of this exogenous shock for his undemocratic purposes (Roque Baldovinos 2021: 246).[30] Contrary to most personalistic plebiscitarian leaders, El Salvador's energetic populist not only managed to avert the health catastrophe and economic collapse threatened by the virus, he also used a rigorous lockdown justified by the pandemic to compress common crime, a crucial scourge afflicting his country. This astounding (albeit temporary) success in combating two acute, severe crises – equivalent to Fujimori's achievements – further boosted his exceedingly high popularity and turned his flimsy party into a steamroller in the midterms. Thus, whereas Bukele had felt compelled to back off from his self-coup attempt in February 2020, he soon thereafter got the chance to pursue his autocratic goals by using his presidential attributions to engineer "miraculous" performance and leverage the resulting plebiscitarian clout for an electoral triumph that gave him a supermajority in Congress. In turn, control over the legislature provided him with an ample repertoire of legal and para-legal instruments for cementing his predominance and destroying liberal pluralism.

How did the health emergency, which stumped so many other personalistic plebiscitarian leaders, enable the Salvadoran upstart to strangle democracy? After all, this massive challenge, which caused enormous disruption and major losses for the broadest sectors of the people, cannot quickly be resolved through bold countermeasures – by contrast to hyperinflation. The pandemic thus posed a major stumbling block for most populist chief executives by making their charismatic claims to "save the people" look hollow. Trying magically to wish away this insurmountable problem, presidents ranging from Bolsonaro to Trump, Erdoğan, and Mexico's AMLO therefore downplayed the pandemic and denied its seriousness, or resorted to quackery and advertised false quick-fixes. By failing effectively to contain the spread of disease and death, these unpromising recipes entailed substantial political costs, probably contributing to Trump's and Bolsonaro's narrow defeats in their reelection bids.

By contrast to this widespread mixture of consternation, wishful thinking, and paralysis, Bukele showed himself to be exceptionally apt in using the

---

[29] An interesting similarity with Fujimori is that Bukele also hails from an immigrant minority that claims greater entrepreneurial spirit and a superior work ethic to the native population, but that has suffered marginalization by the domestic elite (Roque Baldovinos 2021: 239). No wonder that both populists attacked "the establishment" and won vast popular support through pragmatic, energetic, and determined efforts to address urgent problems and produce concrete improvements for the long-neglected majority (see also Meléndez-Sánchez and Levitsky 2021).

[30] I thank Jonatán Lemus for this insight and several of the arguments advanced in the following paragraphs.

enormous challenge of the pandemic to his political advantage (Hallock and Call 2021). Uniquely among populist rulers, he responded to the exogenous shock in resolute and effective ways (Zemmouche 2021: 6–7). While unable to eliminate the virus, he immediately took energetic measures to minimize contagion and protect the citizenry from a potential catastrophe. For this purpose, he quickly imposed and stringently enforced a tight, comprehensive quarantine and lockdown across the country, disrespecting judicial rulings to safeguard basic liberal rights (Tobar 2020: 76–77; Hallock and Call 2021: 1583–84, 1589, 1593–94, 1596–97; Roque Baldovinos 2021: 246–47). This autocratic strategy greatly slowed down the virus's spread, limited disease outbreaks, and forestalled a collapse of the feeble health system.

In 2021, the president followed up by promoting vaccination, giving El Salvador the fourth-highest inoculation rate in Latin America, a significant accomplishment for this relatively poor and underdeveloped nation. Through October 2021, the country indeed suffered a low death rate, at least by official figures,[31] namely fifty-four per thousand, compared to 86 and 104 in neighboring Guatemala and Honduras and the disastrous levels of 223 in Mexico and 286 in Brazil – two countries governed by left-wing and right-wing populists, respectively. Thus, although the nature of the pandemic made it impossible for Bukele to achieve the charismatic miracle of truly resolving the health crisis, he performed much better – at least according to his government's data – than his counterparts among presidents, especially other personalistic plebiscitarian leaders. Consequently, he won ample support for protecting the citizenry relatively well from suffering and death.

Bukele also enacted fairly generous assistance programs to enable the population to survive the lockdown, which constricted their income opportunities. For maximum political payoff, he prioritized the countrywide distribution of food packages. That the government guaranteed families' basic livelihood enhanced his image of caring for the people and boosted his support (IUDOP 2020: 11–14, 19–20). Ironically, the idea of concentrating on food aid emerged from the president's team of Venezuelan consultants, who – though hailing from the self-proclaimed democratic, right-wing opposition to left-wing autocrat Maduro – copied their nemesis's roll-out of a similar assistance program, which kept large numbers of crisis-battered Venezuelans dependent on the ever more dictatorial government and thus helped sustain the disastrous Bolivarian regime (Alvarado 2021; see also Meléndez-Sánchez 2021b: 27–29).[32] While this striking borrowing across a deep ideological divide shows again the opportunism of personalistic plebiscitarian leaders, it greatly strengthened Bukele's standing and helped him push El Salvador toward authoritarian rule.

---

[31] For doubts see Roque Baldovinos (2021: 248) and especially Pearson, Prado, and Colburn (2021: 3–4).

[32] I thank my former student Leonardo di Bonaventura Altuve for this reference and for elucidating the ramifications of this episode.

Furthermore, a crucial additional benefit and likely purpose of Bukele's strict lockdown was that it also brought substantial relief on another enormous problem, namely the crime epidemic that had turned El Salvador into "the most violent country in the world" in 2015 (Rosen 2021: 120; see also Moallic 2020: 123; Wolf 2021: 67; Flores-Macías 2022: chap. 6). In its threat to public safety, large-scale violence, which can surge in drastic spikes, is equivalent in people's minds to the guerrilla challenges bedeviling Peru and Colombia before Fujimori's and Uribe's assumption of power. But whereas organized political violence can be defeated through the capture or killing of the insurgent leadership, which both Fujimori and, eventually, Uribe achieved, common crime constitutes a much more stubborn scourge. Under normal circumstances, it is exceedingly difficult to root out gang violence, given its capillary nature and deep local entrenchment. The strenuous efforts of earlier Salvadoran governments, which escalated their repression to *súper mano dura*, had failed to effect lasting improvements; instead, these tough crackdowns had backfired and ended up breeding even greater violence (Rosen 2021: 119–20; Stelmach 2021: 71–76, 81–82).

Unexpectedly, the COVID-19 pandemic offered a golden opportunity finally to force down violence, albeit temporarily. Legitimated by the health emergency, a strict lockdown with its severe mobility impairments, rigorously enforced by police and military, stopped criminals in their tracks.[33] While domestic violence probably increased, the figures for assaults, robberies, and murders plummeted. Given people's intense fears (Rosen, Cutrona, and Lindquist 2022: 11), Bukele's unprecedented success held tremendous appeal for the long-suffering population (IUDOP 2020: 15–16; IUDOP 2022: 5, 15, 18; cf. Rosen 2021: 122–25). Demonstrating a political brilliance that Machiavelli would have admired, the determined populist thus managed with striking effectiveness to combat another crisis that the prior political class had failed to resolve for countless years.

Bukele's resolute and comparatively successful approach to the pandemic and its major side effect of drastically reducing crime further elevated presidential approval to stratospheric levels of up to 90 percent (IUDOP 2020: 4, 6–7, 15; IUDOP 2022: 4, 9, 11–13, 34). His can-do attitude and pragmatic focus on concrete, urgent problems, and the visible results of his determined, audacious measures in protecting the citizenry, gave him overwhelming support, which allowed his party to sweep the legislative elections of 2021 (Gavarrete 2021: 115; Meléndez-Sánchez 2021a: 19). Propelled by the president's impressive plebiscitarian backing, his totally personalistic movement "New Ideas" succeeded in obliterating the old parties and winning a supermajority (Nayib Bukele consolida su poder 2021). As his vice-president gloated,

---

[33] Behind closed doors, Bukele negotiated a truce with the major gangs as well, as investigative journalists revealed (Havler-Barrett 2020; Stelmach 2021: 80–81). See more on Bukele's anti-crime strategy on pp. 113–114.

"the people sent all [the established politicians] to hell and gave Bukele all [!] the power" (cited in Ballesteros 2021).

Because El Salvador has a unicameral Congress, which limits the number of institutional veto players, this triumph enabled the victorious populist to cement his political hegemony, disable liberal checks and balances, and suffocate democracy (CEC 2021; Hallock and Call 2021: 1590, 1595; Meléndez-Sánchez 2021a: 22). Power-hungry Bukele immediately engineered a sweeping purge of the judiciary, took control of the Supreme Court's constitutional chamber, and soon thereafter induced this body to seize on a legal loophole and effectively suspend the prohibition of presidential reelection (El Salvador: Bukele's Bulldozer 2021; Meléndez-Sánchez and Levitsky 2021; Nilsson 2022: 20–21). Thus, his stranglehold over the legislature has effectively given the charismatic populist control over all three branches of government and opened the door for his self-perpetuation in power,[34] the most fundamental goal of personalistic plebiscitarian leaders. As a result, El Salvador's descent into authoritarianism looks like a foregone conclusion.[35]

To ensure his reelection in the upcoming presidential contest of 2024, Bukele has used the autocratic powers that he has already arrogated for firming up his attack on crime. For this purpose, he combined the heavy-handed approach that he had employed since 2019 with secretive negotiations with the main gangs. In a relatively skillful strategy, he traded reductions in violence for more lenient treatment of incarcerated criminals, yet threatened harsh reprisals in case of gangs' noncompliance with these clandestine deals (Meléndez-Sánchez 2021b: 35–38). Through early 2022, this risky balancing act, which – if publicly exposed – would cost massive drops in popularity (Meléndez-Sánchez 2021b: 33; Moallic 2022: 151–52; Rosen, Cutrona, and Lindquist 2022: 15), managed to compress homicides to much lower levels than before Bukele's assumption of power (Moallic 2022: 143–44).

But a supposed betrayal induced the gangs to blackmail the government with an outburst of indiscriminate killings in early 2022 (Moallic 2022: 143, 145). The aspiring autocrat again turned adversity to advantage by ostentatiously demonstrating his toughness and launching an all-out crackdown on crime. Declaring a state of siege that suspended a host of liberal guarantees, Bukele had the military and police round up tens of thousands of suspected gang members and filled up jails way beyond capacity; moreover, the pliant legislature heightened penalties for crime-related activities (Moallic 2022: 145–46).

---

[34] Bukele Gears up for 2024 2023. In 2022, 78.7 percent of survey respondents agreed or agreed strongly that "the reelection of President Nayib Bukele would be beneficial for the country" (IUDOP 2022: 35).

[35] Landeros 2021: 89–91; Nilsson 2022: 19–20. Democracy ratings show sharp drops under Bukele (Freedom House 2022a: 16; EIU 2023: 6, 13). In 2021, 56 percent of Salvadoran respondents – the highest percentage in all of Latin America – had already expressed their "support for strong and unbounded leadership," that is, authoritarian rule (Paul 2022: 2).

While this return to *súper mano dura* entailed innumerable human rights violations and while its longer-term effectiveness is uncertain,[36] the bold effort to "save the people" at all costs corroborated Bukele's charisma and perpetuated the policy success that he had bolstered during the pandemic. With popularity ratings at stratospheric levels (Moallic 2022: 147; Rosen, Cutrona, and Lindquist 2022: 14–16), the president remains on track for reelection and the consolidation of competitive authoritarianism.

The Salvadoran case demonstrates again that the rare coincidence of conjunctural opportunities provided by two simultaneous crises holds crucial importance for the strangulation of liberal pluralism by right-wing populist presidents. Before he skillfully used the COVID-19 pandemic for boosting his political clout, Bukele, for lack of a legislative majority, could only employ flagrantly illegal means to pursue his autocratic project – but with little success. When he initiated an apparent self-coup in early 2020, he was forced to back off from this direct assault on democracy.

The irruption of the pandemic then marked a tipping point. Because Bukele adroitly managed to turn a dangerous conjunctural challenge into a double opportunity and effectively combated acute, severe problems both in health and in public safety, he enjoyed stratospheric approval, achieved an overwhelming electoral triumph, and then pushed in para-legal ways for smothering democracy. Thus, what sealed the fate of liberal pluralism in El Salvador was an exogenous shock that allowed a Machiavellian president to augment his charisma by bringing dual relief. Unusually among populist leaders, Bukele understood the benefits of a COVID-19 lockdown for greatly containing not only the new viral pandemic but also the longstanding crime epidemic. These noteworthy accomplishments further enhanced his political standing and soon enabled him to control all veto players in El Salvador's unicameral presidentialism (Zemmouche 2021). This savvy use of populist agency differed from the flailing and failing, incoherent and incompetent responses to the pandemic by so many other personalistic plebiscitarian rulers from across the world (Bayerlein et al. 2021; Meyer 2021: 3, 13–14).

Thus, while my theory emphasizes objective conditions and conjunctural opportunities, agency comes into play as well. After all, populist leaders need a great deal of skill to take advantage of the opportunities that come their way. Designing and executing effective responses to serious, pressing, yet resolvable crises is not an easy task, as Collor's striking failure and Menem's early difficulties show. By contrast, Bukele stands out as an extraordinarily capable leader, who pulled off the magic trick of turning two – strictly speaking – unresolvable crises into golden opportunities for vaulting to political supremacy.

---

[36] Even Bukele's critics admit, however, that this heavy-handed approach managed to dismantle gang structures, bringing enormous relief for the hard-pressed population (Impact of Gang Crackdown Acknowledged 2023; Kitroeff 2023: A1, A10; Sin maras y sin democracia 2023).

Yet unfortunately, this unique accomplishment, perpetuated with an unprecedentedly harsh crackdown on crime, has allowed the domineering president to garrote Salvadoran democracy.

CONCLUSION

The preceding sequence of comparative case studies shows that the neoliberal populist path to the asphyxiation of democracy is narrow and steep. Among the numerous leaders examined here, only Fujimori and Bukele managed to realize their hegemonic goals and push their countries into competitive authoritarianism. Many other personalistic plebiscitarian leaders caused only limited problems for liberal pluralism and left the established institutional framework intact. Even Menem and Uribe, who achieved great success and leveraged it to amend the constitution and win reelection, were compelled to step down at the end of their second terms. Thus, as this chapter documents for its neoliberal variant, populism does not constitute as huge a threat to democracy as recent scholars have feared.

After all, neoliberal populists installed nondemocratic regimes only under truly exceptional conditions, namely the coincidence of two dramatic crises. Fujimori was able to establish and maintain his autocratic supremacy only because he resolutely and skillfully confronted both hyperinflation and a virtual civil war, challenges he encountered upon taking office. Thus, an extraordinary set of objective preconditions was required for allowing this personalistic plebiscitarian newcomer to interrupt Peruvian democracy. Similarly, Bukele only managed to cement his hegemony and take complete control of El Salvador's institutions after the exogenous shock of the COVID-19 pandemic gave him the opportunity to avert a true economic and health catastrophe and, simultaneously, impose a temporary "solution" to his country's crime epidemic.

In both of these unusual cases, objective developments that were outside these leaders' control served as necessary conditions for the destruction of democracy, as the many contrasting experiences investigated in this chapter show. Exogenous factors thus delimit the situations in which neoliberal populism can turn into a mortal danger for liberal pluralism. Even these dire conditions are not sufficient for producing such a tragic outcome, however. Instead, personalistic plebiscitarian leaders must also display great skill and aptitude to resolve massive crises. Given the haphazardness of populist agency, which the troubles and travails of Collor, Bucaram, and Serrano exemplify, such success is far from guaranteed. While Fujimori – despite all of his faults and misdeeds – showed outstanding performance by overcoming both hyperinflation and guerrilla insurgency, Bukele had to muster even greater brilliance to take advantage of a sudden shock, contain and avert its catastrophic fallout, and finally make serious (albeit temporary) headway against deeply entrenched crime.

For both reasons – the importance of exogenous developments as necessary conditions, and the additional requirement of well-adapted, effective agency – it is uncommon for neoliberal populists to strangle democracy. Even in presidential systems that command only middling institutional strength and that are subject to para-legal change, liberal pluralism displays a great deal of resilience. As a result, personalistic plebiscitarian leaders encounter substantial obstacles to their authoritarian goals.

Moreover, where charismatic presidents do manage to install competitive authoritarianism, their regime tends to remain uninstitutionalized and brittle, as Fujimori's sudden downfall shows. After all, populist leaders are unwilling to see their autonomy and personal power hemmed in through the "routinization of charisma" (cf. Weber 1976: 142–48, 661–81), that is, the creation of ever firmer organizations and institutional structures (see recently Andrews-Lee 2021: 27–28). Right-wing populists, in particular, refuse to build true parties, for instance, and rely instead on fluid movements and flimsy electoral vehicles (Roberts 2006). This lack of institutional sustenance exposes their nondemocratic regimes to the risk of collapse if they hit a major roadblock, such as an embarrassing corruption scandal or a dramatic drop in performance. Consequently, even more quickly than Peruvian democracy "died," it experienced a revival with Fujimori's ouster – which, although unexpected in its specific timing, was to be expected sooner or later.

This inherent vulnerability is especially likely to turn fatal for the authoritarian regimes installed by neoliberal populists because these leaders receive their essential boost in charisma from the conjunctural opportunities provided by major crises. Yet while success in combating these problems is necessary for winning political predominance and strangling democracy, it is not sufficient for sustaining this unchallengeable hegemony over the long run. Instead, this very accomplishment exposes chief executives to the above-mentioned paradox of success (Weyland 2000; see recently Matovski 2021: 71): As the restoration of normality is increasingly taken for granted, support for the "savior of the people" erodes. Despite their enormous initial achievements, the political fortunes of neoliberal populists therefore trend downward after a few years. Authoritarian regimes that arise along this steep and narrow path lack sustainability, making a renewal of democracy likely.

In conclusion, because of the stringent requirements for the strangulation of democracy documented in this chapter, it is very difficult for neoliberal populists to impose authoritarian rule, and not so difficult for this illiberal rule to collapse. Thus, populism in this version poses less of an effective threat to democracy than some recent observers have claimed.

4

"Bolivarian" and Left-Wing Populism in Latin America

Neoliberal populism was soon followed by a counterwave of left-wing governments, Latin America's famous "pink tide" of the early 2000s (Weyland, Madrid, and Hunter 2010; Levitsky and Roberts 2011; De la Torre 2017b: 196–203; Rovira Kaltwasser 2019: 39–50). While several of these leftist administrations charted a moderate and nonpopulist course, there was also a radical, populist wing led by Venezuela's Hugo Chávez (1999–2013), which embraced a "Bolivarian" approach – a label reflecting Chávez's veneration for independence hero Simón Bolívar. Bolivarian populists sought to reverse market reforms and therefore expanded state interventionism in the economy, including extensive nationalizations. In politics, they pursued a typical personalistic plebiscitarian strategy of determined power concentration and forcefully tried to dismantle checks and balances and take over independent institutions. For this purpose, Chávez and his main disciples, Evo Morales of Bolivia (2006–19) and Rafael Correa of Ecuador (2007–17), convoked constituent assemblies and transformed the constitutional framework to cement their predominance. By invoking popular sovereignty, they leveraged their mass support to weaken or abolish liberal constraints on their rule. Turning the majoritarian component of democracy against its minority-protecting mechanisms, they gradually but systematically undermined liberal pluralism and pushed toward competitive authoritarianism.

Why did those three Bolivarian presidents succeed with their relentless efforts to engineer their political hegemony, whereas other left-wing, (philo-) Bolivarian populists did not manage to overcome liberal constraints? The theory presented in Chapter 2 highlights two crucial factors for this variant of populism, namely grave institutional weakness and a lucky conjunctural opportunity arising from the global commodities boom. First, while many Latin American democracies enjoy middling levels of institutional strength, political crises and serious constitutional conflicts sometimes usher in phases of high instability. Dangerous coup attempts, in particular, can shatter regime solidity and provoke troublesome tensions. The formally questionable, politicized ouster of a president can also set a high-profile precedent and pave the way for further problematic evictions. Where such troubles and travails recur in short order, as happened in Venezuela, Bolivia, and Ecuador in the 1990s and early 2000s, they push a polity into high instability, which makes the constitutional framework unusually vulnerable to populist assaults.

Second, because Venezuela, Bolivia, and Ecuador rely very heavily on hydrocarbon exports, the drastic price increases resulting from the global commodities boom of the early 2000s brought huge revenue windfalls (Fernández and Villar 2014), which enabled personalistic chief executives to boost their plebiscitarian mass support by stimulating the economy, enacting generous social programs, and enhancing public goods provision, for instance through visible infrastructure projects. This cornucopia of benefits raised popular, middle-class, and even elite backing to unusual heights and thus gave the charismatic Bolivarians irresistible clout (Aldaz Peña 2021). Fortified in this way, they managed to strip away the debilitated liberal restrictions on executive authority, starting by pushing through their tailor-made constitutions. A host of power-concentrating machinations and para-legal expedients followed, including the harassment of electoral opponents and independent sectors of civil society.

Thus, the combination of high instability and huge windfall resources, of particularly weak institutions and particularly strong plebiscitarian momentum, allowed these three left-wing populists to spearhead incumbent takeovers and asphyxiate democracy. Due to the biggest and longest-lasting international bonanza of recent decades, this variant of populism turned especially lethal for liberal pluralism (Weyland 2013: 25–31). Yet despite this substantial risk of democratic "death," there were also a number of left-wing populists who did not manage to smother democracy. The present chapter examines these contrasting cases, which lacked the coincidence of high instability and hydrocarbon windfalls, to substantiate my theoretical argument.

Most instructive is the experience of Lucio Gutiérrez in Ecuador (2003–5), who won election as a notorious Chávez imitator; like his role model, he had participated in a recent coup attempt, but then took the electoral route to power. This left-wing populist started his presidency right before the big upsurge in global oil prices, however. Facing fiscal constraints, Gutiérrez saw himself compelled to embark on a drastic policy switch and embraced economic orthodoxy. This striking betrayal of his "Bolivarian" campaign promises undermined the new president's political support and forced him into a downward spiral of ever more opportunistic and precarious congressional alliances, which eventually triggered his protest-driven eviction in 2005.

As fiscal limitations before the commodities boom protected Ecuador's democracy from Gutiérrez's power hunger, even tighter restrictions after the end of this global price cycle brought the surprising termination of Rafael Correa's suffocation of liberal pluralism (see especially Ospina Peralta 2021: 237–50).

Facing serious economic problems exacerbated by his prior spending spree, the Bolivarian populist forewent another reelection in 2017 and instead helped elect a seemingly weak underling, Lenín Moreno. After all, Correa wanted his successor to take the blame for stringent adjustment measures – and pave the way for his own triumphant comeback in 2021, based on his earlier boom-time performance. But imminent economic challenges and widespread revulsion at Correa's autocratic strategy induced and enabled nonpopulist Moreno to break with his overbearing predecessor, reach out to the opposition, and work hard to revitalize Ecuador's democracy.

These Ecuadoran experiences demonstrate the importance of massive revenue windfalls for the capacity of Bolivarian populists to suppress liberal pluralism. As Gutiérrez had been unable to install authoritarianism before the upsurge in international petroleum prices, Correa could no longer maintain his undemocratic rule after their collapse in 2014. Thus, the "oil curse" (Ross 2012), which my theory invokes to elucidate the Bolivarian populist path to the strangulation of democracy, decisively shaped the deleterious regime impact of this variant of personalistic plebiscitarian leadership.

As democracy's changing fate in Ecuador demonstrates the crucial role of conjunctural opportunities, the other component of my explanation, namely the degree of institutional strength, came into play in other cases, such as Argentina. The hard-won democracy restored in 1983 displayed middling institutional robustness, as shown by its resilience to the country's frequent and pronounced policy volatility and to a dramatic bout of governmental instability in 2001–2 (Levitsky and Murillo 2005: 38–39; Pérez-Liñán 2007: 177–82; Roberts 2014: 253). Presidentialism's constraints therefore limited the political latitude of Néstor Kirchner (2003–7), who reoriented the country's longstanding Peronist movement toward the left; they also hemmed in his wife and successor Cristina Fernández de Kirchner (2007–15), who flirted ever more heavily with Chávez-style Bolivarianism. Interestingly, like Venezuela, Argentina profited enormously from the global commodities boom, which gave its extensive agriculture an enormous revenue boost. But whereas Chávez directly controlled the oil industry and single-handedly milked it for his autocratic goals (cf. Ross 2012: 5–8, 33–34, 38–43), Argentina's rural production was in private hands. When Fernández tried to capture a greater share of the windfall profits by raising taxes, landowners protested vigorously. This limitation of rents helped prevent the Kirchners from engaging in massive benefit distribution à la Chávez.

Lacking the Venezuelan populist's steamroller of support, the governing couple did not concentrate power through major institutional transformations. Instead, they planned to perpetuate their control by alternating in the presidency, a formally legal way to avoid term limits. When Néstor's untimely death foiled this ingenious plan, Cristina's core supporters floated the idea of lifting the prohibition on additional consecutive reelections. But given the widow's limited popularity, this institutional constraint proved insurmountable. Although Fernández de Kirchner showed some of Chávez's autocratic tendencies, as evident in her sustained harassment of independent media, she therefore stepped down at the end of her second term in 2015. The Argentine case thus shows that in the absence of high instability and of huge windfall rents flowing directly into government coffers, democracy can survive a dozen years of pushy left-populist governance.

Middling institutional strength and even greater revenue limitations also foiled the populist asphyxiation of democracy in Honduras under Manuel Zelaya (2006–9); but facing the incumbent's relentless pressures, the anti-populist opposition eventually felt compelled to "pull the emergency break" and topple the headstrong president in a civil-military coup. Zelaya, an establishment politician, won election as a right-winger. But as president, he unexpectedly converted to Bolivarian populism, impressed by Chávez's self-perpetuation in power and attracted by the Venezuelan chieftain's offer to share some of the voluminous proceeds of the oil price boom. But these subsidies did not allow Zelaya to replicate the bonanza prevailing in Venezuela. Moreover, Honduras, which had been spared coup attempts and aborted presidencies, was not suffering from high instability. Congress and the courts therefore drew on their independent clout to block Zelaya's stubborn push for a constituent assembly, which the opposition saw as the first step in following Chávez's power concentration script. When the obstinate president kept disrespecting legislative and judicial prohibitions, the military finally ejected him, forestalling his assault on liberal pluralism but interrupting democracy in the process. Thus, due to greater institutional strength and the absence of a massive resource windfall, Honduras' novice in Bolivarian populism did not succeed with his apparent attempt at an incumbent takeover. But tragically, the opposition's desperate efforts to forestall this persistent assault on liberal pluralism provoked the downfall of democracy anyway.

Institutional strength proved even more decisive in Mexico under Andrés Manuel López Obrador (AMLO, 2018–present), who for his third and finally victorious run for the presidency had moderated his initially quite radical populism. A domineering personality convinced of advancing a historical mission, this left-winger would probably have loved to pursue the typical populist goal of self-perpetuation in power. But he encountered neither of the necessary conditions for imposing undemocratic hegemony.

First, when he belatedly captured the presidency, the global commodities boom had long turned to bust. Indeed, with its large population, its diversified economy, and the manufacturing exports boosted by the North American Free Trade Agreement, Mexico had never experienced the massive windfall of Chávez's Venezuela. For these reasons, AMLO lacked the chance to win overwhelming support with generous benefit distribution. Second, the Mexican populist confronted an insurmountable obstacle to extending his tenure, namely the sacrosanct "no reelection" rule of Mexico's longstanding constitution. A major plank of the Mexican Revolution – the foundational juncture of the modern polity – the untouchable one-term limit foreclosed the main path through which personalistic plebiscitarian leaders march to competitive authoritarianism. Due to these two crucial factors, liberal pluralism has survived.

These comparative case studies show that like Latin America's neoliberal populism, the Bolivarian variant also managed to smother liberal pluralism only under restrictive conditions. Again, an unusual coincidence of institutional weakness and conjunctural opportunity was required. But the Bolivarian path to competitive authoritarianism was quite distinctive. What proved decisive was the combination of high instability and huge hydrocarbon windfalls, as the cases of Chávez, Correa, and Morales show. Typically, whereas right-wing populists leveraged the successful resolution of urgent crises and the resulting reversal of losses, their left-wing counterparts relied on the generous distribution of abundant gains.

Yet even during the exceptional times of the global commodities boom, the coincidence of factors that led to democracy's downfall was rare. In Argentina, Honduras, and especially Mexico, higher levels of institutional strength helped to forestall incumbent takeovers. Moreover, conjunctural opportunities were often limited. In Ecuador under Gutiérrez, international hydrocarbon prices had not yet skyrocketed, whereas in Mexico under AMLO, they had already plummeted; in Argentina under the Kirchners, booming commodities were not in government hands; and in Honduras under Zelaya, the windfall benefits provided by foreign subsidies were meager. These resource constraints helped to forestall the populist strangulation of democracy.

Through comparison and contrast, the present chapter thus shows how both high instability and hydrocarbon booms constitute necessary conditions for democracy's strangulation by Bolivarian populists. Because these prerequisites do not frequently prevail and because they rarely coincide, the main finding is – similar to Chapter 3 – that this type of personalistic plebiscitarian leadership also is less dangerous than often feared.

PRESIDENTIAL SYSTEMS WITH HIGH INSTABILITY

A prerequisite for democracy's strangulation by left-wing, Bolivarian populists was the high instability afflicting the liberal institutional framework in Venezuela, Bolivia, and Ecuador before Chávez, Morales, and Correa won election. Obviously, a battered system of checks and balances is comparatively easy to overpower and dismantle, as the new presidents immediately started to do by convoking constituent assemblies, through para-legal pressure in Venezuela and especially Ecuador. Preexisting institutional weakness facilitates the push toward supremacy. Indeed, regime fragility, volatility, and conflict create a widespread longing for the restoration of stability, which majoritarian populist movements promise to fulfill.

How, then, did high instability emerge in those three countries? The medium institutional strength that many presidential systems in Latin America command is sometimes shaken by surges of conflict and constitutional crises. While democracies can recover and even gain strength from a single challenge, as happened in Brazil after Fernando Collor's controversial impeachment in 1992 (see Chapter 3), a series of convulsions undermines institutional resilience. Given the centrality and prominence of the chief executive office under presidentialism, irregular challenges to elected incumbents hold the greatest risk of plunging democracies into such a period of existential uncertainty. Because presidents command ample institutional attributions and coercive capacities, conflicts threatening their permanence in office can easily escalate and turn dangerous. Self-coup attempts can also be destabilizing (Baturo and Tolstrup 2022: 10), but have been less frequent as triggers of presidential crises in Latin America (see Hochstetler 2006: 406–7; Pérez-Liñán 2007: 87–131; Helmke 2017; and see Cameron 1998a on self-coups).

When episodes of contention over the presidency recur in short order, a regime breakdown turns into a distinct possibility. Tottering democracies lack institutional solidity and are prime targets for transformational efforts that under the guise of profound renewal can pursue nefarious goals of power concentration and democratic involution. Populist leaders are in a particularly good position to spearhead such refoundational projects. In typical plebiscitarian fashion, they invoke their majoritarian support to push for a new constitution, which then enshrines their hegemony. To represent "the will of the people" more directly, they seek to weaken and curtail liberal checks and balances. Presenting themselves as the inherent interpreters of the *volonté générale*, they push for strengthening the presidency and for getting the right to self-perpetuate in office. In these ways, a country's descent into high instability paves the way for personalistic plebiscitarian presidents to move systematically toward competitive authoritarianism.

During the decade preceding the election of Chávez, Morales, and Correa, all three countries stumbled into serious instability (Carrión 2022: 57–60, 64–73). Venezuela's seemingly consolidated democracy was first shaken by mass riots in 1989, which erupted in reaction to the unexpected imposition of neoliberal adjustment and which left perhaps a thousand citizens dead. This tragedy and soldiers' involvement in repression then helped to prompt a dangerous military coup attempt in early 1992, which threatened the life of the democratically elected incumbent (Ellner 2008: 94–97; López-Maya 2011: 214–16). A second coup attempt at year's end showed how precarious democracy had become and induced the political establishment to sacrifice the president in order to safeguard the regime. Inspired by Collor's impeachment in Brazil, Congress therefore evicted Carlos Andrés Pérez (CAP, 1989–93) on a technical infraction of financial rules in mid-1993 (Pérez-Liñán 2007: 18–22, 99–103, 157–58).[1] But this desperate rescue attempt did not restore

---

[1] While CAP was notorious for corruption, he was not impeached for personal enrichment; instead, the official charge of financial manipulation was essentially a pretext used by politicians who worried that his permanence in office would endanger democracy.

stability. Instead, the coup leader of 1992, none other than later Bolivarian populist Hugo Chávez, was soon released from prison and started to mobilize countrywide support in order to gain power in the future; profoundly scared, establishment politicians feared new efforts at subversion.[2] Thus, a previously solid democracy quickly became precarious.

In the early 2000s, Bolivia sank into high instability as well. In this geographically fractured country, the state had always faced difficulty commanding reliable authority; contention and protests, roadblocks and "sieges" of major cities, were commonplace. After a massive conflict over privatization, the "water war" in Cochabamba, had rocked democracy in 2000, a new round of contentious protest, the "gas war" of late 2003, escalated even further. Because the effort to break a blockade of the capital city cost dozens of lives, the military refused to engage in further repression, forcing the democratically elected president to resign. Fewer than two years later, his vice-president and successor was pushed out through another upsurge of popular contention. By 2005, therefore, the country seemed to teeter on the edge of ungovernability, if not political chaos.

Similarly, in the decade before Correa's inauguration, Ecuador lost three presidents through irregular means. After Abdalá Bucaram's constitutionally problematic eviction on mental incompetence in 1997 (see Chapter 3), another president was terminated by a civil-military coup in 2000. As a sign of worsening instability, the main military coup maker won the presidential election of 2002. But this left-wing populist and initial Chávez imitator, Lucio Gutiérrez, was then forced out by an upsurge of protests and questionable congressional machinations in 2005 (see later in this chapter). Highlighting the para-legal irregularity of Gutiérrez's and Bucaram's evictions, country experts call these ousters coups as well (Montúfar 2006: 65, 70–71; De la Torre 2015: 126–27). Thus, Ecuador also came to suffer from high instability (Mejía Acosta et al. 2008; Corrales 2018: 170–73).

For analytical reasons, it is crucial to establish the presence of high instability *before* the election of Bolivarian populists who quickly pushed toward illiberalism and competitive authoritarianism. To serve as a causal factor, this necessary precondition stipulated in my theory must antecede the efforts of personalistic plebiscitarian leaders to suffocate democracy. After all, these power-concentrating attempts themselves provoked conflict and exacerbated instability, especially in Venezuela and Bolivia. To avoid a problematic mix-up of cause and effect – the endogeneity much feared by contemporary political science – one must document that regime stability had been shattered before Chávez, Morales, and Correa started their additional wrecking job.

---

[2] When small protests broke out against a renewed adjustment program in 1996 (Weyland 2002: 226–27), the immediate fear was that this unrest had been fomented by Chávez, as I found out during field research in Caracas that year.

FROM CRISIS TO WINDFALL: CHÁVEZ'S MARCH
INTO COMPETITIVE AUTHORITARIANISM

Hugo Chávez's gradual but resolute strangulation of Venezuelan democracy
is of particular importance because it served as a role model for several other
left-wing populists in Latin America. Whereas the region's neoliberal populists operated mostly on their own, lacked close connections, and engaged in
little direct borrowing, Chávez designed the "Bolivarian" variant of populism,
served as a crucial inspiration for aspiring autocrats elsewhere, especially in
Bolivia, Ecuador, Honduras, Nicaragua, and Peru, and ended up leading, coor-
dinating, and generously subsidizing those leftists who managed to win office
(Weyland 2013: 18–19, 30; De la Torre 2017a; subsidies listed in Werz 2007: 9).
Interestingly, a crucial part of Chávez's appeal was not only his high-profile
rejection of neoliberalism and his audacious defiance of US "imperialism," but
also his surprising capacity to survive and eventually overcome pronounced
political instability, impose his unchallengeable hegemony, and engineer his
authoritarian self-perpetuation in power. Chávez's rise, his savvy assault on
liberal democracy, and his ability to win the resulting all-out confrontation are
therefore of particular interest for this book.

Chávez's Relentless Pressure on Liberal Democracy

Before he adopted a populist political strategy, the Bolivarian leader himself
had in 1992 made a major contribution to the high instability that ended up
facilitating his democratic election in 1998 and his subsequent push toward
authoritarianism. After two decades of consolidation since its foundation in
1958, Venezuela's democracy with its two alternating parties had suffered a
mounting loss of popular support in the 1980s because of sustained economic
deterioration, which also made widespread corruption intolerable. The CAP
government's surprising adoption of drastic neoliberal adjustment therefore
provoked a ferocious backlash through a spontaneous outburst of popular
anger and mass contention in 1989. Ordered to suppress this uprising with
brute force, junior military officers came to resent the civilian elite. Led by
Chávez, they eventually tried to unseat the hapless government in a dangerous
and nearly successful coup attempt in 1992 (Ellner 2008: 94–97; López-Maya
2011: 214–16). Because a second putsch later that year turned the institutional framework brittle, civilian politicians sought to save democracy by
ousting the president, whom they impeached on trumped-up charges of financial malfeasance (Kada 2003: 125–27; Pérez-Liñán 2007: 20–21, 101–3, 158;
Bejarano 2011: 239).

These unprecedented challenges and problematic rescue efforts pushed
Venezuelan democracy into high instability. Fears of renewed crowd con-
tention and military plots kept political tensions high in subsequent years.
Recurring economic problems reinforced these concerns. Inflation rose to an

unprecedented 100 percent in 1995, and the economy sank into recession in 1997–98, dragged down by a drastic collapse in international oil prices, on which Venezuela with its massive hydrocarbon exports was utterly dependent. This new exogenous shock contributed to a drop in GDP of almost 6 percent in 1999 (Weyland 2002: 243–45).

The worrisome deconsolidation of Venezuelan democracy, the ground-swell of popular disaffection, the recurring economic problems, and the sharp downturn in 1998 prompted large segments of the citizenry to reject the whole "political class," yearn for a new start, and entrust their fate to an outsider. By far the most daring outsider was former coup maker Hugo Chávez, who therefore won the 1998 presidential election in a landslide after a typically populist campaign (Ellner 2008: 104–5; Roberts 2014: 223–24; on Chávez's populism, see also Hawkins 2010: 50–69). Foiled in his earlier attempt to grab power through military coercion, the Bolivarian leader now reached his goal via the electoral route. And rather than violently attacking democracy from the outside, he could now draw on his democratic triumph to dismantle democracy from the inside.

For this purpose, the new president immediately used the widespread popular revulsion at the enfeebled democracy and pursued his autocratic impulses by convoking a constituent assembly in para-legal ways, pushing aside the constitutional objections of courts and congressional opponents.[3] Based on his majoritarian support and on creative electoral engineering, he won absolute predominance in this body (Bejarano 2011: 245). Consequently, he had his followers disfigure the liberal institutional framework to concentrate power in the presidency, allow for a consecutive reelection, weaken checks and balances, create a unicameral legislature, and close the Congress elected in 1998, in which his partisans were in the minority (Brewer-Carías 2010; Corrales and Penfold 2011: 17–20; Corrales 2018: 118–27; Landau 2018: 161–67). New elections held for all offices in mid-2000 gave Chávez effective political hegemony; his genuine popular support covered up the determined march toward illiberalism. The autocratic populist managed to reduce the number of both institutional and partisan veto players and thus impose his predominance (Corrales 2010: 29–32).

Based on his augmented political clout, the populist president then made ample use of his unilateral attributions to impose a transformation of Venezuela's socioeconomic structures. With a massive package of decrees in late 2001, Chávez mandated land reform and other controversial measures (Weyland 2002: 248; Ellner 2008: 112–15). In 2002, he tried to take over the national oil company, which had enjoyed managerial autonomy and had used it to build up a well-trained body of engineers and achieve high performance in hydrocarbon exploration, production, and export, the central axis of the

---

[3] On Chávez's resolute move toward authoritarianism, see the comprehensive study by Arenas (2009) and the recent overview in Corrales (2022: 33–46).

economy (Ellner 2008: 159–62; Corrales and Penfold 2011: 76–81). By assert-
ing his political control and dismissing an incredible 18,000 recalcitrant engineers, managers, and other employees, Chávez threatened the goose that laid
Venezuela's golden eggs (López-Maya 2009: 36; Corrales and Penfold 2011:
85–90). Together with his other decrees, this power grab therefore provoked
intense resistance from important societal sectors and growing parts of the
citizenry, especially the educated middle classes.

Mounting concerns about Chávez's radical policy measures and his ever
more evident march toward authoritarianism prompted mass demonstrations in April 2002, which seemed to face armed repression from some of
the president's fervent followers. The eruption of violence against peaceful
protestors triggered a coup attempt by large institutionalist segments in the
military, which quickly failed when the interim government was hijacked
by right-wing forces (Encarnación 2002: 42–44; Ellner 2008: 115–18;
Hawkins 2010: 20–21; Coronil 2011: 43–56; Corrales and Penfold 2011:
21–23). Powerful generals therefore reinstalled the temporarily ousted president. After this narrow escape, pushy Chávez confronted an additional
round of fierce opposition in a two-month business lockdown, which the
stubborn populist simply rode out, though at the cost of tremendous damage
to the economy.

Unsuccessful with its extrainstitutional efforts (Gamboa 2017), the desperate opposition sought to take advantage of the drop in presidential popularity
caused by these monumental conflicts and their economic repercussions, especially a deep recession in 2002–3. For this purpose, the anti-populist groupings
tried to enlist an institutional innovation that Chávez's own constitution had
introduced. In trying to cover up the Bolivarian leader's autocratic project with
formally participatory mechanisms, the new charter allowed for a presidential
recall election. In 2003, the incumbent's greatly diminished approval ratings
seemed to make his defeat a foregone conclusion.

Right then, however, global oil prices started a sustained upsurge, rising
by a whopping 50 percent from April 2003 to August 2004. Finding an unexpected lifeline in the sudden influx of additional revenues, savvy Chávez stalled
as long as he could, using his control over Venezuela's electoral authorities to
hinder the opposition initiative and postpone the day of reckoning by more
than a year (Hawkins 2010: 1–3; Corrales and Penfold 2011: 24–25; Carrión
2022: 118–21). In the meantime, he relied on his command over the national
oil company, which he had forcefully imposed in 2002–3, and used the rapidly growing hydrocarbon proceeds to rush the creation of large-scale, widely
advertised social programs.[4] A stunning economic recovery, which raised GDP
by more than 18 percent in 2004, further helped to restore his popularity
(Corrales and Penfold 2011: 24–26).

---

[4] Wilpert 2007: 124–47; Ellner 2008: 122–24; Arenas 2009: 79–82; Corrales 2010: 35–36; Hawkins 2010: 201–2, 217–20.

Therefore, the street-smart populist clearly prevailed when the recall referendum was finally held in August 2004 (Hellinger 2007: 160–63; Roberts 2014: 261–62). For the opposition, this last defeat came after the failure of so many bold and costly efforts to stop Chávez's power grabs and oust the uncontrollable leader (Corrales and Penfold 2011: 27–28). Profoundly demoralized, anti-populist forces struggled for years to settle on a strategy for contesting the autocrat (Morgan 2018: 308–12, 321–24). The victorious Bolivarian, in turn, used his now-unchallenged predominance further to augment his power and complete his takeover of Venezuela's judiciary. The accelerating commodities boom further swelled state coffers (Corrales and Penfold 2011: 54–58), facilitated exorbitant spending sprees, and helped Chávez win another decisive reelection in 2006. After he suffered a surprise loss in a 2007 referendum on ambitious constitutional reforms designed to deepen and cement his authoritarian rule,[5] he blithely pushed through important changes, especially the right to unlimited reelections, in another plebiscite in 2009 (Coronil 2011: 57; Corrales and Penfold 2011: 38–39; López-Maya 2011: 228–33; Carrión 2022: 190–92).

While Chávez advanced gradually with his determined dismantling of Venezuela's democracy, while his frequently high popularity made the descent into authoritarianism difficult to detect, and while the opposition with its contentious countermoves, especially the coup attempt of 2002, muddied the frontlines in these monumental struggles over the country's regime type (Corrales and Penfold 2011: 22–23), most scholars classify Venezuela as competitive-authoritarian from 2006 onward. The Bolivarian populist, who had already acted in undemocratic ways on many earlier occasions, for instance by obstructing the opposition's recall petition in 2003–4, confirmed this rating with his disrespect for the plebiscite defeat of 2007 and for opposition victories in the gubernatorial and municipal elections of 2008. Illiberal moves and the politicized application of rules to harass all independent forces and political adversaries mounted over the years as well (Corrales 2011: 83–88; Corrales and Penfold 2011: 34–37, 142–43; López-Maya and Panzarelli 2013: 252–55, 264; Pappas 2019: 200–2, 208–9).

The Crucial Role of the Hydrocarbon Windfall

As the preceding narrative shows, Chávez initiated democratic backsliding in Venezuela by taking advantage of the high instability of the constitutional framework that he had helped to cause. Moreover, the recession of 1998–99, which came on the heels of two decades of economic deterioration, also played into his hands. Given the weakness of the battered liberal institutions, an economic crisis enabled this populist outsider to initiate the dismantling of checks

---

[5] Werz 2007: 17–21; Arenas 2009: 91–98; López-Maya 2009: 44–49.

and balances. Thus, whereas Latin America's presidential systems of middling institutional strength can be brought down only when two conjunctural opportunities – such as the hyperinflation and guerrilla wars afflicting Peru in 1990 – exceptionally coincide, the major blows befalling Venezuelan democracy in the early 1990s allowed Chávez to start breaching its tottering defenses based on only one crisis: the sharp economic downturn of 1998–99.

Interestingly, when the Bolivarian populist launched his illiberal project, his autocratic end goals were initially not obvious. Instead, the savvy left-winger employed an abundance of participatory and direct-democratic rhetoric to convoke the 1999 constituent assembly and replace the opposition-controlled legislature elected in 1998 through his comprehensive electoral sweep in 2000. While opposition forces distrusted the former coup maker from the beginning and while Chávez frequently used problematic para-legal means, he skillfully depicted his power-concentrating reforms, which included the creation of several plebiscitarian mechanisms, as efforts to transform an ossified, elite-dominated democracy for the sake of greater citizen participation. By hiding his true colors, he thus succeeded in starting his march toward authoritarianism under conditions that depart somewhat from my theory.

But after Chávez's autocratic intentions became glaringly obvious from 2002 onward, he ended up being successful only because the necessary conditions stipulated for the Bolivarian path in Chapter 2 fell into place and Venezuela's high instability came to coincide with an enormous hydrocarbon windfall. After all, the transgressive populist's near-death experiences in 2002–3 suggest that his installation of authoritarianism would most likely have failed if the exogenous opportunity suddenly provided by the global commodities boom had not come to his rescue. Before this huge windfall lifted his sagging fortunes, Chávez faced determined, dangerous opposition from various powerful forces, ranging from business and organized labor to military groupings. Indeed, his enemies almost ousted him through the 2002 coup. These dramatic conflicts and their devastating economic fallout drastically undermined his plebiscitarian support and drove his approval ratings down to a meager 36 percent in late 2003 (Hawkins 2010: 19; Corrales 2011: 75–76). Consequently, the now-unpopular populist seemed destined to defeat in the recall referendum called by the opposition in 2003. Ironically, this plebiscitarian mechanism, which his own 1999 constitution had deliberately introduced, now seemed to turn lethal for its mastermind.

In these dire straits, only the sudden boost in government-controlled hydrocarbon revenues saved Chávez (Corrales and Penfold 2011: 24–26, 138–39). The massive windfall rents enabled the clever populist quickly to roll out large benefit programs for the popular sectors, his main electoral base, and thus defeat the recall petition. Based on this new triumph, he managed to push his populist power concentration project to completion and move from democratic backsliding to the installation of authoritarianism by 2006. Thus, the influx of "over 900 billion [US dollars] in 10 years" (Coronil 2011: 58) allowed the

Bolivarian leader definitely to destroy Venezuelan democracy. While he had already taken major preparatory steps toward this goal by late 2001, the epic conflicts of the subsequent biennium pushed Chávez's rule to the knife's edge and could easily have brought about his downfall. It was the enormous resource inflow produced by the worldwide oil price boom that allowed the left-wing populist to emerge from these stormy seas and consolidate his undemocratic hegemony (López-Maya and Panzarelli 2013).

In sum, Chávez initiated his illiberal plan under special circumstances, facilitated by the obfuscation of his ultimate goal with participatory, direct-democratic slogans. But he could only achieve these autocratic goals because he suddenly encountered the conjunctural opportunity that was crucial for the Bolivarian terminators of democracy, namely the voluminous resource windfall arising from the global hydrocarbon boom. This unexpected gift enabled Chávez to turn predictable defeat in the recall referendum into a clear victory, which finally dealt a knockout blow to the hitherto indefatigable, powerful, and dangerous opposition. Without this exogenous revenue inflow, the acrimonious left-winger would probably have suffered eviction, which would have given Venezuelan democracy a reasonable chance of survival and revitalization.

With the qualifier that illiberal backsliding started under special conditions, the Venezuelan case thus corroborates my theory that the capacity of Latin America's recent crop of left-wing populists to destroy democracy depended primarily on the coincidence of two main factors: High instability created special vulnerability to personalistic plebiscitarian machinations; and an enormous hydrocarbon windfall provided power-hungry leaders with the overwhelming support required for completing the imposition of authoritarian rule.

HYDROCARBON WINDFALLS AND THE MARCH TO COMPETITIVE AUTHORITARIANISM IN BOLIVIA AND ECUADOR

Even more clearly than in the Venezuelan case, the conjunctural opportunities arising from the oil and gas price boom of the mid-2000s provided the crucial impulse for the populist strangulation of democracy in Bolivia and Ecuador, which were also suffering from high instability at the beginning of the new millennium. Because the distribution of massive economic and social benefits greatly strengthened their political clout, new presidents Evo Morales (2006–19) and Rafael Correa (2007–17) managed to augment executive powers, dismantle checks and balances, and prepare their unlimited self-perpetuation in office through unfair means.

As theorized in Chapter 2, a highly brittle institutional framework posed few obstacles to the power hunger of personalistic plebiscitarian leaders. Therefore, they could rely on major governmental efforts to boost popular well-being and did not need to prove their charisma through the extraordinary feat of resolving two acute and severe crises, the task faced and mastered by neoliberal populist Fujimori. With the "manna from heaven" gifted by the global bonanza, they could perform their own miracles, though not quite on the same order of magnitude as Fujimori's unprecedented success in defeating both hyperinflation and a countrywide guerrilla insurgency.

Evo Morales' Strangulation of Democracy in Bolivia

The role of hydrocarbon revenues was particularly important in Bolivia, which in the 1990s, as a result of neoliberal reform and the subsequent increase in foreign investment, had found voluminous new deposits of natural gas. Thus, a country that had long suffered from desperate poverty suddenly seemed to turn rich. Popular expectations and demand-making therefore surged, fueling mass contention that erupted on several occasions in the early 2000s (Gutiérrez et al. 2002; Weyland 2009; Carrión 2022: 64–68). These outbursts in turn pushed a nation that for fifteen years had been governed in an orderly fashion by an oligopoly of three significant parties (Mayorga 1997) into high instability by forcing the ouster of one president in late 2003, and of his vice-president and successor in mid-2015 as well.

This popular effervescence, especially the mobilization and proliferation of often militant social movements, fed into the formation of a new party, the Movement toward Socialism (Movimiento al Socialismo, or MAS) headed by Evo Morales, the leader of a coca growers' union, a crop of questionable legality at the time.[6] The new movement-party pushed for a fundamental transformation of Bolivia's political system, inspired in part by Chávez's Bolivarian project (De la Torre 2017a: 1275–77). For this purpose, the MAS promised not only major socioeconomic improvements for the poor majority, especially indigenous groupings that felt excluded, but also a constituent assembly designed to overhaul the liberal institutional framework. With his forceful demands for profound renewal, Morales surprisingly won second place in the presidential election of 2002. And after his new party and its affiliated multitude of movements fueled the incessant trouble and turmoil of the subsequent years (Stefanoni and do Alto 2006: 71–92), the plebeian leader, by then widely seen as the only chance for restoring some semblance of stability, triumphed in a landslide in late 2005.

After the discovery of natural gas had stirred up bottom-up demand-making and after serious conflicts over gas usage had paved the way for Morales' ascension to the presidency, this personalistic plebiscitarian leader then benefited enormously from the revenue influx resulting from the global hydrocarbon boom. Moreover, the new government's "nationalization" of the gas sector, which effectively meant the imposition of large tax increases, yielded additional resources. Bolivia's previously cash-starved state suddenly had

---

[6] Stefanoni and do Alto 2006: 33–52; Madrid 2012: chap. 2; Anria 2018: 11–19, 62–76, 90–97; see background in Van Cott 2005: chap. 3.

substantial funds to expand social benefit programs and bring relief to the country's large segments of lower-class, poor, and destitute people (Gray Molina 2010: 65–67). Sustained economic growth also allowed for the rise of an extensive new middle and lower-middle class, evident, for instance, in a construction boom.[7]

Facing a precarious institutional framework, flush with gas revenues, buoyed by a strong electoral mandate, and propelled by high popular expectations, Morales quickly followed in Chávez's footsteps, convoked a constituent assembly, and promoted a host of important changes, including – in typical populist fashion – presidential reelection. Due to Bolivia's stark regional divisions, he encountered strong societal and political opposition and did not achieve the total dominance in the constitution-making body that his Venezuelan role model had commanded.[8] But through tense negotiations and serious, sometimes violent conflicts, the personalistic president pushed his power concentration project forward (Lehoucq 2008; Corrales 2018: 158–65). Based on his strong plebiscitarian support, which increased further with the economic and social improvements facilitated by the hydrocarbon windfall, Morales eventually prevailed on several – though not all – issues, including permission to run for an immediate second term in 2009. With another electoral landslide, the incumbent now won unchallenged political hegemony.

In their strenuous struggle for gaining predominance and consolidating it thereafter,[9] Morales and his MAS militants committed numerous infractions against liberal pluralism and thus ended up destroying Bolivian democracy (Rojas Ortuste 2009: 230–34). They pushed through their new constitution with unfair, forceful, and even violent means, for instance by physically blocking the access of other parties to crucial deliberations (Lehoucq 2008; Aboy Carlés 2009: 278). Moreover, they systematically harassed and intimidated a wide range of opposition forces, using formally legal mechanisms in blatantly discriminatory ways (Weyland 2013: 23–24; De la Torre 2017a: 1277–78). As a result, a number of leading politicians ended up in jail or fled into exile to avoid this fate. To facilitate these pressure tactics and shield the government against scrutiny and accountability, Morales took over all of the state's independent institutions, especially the judiciary and the election administration. In these resolute ways, the personalistic plebiscitarian leader pushed Bolivia into competitive authoritarianism.[10]

---

[7] Personal observation, El Alto, Bolivia, July 6, 2018.

[8] Aboy Carlés 2009: 278–81; Mayorga 2009: 191–97; Rojas Ortuste 2009: 225–29, 243; Gray Molina 2010: 58–63; Corrales 2018: 148–53; Carrión 2022: 127–36.

[9] Probably because stronger opposition prevented Morales from enshrining all his power-concentrating proposals in the constitution (Corrales 2018: 148–53, 162–65), the personalistic president and his plebiscitarian supporters in subsequent years used even harsher means than Correa to undermine, attack, and defeat virtually all rival political forces.

[10] Lehoucq 2008; Levitsky and Loxton 2013: 113–14, 117–18; Weyland 2013: 22–24; Sánchez-Sibony 2021; for an unconvincing account see Cameron 2018: 14–15.

Rafael Correa's Strangulation of Democracy in Ecuador

Rafael Correa in Ecuador followed the same Bolivarian script and suppressed liberal democracy as well, based on the two main factors that had also proved decisive in Venezuela and Bolivia. Ecuador had started to descend into high instability with the constitutionally problematic and suspiciously rapid ouster of neoliberal populist Abdalá Bucaram in 1997, which Chapter 3 examined. Only three years later, another president suffered eviction in a civil-military coup; and after the main coup leader, Lucio Gutiérrez, was elected president in 2002, he in turn fell over spiraling mass protests and para-legal congressional machinations in mid-2005, as this chapter analyzes later. This unprecedented "massacre" of chief executives made the institutional framework so brittle that the country looked virtually ungovernable (Pachano 2005; Mejía Acosta and Polga-Hecimovich 2011: 100–4; De la Torre 2015: 118–36).

Because the nation was longing for a strong, Chávez-style leader (Bull and Sánchez 2020: 99; Carrión 2022: 72–73), political outsider Rafael Correa found substantial support for his project of comprehensive socioeconomic and political transformation. Helped by the weakness and fragmentation of Ecuador's party system, the left-wing populist won a convincing second-round victory in the 2006 presidential election. Like his Venezuelan role model and his Bolivian colleague, this personalistic leader, who had advertised his profound aversion to parties by running without a slate of congressional candidates, immediately pushed for a constituent assembly, in rather forceful, impositional, and legally questionable ways (Helmke 2017: 122–24). Remarkably, he broke congressional opposition to his power concentration project by having the government-aligned electoral tribunal simply dismiss and evict a majority of legislative deputies – a brazen purge of this democratically elected body and a frontal assault on checks and balances.[11]

To enable these blatantly para-legal and undemocratic moves, Correa bolstered his political position by using Ecuador's huge oil windfall to initiate a host of ambitious projects, ranging from massive public works, especially the construction of roads and hydroelectric dams, to generous social programs benefiting large segments of the population (De la Torre 2015: 190–93; Aldaz Peña 2021). With these improvements and the oil-fueled economic boom, the personalistic plebiscitarian president earned high approval ratings and managed to push aside the organizationally fluid and politically disparate opposition. To consolidate his political predominance further and promote his prolongation in power, the new charter tailor-made by his supporters concentrated power in the presidency, weakened other branches of government, and allowed for immediate reelection.

---

[11] Conaghan 2011: 271–72; Montúfar 2013: 312–15; Roberts 2014: 268–69; De la Torre 2015: 150–57; Corrales 2018: 178–87; Carrión 2022: 35, 136–41, 145.

Thereafter, the domineering president governed through an abundance of decrees, exerted total control over the national assembly, and commanded a great deal of influence over the judiciary as well (Polga-Hecimovich 2013: 150–53). With systematic pressure and intimidation of the press and frequent attacks on independent social movements and NGOs, Correa governed in autocratic ways and erected a competitive-authoritarian regime (Levitsky and Loxton 2013: 113–14, 120–21; Montúfar 2013; Polga-Hecimovich 2013: 136, 143; De la Torre 2015: 177–79, 200–7; Conaghan 2016; Sánchez-Sibony 2017, 2018; Levitsky and Loxton 2019: 344; for a divergent assessment that is unconvincing, see Cameron 2018: 13–14).

In sum, the combination of factors that had allowed Bolivarian messiah Chávez to complete and consolidate the destruction of democracy in Venezuela was also crucial for enabling his disciples Morales and Correa to replicate this feat in Bolivia and Ecuador. High instability left only feeble obstacles to the self-aggrandizing ambitions of personalistic plebiscitarian leaders; and the enormous support that the three chief executives could obtain by spreading the benefits provided by hydrocarbon windfalls paved the way for removing these hindrances in resolute, forceful ways. Because they won power in presidential systems battered by serious prior blows, the three Bolivarian populists had less difficulty in smothering liberal pluralism than Latin America's neoliberal populists, who governed in democracies of middling institutional strength and who therefore needed the exceptional accomplishment of resolving two profound crises in order to overpower the resulting constraints and impose authoritarian rule.

THE DIVERGENT FATE OF BOLIVARIAN AUTHORITARIANISM

Despite these fundamental commonalities in the factors underlying their creation, and despite the importance of Chávez as a role model, guide, and supporter of Morales and Correa, the authoritarian regimes installed by these Bolivarian leaders eventually diverged in their trajectories. These differences arose in part from a sheer accident, namely Chávez's untimely death from cancer in 2013, which not only put a sudden end to populist governance in Venezuela, but – by felling the coordinator and principal funder of the Bolivarian fraternity – weakened his disciples across the region.

The other main reason for the difficulties soon facing Bolivarian authoritarianism was more foreseeable: In line with my theory, variation in the fates of populist leaders and their regimes emerges mostly from changes in conjunctural opportunities, which are by definition fluctuating. Accordingly, Chapter 3 showed that neoliberal populist Fujimori turned into a victim of his own success: The conjunctural opportunities provided by acute, severe crises naturally disappear once the charismatic populist manages to resolve these problems. Crisis-driven right-wing populism therefore ends up undermining itself, eroding the political foundations of its authoritarian rule. After a few years, Peru therefore managed to restore democracy.

Relying on the hydrocarbon boom starting in 2003, left-wing, Bolivarian populism also stood on shifting ground. Its sustenance depended primarily on exogenous conditions, namely unusually high foreign demand for the three countries' oil and gas exports. When the global commodities boom imploded with the drastic drop of petroleum prices in 2014, Bolivarian authoritarianism suddenly faced substantial resource constraints. With Chávez's death, Venezuela had fallen under the rule of Nicolás Maduro, who – typical for the handpicked successor of a charismatic founder – was a weak lackey without charisma and without the fervent genuine support that Chávez had commanded (Andrews-Lee 2021: 9, 30, 85–87, 141–42). To secure his nonpopulist rule, this hapless disciple therefore felt compelled to employ ever more open and brutal repression. In this way, he pushed Venezuela into full, unadulterated authoritarianism, as well as a Dantean inferno of unprecedented socioeconomic collapse and human catastrophe.[12]

The end of the hydrocarbon boom also created serious problems and challenges for populists Correa and Morales, but they spared their countries Venezuela's dire fate. The two authoritarian presidents responded differently, depending on the organizational sustenance of their support base. In prototypical personalistic plebiscitarian fashion, Correa had exclusively relied on his charismatic leadership. Accordingly, he had refrained from forging a strong, disciplined party (Casullo and Freidenberg 2017: 298–99; Bull and Sánchez 2020: 102–3); moreover, he had antagonized the social movements that backed his first presidential candidacy by charting a distinctly unaccountable, autocratic course in his governance (Conaghan 2011: 274–75; Becker 2014: 135–38; De la Torre 2015: 177–79, 200–7). While this domineering approach had guaranteed Ecuador's Bolivarian president political supremacy during the oil price boom, it left him in a precarious position when the resource windfall disappeared. Indeed, the advent of lean years prompted contention and protest against Correa's desperate efforts to adjust the overheated and debt-ridden economy with fairly drastic austerity measures. Mass demonstrations also sought to block his attempts to prepare his further hold on power (Ospina Peralta 2021: 237–50; Cleary and Öztürk 2022: 216–17).

Moreover, Correa lacked reliable command over the military, which Chávez as a former officer had firmly established in Venezuela and which his challenged successor maintained through juicy perks. By contrast, Correa had a distant relationship with the armed forces, and his efforts to politicize the institution and submit it to his personal control prompted aversion from generals in the military (Bull and Sánchez 2020: 100–1; Polga-Hecimovich 2020: 5, 10–12, 18–19, 29). Because Ecuador's Bolivarian populist could not count on military backing, he refrained from naked repression à la Maduro, which

---

[12] With his haphazard economic policy, his innumerable ideologically driven interventions, and his confrontational political strategy, Chávez himself had decisively put Venezuela on track toward this economic collapse. See, e.g., Rodríguez (2008).

drew growing international criticism and diplomatic pressure even from Latin American governments.

Determined to avoid this opprobrium, Correa sought a smarter way out of his predicament. To maintain political control while shifting the blame for the unavoidable, tough, and painful stabilization of the economy, the three-term president decided to forego another consecutive reelection in 2017 (Bermeo 2016: 17).[13] Instead, he helped elect his former vice-president, nonpopulist Lenín Moreno, while having his supporters pass a constitutional amendment that allowed for his own renewed candidacy in subsequent contests (De la Torre 2018: 78; Carrión 2022: 203–4). With these ingenious moves, Correa sought to have Moreno clear up the economic mess and incur the political costs of this relapse into "neoliberalism." Untainted as the nation's benefactor during the fat years of the hydrocarbon boom, he himself would then make a triumphant return in the 2021 election.

Surprisingly, however, Moreno quickly marked his independence and turned against Correa, going so far as to accuse his predecessor of massive corruption and to foreclose his comeback by promoting a plebiscite to block Correa's chance for reelection. Breaking with Bolivarian populism, the new president also undertook energetic efforts to restore democracy by ending governmental hostility against social movements and lifting the pressure on the media (De la Torre 2018: 78, 83–86; Wolff 2018: 285–88, 295–98). While Moreno predictably suffered the political fallout of economic crisis and austerity, these problems did not erase many citizens' aversion to Bolivarian populism, which Correa's highhandedness had exacerbated. Therefore, Correa's handpicked candidate lost the presidential election of 2021, preserving Ecuador's recently revived and precarious democracy from the renewed threat of personalistic plebiscitarian leadership (Polga-Hecimovich and Sánchez 2021: 6–17). Democracy's surprising resurrection in Ecuador shows the vibrancy of liberal pluralism and people's tendency to get tired of populist confrontation and domination over time.

The unexpected failure of Correa's seemingly savvy plan for riding out the lean years and then resuming his hegemony reinforced the decision of Bolivia's Morales to insist on another reelection so that he could ensure the continuation of his competitive-authoritarian regime. But for this purpose, Morales had to overcome the two-term limit enshrined in his own constitution of 2009, which he had explicitly promised to respect (Assies 2011: 110; Corrales 2018: 162–63; Carrión 2022: 135). Through a counting trick, he para-legally reneged on this promise and won a third term in 2014. But a renewed candidacy in 2019 seemed to require a formal rule change. Morales narrowly lost a plebiscite on this very issue in 2016, however. Therefore, the only way to prepare his prolongation in office was to use his effective control over Bolivia's judiciary and engineer a favorable ruling. Yet the strained argument used by

---

[13] This was an unusual move for a power-hungry populist, whose congressional supporters with their supermajority could probably have pushed through the right of unlimited reelection.

the Constitutional Court, which proclaimed a human right to stand for elections, was so questionable and unconstitutional that it provoked widespread opposition and tainted the Bolivarian populist's 2019 campaign with illegitimacy (Brockmann Quiroga 2020: 33–46; McKay and Colque 2021: 3–4, 9–10; Carrión 2022: 195–99).

Nevertheless, Morales was determined to obtain a fourth consecutive term, counting on his socioeconomic accomplishments and political-organizational strength. After all, by contrast to Venezuela and Ecuador, his economic team had administered the hydrocarbon windfall in fairly prudent and responsible ways, avoiding overspending and subsequent crisis. Thus, while decelerating from the mid-2010s onward, Bolivia's economy continued to achieve modest growth, protecting the enormous socioeconomic benefits that large population segments had received during the preceding fat years, which had boosted the poor country's GDP. Moreover, as another difference from Venezuela and especially Ecuador, Morales combined personalistic plebiscitarian leadership with a vibrant social movement base assembled in a reasonably well-structured political party (Madrid 2012: chap. 2; Anria 2018: 90–97, 130–61). Trusting in his mobilizational capacity and organizational loyalties, the incumbent was confident of achieving a clear reelection victory.

Offended by Morales' highhanded manipulation and averse to his eternal self-perpetuation, however, the opposition won enough votes to endanger his first-round triumph. As ample evidence of direct interference and manipulations of the vote count, together with a wealth of statistical indications of irregularities, suggest,[14] the government therefore resorted to fraud, which prompted a surprising outburst of countrywide mass protest (Lehoucq 2020; McKay and Colque 2021: 3–4, 9–10). Interestingly, many erstwhile MAS supporters were lukewarm and refrained from energetic countermobilization.[15] After weeks of trouble and turmoil, the police finally refused to repress the anti-government manifestations. Morales' rule started to unravel. It imploded soon thereafter, when the Organization of American States (OAS), whom the incumbent himself had enlisted as an arbiter, published a devastating report documenting many irregularities and strong indications of fraud in the vote count (OAS 2019b).[16] Both the country's trade union confederation, which

---

[14] The in-depth analyses by Chumacero (2019), Escobari and Hoover (2020), and Newman (2020) are particularly thorough and comprehensive; contrary to his paper's title, Mebane (2019) also concludes that fraud was decisive. Moreover, Escobari and Hoover (2020: 16, 28) point out significant flaws in the contrasting analysis by Idrobo, Kronick, and Rodríguez (2022).

[15] Kulakevich and Augsburger 2021: 319–20; see also Ortuño Yáñez 2020: 69–75.

[16] The OAS soon backed up this preliminary report with a thorough, comprehensive analysis that documented numerous serious manipulations (OAS 2019a), which the European Union confirmed (EU. EEM 2020: 28–36). Escobari and Hoover (2020: 27–28), Newman (2020: 1–8, 22–23), and Nooruddin (2020) convincingly defend the statistical indications of fraud in the OAS report against flimsy criticism commissioned by an ideological think tank with notorious "Bolivarian" sympathies (Williams and Curiel 2020; see also Johnston and Rosnick 2020: 32–43).

had long supported Morales, and the military high command then asked the personalistic president to resign. He hurriedly absconded into exile (Lehoucq 2020; Wolff 2020).[17]

While after almost fourteen years in power, Morales' competitive authoritarianism collapsed, the haphazard interim government, dominated by right-wingers, failed to restore democracy. With its chaotic tenure and deplorable performance, it ironically paved the way for the MAS to win a convincing victory in the free and fair elections of late 2020. With Morales waiting in the wings, eager to make a comeback in the next presidential contest of 2025, the country's political fate hangs in the balance. Interestingly, the MAS with its combination of populism and social movement activism also harbors several new leaders who are trying to wrest control away from the power-hungry ex-president and who promise to chart a less autocratic course.

In sum, shared conditions, namely the coincidence of high instability and the exceptional hydrocarbon boom prevailing from 2003 to 2014, had undergirded common developments in Venezuela, Bolivia, and Ecuador, namely the descent of Bolivarian populism into competitive authoritarianism. But when the conjunctural opportunity ended that had gifted charismatic leaders with large windfalls and allowed them to win overwhelming support, their political fate began to diverge. In lean times, specific political talents and assets turned decisive. Nonpopulist Maduro's lack of charisma and Correa's typically populist lack of organizational sustenance proved especially important. Moreover, the MAS's social movement base eventually recovered considerable independence and refused to sustain and perpetuate Morales' top-down leadership. For these reasons, while Venezuela sank into full, undisguised dictatorship, democracy enjoyed a precarious revival in Ecuador and has a fighting chance in Bolivia.

ABORTED BOLIVARIAN POPULISM BEFORE THE OIL
WINDFALL: GUTIÉRREZ IN ECUADOR

While Morales and Correa long achieved great political success by following in Chávez's footsteps and while they used their political hegemony to strangle liberal democracy as well, the charismatic politician who emerged as the Bolivarian messiah's most faithful disciple, Lucio Gutiérrez of Ecuador, ended up suffering striking political failure, which temporarily saved his country's battered democracy. The main reason was that this virtual Chávez clone won office right before the upsurge of global oil prices gifted Ecuador a large revenue

---

[17] It is noteworthy that Morales took the decision to step down several hours before the military publicly voiced its suggestion, as his vice-president mentioned in a long interview with Serrano Mancilla (2021: 66). This fact corroborates the conclusion reached by country experts that Morales' downfall did not constitute a coup (Archondo 2020; Lehoucq 2020; Wolff 2020).

windfall. The new president therefore lacked the conjunctural opportunity to boost his support (see Aldaz Peña 2021: 146–48), vault to political supremacy, and smother liberal pluralism.

Instead, Gutiérrez never managed to establish a solid base of political sustenance, and his ever more desperate quest for support inadvertently created more enemies than friends. This imbalance turned politically fatal after fewer than thirty months in office. Yet while Gutiérrez's ignominious eviction through mass protests and congressional machinations preserved democracy in the short run, this renewed irregular eviction of a chief executive – the third problematic ouster within a mere nine years – exacerbated Ecuador's political instability (Montúfar 2006: 69, 71, 73). This further weakening of the institutional framework helped pave the way for the quickly following rise of Rafael Correa, who, benefited by the roaring commodities boom, did manage to proceed with the populist installation of authoritarianism.

Exactly like Chávez, Gutiérrez did not vault to political prominence as a democratic politician – just the opposite. As a junior army officer, he acted like his Venezuelan role model and played a leading role in a civil-military coup against a neoliberal president in 2000 (Polga-Hecimovich 2020: 13–14). This blatantly extraconstitutional move actually succeeded in toppling the democratically elected incumbent. Domestic opposition and intense US pressures, however, led to a precarious restoration of the constitutional order and the succession of the vice-president; the coup monger landed in jail, albeit for a mere six months.

Like the Venezuelan inventor of Bolivarianism, Gutiérrez became a symbol of defiance against a discredited political class and an unstable democracy with endemic governance problems (Roberts 2014: 267). Ostentatiously highlighting his leading role in the coup, the Chávez replica ran in the presidential election of 2002, winning a clear victory in the second round. While in Ecuador's fragmented party system, Gutiérrez had not achieved the massive triumph of his Venezuelan role model, the country prepared itself for a repetition of Chávez's political script.

But while benefiting from Ecuador's rapid descent into institutional instability, the new populist president lacked the conjunctural opportunities for successfully pursuing this daring and risky path toward Bolivarian authoritarianism. Chávez's recent near-death experiences, the temporarily successful coup attempt of April 2002, and the dangerous business strike at year's end, which occurred shortly before Gutiérrez's inauguration, served as a telling note of caution. After all, despite lingering economic problems, Ecuador was not suffering from an acute, serious crisis. Nor was the country benefiting yet from an enormous resource windfall; instead, Gutiérrez took office in January 2003, just a few months before the sustained upsurge in the price of Ecuador's main export: petroleum (Corrales 2018: 170; Aldaz Peña 2021: 146–48). Consequently, Gutiérrez narrowly missed the chance of replicating the Bolivarian blueprint.

Instead, facing a recent increase in fiscal deficits, Gutiérrez undertook a drastic policy shift that his left-wing and indigenous core supporters condemned as a betrayal (Acosta 2005: 50–52; Villegas Aldas 2010: 15, 18–21; Madrid 2012: 101–2; Roberts 2014: 267). Like many other Latin American presidents who encountered economic difficulties after campaigning on non-neoliberal platforms (Stokes 2001), he quickly changed course, embraced economic orthodoxy, and entered into negotiations with the main enforcer and notorious symbol of neoliberalism, the International Monetary Fund (Correa 2003: 6–10). Thus, rather than imitating Chávez, Ecuador's new president felt compelled to act more like neoliberal populist Carlos Menem of Argentina, allying with forces that were anathema to the Bolivarian left.

But the absence of an urgent, severe crisis made Gutiérrez's adoption of austerity measures unpalatable to the surprised population. Moreover, Gutiérrez differed from Menem in lacking any organizational sustenance, which the Argentine president had commanded through his leadership of the country's massive Peronist movement (Corrales 2002). Instead, as a newcomer to politics, Gutiérrez had hurriedly cobbled together a flimsy, heterogeneous electoral alliance, which his blithe abandonment of his campaign pledges now shattered (Villegas Aldas 2010: 16, 25–27).

With this loss of left-wing and indigenous support and with Gutiérrez's diminishing popularity ratings (Villegas Aldas 2010: 40–43), any plan to follow in Chávez's footsteps, overturn the liberal institutional framework through a constituent assembly, and thus engineer undemocratic predominance was out of the question. Instead, the chameleonic populist was compelled to govern inside the existing system of checks and balances, however unstable it was. For this purpose, the new president tried hard to build a legislative coalition (Villegas Aldas 2010: 28–33), using all kinds of means, including the shady "deals" and patronage payoffs for which he had attacked the domestic political establishment.

In Ecuador's fragmented multiparty system, which the struggling populist was unable to sweep away like Chávez had done and Morales and Correa would soon do, these opportunistic bargains and shifty collaborations set in motion a virtual dance of alliances that further weakened government performance (Montúfar 2006: 23, 27–30; De la Torre 2015: 115–16). As popular discontent grew and Gutiérrez fell out with one legislative grouping after the other, he eventually saw no other option but to strike an agreement with the supporters of neoliberal populist Abdalá Bucaram (see Chapter 3). This unsavory deal included the dropping of legal charges against this notoriously corrupt politician and thus enabled the disgraced ex-president to return to his home country (Villegas Aldas 2010: 46–50; Mejía Acosta and Polga-Hecimovich 2011: 102–3).

This desperate move proved to be Gutiérrez's undoing: It required a heavy-handed intervention in the judiciary, especially the blatantly para-legal imposition of judges who would clear Bucaram, as well as other politicians involved in shameless bribery (Acosta 2005: 44–46; Montúfar 2006: 23–24, 30–31, 58). Popular revulsion prompted growing protests against Gutiérrez's increasingly undemocratic machinations (Pachano 2005: 43–46; Montúfar 2006: 36–42). Fueling this escalation, Bucaram's triumphant homecoming parade (De la Torre 2015: 98–99, 119) provoked an explosion of popular contention, which quickly sealed the incumbent's fate (Montúfar 2006: 42–58). Congress removed him from office under a constitutionally questionable pretext (De la Torre 2015: 119–26), further aggravating Ecuador's high instability.

Thus, without the conjunctural opportunity provided by a huge hydrocarbon windfall, Gutiérrez suffered the kind of political failure that Chávez only narrowly averted in 2002–4. Whereas skyrocketing oil prices enabled Venezuela's Bolivarian populist to escape from the opposition's trap of a recall referendum, Ecuador's incumbent fell in the absence of such largesse. Indeed, the lack of surplus revenues at his inauguration had induced Gutiérrez early on to abandon Chávez's script, which he had so closely followed during his ascent to power. Rather than trying proactively to overturn the liberal institutional order, he was initially compelled to govern inside it. His embrace of fiscal responsibility betrayed his campaign promises, however, and left him bereft of reliable support. This predicament, in turn, set in motion a downward spiral of fleeting opportunistic alliances that eventually induced Gutiérrez to resort to autocratic moves in despair, in a vain effort to sustain his tottering government in Ecuador's ever more unstable polity.

The absence of the conjunctural opportunity that miraculously saved Chávez thus pushed Gutiérrez onto a political trajectory that culminated in his striking political failure. The shifty populist's downfall gave Ecuador's clobbered democracy an additional lease on life – but only for a short time, as the analysis of Correa's push toward authoritarianism showed earlier.

EVICTED BOLIVARIAN POPULISM WITHOUT AN OIL WINDFALL: ZELAYA IN HONDURAS

Whereas Ecuadoran left-winger Gutiérrez surprisingly betrayed Chávez's Bolivarian gospel, Honduran right-winger Manuel Zelaya surprisingly embraced it. In their inherent shiftiness and opportunism, the two personalistic plebiscitarian leaders undertook these unexpected policy switches based on the conjunctural opportunity that is so decisive for Bolivarian populism: When taking office in early 2003 right before the upsurge in global oil prices, Gutiérrez did not encounter a revenue windfall; by contrast, Zelaya noticed from 2006 onward that he could benefit from Venezuela's huge windfall because Chávez offered Honduras generous subsidies (Cunha Filho, Coelho, and Pérez Flores 2013). Consequently, whereas as president, Gutiérrez had abandoned Chávez's political strategy and refrained from convoking a constituent assembly to start dismantling liberal pluralism, Zelaya toward the end of his term decided to bet on this script, most likely in a belated effort to engineer his perpetuation in power. This is, at least, what Honduras' strong opposition suspected, prompting determined resistance to Zelaya's stubborn push, which eventually led to the military eviction of this new convert to Bolivarian populism.

Zelaya, a typical product of Honduras' centenarian two-party system, won the 2005 election with a center-right platform and started his government with this orientation. In his second year, however, this elite politician began to chart an ever more left-wing and populist course (Ruhl 2010: 98–100). Now depicting himself as an advocate of the poor, he tried hard to win a mass following with surprisingly generous social concessions, including a whopping 30 percent increase in the minimum wage. Marking ever starker distance from Honduras' traditional political class, including his own party, the chameleonic president increasingly turned to Venezuela's Chávez, who – flush with petrodollars – worked tirelessly to win friends in Latin America by providing enormous financial support.[18] Chávez could also serve as a political role model because in 2006, he had .won a second consecutive reelection, had established his undemocratic supremacy, and was preparing his continuing self-perpetuation in office. No wonder that an ambitious personalistic leader such as Honduras' new populist took inspiration from the inventor of Bolivarian populism (De la Torre 2017a: 1281–82).[19]

What attracted Zelaya, however, scared his opponents, who were well entrenched in Congress, the courts, most of the party system, large segments of civil society, private business, and the military (Cunha Filho, Coelho, and Pérez Flores 2013: 525–26). These center-right forces, who had long dominated Honduran politics, resented Zelaya's betrayal and unexpected turn to the left. They feared that an emulation of Chávez's script would disrupt and overturn Honduras' oligarchical democracy and bring a slide into authoritarianism under an unaccountable and uncontrollable leader. When Zelaya began to propose steps toward the convocation of a constituent assembly – precisely the mechanism that Venezuela's Bolivarian populist had used to start bending and breaking liberal institutions – Congress and the courts dug in their heels and consistently blocked the pushy president's repeated forays (Llanos and Marsteintredet 2010: 182–85; Ruhl 2010: 100–2). The very fact that Zelaya stubbornly persisted with his transgressive initiatives, which were formally unconstitutional, aggravated the fears of the opposition. Because neither side gave in, the conflict escalated in mid-2009. After the president's ever more

---

[18] Cunha Filho, Coelho, and Pérez Flores 2013: 524–25, 531–35; Llanos and Marsteintredet 2010: 180–81.

[19] Thus, Zelaya constituted the Bolivarian counterpart to Guatemala's neoliberal populist Serrano, who tried to emulate Fujimori's 1992 self-coup, yet failed as well (see Chapter 3). Both of the Central American populists sought to enact the mechanism of incumbent takeover that their South American role models had introduced – left-wingers via a constituent assembly, right-wingers via military imposition.

aggressive steps, the military finally deported Zelaya from his own country, allegedly on high-court orders.[20] Congress installed its speaker as interim president, following the constitutional line of succession. These drastic moves precluded Honduras' feared descent into Bolivarian authoritarianism – but tragically overthrew democracy in the process.

Why did Zelaya fail, whereas Chávez, Morales, and Correa managed to prolong their rule by asphyxiating liberal pluralism? Honduras differed in both of the factors that my theory highlights as decisive for democracy's suffocation by Bolivarian populism. On the institutional front, the Central American nation was not suffering from high instability. Instead, since the installation of democracy in the early 1980s, every president had served out his full term, had faithfully handed over power to his successor, and had not tried to overturn the constitutional framework. No dangerous coup attempts or mass protests had shaken the established order (Ruhl 2010: 93, 104).

Middling institutional strength gave Honduras' presidential system a great deal of resilience against Zelaya's controversial reform efforts. Whereas high instability had enabled Chávez and Correa to push through their demand for constituent assemblies in flagrantly para-legal, if not illegal ways, the greater solidity of the Central American polity sustained determined and insurmountable resistance to the Honduran populist's planned replication of the Bolivarian script. The opposition in Tegucigalpa refused to be steamrolled, and it commanded the clout to block Zelaya's variegated advances, different from their counterparts in Caracas and Quito. Based on their democratic legitimacy and electoral mandates, the Honduran conservatives did not cede to populism's invocation of popular sovereignty as a self-serving justification for dismantling the liberal institutional framework (Ruhl 2010: 100–2).

Indeed, due to Honduras' second difference from Venezuela, Bolivia, and Ecuador, Zelaya lacked majority support; in particular, he was far from enjoying the overwhelming strength that Chávez, Morales, and Correa obtained with the help of their hydrocarbon windfalls. Instead, when the Central American Chávez disciple initiated his relentless push for a constitutional overhaul, his popularity ratings hovered around a meager 30 percent (Ruhl 2010: 99; Cunha Filho, Coelho, and Pérez Flores 2013: 536). Typical of populism, the Honduran president probably hoped to boost his political standing by resolutely defying the entrenched establishment and by fueling constant confrontation. But even after the unconstitutional coup that turned this aggressor into a victim, he never achieved lopsided popular backing; instead, the country was split right down the middle, with substantial parts of the citizenry expressing relief at his ouster (Ruhl 2010: 102).

A principal reason for Zelaya's low approval was that continuing resource constraints hindered his efforts to attract lower-class followers through

---

[20] Llanos and Marsteintredet 2010: 174–75, 184–85, 189; Ruhl 2010: 93, 101–2; Kuehn and Trinkunas 2017: 871–72; Ginsburg and Huq 2018b: 63, 186.

massive social benefits. While he could mandate a big increase in the minimum wage and have business pay a large part of the cost, he lacked the funds to create new social programs or start mega-investments on the order of Chávez and Correa. After all, though comparatively generous (Cunha Filho, Coelho, and Pérez Flores 2013: 531–35), the subsidies sent by Venezuela's president were far from providing the virtually unlimited resource abundance that the Bolivarian chieftain himself enjoyed. While borrowing some of Chávez's good fortune, Zelaya therefore did not have nearly the same conjunctural opportunity to boost his political supremacy and push aside all obstacles. For these reasons, the Central American populist proved clearly unable to follow in the footsteps of his Venezuelan role model, overcome the much firmer institutional constraints he encountered, and smother liberal pluralism in Honduras.

Tragically, however, in their desperate attempt to stop Zelaya's persistent assault, his opponents ended up killing the prospective victim themselves. By pulling the emergency break, they prevented a frontal collision but caused the train to derail. Thus, in this unusual case, which reveals the dilemmas caused by populist politics, a populist effort to strangle democracy failed, but populism indirectly provoked democracy's execution.

WEAK POPULISM WITH LIMITED WINDFALL RENTS: PERU'S HUMALA AND CASTILLO

Similar to Zelaya, the political-institutional and socioeconomic context facing left-wing populists in Peru, especially Ollanta Humala in 2011, also differed fundamentally from the propitious conditions that enabled Bolivarian leaders Chávez, Morales, and Correa to suffocate liberal democracy. As regards the institutional framework, Peruvian democracy enjoyed a strong recovery after the stunning downfall of neoliberal populist Fujimori and the implosion of his competitive-authoritarian regime in 2000, which Chapter 3 examined. The interim administration of Valentín Paniagua (2000–1) eagerly revived liberal pluralism. The restoration of free and fair elections gave subsequent presidents sufficient legitimacy to serve out their full terms despite quick and drastic drops in their popularity. Thus, while governments were weak, the revived democratic regime proved relatively robust.

Peru has also lacked the conjunctural opportunities that allowed Chávez, Morales, and Correa to boost their support through the politically targeted distribution of vast hydrocarbon rents. Moreover, the absence of urgent, profound crises has foreclosed any chance for presidents to turn into the charismatic "savior of the people." Instead, the market model implanted by Fujimori guaranteed price stability, produced two decades of sustained economic growth, and after the early 2000s yielded substantial reductions in poverty as well. At the same time, Peru's heavy reliance on primary exports was quite diversified and largely in private and foreign hands (Lust 2016: 200–1). Moreover, many of these products lacked the symbolic prominence of hydrocarbon extraction in Venezuela, Bolivia, and Ecuador. Therefore, the commodities boom did not provide the state with the huge revenue windfalls that the massive oil and gas industry of Venezuela, Ecuador, and Bolivia gifted to the three Bolivarian terminators of democracy (see in general Ross 2012: 5–8, 27–62).

Certainly, however, pronounced social and regional inequality, especially the longstanding gulf between the Lima metropolitan area and the neglected and underdeveloped Andean hinterland, bred festering discontent that left-wing populists could mobilize (see Cameron 2011: 382–83). Ollanta Humala, a former military rebel and left-wing nationalist, tapped into this potential when running for president in 2006. Just like Chávez and Ecuador's Gutiérrez, Humala had vaulted to national prominence by spearheading an armed uprising. Because he took this daring step in the dying days of the Fujimori regime and framed it as resistance to authoritarianism and corruption, he was amnestied (Nesbet-Montesinos 2011: 81–85).

Given the strong similarities to Venezuela's Bolivarian leader and Chávez's energetic efforts to spread his political-ideological project across Latin America, Humala's campaign received vocal backing from his role mode, and probably financial subsidies as well. The Peruvian populist, in turn, proposed the *chavista* script of profound socioeconomic transformation and a complete institutional overhaul through a constituent assembly.[21] But due to the good performance of Peru's market model and the risk aversion of a rising middle class, Humala's closeness to the Bolivarian chieftain backfired. In particular, Chávez's impetuous trading of insults with his disciple's second-round opponent may well have cost Humala the victory (Cameron 2011: 385–87; Madrid 2012: 136–42).

The lackluster performance of president Alan García (2006–11), who failed to make a dent in Peru's social and regional inequality (Cameron 2011: 389–94), enabled Humala to run again in 2011. This time, he faced primarily the neoliberal populism of Fujimori's daughter Keiko, who remobilized her father's supporters and thus commanded considerable strength in Peru's exceedingly fluid party system. Because the resulting left–right polarization was dividing the country right down the middle, Humala made a strategic move toward the center and greatly softened his Chávez-style platform. Accordingly, he sought to reassure liberal middle-class voters by shelving his longstanding proposal of a constituent assembly, which in Venezuela, Bolivia, and Ecuador had served as the first step toward the Bolivarian strangulation of democracy (Levitsky 2011: 89–90; PNP 2011: 1–2; Tanaka 2011: 81–82; Madrid 2012: 142–44; McClintock 2013: 233–37).

Despite this crucial accommodation, Humala won only narrowly. Consequently, he had no mandate for spearheading profound changes, nor the opportunity to augment his own autonomy and power. At the same time,

[21] Vergara 2007: 86–90; Dargent 2009: 84–85; Levitsky 2011: 85; Nesbet-Montesinos 2011: 84–88; McClintock 2013: 225–33.

the weak president faced an institutional framework of middling strength and lacked the conjunctural opportunities that hydrocarbon windfalls had provided to his erstwhile Bolivarian role models. While the commodities boom increased tax revenues (Lust 2016: 198–99, 203–6), these extra rents remained limited. Hemmed in from all sides, the hapless populist made further concessions and avoided any challenges to liberal-democratic principles and Peru's institutional parameters, as well as to the market model imposed by Fujimori (Rathbone 2011; Vergara 2013; Muñoz and Guibert 2016: 333–35).

By refraining from the transgressive efforts and power concentration project with which Honduras' Zelaya provoked an anti-populist coup, Peru's former coup monger guaranteed political tranquility. In contrast to his Central American counterpart, Humala acquiesced to the institutional constraints and limited conjunctural opportunities that he was facing (Nesbet-Montesinos 2011: 88–89; Murillo Ramírez 2012: 4–6). As a result, the tamed populist managed to serve out his term, despite rising accusations of malfeasance and diminishing popularity ratings (Murillo Ramírez 2012: 11–13; Muñoz and Guibert 2016: 313–14, 317, 326–28, 334–35). Conversely, Humala's abandonment of autocratic aspirations and his crippling debility meant that his government did no damage to liberal democracy.[22]

In 2021, left-wing populism obtained another chance in Peru with the surprising rise of union radical Pedro Castillo in a phenomenally fragmented welter of utterly flimsy, fluid "parties." Like Humala, the new president found widespread, intense support in Peru's mountainous and rural hinterland, which has long felt excluded from the growing prosperity of the coastal areas,

---

[22] From the beginning, leftist ex-bishop Fernando Lugo (2008–12) in Paraguay was in an even weaker position after managing to defeat the long-ruling Colorado Party in 2008. Certainly, Paraguay's democracy, which had arisen from an anti-dictatorial coup in 1989, had suffered from considerable instability in the 1990s and early 2000s, with a barely averted coup attempt in 1996, the assassination of the vice-president and subsequent impeachment-driven resignation of the president in 1999, and another presidential impeachment in 2001. But the absence of a huge hydrocarbon windfall and the control of Paraguay's large-scale agriculture by private proprietors, which restricted the state's tax take, deprived Lugo of conjunctural opportunities for boosting his mass support. Indeed, entrenched elite dominance and the wide-ranging patronage machine of the Colorado Party limited the space for plebiscitarian mobilization.

Moreover, given the Colorados' entrenched strength, Lugo had won the presidency only through an alliance with another old establishment party, which dominated his coalition's congressional delegation. Therefore, the left-wing leader did not succeed in approving many substantive reforms, not to speak of power-concentrating institutional changes; the convocation of a constituent assembly for purposes of regime transformation was out of the question. In fact, when in the run-up to the 2013 presidential contest, Lugo seemed to renege on an alternation deal with his main alliance partner, that party defected and in cooperation with the Colorados evicted Lugo in a procedurally problematic express impeachment in 2012 (Marsteintredet, Llanos, and Nolte 2013: 112–14; Ezquerro-Cañete and Fogel 2017: 286–93). This new irregularity did not shake the still quite oligarchical democracy, however; it simply ended up allowing the Colorados to resume their long-running dominance by winning the presidential election of 2013. Left-wing populism in Paraguay thus remained an inconsequential episode.

especially Lima. While Castillo was supported by an avowedly Marxist party, he had considerable similarities to Bolivia's Morales. Moreover, Peru's new advocate of Bolivarian populism faced a more propitious institutional context for transformative initiatives than Humala had encountered.

After all, institutional stability had cracked from 2016 onward, when Keiko Fujimori, backed by her father's revitalized populist movement, had lost her second presidential election, now by a painfully narrow margin (0.24 percent). Yet in the same contest, her party won a clear majority in Congress. Frustrated at her own defeat, Keiko and her supporters stubbornly obstructed and frequently contested new president Pedro Pablo Kuczynski and eventually pushed him to resign on politicized corruption charges in a chaotic double impeachment effort in 2017–18. His constitutional successor Martín Vizcarra counterattacked with anti-corruption measures directed against congresspeople and other politicians. As the conflict escalated, the new president ended up dissolving the legislature and calling new elections in a strained interpretation of the constitution. The new Congress, beset by deep party fragmentation, then evicted Vizcarra in 2020. As his controversial successor was quickly forced out by popular protests, Congress was compelled to fill the void with an interim president. With all these acrimonious conflicts, irregularities, and interruptions of presidential tenure, Peru was quickly sliding into high instability (Dargent and Rousseau 2021: 379–80, 385–96; Muñoz 2021: 50–54; Barrenechea and Encinas 2022: 416–18).

Yet while populist Castillo faced this debilitated institutional framework, he lacked the conjunctural opportunities for boosting his plebiscitarian support and extending it beyond the unenthusiastic following that he had assembled during the highly polarized presidential runoff campaign. After all, Peru was not benefiting from a huge revenue windfall. As mentioned earlier, hydrocarbons, the main commodities singled out in the resource curse literature (Ross 2012), provided only a limited portion of export revenues, and mineral extraction was largely in private hands. The state's resulting resource constraints foreclosed a massive program of economic expansion or social distribution with which Castillo could have attracted additional backing.

At the same time, Peru was not in the depths of an acute yet resolvable crisis – the other conjunctural opportunity through which a personalistic plebiscitarian leader can potentially establish political supremacy. Certainly, the COVID-19 pandemic had caused a sharp economic contraction, driving down Peru's GDP by 11.1 percent in 2020. But by Castillo's inauguration in mid-2021, an equally strong recovery had already gathered steam and erased the pre-year losses (Barrenechea and Encinas 2022: 413–16). Consequently, the new president came too late to turn into "the savior of the people": He could not miraculously overcome a severe crisis and therefore lacked the other magic key for boosting his support. In sum, the left-wing populist did not encounter the conjunctural opportunities for exploiting Peru's high instability and resolutely pursuing power concentration.

While facing an unfavorable conjunctural context, Castillo's political standing also suffered from populism's typical agency problems. Indeed, he was a complete outsider who even lacked firm insertion in the hard-core left-wing party that had used him as a figurehead for the presidential election. As personalistic leaders commonly do, he surrounded himself with friends, loyalists, and cronies of unimpressive caliber, while remaining distant from the more "established" and powerful government ministers whom he felt politically compelled to install. Consequently, his decision-making was extremely haphazard. Ill-considered appointments, quickly blocked initiatives, corruption, and scandals abounded (Dargent 2021; Santander 2021; Peru: Jobs for the Comrades 2021). Certainly, this unceasing series of stumbles, conflicts, and governmental crises reflected in part the tremendous fluidity of Peru's party system, a lasting product of Fujimori's anti-organizational populism exacerbated by subsequent personalistic plebiscitarian leaders such as Humala. But Castillo's inexperience, badly prepared and unconsulted choices, and unpredictable twists and turns – typical of populist outsiders – made his government performance exceedingly rocky and his grip on power precarious (Barrenechea and Encinas 2022: 428–33). Given Peru's high instability, a president who clearly was not up to the task had to fear for his political survival, as congressional impeachment efforts showed.

The risk of premature downfall can induce presidents, especially populist leaders, to attempt a "flight forward" and go on the attack (Helmke 2017). In April 2022, Castillo's fourth prime minister – in less than one year in office – indeed initiated such a potential assault on liberal pluralism by proposing a referendum on a constituent assembly. This apparent effort to replicate Hugo Chávez's strategy for gaining political preeminence and strangling democracy was stillborn, however. With approval ratings hovering around 20 percent, Castillo was unlikely to win majoritarian support with rhetorical broadsides against Peru's dysfunctional political class. Indeed, before the president could even start any plebiscitarian mobilization, Congress quickly rejected the referendum project.

Yet as Congress kept seizing on governmental corruption and preparing moves to evict the embattled president, Castillo panicked in December 2022 and tried to decree a self-coup à la Fujimori. Given his abysmal government performance, however, this blatant move toward authoritarianism lacked serious support and was quickly disavowed by the military. Like the equally ill-considered attempt of Guatemala's Serrano (see Chapter 3), Castillo's desperate wager quickly failed; indeed, the aspiring dictator landed in jail (Castillo Impeached and Arrested 2022; Vivas 2022).

In sum, Castillo's inexperienced, haphazard leadership and his tremendous political weakness prevented this philo-Bolivarian populist from taking advantage of the pronounced institutional weakness prevailing in contemporary Peru for advancing his autocratic inclinations. This case of populist failure shows that high instability is not a sufficient condition for the downfall of democracy; on its own, without the conjunctural opportunities specified in my theory, it does not automatically bring an authoritarian involution. Though precarious, democracy therefore survived Castillo's machinations as well as his dramatic eviction, sealed with the constitutional succession of his vice-president. Given Peru's high instability, however, liberal pluralism could potentially fall prey to a more competent populist, if conjunctural opportunities were to appear. The violent countrywide protests that have persisted after Castillo's ouster, for instance (Peru: A Country Tearing Itself Apart 2023), may eventually cause a double crisis in the economy and in public security, which could pave the way for a right-wing, Fujimori-style populist, perhaps his daughter Keiko, to restore the kind of autocracy that the Andean Samurai had imposed.

CONTAINED POPULISM WITH LIMITED WINDFALL RENTS:
THE KIRCHNERS IN ARGENTINA

Like Peru's recent populists, Argentina's couple of left-wing Peronists, Néstor Kirchner (2003–7) and Cristina Fernández de Kirchner (2007–15), were hindered by the absence of a massive hydrocarbon windfall. As in the Andean country, the global commodities boom benefited primarily private producers, whereas governments faced limitations in their tax take and their corresponding capacity to garner support through massive benefit programs. Moreover, like Peru's Humala, the Kirchners faced an institutional framework of medium strength, which they proved unable to dismantle or bend toward authoritarianism. For these two reasons, liberal pluralism in the Southern Cone country survived a long stretch of personalistic plebiscitarian governance.

As regards institutional constraints, the democracy restored in 1983 after seven years of exceptionally brutal military rule commanded great legitimacy and a good deal of strength. To leave behind the anomaly of a cruel dictatorship, Argentina reinstated its longstanding constitution of 1853. A broadly representative assembly then reformed the old charter in 1994, based on a negotiated agreement among the country's two major parties. This balanced deal allowed for one immediate reelection but limited presidential powers, such as executive decree authority (Negretto 2013: 140–65; Corrales 2018: 60–61; see Chapter 3). A vibrant civil society sustained by a strong educated middle class and a comparatively well-organized labor movement stood ready to defend liberal pluralism with fierce determination. The democratic framework indeed proved its resilience by surviving years of economic stagnation after 1998 and a traumatic crash in 2001–2. While four presidents fell in quick succession in a two-week spasm, Congress quickly closed this hiatus of instability by installing an experienced leader of the powerful Peronist movement as interim president. Therefore, the regime as such did not face serious challenges (Diamint 2006: 163–64, 173–76; Epstein and Pion-Berlin 2006: 12).

Given its middling institutional strength, Argentina avoided the fate of Venezuela, where Hugo Chávez had initially benefited from the severe downturn of 1998 and the country's high instability to launch his resolute march into competitive authoritarianism (see earlier). By contrast, the robustness of Argentine democracy impeded such a radical new start, including the emergence of a total outsider like the Venezuelan coup monger. Instead, Néstor Kirchner won in 2003 as one of three presidential candidates simultaneously fielded by the Peronist movement, which had recently governed under neoliberal populist Carlos Menem (1989–99), as examined in Chapter 3 (Levitsky and Murillo 2005: 40–42). Yet Kirchner ended up with a weak mandate because he garnered only 22 percent of the vote in the contest's first round; and his strongest rival, ex-president Menem, anticipated certain defeat and withdrew from the runoff, thus depriving the victor of a clear triumph (Cheresky 2006: 216–20; Epstein and Pion-Berlin 2006: 13; Mora y Araujo 2011: 100–1, 135–37; Roberts 2014: 255).

To compensate for this lame start and demonstrate charisma, Kirchner quickly used his presidential attributions to fortify his leadership through a burst of bold initiatives and deliberate confrontations with established power centers (Levitsky and Murillo 2005: 42–43; Cheresky 2006: 205–8; Mora y Araujo 2011: 141–42; Ollier 2015: 66–72; Andrews-Lee 2021: 184–85). But despite these typically populist efforts to boost his clout, the new president left the institutional framework intact and did not promote an overhaul of the constitution, contrary to Chávez. In the hard-won democracy, any forceful effort to dismantle checks and balances and propel executive aggrandizement looked unpromising and was bound to provoke ample resistance. The country's electoral procedures and guarantees of free and fair contests also remained untouched. Argentina's medium degree of institutionalization thus helped protect democracy from the temptation of a populist assault.

In fact, Kirchner did not even need to push for institutional change in order to achieve populists' most basic goal, namely perpetuation in power. Because his wife Cristina Fernández de Kirchner was also a prominent politician, the power couple could avoid term limits by simply alternating in the presidency (Morales Solá 2007; Schamis 2013: 173–74; Ollier 2015). This conjugal arrangement allowed for a lengthy stretch of populist governance. Thus, it lowered the Kirchners' incentive to distort regime institutions, impose political hegemony with para-legal means, and move toward competitive authoritarianism.

The substantial yet limited political payoffs of the global commodities boom seemed to make this savvy strategy viable and realistic. After the near-collapse of 2001–2, Argentina's economy recovered very quickly from mid-2002 onward (Mora y Araujo 2011: 134, 138), for two reasons. First, marking distance from fellow Peronist and neoliberal populist Carlos Menem, Néstor Kirchner rejected market-oriented adjustment and instead charted an interventionist and nationalist course. In particular, employing typical populist boldness, he renegotiated his country's huge foreign debt at a steep discount and thus reduced the outflow of resources.[23] Second, Argentina's large agricultural sector benefited from China's hunger for foodstuffs and the corresponding jump in international prices (Calvo and Murillo 2012: 151). With production soaring and GDP growth reaching 8–9 percent from 2003 to 2007, this bonanza boosted Néstor Kirchner's popularity ratings, strengthened his political support, and fueled Cristina's clear presidential victory in 2007 (Mora y Araujo 2011: 25, 101–2, 136, 140–44, 151–52).

The Argentine power couple never achieved the unstoppable predominance of Hugo Chávez, however, nor his prowess in the electoral arena (Mora y Araujo 2011: 142–43, 148–49, 156–57). Indeed, Cristina Fernández did not even win a majority in 2007; her 45.3 percent of votes paled before Chávez's initial 56.2 percent in 1998 and his reelection with 59.8 percent in 2000. One main reason was that Venezuela's oil industry was state-owned, which gave the Bolivarian populist direct and full control over the massive revenue influx. By contrast, like much of Peru's diversified export sector, Argentine agriculture was in private hands. Therefore, only in indirect ways did the unprecedented boom provide the Kirchners with windfall rents, namely via taxation. When Cristina tried to push the limits with a substantial rate increase, landowners offered ferocious resistance.[24] Facing fiscal constraints, the left-wing Peronists never enacted the variety of generous benefit programs with which Chávez raised his support to stratospheric levels (Etchemendy and Garay 2011: 295–96; Wylde 2011: 441). For all of these reasons, the Kirchners intended to confine themselves to dominating the government with their scheme of presidential alternation, but did not seriously undermine, distort, or smother democracy (Gervasoni 2015: 23–27).

The limited political payoffs of the commodities boom and the resulting absence of overwhelming clout then precluded an assault on liberal pluralism when a personal accident obliterated the Kirchners' savvy plan of perpetuation in the presidency: Unexpectedly, Néstor died in 2010. While this tragedy helped the mourning widow win reelection in 2011 (Mora y Araujo 2011: 95–96, 152; Schamis 2013: 175; Cherny 2014: 156; Andrews-Lee 2021: 186), the problem now was how to secure populist governance for the long term. For this purpose, Cristina Kirchner's diehard supporters sought to abolish the two-term limit enshrined in the reformed constitution of 1994 (Los ultra K quieren reformar la Constitución 2011; Corrales 2018: 212).

But this plan never went beyond a trial balloon, which drew fierce resistance, including large-scale protests in 2012. By then, the incumbent enjoyed limited popularity due to her typically populist penchant for confrontation (Ollier 2015: 81). Because the lack of massive benefit distribution had precluded her from winning widespread backing, she had brashly pushed her

---

[23] Broder 2005: 144–48; Etchemendy and Garay 2011: 289–90; Wylde 2011: 436–39, 447–48.
[24] Kirchners v the Farmers 2008; Calvo and Murillo 2012: 153–54; Wylde 2016: 334–36.

weight around, engaged in incessant conflict, and put growing pressure on independent media (Gervasoni 2015: 24–44). Given many Argentines' aversion to autocratic behavior, Fernández de Kirchner did not manage to achieve a convincing victory in the congressional midterm contest of 2013. Therefore, her supporters lacked the votes to engineer a constitutional amendment on continued reelection. As a result, this left-wing populist was compelled to step down after her second term in 2015.[25]

In conclusion, Argentina's middling levels of institutional solidity protected its democracy against populism's illiberal designs. Consequently, the economic collapse of 2001–2 did not allow President Kirchner to impose his total predominance. As his Peronist predecessor, neoliberal populist Menem, had noticed a decade earlier, a single deep crisis was not sufficient for strangling democracy; only the simultaneous double crisis that Fujimori encountered in Peru paved the road toward competitive authoritarianism.

In the absence of high instability, the global commodities boom did not allow for a successful assault on democracy à la Chávez either. Indeed, in Argentina, the international bonanza benefited primarily private business people, who limited state extraction by strongly opposing tax increases. Thus, the Kirchners did not have the same conjunctural opportunity that a windfall of state-controlled hydrocarbon rents gifted to the Bolivarian leader. For all of these reasons, liberal pluralism survived a dozen years of populist government in Argentina.

POPULISM FACING AN INSURMOUNTABLE INSTITUTIONAL CONSTRAINT: AMLO IN MEXICO

Andrés Manuel López Obrador in Mexico (2018–present) has faced even greater constraints to his evident power hunger than the Kirchners in Argentina. When the persistent populist finally won the presidency on his third attempt, the global commodities boom had clearly passed, so he could not benefit from a resource bonanza. Moreover, Mexico's 1917 constitution enshrined a particularly strong institutional obstacle to the driving ambition of personalistic plebiscitarian politicians, namely a sacrosanct prohibition of presidential reelection. In the absence of truly overwhelming support, Mexico's charismatic leader has not managed to eliminate or bend this ironclad rule and prepare his self-perpetuation in power. Thus, the headstrong president has encountered neither one of the necessary preconditions for the populist suffocation of democracy: neither institutional weakness nor a propitious conjunctural opportunity. As a result, liberal pluralism is likely to survive his six-year term.[26]

---

[25] The ex-president made a comeback in 2019, but only as vice-president under a non-populist president from her Peronist Party (Murillo and Zarazaga 2020).

[26] I thank German Petersen and especially Jonatán Lemus for many interesting comments, observations, reflections, and newspaper articles on the Mexican case.

Different from most other left-wing populists, AMLO did not rise as a political outsider. Instead, he had earned his political spurs as a member of Mexico's long-governing Institutional Revolutionary Party (PRI), which had "routinized" the charismatic, populist legacy of mythical president Lázaro Cárdenas (1934–40) by building a nationwide organizational apparatus that controlled major interest groups and population sectors through state-corporatist arrangements (Reyna and Weinert 1977). As the PRI ceded to the urgent economic need of imposing neoliberal adjustment and structural market reform in the 1980s, AMLO joined the breakaway faction committed to the party's original state-interventionist and social-distributive project, which formed the Party of the Democratic Revolution (PRD) (Bolívar Meza 2017: 108–9).

AMLO charted a distinctly personalistic, populist path, however, for which his election as head of Mexico City's federal district (2000–6) gave him a prominent platform. Headstrong, independent-minded, and driven by the goal of establishing his political supremacy, AMLO ran as the PRD candidate in the presidential election of 2006. Refusing to accept his exceedingly narrow loss by 0.56 percent of the vote, he spearheaded months-long protests against alleged fraud and inaugurated himself as the country's "legitimate president" in a makeshift ceremony on Mexico City's huge central square (*Zócalo*) right outside the presidential palace. The fervent mobilization of his core following, and the support networks that he had taken from the PRI into the PRD (cf. Petersen and Somuano 2021: 366–68) and that he had further extended as head of the federal district, allowed AMLO to survive his 2006 defeat and run again in 2012. After a renewed loss, this time by a more decisive margin, his domineering leadership started to face serious questions inside the PRD (Bolívar Meza 2014: 29–35).

In typical populist fashion, however, AMLO was determined to pursue his personalistic goal of becoming president. Therefore, he broke away from the PRD and formed his own electoral vehicle, the Movement of National Regeneration (MORENA; also an appeal to Mexico's darker-skinned – *morena* – mestizo majority, see Elizondo 2021: 84). Predictably, the new formation has lacked firm institutionalization and has remained under AMLO's complete control (Navarrete Vela, Camacho Sánchez, and Ceja García 2017: 21; Bruhn 2021).

In turn, the continuing challenge from this populist maverick (Bruhn 2012) helped induce Mexico's established parties, which by now included the remainder of the PRD, to undertake a major effort to overhaul the country's development model, stimulate economic growth, and promote greater social equity through profound regulatory, fiscal, and educational reforms. President Enrique Peña Nieto (2012–18) therefore managed to forge a novel "Pact for Mexico" among the country's three main parties, which paved the way for the congressional approval of several ambitious structural transformations (Elizondo 2021: 259–60, 364–70, 417–18, 422–23). These promising

initiatives encountered considerable opposition, passive resistance, and inertia in the implementation phase, however. Moreover, Peña Nieto suffered
increasing disrepute because of rampant corruption in his entourage and in
the governing PRI.

As the incumbent's star fell, AMLO's political fortunes rose again. After
all, the cooperation of the main established parties through the reform pact
had turned the left-wing populist into the single most outstanding opposition
leader (Elizondo 2021: 17). Growing revulsion against Mexico's "political
class" and popular disaffection at the meager political and socioeconomic payoffs of the country's democratic transition of 2000 enabled AMLO to win the
2018 contest in a landslide. As this charismatic leader captured the presidency
by more than thirty percentage points ahead of his main rival, his fledgling
movement, MORENA, together with some smaller allies, also won majorities
in the bicameral Congress, including a supermajority in the lower chamber
(Elizondo 2021: 91–95, 102–4).

Because AMLO already controlled all the elected branches of government,
he initiated a systematic, patient effort to take over the sole remaining veto
player at the national level, namely the judiciary. Slowly but surely, he used
his appointment powers and his partisan support in Congress to promote new
judges aligned with his movement, while trying to push out some magistrates
nominated by his predecessors (Elizondo 2021: 143–54; Aguilar Rivera 2022:
370). He also leaned hard on Mexico's electoral authorities and sought to
subdue them through accusations and intimidation (Petersen and Somuano
2021: 362–65; Dresser 2022: 84). Besides fully exploiting his presidential
attributions and his majority backing in the legislature, AMLO also leveraged
his impressive popularity: After a slow decline from their initial sky-high levels, his approval ratings stabilized at around 60 percent from 2020 onward,
despite the sharp economic recession caused by the COVID-19 pandemic and
the government's incompetent and unnecessarily costly response to this massive health challenge (Buendía and Márquez 2021: 3; Sánchez-Talanquer and
Greene 2021: 66–67).

Yet despite these important strengths, which created grave concerns about
the autocratic inclinations of this headstrong populist (see, e.g., Silva-Herzog
Márquez 2020: 151, 171, 179), AMLO has not succeeded in strangling
Mexico's democracy and imposing his personalistic supremacy (contra Aguilar
Rivera 2022; Dresser 2022). While eagerly concentrating power, attacking
other political forces with broadsides and insults (Espino 2021: 175–88), and
pressuring and straining various liberal institutions and civil society groupings
(Elizondo 2021: 138–54, 161–68; Petersen and Somuano 2021: 355–65), he
has not managed seriously to disadvantage the partisan opposition or skew the
electoral arena. Instead, the crucial midterm elections of 2021 were free and
fair – and they produced a setback for MORENA and its allies, which made
it impossible for the president to rely on supermajorities and single-handedly
change the constitution (Sánchez-Talanquer and Greene 2021: 61–62, 65,

68–69; Aguilar Rivera 2022: 364–67, 377). With the direct route to amending Mexico's charter foreclosed, AMLO has – despite a variety of trial balloons, initiatives, and forays – not found a way to overcome the strict limit on every populist's most fundamental ambition, namely Mexico's deeply entrenched prohibition on presidential reelection.

In line with my theory, the two fundamental reasons that have impeded AMLO's self-perpetuation in power are Mexico's significant institutional strength and the absence of propitious conjunctural opportunities. First, while Mexico's democracy is still fairly young, its vulnerability to institutional manipulation is low and the liberal framework has proven resilient. For instance, a governmental effort to block AMLO's first presidential candidacy through a trick of discriminatory legalism failed – and backfired – in 2005 (Elizondo 2021: 35–36). Also, the fear that the 2012 presidential victory of the PRI, the mainstay of Mexico's authoritarian regime for seven decades, would usher in a regression to nondemocracy did not come true. Indeed, in 2018 the PRI incumbent made no effort to hinder AMLO's electoral campaign or block his victory (Elizondo 2021: 10, 112, 138).

While these experiences demonstrate the general resilience of Mexico's democracy, the strongest institutional obstacle against the populist march toward illiberalism and authoritarianism is the constitutional prohibition of presidential reelection, the iron law of Mexican politics. Its deep historical roots make this rule virtually insurmountable. Fueled by strident opposition to a long-ruling personalistic dictator (Porfirio Díaz, 1876–1911), "no reelection!" emerged as a major battle cry of the Mexican Revolution, the critical juncture giving rise to modern Mexico (see recently Corrales 2018: 194). Since 1910, this basic limitation on executive predominance has been upheld so fervently that violators risk death: When post-revolutionary president Álvaro Obregón (1920–24) engineered his reelection in 1928, an assassin violently forestalled his return to power. This drastic enforcement further enshrined the prohibition, such that supremely popular president Lázaro Cárdenas (1934–40) decided to forego another candidacy, despite the near-certainty of an electoral triumph. Like this revered founder of Mexico's institutionalized regime, every subsequent president, even during the height of authoritarian rule (1940s–1970s), governed for exactly six years, and then stepped down right on schedule. This taming of the quest for personalistic preeminence, which is highly unusual for a long-running autocracy (cf. Svolik 2012), proves the strength of the one-term limit.

All these precedents turned the principle of no presidential reelection rock solid and exceedingly difficult to overcome, even for a personalistic plebiscitarian leader. Facing this brick wall to his populist urge to stay in power beyond Mexico's sacrosanct six-year term, AMLO floated some ideas and proposals that could, perhaps, enable him to evade this limitation. As Venezuela's Chávez had done in his new 1999 constitution, the Mexican leader had his congressional followers institute a presidential recall election.

Was the underlying plan that AMLO could stay on beyond 2024 unless he were recalled – which his stable majority support would prevent (Elizondo 2021: 532; Mexico Election Outcome Forces Recall Referendum Rethink 2021)? Opposition concerns grew when AMLO's partisans in Congress, in an openly unconstitutional way, lengthened the term of the Supreme Court head, a presidential ally. Could this precedent be applied to the presidential mandate as well, and would the lead judge, now in office through 2024, legitimate and certify such an extension?

All these exploratory forays and potential preparations came to naught, however, with the disappointing vote haul of MORENA and its coalition partners in the midterm elections of 2021. Without supermajorities in both houses of Congress, constitutional limitations were much harder to evade, bend, or eliminate (Sánchez-Talanquer and Greene 2021: 61–62, 65, 68–69). Indeed, when AMLO tried to regain the initiative by spearheading a politicized referendum against Mexico's old political class, he suffered an embarrassing defeat by achieving a strikingly low turnout of only 7 percent of eligible voters.[27] Weakened in his political standing, the incumbent backed away from forays toward self-perpetuation and started instead to nominate and vet pre-candidates for his succession in 2024. Furthermore, the head of the Supreme Court closed one of the potential loopholes by refusing to accept the unconstitutional extension of his own term (Mexico: Power Struggles in Judiciary 2021: 11). Indeed, his replacement by an independent-minded judge in early 2023 deprived AMLO of a strategically placed ally, reaffirmed judicial autonomy, and thus resuscitated Mexico's eroded system of checks and balances (Judicial Independence Stressed 2023; cf. Aguilar Rivera 2022: 370).

In sum, AMLO faced an unusually strong institutional obstacle to populist self-perpetuation in Mexico's fundamental no reelection rule. Any prospect of suspending or overcoming this hurdle was foreclosed by the political setbacks of mid-2021. Why, however, did the charismatic president suffer these setbacks, rather than sweeping the midterm elections and obliterating the partisan opposition through a massive referendum victory? In line with my theory, the second crucial limitation to AMLO's personalistic power hunger arose from the absence of conjunctural opportunities for winning huge, truly overwhelming support. The incumbent benefited neither from a huge revenue boost nor an acute, severe crisis that he could miraculously resolve.

Although Mexico is a major oil exporter, the end of the commodities boom prevented the government from receiving the enormous windfall that had boosted the political fortunes of Chávez, Correa, and Morales (Sánchez-Talanquer and Greene 2021: 67–68). By the time AMLO finally won the presidency, the bonanza of the early third millennium had busted. Moreover,

---

[27] Aguilar Rivera 2022: 369. Similarly, when AMLO held his recall referendum in early 2022, turnout only reached an anemic 17.8 percent (Reading into Mexico's Recall Result 2022).

whereas the Venezuelan populist had taken office during a sharp economic crisis, which had boosted his capacity to initiate profound change, Mexico in 2018 was in much less dire straits with its economic stability and modest growth. And when a catastrophic shock did irrupt in 2020, it came in the form of the COVID-19 pandemic, which was not susceptible to any quick, magic resolution. Instead, like so many other populist chief executives, including Trump and Bolsonaro, AMLO clearly failed to cope with this unprecedented health challenge in a competent and effective way. The resulting human costs have been enormous, amounting to over 600,000 excess deaths.[28] Because his charismatic prowess did not save Mexico, the left-wing populist did not manage to turn adversity into advantage and obtain political payoffs from this dangerous challenge.

Without propitious conjunctural opportunities, AMLO never achieved the extent and intensity of support that would have allowed him to bend or break the institutional obstacles he encountered, especially the reelection rule. While his personal aura and skillful populist discourse (Espino 2021) guaranteed high popularity levels of approximately 60 percent (Buendía and Márquez 2021: 3), the incumbent did not succeed in giving his backing the force of an irresistible steamroller, with which Chávez, Correa, and Morales had pushed through their illiberal, authoritarian designs. Indeed, from the beginning of his term, AMLO's support was not massive enough to allow for the complete overhaul of the established institutional framework through a constituent assembly (Elizondo 2021: 528; Aguilar Rivera 2022: 371; see also Carrillo Nieto 2020: 300–5, 312), the mechanism that the three Bolivarian populists had used to initiate the strangulation of democracy and that AMLO himself had advocated during his first presidential campaign in 2006.

For these reasons, Mexico's headstrong populist has not smothered liberal pluralism. Despite the substantial clout that he gained from the disrepute of the established parties and despite the majorities that MORENA for years commanded in Congress, the charismatic president did not manage to push aside liberal constraints on his power hunger and engineer his self-perpetuation. Instead, the absence of promising conjunctural opportunities, especially a hydrocarbon windfall or a drastic, yet resolvable crisis, prevented him from achieving the massive, fervent support that a profound transformation of Mexico's constitutional framework would have required. Indeed, the untouchable no reelection maxim posed an enormous obstacle to self-perpetuation and may have been sufficient on its own for protecting liberal pluralism against populist asphyxiation.

---

[28] Mexico's Populist President 2021: 19; Dresser 2022: 77; see also Elizondo 2021: 74–75, 273–76, 439–54; Espino 2021: 101–17; Sánchez-Talanquer and Greene 2021: 67; see in general Bayerlein et al. 2021; Meyer 2021: 3, 13–14; Foa et al. 2022.

CONCLUSION

As the variegated experiences examined in this chapter show, left-wing, Bolivarian populism in Latin America has been similar in its regime impact to the preceding right-wing, neoliberal variant. Despite their shared autocratic inclinations, both types of personalistic plebiscitarian leadership have asphyxiated liberal pluralism only under special, restrictive conditions. Some form of institutional weakness has to coincide with a specific conjunctural opportunity for charismatic chief executives to gain the overwhelming clout required for imposing their supremacy. Where either one of these necessary prerequisites is missing, democracy has a great chance of surviving, although it may suffer some damage. My interactive argument, corroborated through the comparative analysis of a comprehensive set of cases, means that the real danger that populism poses to liberal pluralism is not as severe as recent commentators have feared. Instead, democracy "dies" only in a minority of cases, as Chapter 3 found as well.

The constellation of factors that enable left-wing, Bolivarian chief executives to smother democracy are distinctive, however. Whereas right-wingers try to exploit severe crises and avert looming losses to achieve their fundamental conservative goal of restoring and safeguarding order, left-wingers depend on windfall gains to promote progressive change, especially social improvements. They use the abundance of resources provided by hydrocarbon booms, which allow them to boost the distribution of socioeconomic benefits and thus earn strong and widespread backing. With this powerful tailwind, they can take advantage of high institutional instability, push aside the remaining checks and balances, and achieve their hegemonic ambitions. This exceptional combination of huge revenue inflows and pronounced institutional debility allowed the three main Bolivarians – Chávez, Morales, and Correa – to install competitive authoritarianism.

By contrast, the absence of one of these necessary conditions protects liberal pluralism from assaults by left-wing populists. As the fate of Ecuador's Gutiérrez and the declining fortunes of his successor Correa in the mid-2010s show, before and after the global commodities boom of 2003–14, Bolivarian populism did not destroy democracy and had difficulty prolonging authoritarian rule; Bolivia's Morales was also weakened by the end of the bonanza. Where resource limitations coincide with middling institutional strength and stability, as in Argentina under the Kirchners, Peru under Humala, and Mexico under AMLO, liberal pluralism is even safer; because populism with its penchant for incessant confrontation faces constraints, the level of political conflict is lower. The exception was Honduras, where, despite such an unpropitious constellation, new Bolivarian convert Zelaya stubbornly pushed his power concentration project, and the opposition, excessively scared by the precedent of Chávez's assault, overreacted as well.[29] In this tragic case, a

---

[29] Chapter 7 discusses the role of diffusion in this case, in which a foreign model served as inspiration for one side of the ideological divide, yet as a deterrent for the other.

populist attempt at incumbent takeover failed, but only via a military coup. Thus, personalistic plebiscitarian leaders hailing from the left can provoke trouble for liberal pluralism not only through their own nefarious actions, but also by challenging their powerful opponents among elites and prompting them to defend their interests with all means, even by overthrowing democracy themselves.

5

Right-Wing and Traditionalist Populism in Europe

In analyzing populism's repercussions for democracy in Latin America, Chapters 3 and 4 have examined under what conditions presidential systems of government allow personalistic plebiscitarian leaders to undermine and eventually strangle liberal pluralism. This investigation found that, while high institutional instability carries particular risks, presidential systems of middling institutional strength create significant checks and balances that – while not hard to bend – prove quite difficult to crack.

By featuring mostly parliamentary (and some semi-presidential) systems of government, European democracies have a different institutional set-up. With the attenuated separation of power resulting from the political integration between parliamentary majorities and prime-ministerial governments, parliamentarism lacks the number of institutional veto players embodied in presidentialism's checks and balances. Consequently, institutional constraints on executive power tend to be significantly looser than under presidentialism, depending on the type of legislature (unicameral vs. bicameral), on the degree of judicial autonomy and strength, and, as a last line of defense, on constitutional rigidity.

However, by making governmental stability rest on ongoing party support in the legislature, parliamentarism empowers partisan veto players (Tsebelis 2002), whose number is shaped by societal cleavages and the electoral system. With the increasing complexity of post-industrial societies and the frequent use of proportional representation, the effective number of parties can be substantial. Accordingly, a single party rarely wins a majority that can sustain the government on its own. Instead, prime ministers must usually find partisan allies, which can be quite unreliable, due to programmatic and ideological differences or for strategic reasons, namely to use their pivotal position for extracting special concessions.

With this political-institutional configuration, parliamentary systems are formally quite open to transformative change; but chief executives' effective political clout – and the corresponding threat that a populist leader can pose to democracy – depends on their partisan powers. Accordingly, the risks arising from parliamentarism's institutional susceptibility to change are usually counterbalanced by party fragmentation, which impedes resolute power concentration by an ambitious prime minister. This obstacle only falls away if a populist leader can win a safe single-party majority, especially a supermajority that allows for an overhaul of the constitution.

Therefore, the second type of factor highlighted in my theory becomes crucial again, namely the conjunctural opportunities for personalistic politicians to win massive support. In Europe, acute economic crises have proven essential for populist leaders to achieve decisive victories over the established parties and obtain parliamentary majorities, if not supermajorities. Urgent economic problems that hurt large sectors of the population discredit the incumbent government and the forces sustaining it. By arousing demands for a new beginning, they open the door for challengers who promise to "save the people" from losses and chart a new course. Severe hardship gives resonance to charismatic appeals and enables personalistic plebiscitarian leaders to sweep the electoral arena.[1]

The "easy changeability" of parliamentarism means that a single pressing, yet resolvable crisis is sufficient for boosting the power of populist leaders to the levels required for smothering democracy with their hegemonic machinations.[2] This is a noteworthy contrast to Latin America's presidential systems of middling institutional strength, where only the unusual coincidence of two urgent crises paves the populist road to authoritarianism. Thus, the attenuated separation of powers embodied in parliamentarism makes it easier for personalistic politicians to assert their predominance; because they need less of a massive plebiscitarian boost, the conjunctural preconditions for achieving their nefarious goals are not as restrictive. Consequently, parliamentarism poses substantial risks for the maintenance of liberal pluralism.

This unexpected finding casts doubt on the criticism of presidentialism and advocacy of parliamentarism spearheaded by Juan Linz (1990; Linz and Valenzuela 1994). While the direct mandate and institutional autonomy of

---

[1] Europe, even its less developed eastern half, has not suffered from major public security crises during the time period under investigation. States command control over the national territory and thus forestall massive crime or political insurgencies; even terrorist attacks (as in Paris in November 2015) have remained sporadic. In the rare cases in which serious political violence did erupt, namely Yugoslavia and Moldova, open conflict was ended through the formal or informal dissolution of these countries, including the internal division of Bosnia and the separatism of Transnistria.

[2] Because European countries do not rely for their economic well-being on voluminous hydrocarbon exports, they cannot benefit from huge revenue windfalls. Therefore, the suppression of democracy by Latin America's Bolivarian presidents Chávez, Morales, and Correa, who garnered overwhelming support with the massive distribution of benefits and therefore managed to push aside the weak institutional constraints remaining under highly unstable presidentialism, has had no parallel in Europe.

popularly elected presidents can provide a propitious platform for the ambitious power drive of populist leaders, parliamentarism's weak checks and balances and the centrality of prime ministers offer such leaders a great deal of latitude and dominance as well. Consequently, my investigation finds that the rate at which populist chief executives asphyxiate democracy is, overall,[3] quite similar across the two different systems of government. Institutions clearly matter, but personalistic plebiscitarian politicians are savvy and take advantage of any available opportunity to augment their clout. Therefore, they can flourish in a variety of institutional settings – to the detriment of liberal pluralism.

The following sections demonstrate the importance of parliamentarism's institutional openness and the crucial role of economic crises by examining a broad set of populist administrations in Western and especially Eastern Europe. As in Chapters 3 and 4, the cases of personalistic plebiscitarian leaders who did suppress democracy, namely Recep Tayyip Erdoğan in Turkey (2003–present) and Viktor Orbán in Hungary (2010–present), anchor this discussion. Comparison and contrast then show how other cases differed in outcome because one or both of the factors highlighted in my theory were absent.

In their energetic quest for political hegemony, both Erdoğan and Orbán took advantage of the prime-ministerial powers provided by parliamentarism and the plebiscitarian opportunities arising from a sharp economic crisis. The Turkish leader, however, felt compelled to take a slow, winding road toward authoritarian rule. While the recession of 2001 enabled him to win a strong parliamentary majority, it was insufficient for unilateral changes of the constitution. Even more importantly, the new prime minister faced a dangerous informal veto player, namely an interventionist military. Erdoğan therefore needed many years for using his electoral prowess to impose his undemocratic preeminence, through a variety of deceptive tactics and unsavory machinations.

By contrast, the fallout of the global recession of 2008, which hit Hungary hard, gave opposition leader Orbán a groundswell of support, which the electoral system translated into a supermajority. As a result, the Magyar populist managed quickly to concentrate power by having his supporters approve a tailor-made constitution and by taking over all independent institutions, especially the judiciary. In smooth and formally legal ways, Orbán thus succeeded in advancing toward competitive authoritarianism. Because Hungary's personalistic plebiscitarian leader moved so fast and broke no official rules, the European Union found no way to block this descent into illiberalism and nondemocracy.

In other East European cases, by contrast, the absence of serious economic crises did not allow political outsiders to win clear majorities, especially supermajorities. Populists' limited clout has protected democracy from their hegemonic ambitions and autocratic projects. In contrast to Hungary, Poland is

---

[3] This assessment considers presidential systems of both middling institutional strength and those suffering from high instability.

particularly interesting with its ongoing struggles over liberal pluralism. Given sustained economic growth, the Law and Justice Party led by populist Jarosław Kaczyński won only the narrowest of majorities in 2015, which precluded a constitutional transformation à la Orbán. Moreover, Poland's democracy with its semi-presidential system and its bicameral legislature features a greater number of institutional veto players than Hungary. Consequently, the Warsaw government could not follow in the Magyar populist's footsteps. Instead, it resorted to a variety of para-legal machinations to push toward illiberalism. These controversial tactics provoked strong domestic opposition and mass contention, however, which together with intensifying European Union pressures have prevented a descent into authoritarian rule.

By contrast to Poland in the 2010s, Slovakia did face a huge economic crisis in the 1990s, but populist prime minister Vladimír Mečiar (1990–91, 1992–94, 1994–98) had no way of resolving it. After all, while the collapse of communism caused a catastrophic downturn, its deep structural roots precluded any quick recovery. Because he was unable to "save the people," this openly autocratic leader could not win parliamentary majorities. Weakened by unreliable coalition partners, the Slovak populist pursued his undemocratic goals with blatantly transgressive means. In reaction, an upsurge in support for the opposition brought his electoral defeat in 1998 and relieved Slovak democracy of authoritarian pressures.

As the absence of a resolvable crisis hobbled and cut short Mečiar's attack on democracy, the same lack of a propitious conjunctural opportunity limited the political clout of numerous other populist prime ministers in Eastern Europe, including Mečiar's eventual successor Robert Fico (2006–10, 2012–18), Romania's Traian Băsescu (2004–7, 2007–12, 2012–14), Bulgaria's Boyko Borisov (2009–13, 2014–17, 2017–21), Slovenia's Janez Janša (2004–8, 2012–13, 2020–22), and the Czech Republic's Andrej Babiš (2017–21). Because their parties did not command legislative majorities, these chief executives had to depend on other political forces as coalition partners. The resulting limitations on their power precluded major political-institutional transformations, especially constitutional changes that could have done serious damage to democracy. Instead, the populist leaders confined themselves to advancing their own interests and benefiting their cronies through informal machinations, shady patronage deals, and growing corruption, which eventually led to their downfall, mostly via electoral defeat, but in Slovakia via mass protests in 2018. While soiled and sullied, democracy therefore survived populist governance in a number of East European countries.

Interestingly, the same process unfolded in Italy, where the party system's collapse in a monumental corruption scandal opened the door for billionaire tycoon Silvio Berlusconi to vault into the premiership in 1994. But in the absence of an economic crisis, the flashy populist was far from winning a parliamentary majority for his electoral vehicle. Instead, during his three stints as chief executive (1994–95, 2001–6, 2008–11), Berlusconi had to hold together coalition governments. He therefore lacked the predominance required for dismantling democracy and moving toward illiberalism. Indeed, with his polarizing discourse, his conflicts of interest, and his personal indiscretions, the Italian populist provoked so much resistance from independent institutions, especially the judiciary, and vocal opposition from civil society that democracy escaped unscathed from his many years in the premiership.

The comparative case studies thus show that in Europe's parliamentary systems with their attenuated checks and balances, the populist suffocation of democracy depends on the irruption of a grave and pressing, yet resolvable economic crisis. Downturns of this type enabled Orbán and Erdoğan to win clear parliamentary majorities and push toward authoritarian rule. By contrast, a structural collapse that was not easy to overcome, or fairly normal, noncrisis conditions, precluded personalistic plebiscitarian leaders from obtaining the overwhelming clout needed to impose their power concentration projects. As in Latin America, the interaction of a specific form of institutional weakness and of distinctive conjunctural developments shaped the effective threat of populism. Because these necessary preconditions for the suffocation of democracy do not often coincide, the fate of liberal pluralism is less dire than often feared.

As the specific causal factors that condition the regime outcomes of populist experiences in Europe differ from Latin America, most of Europe's charismatic politicians also diverge in their political orientation from the two groups of personalistic plebiscitarian leaders examined in Chapters 3 and 4. Historically speaking, populism in Latin America tended toward the nationalist, state-interventionist, moderately redistributive left of the political-ideological spectrum (see recently Rovira Kaltwasser 2019: 37–39; Souroujon and Lesgart 2021: 56–59). The Bolivarianism of the 2000s in many ways resumed and modernized this tradition, as indicated by Hugo Chávez's reliance on an Argentine Peronist as one of his main early advisers (Ceresole 2000). Unusually, the regional debt crisis and hyperinflation of the late 1980s and early 1990s gave rise to a right-wing version of populism, which had a distinctly neoliberal bent.

By contrast, European populism tends to be right wing, but nationalist and increasingly state-interventionist in its economic orientation. Moreover, it is culturally conservative, if not reactionary, and xenophobic and exclusionary in its growing animus against immigrants and Muslims.[4] While there is considerable variation among Europe's personalistic plebiscitarian leaders of the last three decades – with Italy's Berlusconi more centrist and Poland's Kaczyński hard-core right wing – many of these populists, especially in recent years, have embraced some version of cultural traditionalism.[5]

---

[4] For a systematic presentation of these orientations by a populist "ideologue," see Legutko 2018; for an insightful and provocative interpretation, see Krastev and Holmes 2019: chap. 1; see also Bill and Stanley 2020; Enyedi 2020; Coman and Volintiru 2021.

[5] Left-wing populists have rarely won chief executive office in Europe. The emblematic exception is Alexis Tsipras in Greece (2015, 2015–19), whose radical-left movement-party

A LONG AND WINDING ROAD TOWARD POPULIST
AUTHORITARIANISM: ERDOĞAN IN TURKEY

The institutional and conjunctural factors highlighted in my theory came together in the early 2000s in Turkey, enabling populist leader Recep Tayyip Erdoğan to smother democracy over the course of his lengthy tenure in office. Specifically, a deep economic crisis at the turn of the millennium allowed his Islamist party to win a clear legislative majority, which then faced weak checks and balances in the country's parliamentary system. Leveraging the resulting predominance, the "new Sultan" (Cagaptay 2017; see also Yavuz 2021: 136, 243, 317) extended his political clout and institutional attributions step by step. Once he had established authoritarian hegemony, he tried to secure his command over the government by replacing Turkey's parliamentarism with a (hyper)presidential system. While consistently pursuing the typically personalistic goal of enhancing his own autonomy and power, Erdoğan was forced, however, to take an unusually sinuous route in order to remove a peculiar obstacle, namely the military's tutelary role over Turkish democracy, as explained shortly.

In his effort to win political supremacy, Erdoğan was initially helped by "the worst economic and financial crisis in modern Turkish history," which caused GDP to drop by 6 percent in 2001 (Özel 2003: 82; see also 82–86; Aytaç and Öniş 2014: 48–50; Cagaptay 2017: 84–85; Yavuz 2021: 14–17, 97, 129–33). This sharp recession further undermined popular support for the established, rather corrupt secularist parties, which had seen their standing eroded over the years by the irresistible advance of political Islam, its ever stronger bid for power, and the resulting political divisions and governability problems. By promising economic recovery and political renewal, the

surprisingly forged a governing alliance with a formation of radical-right populists (Aslanidis 2021). Interestingly, the political-regime impact of this unusual experience conforms to my theory. Tsipras achieved electoral victory in 2015, years after the country's massive economic crisis had hit rock bottom in 2011; indeed, 2014 had brought slight growth. More importantly, the bailout conditions imposed by external creditors and the EU forced additional austerity measures and thus precluded any expansionary boost through which the populist prime minister could have brought quick and decisive relief and proved his charisma; instead of expanding, his plebiscitarian support therefore shrank (Rori 2020: 1024, 1028–29; Tsatsanis, Teperoglou, and Seriatos 2020: 505–6). The political weakness resulting from the impossibility of resolving the crisis prevented the government from pushing through institutional and constitutional changes (Pappas 2020: 62). As Tsipras could augment his autonomy and clout only through controversial efforts to intimidate the press and undermine judicial independence, the main opposition party, which raised the banner of defending liberal democracy, won increasing backing (Pappas 2020: 63–65). Weakened by a courageous foreign policy decision, which finally exploded his ideologically incongruent coalition (Aslanidis 2021: 643–44), Greece's personalistic leader lost the parliamentary elections of 2019 in a landslide, paving the way for the recovery of liberal pluralism (Rori 2020: 1031–34; Tsatsanis, Teperoglou, and Seriatos 2020: 521–28).

charismatic Erdoğan led his new, moderately Islamist party, over which he has exerted total personalistic predominance (Baykan 2018: 106, 122, 132–34, 167–88, 213–17, 226, 231, 251–52), to a convincing victory in the 2002 elections. Because Turkey's electoral system translated the 34.3 percent vote plurality of this Justice and Development Party (AKP) into a parliamentary seat majority of 66 percent, the new prime minister could take advantage of the institutional openings provided by the country's parliamentary system and its fairly flexible constitution (Yegen 2017).

Initially, however, Erdoğan faced an unusual roadblock and saw himself compelled to take a tactical detour in order to protect his populist project from a potentially lethal threat. After all, the populist leader's Islamist background and inclinations threatened to provoke a forceful intervention by Turkey's military, the longstanding guardian and enforcer of the secularism that Mustafa Kemal Atatürk had imposed at the foundation of the republic in the 1920s and 1930s (Turan 2015: 47–48, 52–53, 191–96). To stem the resurgence of political Islamism from the 1970s onward, the armed forces had on several occasions prohibited religious parties and pressured their governments, most recently by pushing Islamist prime minister Necmettin Erbakan from office in 1997 (Özel 2003: 87–88; Phillips 2017: 17–21; Baykan 2018: 48–50). Indeed, Erdoğan himself suffered four months of imprisonment in 1999 because as mayor of Istanbul he had publicly read an inflammatory fundamentalist poem at a mass rally (Guiler 2021: 179–81; Yavuz 2021: 123–26). When he took over the government in early 2003, he could feel the generals' watchful eyes on his neck. In the following years, his government and his party indeed faced serious challenges from military circles and their allies entrenched in state institutions, especially the judiciary, in 2007 and 2008 (Baykan 2018: 54–58; Yavuz 2021: 21–23, 99–100, 142–58; Cleary and Öztürk 2022: 214).

To safeguard his personalistic leadership against this extra-official "veto player" (cf. Tsebelis 2002: 81) and gain the necessary latitude for advancing his populist and Islamist project, Erdoğan had to break the military's stranglehold. For this purpose, he cleverly invoked the basic democratic principle of popular sovereignty to contest the tutelage of the unelected military. In this way, he targeted the Achilles' heel of Turkish secularism. After all, while Atatürk's purge of Islam from the public sphere had played a crucial role in allowing Turkey to become much more democratic than most other countries in the Middle East, the gradual advance of Islamism among the mass citizenry, especially in the vast Anatolian hinterlands (Çarkoğlu and Hinich 2006: 370–75), made the maintenance of secularism dependent on military enforcement, a practice of questionable democratic legitimacy.

Erdoğan skillfully exploited this glaring paradox by initially appealing to liberal pluralism in order to push the armed forces out of politics and thus remove the sword of Damocles hanging over his head. With these goals in mind, the new prime minister sought and obtained support from domestic and foreign pro-democratic forces, including the European Union (Goodman 2018; Yavuz 2021: 134–35, 1139–40, 149, 289, 315). He then leveraged this backing for sustained efforts to break the military's independent clout, culminating in mass trials of generals on trumped-up and manipulated charges of conspiracy against his democratically elected government (Esen and Gumuscu 2016: 1584–86; Cagaptay 2017: 94, 106–17; Phillips 2017: 23–28; Yavuz 2021: 158–60, 195–96, 211–18, 224).

Once he had shoved the armed forces back into the barracks and thus secured his own tenure in office against the risk of sudden interruption, Erdoğan made a fundamental and sustained turnaround, abandoned liberal-pluralist initiatives, and systematically propelled his hegemonic project (Cagaptay 2017: 115–29; Somer 2019: 48–55). For this purpose, he drew on the strong and intense plebiscitarian support that he gained from fomenting Turkey's economic recovery and subsequent boom (Cagaptay 2017: 91–93). Moreover, this backing rested on his cautious but steady promotion of Islamist practices, their official recognition by the state, and their readmission into the public sphere (Yavuz 2021: 77–95, 130–32). This traditionalist cultural project was symbolized by the stepwise transformation of Hagia Sophia, the country's most famous religious monument, from a museum back into a mosque, a striking reversal of a high-profile act of Atatürk's imposition of secularism. By also building huge new mosques in visible locations, such as Istanbul's iconic Taksim Square and a hill majestically overlooking the Bosporus (Cagaptay 2017: 29, 128–29), the prime minister appealed to the numerically strong Muslim segments of the population, who had felt excluded and oppressed by Atatürk's eviction of religiosity from the public realm (Çarkoğlu and Hinich 2006: 370–75). Erdoğan's economic accomplishments and anti-secularist measures combined to strengthen the same large groupings in Turkey's vast provinces, especially a prospering Anatolian business and middle class (Hadiz 2014: 125–35; Baykan 2018: 83–87).

The resulting strong and firm popular backing allowed Erdoğan to proceed with his illiberal turnaround (Dinçşahin 2012: 630–39). Slowly but surely, he cemented his political hegemony and command over the state, co-opted, divided, and combated the opposition, and put increasing pressure on the press and civil society (Esen and Gumuscu 2016: 1586–95). Because the prime minister already controlled the executive and legislative branches in Turkey's parliamentary system, the crucial target of his push for supremacy was the judiciary. The new Sultan therefore used his appointment powers and informal pressures to spearhead a systematic takeover of the country's courts (Yavuz 2021: 160–62). His overbearing influence over jurisdiction then enabled Erdoğan to harass and intimidate political opponents and independent forces in civil society. After he had employed this discriminatory legalism in the trials against leading generals mentioned earlier, he turned it into an increasingly forceful and effective weapon against civilian adversaries during the 2010s, especially after the 2016 coup attempt discussed later.

Once Erdoğan had gained political hegemony and established a stranglehold over Turkey's suffocated democracy, he pushed hard for a transformation of the system of government. Whereas parliamentarism with its comparatively easy changeability had allowed the power-hungry populist to dismantle the remaining constraints on his latitude and accumulate predominant power, he now sought to cement his supremacy by securing his hold over the executive branch. To become independent of potentially changeable majorities in parliament, he wanted to create and then occupy a directly elected, powerful presidency: an institutionally safer base that also augmented his prestige by making him head of state. In the typically populist quest for preeminent power, he sought to erect a hyper-presidential system with a chief executive unencumbered by effective checks and balances (Yavuz 2021: 25, 136, 196–97, 249–52).

While Erdoğan faced resistance against this centralizing constitutional overhaul from opposition parties and civil society, and even from some leaders of his own party, his plebiscitarian mass base was strong and broad enough to guarantee victory. Sustained economic success and popular appreciation for the reassertion of Islam, especially in Turkey's far-flung heartland, allowed him to outflank his liberal critics in the country's urban centers, especially cosmopolitan Istanbul (Baykan 2018: 83–95). Consequently, the populist leader had the clout to repress pro-democratic protests that erupted in major cities in 2013 and to defeat a dangerous and bloody military uprising, a last-ditch effort to block his power concentration project, in 2016 (Öniş 2015: 28–31; Phillips 2017: 36–41, 165–74).

Indeed, with fierce determination, Erdoğan took advantage of the ill-planned and ill-fated coup attempt to rally the mass citizenry around his flag. After the failed rebellion, he greatly intensified his attack on liberal pluralism with large-scale purges and innumerable arrests.[6] In this resolute fashion, he removed any suspected critic or potential defector from the public administration, especially the military, and severely intimidated the remaining personnel. He also cracked down on the political opposition, especially the pro-Kurdish People's Democratic Party (HDP), which had spearheaded a liberal-democratic challenge to his increasingly autocratic rule in mid-2015; this HDP initiative had helped to inflict on the AKP a surprising electoral defeat, which Erdoğan skillfully reversed in a new contest a few months later (Öniş 2016; Cagaptay 2017: 180–82). To forestall any such threat to his political predominance in the future, the victorious populist used the groundswell of support that he

---

[6] Baykan 2018: 245–48; Christofis 2020: 2–3; Cleary and Öztürk 2022: 215. To what extent Erdoğan himself helped to provoke or even engineer this badly executed challenge remains unclear. In his thorough and exceedingly well-researched analysis of Erdoğan's government and regime, Yavuz (2021: 230–48) carefully examines various hypotheses and concludes that the president cornered coup mongers into making a desperate and risky move that played strongly into his own hands and ended up sealing the fate of Turkey's democracy (Yavuz 2021: 248–55).

gained after the military uprising and engineered the imprisonment of the HDP's leader on massively trumped-up charges in late 2016.

Widespread revulsion at the shocking coup attempt also gave Erdoğan the clout to overcome the lingering resistance to his constitutional transformation and push through the switch from parliamentarism to hyperpresidentialism; consequently, the office that he had won in a direct popular election in 2014 now became all-powerful.[7] In these ways, the personalistic plebiscitarian leader managed to seal his hegemony and bury democracy. After strangling liberal pluralism gradually since 2007, Erdoğan broke its neck after the military challenge of 2016 and instituted a competitive-authoritarian regime (Esen and Gumuscu 2016), if not a full-scale dictatorship (e.g., Phillips 2017). While the new Sultan's political position has weakened in recent years with a drastic economic downturn and more determined opposition efforts to form a unified coalition, his institutional grip over the Turkish polity is so firm and well entrenched that he may be difficult to dislodge in future electoral contests, which he is starting to skew significantly, for instance by banning opposition politicians (Topcu 2022; Erdogan's Empire 2023: 4, 11).

Erdoğan's asphyxiation of democracy thus exemplifies and substantiates the third path to the populist abolition of liberal pluralism that my theory specifies. Starting out in a parliamentary system with weak checks and balances, Turkey's Islamist populist profited from a severe economic crisis that enabled his party to win a clear legislative majority. The savvy leader used the resulting concentrated power in the beginning of his long tenure to eliminate an unusual obstacle to his quest for political hegemony, namely the effective veto power of the military, the custodian of Atatürk's imposed secularism. In this struggle against the unelected generals, the clever prime minister initially raised the banner of liberal democracy for tactical reasons.

But as soon as he had vanquished the top brass, Erdoğan showed his true colors and increasingly put the squeeze on democracy. He drew the necessary strength for this autocratic project from the economic recovery over which he presided and from his systematic promotion of Islamist practices and symbols. Intense plebiscitarian support allowed him to survive opposition challenges and a military coup attempt, which he then exploited for completing the destruction of democracy. Interestingly, while the weak institutional constraints of parliamentarism were crucial for enabling him to pursue this steady concentration of power, once he had achieved clear political hegemony, he decided to safeguard his predominance by pushing through an unbalanced presidential system and occupying this supremely powerful office (see comprehensive analysis in Yavuz 2021).

---

[7] Baykan 2018: 248–49; Bilgin and Erdoğan 2018; Esen and Gumuscu 2018: 44–47; Aytaç and Elçi 2019, 93–101.

THE QUICK AND FORMALLY LEGAL SUPPRESSION
OF DEMOCRACY: ORBÁN IN HUNGARY

Compared to his Turkish counterpart, Viktor Orbán had a much more straightforward and unimpeded path toward the suffocation of liberal pluralism in Hungary. After all, a serious economic crisis knocked out his partisan adversaries and gifted him a supermajority, unicameral parliamentarism with particularly weak checks and balances facilitated change, and no overbearing military looked over his shoulder. Whereas Erdoğan needed more than a decade to cement his hegemony and install authoritarianism, the Magyar populist steamrolled democracy with tremendous efficiency and disturbing speed (there is an excellent, comprehensive analysis in Körösényi, Illés, and Gyulai 2020). In this way, he pushed through a deeply illiberal project rooted in traditionalist conservative values (Buzogány and Varga 2021: 3–8).

Orbán's strikingly easy asphyxiation of liberal pluralism stands out as a worrisome precedent, for three reasons. First, Hungary, together with the Czech Republic and Poland, was widely regarded as a paragon of post-communist transformation, with its full and sustained embrace of market economics, societal pluralism, and free political competition, which appeared to take firm roots and over time improve in democratic quality.[8] That such a seemingly consolidated, fairly healthy democracy could be dismantled, and that it would be dismantled by a former liberal turned populist, came as a shock to scholars and political observers, including the officials of the European Union.

The second shock was that the Magyar populist managed to push through this regressive involution so quickly and lock it in so tightly that it looks difficult to reverse. Third and related, Orbán engineered Hungary's descent into authoritarianism in completely legal ways (Scheppele 2018: 545–48, 573–79), without any of the para-legal, if not illegal pushing and shoving to which all the other autocratic populists – Fujimori and Bukele; Chávez, Morales, and Correa; and Erdoğan – resorted. Parliamentarism's openness to change allowed Hungary's newborn populist to achieve undemocratic supremacy smoothly, without any violation of the existing rules and without the years of serious, dangerous contestation that Chávez and Erdoğan, in particular, only narrowly survived.

The root cause was that Orbán encountered a particularly propitious institutional setting for his typically populist goal of power concentration because Hungary's parliamentarism features an unusually weak separation of powers. The populist prime minister faced an indirectly elected president with limited attributions and minimal political clout. Unicameralism embodies only one institutional veto player, greatly facilitating domination by a majoritarian force.

---

[8] Carpenter 1997: 205–6; Krastev and Holmes 2019: 19–33, 52–62, 70–75; Bernhard 2021: 585–88; for Hungary, see Bartlett 1997; for Poland, see Gwiazda 2016: 68–70, 135–36, 143–48, 152–53; Sadurski 2019: 2, 162.

Moreover, Hungary is a unitary state where the central administration sets the rules for the whole country. Therefore, if one party won a parliamentary majority, "the [national] government was entitled to command a particularly strong and dominant vertical power structure with no institutionalized political rival on the scene. There has been no upper house, no directly elected president of the republic, and no strong regional self-governments either" (Ádám 2019: 391; see also 390, 397; Bernhard 2021: 607). Arguably, therefore, Hungary was Eastern Europe's "most majoritarian" democracy (Bogaards 2018: 1490).

What allowed Orbán to exploit the exceptionally sparse checks and balances in Hungary's parliamentary system for his undemocratic designs was that his party won a crushing majority in 2010. After all, the incumbent government, already discredited by meager economic performance and a blatant admission of lying to the public, suffered a devastating blow with the global recession of 2008 (Bozóki 2015: 11–12; Lendvai 2017: 53–65, 78–80; Csehi 2019: 1015–16; Bernhard 2021: 598). This exogenous shock, which caused GDP to drop by 6.6 percent in 2009, served as the coup de grâce for the ruling parties, especially the prime minister's socialists. The economic crisis gave Orbán's Fidesz a clear vote majority in the parliamentary elections of 2010, which translated into a constitutional supermajority of 68 percent of seats (Bogaards 2018, 1490–91; Körösényi, Illés, and Gyulai 2020: 38, 49, 55, 76–77).[9]

The new prime minister, who in the 2000s had established total personalistic control over the party that he had helped to found (Körösényi, Illés, and Gyulai 2020: 66, 98, 125; Metz and Várnagy 2021: 323–25), resolutely seized this unusual opportunity and took advantage of the institutional flexibility of Hungarian parliamentarism to push through a determined project of power concentration.[10] In 2011, without any thorough consultation and deliberation, he already had his partisan majority in parliament approve a new constitution that increased prime-ministerial attributions and weakened liberal safeguards (Körösényi and Patkós 2017: 324–25; see also Tsebelis 2022: 290). Moreover, Fidesz systematically packed the courts, especially the Constitutional Court (Lendvai 2017: 103–7; Scheppele 2018: 550–52). In this way, the ambitious leader eroded judicial independence, liberal pluralism's last line of defense in Hungary's parliamentary system.[11] By overcoming particularly weak checks

---

[9] Like other populist chief executives in the EU's East European member states, Orbán has also benefited from windfall rents that are in principle similar to the petrodollar bonanza gifted to Venezuela's Chávez by the global commodities boom, namely plentiful fiscal subsidies provided by Brussels. Amounting to a maximum of 4 percent of GDP, however (Ádám 2019: 394, see also 395, 397; Neuwahl and Kovacs 2021: 25), this influx was much less voluminous than the overabundance benefiting Chávez. More importantly, because other East European EU members received similar subsidies, this factor does not provide much help in explaining the populist strangulation of democracy in Hungary, by contrast to its frequent survival elsewhere.

[10] Scheppele 2018: 549–50; Pappas 2019: 194–95, 202–4, 209, 253–55; Körösényi, Illés, and Gyulai 2020: 79–90; Bartels 2023: 194–99.

[11] Bánkuti, Halmai, and Scheppele 2015: 38–39; Bozóki 2015: 18; Freedom House 2022b: 15–16.

and balances, the Magyar populist thus advanced toward authoritarianism with great speed and shocking ease. Given the perfect legality of his machinations, the European Union proved unable to stop this rapid suffocation of democracy (Neuwahl and Kovacs 2021: 17–19).

As Scheppele (2018: 545–48, 573–79) has emphasized by invoking the concept of autocratic legalism, Hungary's personalistic plebiscitarian leader employed the official institutional mechanisms to dismantle democracy from the inside and institute an autocratic system. That the savvy populist did not violate any formal rules in quickly cementing his predominance prevented his liberal domestic opponents and their supporters abroad from blocking his illiberal advance. Sporadic protests by civil society movements, which occasionally reached substantial size, proved no match against Orbán's march toward political hegemony.[12] The Magyar populist also engineered a plebiscitarian façade for his rule by holding sham "consultations" with the population and by conducting referenda with highly suggestive, manipulative questions (Csehi 2019: 1020–21).

To secure his stranglehold further, Orbán also used his rapidly growing supremacy to skew political competition in his favor (Gomez and Leunig 2022: 674–75; Bakke and Sitter 2022: 26–27). An early reform accentuated the majoritarian features of Hungary's electoral system, allowing the largest party – his own Fidesz – to translate a mere plurality of the vote into a lopsided parliamentary majority. With the help of this institutional engineering and heavy gerrymandering (Scheppele 2022: 52–53, 57), the governing party retained its constitutional supermajority even after suffering substantial vote losses in the 2014 elections (Bánkuti, Halmai, and Scheppele 2015: 37–45; Bozóki 2015: 16–21; Lendvai 2017: 127–31). With disturbing predictability, the 2018 contest yielded another triumph for the well-entrenched populist; and despite the opposition's efforts to unify, he won in 2022 as well (Scheppele 2022: 45–49, 54–55).

Interestingly, while the Hungarian leader exploited the easy changeability of parliamentarism to establish his political predominance, he has in recent years tried to enshrine this hegemony by employing counter-majoritarian mechanisms; thus, he has used his current supermajority to secure his party's grip on power and constrain any future opposition majority. For this purpose, the new autocracy strengthened supposedly independent institutions and packed them with its cronies for unusually long terms. These lock-ins could only be reversed through a supermajority, which the present opposition is exceedingly unlikely to win. In this savvy way, Fidesz has sought to cement its dominance and create institutional bastions to exert continued influence even if Hungary were to return to democracy; these authoritarian enclaves would limit the latitude of any future liberal-pluralist government.[13]

---

[12] Petőcz 2015: 207, 225–26; Van Til 2015: 374–75; Protests in Hungary 2019; Bernhard 2020: 354–55.

[13] Grzymala-Busse 2017: S7; Bogaards 2018: 1488–89; Körösényi, Illés, and Gyulai 2020: 86, 89; Gomez and Leunig 2022: 670–71, 675.

Thus, after initially exploiting the unusual plasticity of Hungarian parliamentarism for boosting his own overwhelming power, Orbán then deliberately hardened institutions that he now controlled to reduce the corresponding risk to his own supremacy. Interestingly, whereas Erdoğan exacerbated majoritarianism in Turkey by pushing through the installation of omnipotent presidentialism, Orbán used his super-majoritarian command for potentially counter-majoritarian institutional changes – a smart strategy for perpetuating his overbearing influence where a move to hyperpresidentialism is unthinkable.

Orbán's rapid and formally legal advance toward illiberalism surprised external defenders of democracy and seriously hindered their exertion of leverage – until it was too late. Overestimating the consolidation of liberal pluralism after twenty years of post-communist development in Eastern-Central Europe, the European Union, in particular, did not manage to protect Hungarian democracy. Although the country depends on voluminous financial subsidies from Brussels (Körösényi, Illés, and Gyulai 2020: 127), which have helped Orbán to cement his support through extensive social benefit programs, the EU failed to use this source of influence effectively (Krekó and Enyedi 2018: 45). Because with his supermajority of 2010, Hungary's populist leader enacted his autocratic project with great speed and without any rule violation, Brussels was quickly confronted with a fait accompli and found it exceedingly difficult to invoke broader liberal-democratic principles to contest, not to speak of reversing, the constitutional transformation that Orbán had so smoothly engineered. Because the ever more authoritarian prime minister also started to turn to Russia's Vladimir Putin for support (Buzogány 2017: 1315–19; Lendvai 2017: 223–27), the EU was reluctant to put heavy pressure on Hungary and engage in brinkmanship.

Its disappointing ineffectiveness in Hungary, however, induced the EU to make more resolute efforts to stem the tide of autocratic populism in Eastern Europe by exerting earlier and stronger leverage on the right-wing populist government of Poland (2015–present), in many ways the pivotal case for the fate of liberal pluralism in contemporary Europe. Indeed, after mobilizing against this additional threat and creating fine-tuned mechanisms for exerting well-calibrated influence, Brussels has finally begun to take more energetic steps against Orbán's authoritarianism as well (EU eröffnet Verfahren gegen Ungarn 2022; Riegert 2022).

THE ONGOING STRUGGLE OVER LIBERAL DEMOCRACY IN POLAND

The populist Law and Justice Party (Prawo i Sprawiedliwość, or PiS), which is stage-managed from behind the throne by surviving party co-founder Jarosław Kaczyński,[14] has systematically tried to follow the playbook of Hungary's

---

[14] Pakulski 2016: 61; Grzymala-Busse 2018: 96, 100–1; Stanley 2020: 179–80, 186; Pytlas 2021: 340, 342, 347–50. After Kaczyński's twin brother died in a plane crash in Russia in 2010, the

Orbán (Bodnar 2018: 640; Sadurski 2019: 3–4, 14–15, 163).[15] After a brief and turbulent stint in power from 2005 to 2007 (Stanley 2016), PiS and its highly personalistic leader have since 2015 led a conservative-traditionalist government that has tried hard to move away from liberal democracy as well.[16] Like its counterpart in Budapest, the right-wing administration in Warsaw has persistently sought to take over the judiciary and has put great pressure on civil society (Grzymala-Busse 2018; Sadurski 2018: 121–58). At the same time, PiS has emulated the Magyar leader by strengthening its support through the provision of fairly generous social benefits to poorer population segments. Moreover, intense appeals to traditional Catholic values, which are especially well entrenched in rural areas and small towns,[17] and withering rhetorical attacks on Poland's Western-oriented liberal sectors, have helped the PiS-led coalition to win narrow reelection victories in the legislative contest of 2019 and the presidential race of 2020.

In Poland, however, the populist authoritarian project faces much greater obstacles than in Hungary, due to differences in both of the types of causal factors highlighted by my theory.[18] First, in institutional terms, the country along the Vistula is distinguished from Magyar unicameralism by featuring a bicameral legislature. The upper chamber has substantial – albeit not co-equal – attributions. This additional veto player makes decision-making more complicated and hinders the imposition of controversial change. Under the governments controlled by populist Kaczyński, this institutional obstacle has assumed greater relevance after PiS lost its Senate majority in the 2019 elections.[19]

Moreover, by contrast to Hungary's parliamentarism, Poland has a semi-presidential system of government (Castle and Taras 2002: 190, 195–97, 203; Sydorchuk 2014; Gwiazda 2016: 117–21). Directly elected by popular

---

Polish populist has not only propagated anti-Russian conspiracy theories, which for painful historical reasons have great resonance in Poland, but has also promoted a personality cult that officially focuses on the accident victim but extends to himself as well.

[15] I thank Wojciech Sadurski and Ben Stanley for many interesting comments, observations, and reflections on the Polish case.

[16] See the comprehensive criticism of liberal democracy by party intellectual Legutko (2018) and the analysis by Buzogány and Varga (2021: 3–5, 8–11). During its earlier tenure in government (2005–7), PiS had resolutely pursued illiberal power concentration as well (Sydorchuk 2014: 135–36), yet faced domestic protests and external pressures that, together with serious tensions in the governing coalition, led to its quick downfall (Stanley 2016).

[17] Castle and Taras 2002: 53–54, 110–16, 142–45, 158–60, 174; Pakulski 2016: 56–57; Kotwas and Kubik 2019; Stanley and Cześnik 2019: 81–82; Bill and Stanley 2020: 387–89; historical background in Davies 2005: 467, 499.

[18] PiS ran afoul of these obstacles during its first attempt at populist governance from 2005 to 2007 (Stanley 2016). Yet this very failure induced Kaczyński to redouble his illiberal efforts after the party's reelection in 2015 (Pytlas 2021: 342), and to proceed in a more targeted, strategic, and therefore dangerous fashion on second try (Stanley 2020: 182–83, 186–87).

[19] I thank Wojciech Sadurski, University of Sydney, for highlighting this point (personal communication, April 17, 2022).

vote, the head of state enjoys some institutional independence, which he used on several occasions, especially in 2017 and 2021, to hinder some of the PiS government's illiberal initiatives through presidential vetoes. In political practice, however, this independent role is muted by the firm command that PiS's charismatic leader Kaczyński exerts over his populist party and its public officials, including the head of state (Tworzecki 2019: 102; Pytlas 2021: 340, 342, 347–50). Usually, therefore, the president and the prime ministers selected by party hegemon Kaczyński push in the same illiberal direction (Sadurski 2018: 113).

Second, PiS has not enjoyed the crucial conjunctural opportunity that enabled Hungary's Orbán to obliterate the incumbent parties and win a parliamentary supermajority in 2010. Instead, Poland's populists came to power in good economic times in 2015 (Grzymala-Busse 2018: 98–99). Accordingly, they squeezed out only a narrow victory, with 51 percent of the seats in parliament. While this result, for the first time in Poland's post-communist democracy, allowed the populist party to govern on its own, unencumbered by potentially troublesome allies (Grzymala-Busse 2019: 708), the slim majority prevented power-hungry Kaczyński from pushing through constitutional transformations, not to speak of engineering a new charter, as Orbán had managed to do right away and as the Polish populist would have wanted to do as well.[20] Therefore, Poland's personalistic plebiscitarian leader was unable to imitate the central part of Orbán's strategy of quickly and smoothly suffocating democracy.

Instead of gaining a rapid stranglehold over liberal pluralism along the Vistula, the PiS government saw itself compelled to pursue its authoritarian project in a series of small, sequential steps, which – for lack of a constitutional supermajority – were often of a para-legal nature (Pirro and Stanley 2022: 92, 95, 97). Because Kaczyński already controlled the elected branches of government, his main target was the judiciary. In a variety of ways, including the use of appointment powers and the creation of politically dominated oversight institutions, PiS has tried hard to erode judicial independence.[21] These illiberal initiatives first sought to paralyze the decision-making of the constitutional tribunal in order to obstruct effective judicial scrutiny of governmental and parliamentary actions; thereafter, court packing tried to turn the top judiciary into an instrument of the populist project (Sadurski 2019: chaps. 3–4; Pirro and Stanley 2022: 93, 95; see also Harper 2021: 103–4; Freedom House 2022c: 15–16; Sadurski 2023).

But because many of these efforts were of questionable legality and reeked of arbitrariness, they did not advance smoothly. Instead, judges across the

---

[20] Sadurski 2018: 107–9, 113–17; Tworzecki 2019: 99; Bill and Stanley 2020: 383–85; Csehi and Zgut 2021: 60–61.

[21] Sadurski 2018: 121–40; Grzymala-Busse 2019: 710–11; Harper 2021: 103–4; Issacharoff 2023: 143–44. As Harper (2021: 34, 41–42, 48) highlights, however, the politically more liberal predecessor government had already initiated the political manipulation of judicial appointments.

various courts have strenuously defended their professional autonomy (Bodnar 2021: 104; Gliszczyńska-Grabias and Sadurski 2021: 149–50), which was hard won after the fall of communism (Castle and Taras 2002: 208–9). These acts of passive resistance and active opposition have not deterred populist Kaczyński, however; instead, he has redoubled his strangulation attempts (Stanley and Cześnik 2019: 79–80). To achieve their illiberal goals, the PiS governments have resorted to a host of unsavory machinations and tricks, targeting independent forces and especially political opponents with "discriminatory legalism."[22]

To propel this sustained assault on liberal pluralism, PiS has also acted as a majoritarian steamroller in parliament. Rather than engaging in consultation and negotiation with opposition forces, it has resolutely forced through its bills through loose, expansive usage of legislative fast-tracking, which marginalized any input from other parties. Moreover, procedural tricks excluded deputies not aligned with the government from crucial decisions, such as the approval of the budget in 2017 (Sadurski 2018: 150–52). Thus, in typically populist fashion, Kaczyński's party acted as the self-appointed mouthpiece of "the people" and abridged the rights of alternative political groupings.

Last but not least, PiS has sought to preserve and expand its slim parliamentary majority and boost its electoral results by skewing Poland's voting rules. For this purpose, it engaged in gerrymandering and other manipulations (Grzymala-Busse 2018: 98; Sadurski 2019: 140–43). Its programs of social protection, which are strongly family-oriented and thus try to promote traditionalist Catholic values, are designed to tighten its grip over its main electoral base in Poland's extensive rural areas and small towns. In all of these ways, Kaczyński has hoped to marginalize the partisan opposition and safeguard his fairly precarious control.

Yet these opportunistic moves and especially the use of unfair para-legal measures have exacted a steep political price that has hindered Kaczyński's push toward authoritarianism. The absence of a parliamentary supermajority and the resulting inability to replicate the formal-legal approach of Hungary's Orbán and proceed with the frictionless asphyxiation of democracy have led to ample and fervent countermobilization by Poland's relatively vibrant and contentious civil society (Sadurski 2018: 152, 177; Bernhard 2021: 605; less sanguine Gwiazda 2016: 77–84). Frequent protests have slowed the march into illiberalism and forced the populist governments to shelve or at least postpone a number of anti-pluralistic initiatives (Bernhard 2020: 354–55; Matthes 2021: 267–75). Recurrent manifestations of contention have expressed especially strong opposition to PiS's systematic efforts to take control of the judiciary through problematic tricks. Numerous other street demonstrations have

---

[22] Bodnar (Bodnar 2021; see also Bodnar 2018: 641–50) and Sadurski (Sadurski 2022: 5; Sadurski 2023) systematically employ my concept (Weyland 2013: 23–25) to elucidate Kaczyński's machinations.

contested Kaczyński's sustained attempts to push fundamentalist cultural values and abridge the liberal rights claimed by progressive sectors (Gliszczyńska-Grabias and Sadurski 2021: 131, 152).

By drawing international attention to PiS's legally questionable manipulations, these incessant conflicts have also facilitated the exertion of pressure by the EU, which has tried to forestall another undemocratic involution in Eastern Europe and stop the trend set in motion by Orbán's populist takeover in Hungary (Sadurski 2019: 202, 225). Thus, as in Latin America, where the OAS responded with particular energy and effectiveness to the emulation of Fujimori's 1992 self-coup by Guatemalan President Jorge Serrano in 1993 (see Chapter 3), the EU was determined to block Kaczyński's sneaky attempts to follow in Orbán's illiberal footsteps. Precisely because regional organizations can be taken by surprise by an initial undemocratic precedent, such as Fujimori's bold power grab or Orbán's unexpectedly quick and uncontested advance, they then make extra efforts to act more quickly and energetically to impede the diffusion of this deleterious precedent (Matthes 2021: 263–64).

For this purpose, the EU fine-tuned its instruments for putting pressure on governments that stray from liberal pluralism. Because its earlier mechanisms of intervention were too heavy-handed, they had not proved very usable;[23] member governments' veto power had tended to block their application, especially as undemocratic populism started to spread across the region in the 2010s, after the Hungarian precedent. To escape from this predicament, the EU introduced a new procedure designed specifically to defend and bolster the rule of law (Sadurski 2019: 213–18; Neuwahl and Kovacs 2021: 22–29). By employing this novel mechanism first, and then increasing its pressure with higher-caliber weaponry, the EU has contained the Kaczyński government's infringements to some extent (Sadurski 2019: 218–27; Bakke and Sitter 2022: 32–33; Rule of Law in Poland 2023). Moreover, Brussels has probably exerted a deterrent effect and made further violations less likely, inside Poland and across the region. Most importantly, the frequent outspoken criticism by several European institutions has encouraged liberal sectors in Poland to oppose and protest their governments' unsavory machinations. In these ways, the domestic and international defenders of liberal pluralism have reinforced each other.

As a result of all these obstacles and counter-pressures, PiS's undemocratic project has advanced much less far than Orbán's quick march toward authoritarianism (Bernhard 2020: 349). While degraded and imperiled, Polish democracy has survived so far and deserves a substantially higher international democracy ranking than Hungary. Whereas Orbán has established electoral hegemony and an institutional stranglehold over political life, an intense and open-ended struggle between Kaczyński's pushy illiberal government and determined opposition forces continues to rage. Consequently, Freedom House

---

[23] The PiS governments have often reacted to EU pressures in allergic and contentious ways (see Legutko 2018: 85–91).

(2022b, 2022c) in its most recent assessments rated Poland as "free" with a score of 81/100, by contrast to Hungary's 69/100.

The fact that both the 2019 parliamentary elections and the 2020 presidential contest were highly competitive shows that PiS has not succeeded in suppressing other parties and smothering democracy (Petrović 2020: 59; Freedom House 2022c: 3–6; EIU 2023: 51).[24] Indeed, the opposition broke PiS's majority in the Senate in 2019, putting another – albeit limited – roadblock in the path of Kaczyński's hegemonic project (Bodnar 2021: 106; Bakke and Sitter 2022: 30; see also Bartels 2023: 205–6). An additional source of friction is that despite the populist leader's internal dominance, PiS is far from unified. Factional disagreements and conflicts are intense (Harper 2021: 181–86; Pytlas 2021: 348, 350).

In conclusion, while Polish democracy faces acute danger, it has hitherto demonstrated a great deal of resilience and has a strong fighting chance to survive this long stretch of typically illiberal populist governance. In this ongoing experience, my theory would predict such a salutary outcome. After all, the country's semi-presidential system with its bicameral legislature is less vulnerable to power-concentrating change than regular parliamentarism, especially its highly majoritarian Hungarian version. And the absence of a severe economic crisis kept opposition parties viable and prevented Poland's personalistic leader from winning overwhelming mass support. The resulting obstacles, which have precluded the country's descent into authoritarianism so far, are likely to do so in the future as well.

LIMITATIONS OF AN AUTOCRATIC POPULIST: MEČIAR IN SLOVAKIA

As just demonstrated by comparison to Hungary, a crucial underlying cause for the incapacity of Poland's illiberal populism to sweep aside political-institutional obstacles has been the absence of a sharp economic crisis. Interestingly, Slovak populist Vladimír Mečiar did encounter a massive economic downturn, but nevertheless ended up failing with his forceful and particularly unsavory efforts to strangle his newborn country's fledgling democracy during his three stints as prime minister (1990–91, 1992–94, 1994–98). Why?

Mečiar won a good deal of electoral backing and political influence by emerging as a typically populist leader immediately after the unexpected collapse of Czechoslovakia's hard-core communist regime (Abrahám 2000: 142–44, 161–62; Haughton 2001: 747, 763–64; Deegan-Krause 2012: 182–90). The institutionally fluid setting of the monumental "triple transition" (Offe 1991) seemed to offer a golden opportunity for a personalistic plebiscitarian politician who eagerly and in rather autocratic ways strove for power concentration.

---

[24] Based on recent polls, Sadurski (2023) foresees the potential of a tight race in the upcoming parliamentary elections of late 2023 as well.

While Mečiar initially became head of government in the Slovak half of the still-unified country, the "velvet divorce" of 1993 released him from federal supervision and seemed to give him free rein. Indeed, the new Slovak Republic featured a parliamentary system with an indirectly elected president, who lacked unmediated democratic legitimacy;[25] the institutional requirements for constitutional change were comparatively easy as well. For these reasons, Mečiar faced weak institutional constraints to his typically populist quest for augmenting his clout and imposing political predominance (Fish 1999: 53–54).

Moreover, the ambitious prime minister started his first two governments in the midst of a grave economic crisis. But of course, to derive a big political boost from such a crisis, which would allow for the suffocation of democracy, a personalistic plebiscitarian politician must manage to resolve the problem. Only substantial relief from their suffering induces large numbers of people to see the leader as a charismatic savior and offer their intense, fervent support. Thus, "miraculous" success is a necessary precondition for the establishment of undemocratic hegemony and the strangulation of liberal pluralism.

The economic meltdown accompanying the fall of communism, however, was not a resolvable conjunctural crisis that a bold adjustment plan could quickly overcome. Instead, it amounted to a near catastrophe resulting from the implosion of the whole development model (Leff 1997: 183, 188; Hofbauer and Noack 2012: 77, 94–95, 104–5). Any turnaround required complex structural reforms, such as the privatization of bloated, utterly inefficient state enterprises, which would take a while to bear fruit. The transitional pain caused by such an unavoidable overhaul was huge and bound to last for years. Consequently, the populist leaders emerging in early post-communism – a fairly rare breed[26] – could not gain the political leverage for smothering the fragile new democracies.

Best positioned was Lech Wałęsa in Poland, the hero of the Solidarity Movement, which had courageously shaken the communist system from 1980 onward and helped to prepare the demise of communism across Eastern Europe (Staniszkis 1984; Bernhard 1993). Moreover, the Solidarity government that won office in 1989 and succeeded in electing Wałęsa as president in 1990 enacted a bold "shock plan" to dismantle communism's economic model as quickly as possible and put the country on a path toward capitalist prosperity (Weyland 1999: 395–96). But even this courageous adjustment and accelerated restructuring could not avoid a major transitional decline that brought a great deal of social pain. These serious strains facilitated the surprisingly quick electoral comeback of the former communists, who retook the government in 1993 and then defeated power-hungry and pushy Wałęsa in his presidential reelection bid in 1995 (Grzymala-Busse 2002: 160–71, 212–15, 249–58).

---

[25] A constitutional change in the late 1990s introduced direct presidential elections.

[26] Stanley (2017: 140–46). The upsurge of political liberalism during the heady days of early post-communism hindered the rise of populist leaders at that time.

The failure of Wałęsa, the paragon of post-communist populism, to leverage the economic crisis of the early 1990s for establishing political hegemony and moving toward illiberalism shows that this structural collapse lacked the quick resolvability of a conjunctural crisis; it differed fundamentally, for instance, from the hyperinflation that helped Peru's Fujimori to boost his political fortunes and impose competitive authoritarianism (see Chapter 3). Therefore, the Polish populist did not have a chance to smother democracy – and Mečiar did not encounter such a conjunctural opportunity either.

Indeed, the Slovak prime minister did not even try to effect quick, dramatic relief from the deep crisis caused by communism's breakdown. He rejected the "big-bang" reforms adopted in Poland and in his own Czechoslovakia (Leff 1997: 180–85). Mečiar did not want to dismantle the communist development model in a concentrated burst and install market capitalism at lightning speed. Instead, he sought to avoid the severe pain of a shock program, which would hit Slovakia with its concentration of uncompetitive heavy industry especially hard. Therefore, Mečiar promoted a gradualist approach to marketization, for instance by blocking fast-track privatization programs (Leff 1997: 188, 193–95; Hofbauer and Noack 2012: 91–94, 118–19, 166). This effort to limit short-term costs also reflected Mečiar's initially precarious political position, as evident in the quick breakup of his first two governments, in 1991 and 1994. While this fragility made the imposition of a painful shock program politically risky and inadvisable, Mečiar's drawn-out adjustment program precluded a rapid recovery and prolonged transitional losses (Carpenter 1997: 217).

For these reasons, Mečiar did not become Slovaks' "miraculous" savior from the post-communist depression. Consequently, he did not win overwhelming support. His party never reached 40 percent of the vote (Haughton 2001: 746). Failing to obtain a majority of seats in the Bratislava parliament, Mečiar always needed allies. But the populist leader could not reliably count on his ideologically divergent coalition partners. Despite their relative weakness, these smaller parties blocked some of his power-concentrating projects, especially an "electoral reform ... moving from proportional representation to a more plurality-based system," which promised disproportionately to strengthen the prime minister's own party (Haughton 2002: 1334; see also 1332–33). This intracoalition resistance prevented Mečiar's party from gaining the predominance that a similar change later cemented for Orbán in Hungary. His failure to skew the electoral system also contributed to the Slovak populist's defeat in the 1998 contest, which ended his pressure on democracy.

Throughout his three terms in office, the need to find coalition partners among Slovakia's fluid parties kept Mečiar's hold over the government precarious, especially during the early 1990s. The prime minister's populist movement, which typically did not congeal into an institutionalized party (Haughton 2001: 747), suffered waves of defection. These desertions were driven in part by revulsion at the overbearing personalistic leadership of Mečiar, who did not accept disagreement or criticism and who vengefully attacked all "traitors"

(Abrahám 2000: 165–69; Haughton 2001: 754–57; see also Fish 1999: 47). The hemorrhages that the domineering populist provoked shrank his own movement and its allied parties and prompted his government's downfall in 1991 and again in 1994 (Pehe 1991; Carpenter 1997: 212–13; Leff 1997: 148–49).

Yet despite his fights with Slovak politicians, which turned rather nasty, Mečiar's personal charisma (Grzymala-Busse 2002: 197), his populist promises, and his appeal to the losers of Slovakia's triple transition guaranteed him a good deal of popular support, which brought his reelections in 1992 and 1994 (Carpenter 1997: 212; Haughton 2001: 759–60). After the latter victory, he sought to consolidate his grip over the government by forging a broader coalition. Typical of populist leaders, who lack firm commitments to programmatic preferences and ideological principles, he reached out both to a hard-left workers' party and a hard-right nationalist party (Haughton 2002: 1321–22; Hofbauer and Noack 2012: 110–11).

Even this alliance, however, which remained conflict-ridden (Leff 1997: 153–56; see also Haughton 2002: 1329, 1332–34), did not give the reinstalled prime minister a supermajority that would have enabled him to enact constitutional changes. In his relentless quest for concentrating power, the autocratic Mečiar frequently used para-legal, if not illegal means during his third term in office (1994–98). For instance, his governing coalition immediately took almost complete control of parliament, abridging opposition parties' rights of participation (Grzymala-Busse 2002: 247). The headstrong leader also attacked the press, assailed his political adversaries, and sought to break or bend democratic institutions (Deegan-Krause 2012: 194–96; Deegan-Krause 2019: 63–66; FES n.d.).

Mečiar used harassment, intimidation, and even coercion to discipline his own movement and its coalition partners, to combat earlier defectors who now opposed his machinations, and to cow independent institutions, such as the judiciary, into submission (Grzymala-Busse 2002: 151–52, 159, 197–98, 203–4, 247). For instance, Slovakia's president, a former crony whom the prime minister had helped elect in 1993, quickly took an independent stance, opposed Mečiar's infringements of liberal norms, and mustered the courage to advocate the no-confidence vote that felled the populist leader's government in 1994 (Zifcak 1995: 61–64; Haughton 2003: 272–78). Determined to deter any such treason after his reelection in late 1994, the personalistic plebiscitarian prime minister frontally attacked the president and went so far as to have the police kidnap his adversary's son for extradition to Germany, where the youngster was under suspicion of illegal activities. While the government claimed to enforce the law, domestic and international public opinion was aghast at this unprecedented act of political discrimination and blatant vendetta.[27]

---

[27] Abrahám 2000: 179–84; for a more Mečiar-friendly interpretation, see Hofbauer and Noack (2012: 100–1).

The prime minister's openly autocratic approach led to an even worse infraction of liberal-democratic rules when another parliamentary deputy left his populist movement in 1996. Fearing a new wave of defection that could undermine his hold on power, as had happened in 1991 and 1994, Mečiar had his co-partisans and allies expel the deserter from the legislature. When the Supreme Court declared this political punishment unconstitutional, the government blithely ignored the ruling (Abrahám 2000: 185–89). From then on, the personalistic plebiscitarian leader refused to comply with judicial decisions on several other occasions (FES n.d.). As attacks on the press increased as well, Slovakia seemed to be heading toward competitive authoritarianism.

By committing open infractions of liberal rules and procedures, which sought to compensate for his precarious political position and which were therefore more blatant than the discriminatory legalism of Kaczyński's majoritarian PiS in Poland, Mečiar eventually provoked an even stronger pushback than the populist in Warsaw has faced in recent years. After a long stretch of fearful inactivity and striking quiescence (Carpenter 1997: 215–17), a wide range of civil society groupings mobilized against the personalistic plebiscitarian leader and his autocratic machinations (Bútora and Bútorová 1999: 81–84, 88–90; FES n.d.). And after long being intimidated by Mečiar's assaults, opposition parties from 1997 onward decided to take countermeasures as well (Grzymala-Busse 2002: 204, 247–48; Vachudova 2005: 170–75). Facing the imminent danger of a descent into authoritarianism, they overcame their deep political and ideological disagreements and negotiated electoral alliances. Interestingly, Mečiar's desperate effort to undermine this opposition cooperation by pushing through an electoral reform that disadvantaged party groupings backfired. Instead, the two alliances that had just formed quickly unified forces and turned into parties. Together, they went on to defeat the populist leader in the 1998 contest (Abrahám 2000: 211–12, 219; Nemčok and Spáč 2020: 245).

While domestic forces in civil society and the partisan arena were decisive for stopping Mečiar's resolute march toward autocracy, a specific conjunctural factor, namely external pressures from West European countries, played a crucial supporting role (Vachudova 2005: 156–59, 162–65, 170–75). Because many Slovaks were interested in joining the European Union and NATO, as the bulk of Eastern Europe's post-communist nations tried so hard to do, the EU commanded particular leverage during the late 1990s. As preconditions for accession, EU leaders demanded not only major progress toward instituting a market economy but also firm guarantees of liberal democracy. Consequently, the West European club of rich countries punished Mečiar's worsening infractions in 1997 by leaving Slovakia off the candidate list for early accession (Abrahám 2000: 225–29; Hofbauer and Noack 2012: 98–102, 145–48). This painful socioeconomic sanction and embarrassing symbolic snub weakened the autocratic prime minister's legitimacy and fired up his opponents in civil society and the party system. By mobilizing domestic resistance, foreign influence contributed significantly to the downfall of authoritarian populism in the 1998 elections.

These external pressures had special weight during Slovakia's quest for inclusion in the EU and NATO; after all, conditionality is comparatively easy to enforce when the accession process can be delayed or canceled (Bernhard 2021: 596). By contrast, international actors have much less leverage once countries gain membership, as the cases of Orbán's Hungary and Kaczyński's Poland mentioned earlier show. Indeed, the new members can use their participation in the EU's consensus-oriented decision-making for self-protection or mutual support against sanctions, while threats of expulsion have low credibility.[28] Thus, in addition to the main factor highlighted in my theory, namely the absence of a severe, acute crisis that a personalistic plebiscitarian leader could resolve and thus use for winning overwhelming support, a particular conjunctural factor also proved important for the survival of liberal pluralism in Slovakia.[29]

In conclusion, Mečiar's persistent and worsening attacks on Slovakia's fledgling democracy failed despite the easy changeability of parliamentarism, which was exacerbated by the institutional fluidity of the new polity, and despite the presence of a huge economic crisis. But although this volatile setting favored the rise of an autocratic populist, one necessary precondition for the installation of authoritarianism was missing, namely the resolvability of the crisis: According to my theory, success in combating and reversing deep losses is crucial for populist leaders to win overwhelming mass support and push aside all opposition forces and institutional constraints. Only if they manage to bring dramatic relief can personalistic plebiscitarian politicians take advantage of the political opportunity provided by an acute, severe crisis.

The collapse of the communist development model, however, differed fundamentally from a conjunctural recession or hyperinflation, which a bold adjustment plan can quickly end. Therefore, Mečiar did not succeed in winning the vote shares required for a parliamentary majority, not to speak of a constitutional supermajority. Unable to advance his autocratic designs in the smooth, formally legal ways of Hungary's Orbán, the Slovak premier resorted

---

[28] Sadurski 2019: 200–2, 222–23; Theuns 2022; Bakke and Sitter 2022: 32–33.

[29] This particular constraint also hemmed in Bulgaria's former Tsar, Simeon Borisov von Saxe-Coburg-Gotha, who after his return from decades in exile won the premiership with a populist strategy in 2001. After all, the post-communist country in the early 2000s was eager to join the EU and NATO, and the new prime minister defined accession as his main priority. Because the West demanded full respect for democracy, the ex-monarch's hands were tied (Barany 2002: 145–46; Vachudova 2005: 211–12). In addition, domestic factors also precluded the suffocation of liberal pluralism. While Bulgaria lacked a solid institutional framework, the absence of a deep yet resolvable crisis prevented the new prime minister from pursuing any hopes for boosting his powers, not to speak of restoring his earlier monarchical glory. Indeed, his flimsy electoral movement gradually dissipated, such that he lost the premiership in the 2005 elections. For these reasons, the fleeting reign of the populist ex-autocrat did no damage to Bulgaria's low-quality democracy (Barany 2002: 148–49; Ghodsee 2008: 28–30; Cristova 2010: 224; Zankina 2016: 189–90).

to open discrimination and ever more blatant infractions, which eventually provoked a powerful backlash from domestic civil and political society and strong international pressures. Mečiar therefore failed with his strangulation of democracy.

SERIAL POPULISM AND THE SURVIVAL
OF DEMOCRACY IN SLOVAKIA

After Mečiar's electoral ouster, Slovak democracy recovered quickly, and liberal pluralism gained a new lease on life (Vachudova 2005: 185, 201; Bakke and Sitter 2022: 24). Yet the continuing plasticity and fragmentation of the party system and the resulting electoral volatility kept the door open for the emergence of new personalistic plebiscitarian leaders. Accordingly, "soft populist" Robert Fico (Walter 2017: 176) won the parliamentary elections of 2006. Without a majority, the new prime minister sustained his government in part through an alliance with Mečiar, whose political fortunes had kept sinking (Haughton and Rybář 2008: 248–52; Walter 2017: 176–78). Interestingly, Fico soon turned into a "light" version of Mečiar. While hailing from the social-democratic left and tempering economic liberalism with social programs and state interventionism (Hofbauer and Noack 2012: 180–85, 200–7), he also moved toward nationalism and worked hard to establish his political hegemony.[30] After an electoral defeat in 2010, Fico skillfully managed to engineer a new contest in 2012, which he won decisively; and he emerged victorious in 2016 as well, albeit with a declining vote share and the need for coalition partners.[31]

Yet while dominating Slovak politics for many years (2006–10, 2012–18), Fico refrained from assaulting liberal democracy as Mečiar had done.[32] After all, his main election triumphs of 2006 and 2012 occurred at times when his country was not suffering from any deep economic crisis (Haughton and Rybář 2008: 242–45; Hofbauer and Noack 2012: 216–17; Rybář and Spáč 2017: 153). In line with my theory, the soft populist therefore lacked the opportunity to win massive backing and push toward authoritarian rule. Perhaps learning from Mečiar's failure as well, Fico respected the basic framework of liberal democracy.

But the powerful prime minister pursued his personalistic goals by building up networks of cronyism and patronage. This web of nepotism and corruption grew like a cancer and came to involve organized crime as well (Hofbauer and Noack 2012: 198–99, 209). Shockingly, a courageous journalist who investigated this government-abetted swamp was assassinated in 2018. This

[30] Hofbauer and Noack 2012: 174–79; Mesežnikov and Gyárfášová 2018: 83.
[31] Rybář and Spáč 2017; see also Szomolányi 2016: 71, 79–80; Nemčok and Spáč 2020: 242.
[32] Deegan-Krause 2012: 197–201; Szomolányi 2016: 71, 79–80; Haydanka 2021: 10; Bakke and Sitter 2022: 22, 29.

unprecedented crime provoked massive mobilization in Slovak society, which quickly forced Fico to step down; as in 1998 with Mečiar's electoral defeat, blatant transgression felled another Slovak populist.[33] Fico's discredited party, which the power-hungry leader continued to head, also lost the presidential elections of 2019 and the parliamentary contest of 2020 (Gyárfášová and Učeň 2020: 327; Rossi 2020: 236, 239, 243).

Rather than immunizing Slovakia against populism, however, the ignominious demise of Fico and the weakening of his party fueled the churn of the country's fluid, organizationally weak party system. Consequently, another personalistic plebiscitarian leader won the elections of 2020 (Rossi 2020: 235–38). Because he seemed most determined to root out widespread, entrenched corruption and because he vociferously spearheaded the citizenry's profound demand for change, headstrong populist Igor Matovič emerged victorious in a divided field and took the helm, precariously sustained by a heterogeneous alliance (Gyárfášová and Učeň 2020: 328–31; Nič 2020: 2–3; Rossi 2020: 237–38, 244; Smolecová and Šárovec 2021: 39–41).

Within a mere year, however, this unpredictable maverick saw his own government submerged in scandals. Moreover, he quickly demonstrated an obvious inability to cope with the COVID-19 pandemic, as evident in Slovakia's unusually high death toll. The deep crisis caused by the coronavirus, which resists any quick, thorough resolution, has revealed the hollowness of populist leaders' promises to "save the people" in many countries across the globe, as Chapter 2 explained and various studies document (Bayerlein et al. 2021; Meyer 2021; Foa et al. 2022). Because COVID-19 quickly deflated Matovič's claims to charisma, a questionable, secretive prime-ministerial decision shook Slovakia's feeble coalition government and forced Matovič to resign in early 2021.[34] The ambitious populist stayed on as a government minister until late 2022, however, probably waiting for the opportunity to make a comeback, which the openness of Slovakia's electoral arena may yet provide.

In sum, Slovakia experienced a series of populist governments, but they posed diminishing threats to democracy. The underlying reason for both of these developments is that personalistic plebiscitarian incumbents with their anti-organizational tendencies further destructure the weak party system that allowed for their emergence in the first place. Therefore, after the first leader's eventual downfall, the rise of another populist is likely. This path dependency can yield a sequence of personalistic plebiscitarian chief executives. Yet precisely because persistent party weakness facilitates the rise of charismatic outsiders, they can emerge with relative ease under fairly normal conditions. Consequently, they take office without encountering the

---

[33] Mesežnikov and Gyárfášová 2018: 78–80, 84; Bútorová and Bútora 2019: 83–86, 94–95; Nemčok and Spáč 2020: 247, 261.

[34] Slowakei: Ungewöhnlicher Rücktritt 2021; Petrović and Jeremić 2021: 720–21.

crisis situations that would provide opportunities for establishing total predominance and strangling democracy. For these reasons, serial populists as in Slovakia do not tend to do massive, lasting damage to liberal pluralism (Weyland 2022a: 37–38).

POPULISM WITHOUT CRISIS IN EASTERN EUROPE: THE SURVIVAL OF NOT-VERY-LIBERAL DEMOCRACIES

Several other populists in contemporary Eastern Europe faced the same constellation as Robert Fico in Slovakia, namely relatively weak institutional constraints but the absence of drastic resolvable crises that would have enabled them to impose their personalistic hegemony and smother democracy. While these chief executives used their political clout to promote cronyism and let corruption fester, they did not manage to enact major institutional change, not to speak of engineering a new constitution; nor did they seriously skew the electoral arena and undermine or marginalize the opposition. Because citizens sooner or later became disaffected with the cancerous growth of incompetence, nepotism, and malfeasance, these leaders sooner or later saw their plebiscitarian support shrink. Consequently, they faced serious challenges along the way, including mass protests or impeachments, and eventually lost power in an electoral upset. After their demise, democracy – though (further) diminished in quality – recovered from populist pressures.

This temporary yet limited backsliding, which did not impose authoritarianism, occurred in the Czech Republic under Andrej Babiš (2017–21), in Romania under Traian Băsescu (2004–7, 2007–12, 2012–14), in Bulgaria under Boyko Borisov (2009–13, 2014–17, 2017–21), and in a more pronounced but very temporary way in Slovenia under Ivan "Janez" Janša (2004–8, 2012–13, 2020–22) during his third government – to name and analyze only the more prominent cases. All of these personalistic plebiscitarian leaders encountered institutional systems of relative plasticity, one of the necessary conditions for successful assaults on democracy according to my theory. The Czech Republic and Slovenia feature parliamentary systems (Hanley and Vachudova 2018: 280–81), characterized by relatively easy changeability, as explained in Chapter 2. Specialists classify Romania's system of government as parliamentarism or weak semi-presidentialism because the head of state's political clout depends on the partisan constellation in parliament (Dragoman 2013: 39–40; Ştefan 2021: 481–83, 485–86, 493). Bulgaria has a semi-presidential system (Ganev 1999). Yet the farther one moves away from Central Europe toward the Balkans, the weaker is the rule of law. Consequently, the somewhat stronger institutional constraints in Romania and especially Bulgaria are easier to bend or overcome in para-legal ways, compared to the Czech Republic and Slovenia with their greater compliance with official rules. Overall, therefore, the institutional arena is relatively open for populist machinations in all of these nations.

What has been missing, however, is the second precondition for the strangulation of democracy, namely acute and severe crises that populist chief executives can overcome with bold countermeasures. Only in this way could personalistic leaders win overwhelming plebiscitarian backing that would allow them to push aside the remaining institutional strictures, energetically concentrate power, and abolish democratic competitiveness. Babiš, Băsescu, Borisov, and Janša, however, did not emerge in such a crisis setting.[35] They were not catapulted into power by a catastrophic challenge that enabled them to blame and attack their predecessors and become their country's savior.[36] Instead, they arose in fragmented, fairly fluid party systems, which dogged the socioeconomic and political performance of preceding governments and left considerable room for relative newcomers – but which would create substantial problems for the victorious populists as well.

The absence of conjunctural opportunities for garnering massive backing limited the clout of these populist chief executives and, correspondingly, the damage they could do to liberal pluralism.[37] As a result, the survival of democracy was not endangered, although its quality suffered (Guasti 2020: 476–82). All of these personalistic plebiscitarian politicians used their prime-ministerial attributions and their substantial influence in parliament to pass some illiberal policy measures, such as restrictions on immigration. Moreover, they showered economic perks and privileges on their supporters, friends, and family members. These self-serving shenanigans skewed market competition and brought a good deal of illicit enrichment and corruption.[38] To cover up these political manipulations and the resulting misdeeds, the populist governments criticized investigative journalists, sought to expand their own command over media outlets, and tried to restrict the operation of civil society groupings (Hanley and Vachudova 2018: 286–87; Delić 2020; Petrović 2020: 61–62).

But these personalistic plebiscitarian leaders never enjoyed the unaccountable predominance that would have enabled them to dismantle democracy and ensure their self-perpetuation in power. Instead, because they had not rescued their countries from impending doom and therefore did not benefit from a groundswell of support, their electoral vehicles never won majorities (Hanley and Vachudova 2018: 277, 283, 289; Tsai 2019: 1465). In the

---

[35] During the year of Borisov's first election in 2009, Bulgaria suffered a moderate recession (–3 percent growth, per World Bank), which was clearly less than the crisis threshold of –5 percent used in this study. Therefore, the populist leader's crisis discourse (Gurov and Zankina 2013: 8–9) and his subsequent economic adjustment measures (Kostadinova and Giurcanu 2015: 802) found only limited resonance and support among citizens and voters.

[36] Strikingly, in Romania and Bulgaria, the years of the Great Recession (2008–12) saw better economic indicators overall than the pre-crisis years (Kostadinova and Giurcanu 2015: 791, 810).

[37] On Babiš's ideas and plans, see Havlík 2019.

[38] Hein 2015; Hanley and Vachudova 2018: 283–88; Mungiu-Pippidi 2018: 108, 111; Cirhan and Kopecký 2020: 104–5.

fragmented party systems facilitated by the proportional representation prevailing in Eastern Europe (Cristova 2010: 223–28; Cabada and Tomšič 2016: 34–40), populist leaders commonly need coalition partners in order to win and retain the premiership (unless they rely on minority cabinets, which are even weaker).[39] These alliances often lack solidity. After all, populism has vague and fickle programmatic and ideological commitments; and while this fluidity allows for reaching out across the ideological spectrum, it limits the glue that keeps governments' base of sustenance together.[40] Moreover, personalistic plebiscitarian politicians are domineering alpha males, who have difficulty negotiating and keeping compromises with other leaders – and even holding together their own electoral vehicles (Gherghina and Soare 2021).

For these reasons, the coalitions sustaining populist prime ministers remained fairly precarious. While the quest for power, patronage, and corruption provided incentives for cooperation, this malfeasance also increased the risk of scandals. Intracoalitional squabbles reduced the chief executives' clout and hindered their pursuit of self-aggrandizement. Without a firm support base, assaults on democracy are unpromising. In fact, every few years, alliances headed by populists collapsed, leading to their ouster.

Accordingly, Romania's Băsescu suffered two impeachments and temporary suspensions from office. While he survived ("won") the subsequent referenda and was quickly reinstalled, the second impeachment, which proved his lack of popularity, left "his charisma in tatters."[41] Similarly, the domineering approach of Bulgaria's Borisov inside his first government, which included a push for stringent austerity measures, hurt his public standing and helped to provoke protests that led to his resignation in 2013 (Bankov 2020: 55–56, 60–63; see also Gherghina and Soare 2021: 66). A comeback effort was initially unsuccessful, but the Bulgarian populist won a limited victory in the 2014 elections and resumed office. His party's defeat in the presidential contest of 2016 prompted his second resignation in 2017, but he won the subsequent snap election, forming another wide-ranging coalition government (Kanev 2013: 21–35; Tsai 2019: 1465; Spirova and Sharenkova-Toshkova 2021: 436–45; see also Ganev 2018: 91–103).

Standing on even weaker ground, the Czech Republic's Babiš (2017–21) headed a minority coalition government that only narrowly survived a no-confidence vote in 2018 (Hanley and Vachudova 2018: 277, 283, 289).

---

[39] As mentioned earlier, the political clout of Romanian presidents depends on their "convergence" with the majority coalition in parliament as well (Ştefan 2021: 481–83, 493). On the president's frequent predominance over the prime minister, see Kostadinova and Giurcanu (2015: 804–5).

[40] Cholova and De Waele 2011: 28–34, 42–44; Gurov and Zankina 2013: 5; Hein 2015: 752–53, 758–71; Cabada and Tomšič 2016: 44–45; Zankina 2016: 190–91; Mungiu-Pippidi 2018: 111, 113; Spirova and Sharenkova-Toshkova 2021: 436–45; Ştefan 2021: 490–91.

[41] Tismaneanu 2013: 87; see also 85–86; Deloy 2012; Dragoman 2013: 38–40; Mungiu-Pippidi 2018: 108, 113; Klašnja and Pop-Eleches 2022: 742.

Similarly, the political position of Slovenia's Janša grew increasingly precarious over the course of his three stints in government. As the Ljubljana populist turned more autocratic, he faced stricter containment from Slovenia's strong and independent Constitutional Court, and fiercer challenges from the country's vibrant civil society. Consequently, a corruption scandal and subsequent no-confidence vote felled him one year into his second premiership in 2013; and he faced – but survived – another no-confidence vote in 2021, barely one year after his third inauguration (Petrović 2020: 60–63).

While lacking firm political sustenance, these populist chief executives also had tension-filled relationships with the political opposition and civil society. Babiš, for instance, a Czech version of Berlusconi (Hanley and Vachudova 2018), faced huge protests over the years, which targeted his shady business dealings and his conflicts of interest as prime minister (Guasti 2020: 480–81). Popular revulsion against his uncouth behavior also contributed to the opposition victory in the parliamentary elections of late 2021 (Higgins 2021), which ended his pressure on democracy; his comeback effort in the presidential elections of early 2023 clearly failed as well (Palata 2023; Charlemagne: Return to Centre 2023). Similarly, Bulgaria's Borisov faced several opposition challenges, including no-confidence votes, over the years (Spirova and Sharenkova-Toshkova 2021: 438–43). Moreover, after the popular protests of 2013, a new round of mass demonstrations took aim at the Balkan populist in 2020 and contributed to his lack of electoral success and eventual defeat in a series of initially inconclusive contests in 2021.

Slovenia's Janša stirred up particular tension by making a drastic turn toward autocracy during his third term (2020–22). In open imitation of Donald Trump and Hungary's Viktor Orbán, he attacked journalists and used the COVID-19 pandemic to tighten his grip over the small nation, which therefore suffered the biggest drop in its liberal democracy score (2018–21) among all European countries (Guasti and Buštiková 2022: 5–6). But these transgressions provoked fierce resistance, including mass protests, which contributed to the no-confidence vote in 2021, mentioned earlier, and paved the way for Janša's stinging defeat in the parliamentary elections of 2022 (Murphy 2022).

All these limitations and weaknesses deprived the populist prime ministers of the clout to steamroll liberal pluralism and move toward competitive authoritarianism. In particular, they never commanded Orbán's capacity to distort the institutional framework quickly and legally by forging a new constitution; lacking the supermajority that the Magyar leader won due to Hungary's deep recession in 2008, they could not smoothly undermine and abolish democracy. Therefore, the Czech leader Babiš, for instance, was not able to push through his undemocratic project of installing "a strongly majoritarian, centralized system that eliminated checks and balances" through "the abolition of the Senate ... and a move to a first-past-the-post electoral system" (Hanley and Vachudova 2018: 282; see also 283), which could have guaranteed his party a parliamentary majority.[42] Similarly, the weak support base of Slovenia's Janša, whose party commanded barely 28 percent of parliamentary seats, made institutional reforms and especially a constitutional transformation impossible.

While the lack of overwhelming popularity and strong electoral mandates precluded authoritarian regressions via constitutional transformation, open infractions and violations of liberal rules were risky, as the political fate of Slovakia's Mečiar had shown. Many East European populists, especially Babiš and Băsescu, therefore refrained from forcing illiberal projects in autocratic ways. Even Borisov in Bulgaria, where there was most room for para-legal change and arbitrary machinations, did not undertake any serious effort to distort the electoral arena and skew the vote count in order to guarantee his own perpetuation in power (Ganev 2018: 92). Instead, these personalistic prime ministers confined themselves primarily to enjoying the ample perks of office, as long as their fragile coalitions kept them in power. When Slovenia's Janša departed from this self-restraint during his third term (2020–22) and initiated a more frontal attack on democracy, he provoked a substantial backlash and clearly lost the subsequent election. Thus, whereas he sought to follow in the footsteps of Hungary's Orbán, he actually ended up in the political wilderness like Slovakia's Mečiar; and as had happened in Slovakia, Slovenia's democracy quickly recovered.

For these reasons, liberal pluralism has managed to persist in most of Eastern Europe. While temporarily depressed in quality during the rocky stretches of personalistic plebiscitarian leadership, democracy gained a new lease on life after their downfall. The absence of dramatic yet resolvable crises prevented many personalistic prime ministers from taking advantage of the variegated institutional weaknesses of their governmental systems; they could not resolutely concentrate power, cement their own hegemony, and destroy democracy along the way (Ganev 2018: 91–92, 96–101). These cases thus provide further corroboration for my theory on the interaction of institutional weaknesses and conjunctural opportunities, which Chapters 3 and 4 assessed for Latin America and which applies to Eastern Europe with its fairly weak democracies as well.

POPULISM IN SOUTHERN EUROPE: BERLUSCONI IN ITALY

The populist governance of Silvio Berlusconi (1994–95, 2001–6, 2008–11) played out in quite similar ways, and with similar outcomes, as personalistic plebiscitarian experiences did in Eastern Europe. Like Babiš in the Czech Republic,[43] Băsescu in Romania, and Borisov in Bulgaria, *Il Cavaliere* faced an institutional setting that was fairly favorable for the typically populist goal

---

[42] For similar ideas and projects in Romania, see Dragoman (2013: 33–36).

[43] In fact, as a political newcomer who drew heavily on his ownership of a major media empire for his electoral rise, Berlusconi shares particular similarities with Babiš, who in turn has been called "Babisconi" (Cirhan and Kopecký 2020: 99).

of power accumulation and political hegemony. Above all, parliamentarism left the door open for institutional change, including efforts at constitutional transformation. But like Babiš, Băsescu, Borisov, and Janša, Berlusconi did not encounter the second necessary condition for achieving political predominance and strangling democracy, namely a sharp, severe, yet resolvable crisis. Because the charismatic prime minister could not heroically save his compatriots from impending doom, he never counted on overwhelming backing, and his power concentration efforts failed. Consequently, his government did not significantly damage Italian democracy (Taggart and Rovira 2016: 351–52; Newell 2019: 191–92, 199). Berlusconi's ultimate "failure" (Newell 2019) thus shows the broad validity of my theory, which extends to advanced industrialized countries as well.[44]

Indeed, the fact that this personalistic plebiscitarian leader was far from suffocating liberal pluralism is especially noteworthy because Berlusconi occupied the premiership in a particularly fluid institutional setting. In the early 1990s, Italian politics had suffered a veritable earthquake: A huge corruption scandal that tainted large segments of the entrenched "political class" shattered the party system and prompted the implosion and dissolution of the mainstays of the post-World War II democracy, most prominently Christian Democracy, which had for decades anchored governments (Shin and Agnew 2008: 46–59; Newell 2019: 55–60; Pappas 2019: 146–48). Besides allowing for the sudden rise of political outsiders such as media tycoon Berlusconi, this organizational collapse opened up extra opportunities for institutional, if not constitutional transformation. Desperate to emerge from the crisis through political renewal and relegitimation, the surviving politicians tried out electoral reform, for instance, changing the voting system repeatedly.

The resulting institutional plasticity reinforced the easy changeability inherent in parliamentarism. With a formally weak president, Italian prime ministers who command majorities in parliament have comparatively free rein and can, in principle, enact a wide range of changes. While the courts impose constraints, appointment powers can over time erode these impediments as well. The profound shock of Italy's mega-corruption scandal provided a special impetus and additional legitimacy for efforts to push through transformations. And the meltdown of established party organizations could allow a new charismatic leader to attract wide-ranging support.

These possibilities can only become realities, however, if a personalistic plebiscitarian leader finds a special opportunity for boosting his charisma through heroic deeds. Yet what miracles could Berlusconi perform? Italy achieved middling economic growth during the 1990s, and a small dip in 1993 did not lend itself to dramatic rescue efforts. Thus, the *Cavaliere* was unable to bring

---

[44] In West European countries where populist parties form part of coalition governments and their leaders often do not hold the premiership, their impact on democracy is only minimal (Akkerman 2017).

the big relief that would have proven "magical" prowess. During Berlusconi's subsequent governments in the 2000s, the growth rate trended downward; but the main causes were deep-rooted structural problems that the charismatic populist could not quickly resolve. Also, the center-right politician won his last electoral triumph in early 2008, before the Great Recession hit Italy hard. Because the painful fallout appeared in 2009 under his own stewardship, he could not blame the predecessor government and use this economic challenge for boosting his own political fortunes.

For these reasons, Berlusconi's new party Forza Italia (FI)[45] never managed to win an electoral majority; indeed, it did not even reach 30 percent of the vote. To capture the premiership, the flamboyant business and media tycoon therefore needed to form coalitions. Given continuing ideological divisions – a legacy of the decades-long standoff between mainstream Christian Democracy and a large, "suspect" Communist Party – Berlusconi was compelled to find these allies among regionally and doctrinally divergent right-wing formations (Verbeek and Zaslove 2016: 309). For this purpose, he linked up both with an ever more populist party advancing the special interests of the country's economically advanced and dynamic north, and a party slowly emerging from neo-fascism that was centered in the poor, "backward," and state-dependent south (Shin and Agnew 2008: 66, 72–74, 97, 101–2, 132; Fracanzani 2021: 47–48, 184–85, 192).

On his first try in 1994, political newcomer Berlusconi managed this tricky balancing act only for a few months. The Northern League had its own populist strongman, who feared being outshone and therefore bolted in late 1994 (Shin and Agnew 2008: 85–86; Newell 2019: 65–66). This quick defection cost the prime minister his job and sent the FI leader into the opposition for years. But because the recalcitrant Lega paid a big electoral price in subsequent years, it turned into a more reliable partner for Berlusconi after the right's electoral victory in 2001. This loyalty helped the *Cavaliere* achieve the unusual feat of staying at the helm for five years – an Italian record. Yet the downside was constant infighting among his coalition partners because the Lega highlighted its own populist credentials by frequent feuding with its two allies, especially the (by then) post-fascists from the south (Albertazzi and McDonnell 2005: 956–59, 969–70). These disagreements and conflicts weakened Berlusconi's governments throughout their longer tenures in the 2000s.[46]

With such pugnacious, obstreperous partners, Berlusconi had to exert considerable effort to keep his heterogeneous coalitions together (Pasquino 2007: 43–44). Consequently, the populist leader lacked the solid foundation for resolutely promoting his own quest for unchallenged predominance. In particular, FI's wobbly alliances could not transform Italy's institutional order in an undemocratic direction (Körösényi and Patkós 2017: 319, 324). Intracoalitional

[45] This means "Forward Italy," the battle cry of the historically successful national soccer team.
[46] Shin and Agnew 2008: 43–44, 100, 107–8; Fella and Ruzza 2013; Newell 2019: 2, 11, 65–66, 93, 99, 106–8, 166, 200.

disagreements marred a major effort at constitutional reform, which sought to strengthen prime-ministerial power and reduce parliamentary and judicial prerogatives – potentially, a crucial step toward illiberalism (Blokker 2020: 24, 31–32). Yet Berlusconi's divergent partners insisted on various other amendments; the Northern League pushed for more decentralization, whereas the post-fascists of the poor south, hungry for governmental patronage, advocated centralization (Albertazzi and McDonnell 2005: 966–67). Because the overall reform package turned into an incoherent, unwieldy Frankenstein's monster, and because differences among the allied parties weakened their campaign efforts and voter mobilization, the constitutional referendum suffered defeat in 2006.[47]

Moreover, Berlusconi's illiberal and hegemonic tendencies were held in check by a judiciary that had gained legitimacy and strength from the prosecution of massive corruption in the early 1990s (Dallara 2015; Fracanzani 2021: 143–44). Due to his own notorious conflicts of interest, the billionaire businessman was ill-positioned to spearhead an anti-bribery crusade, take the limelight away from the judiciary, and claim the typically populist mantle of the moralizing hero. Because the populist prime minister could therefore not use his appointment powers for gradually transforming and eventually controlling the judiciary, the third branch remained a thorn in his side: Judges eagerly scrutinized Berlusconi's decisions and contained his expansive tendencies (Fracanzani 2021: 153–61).[48] Indeed, facing the unusual challenges emanating from personalistic plebiscitarian leadership, even Italy's presidents assumed a more active and independent role and helped to restrain Berlusconi (Furlong 2015; Verbeek and Zaslove 2016: 310–12; Pasquino 2021: 169). Furthermore, the independent media and civil society did not tire in exposing the prime minister's personal and political scandals, which contributed to electoral losses and the defection of partisan allies, and finally forced Berlusconi to resign in 2011.[49] His subsequent comeback efforts failed as his party's vote shares steadily diminished (Pappas 2019: 256).

In conclusion, Berlusconi lacked the crucial conjunctural opportunity to take advantage of Italy's relative institutional openness and push through changes that would have established his predominance and enabled him to asphyxiate democracy. By contrast to Turkey's Erdoğan and Hungary's Orbán,[50] the *Cavaliere* did not rise in a crisis situation that would have allowed him

---

[47] Bull 2007: 100–4, 107–9; Pasquino 2007: 44–47; Shin and Agnew 2008: 67, 123, 128–32; Newell 2019: 165–67, 174–75, 191–92.

[48] Even the UK's new Supreme Court with its as yet unclear constitutional role served as a crucial safeguard by striking down the attempt of populist Prime Minister Boris Johnson to prorogue parliament and unilaterally force through the controversial Brexit decision in 2019 (Issacharoff 2023: 138–40).

[49] Shin and Agnew 2008: 104–5; Fella and Ruzza 2013: 39–42, 45, 48; Verbeek and Zaslove 2016: 311–18; Newell 2019: 94–99, 104–8, 203.

[50] In their interesting and insightful comparison of Orbán and Berlusconi, Körösényi and Patkós (2017) foreground populist leaders' agency and therefore attribute the divergent regime

miraculously to rescue his compatriots and, as a reward, earn overwhelming support. Instead, Berlusconi's own party never even won a majority of votes. Dependent on recalcitrant allies and weakened by intracoalitional tensions and conflicts, Italy's personalistic plebiscitarian leader had no way of enacting the constitutional transformations that pushed Turkey and Hungary into competitive authoritarianism. Therefore, his many years in the premiership left Italian democracy virtually unscathed, despite all the shady dealings and embarrassing scandals. Indeed, Newell (2019) subtitles his major analysis of Berlusconi's reign "a study in failure."

As in Slovakia, however, the two decades during which Italian politics revolved around Berlusconi's populism kept the party system fragmented and fluid, which enabled other populist leaders to rise (Verbeek and Zaslove 2019: 93–98; Fracanzani 2021: 210–12). Accordingly, the Mediterranean nation sank into serial populism. Personalistic plebiscitarian politicians emerged across the political and ideological spectrum. Besides the emergence of a particularly diffuse left-of-center grouping, the Five Star Movement (Vittori 2018: 82–87), the Northern League fell under an especially resolute and strident, yet charismatic right-winger, Matteo Salvini, who followed Europe's ever more numerous ethno-national populists in embracing a hard-core anti-immigration stance.

Despite their ideological divergences, these two populist formations formed a typically fractious coalition after the 2018 elections (Baldini and Giglioli 2020). While the rudderless Five Star Movement, whose support quickly dissipated, posed no threat to liberal democracy, pushy Salvini with his clearly illiberal project overplayed his cards. Unwilling to remain the alliance's junior partner, the impetuous chieftain of the Northern League tried in 2019 to grab control of Italy's government. But because there was no crisis that could have turned him into a magical savior, Salvini did not marshal a massive upsurge of support; instead, his power-hungry maneuver backfired drastically. When he sought to force new elections in mid-2019 by brashly breaking his rocky coalition with the Five Star Movement, he inadvertently provoked the formation of a new governing alliance, which expelled him into the political wilderness (Chiaramonte, De Sio, and Emanuele 2020: 151; Pasquino 2021: 165–66). Since then, his political star has quickly faded (Welcome to Normal Politics 2020; Bartels 2023: 176; Jones 2023: 31), a common fate for personalistic plebiscitarian leaders, whose reliance on charisma and plebiscitarian acclamation exposes them to drastic ups and downs in their political fortunes. While the enormous volatility of Italian politics and the continuing fluidity of the party system make forecasts uncertain, the country's liberal pluralism has, thus, managed to survive various populist experiences so far.

---

developments to differences in goals and styles. But especially where goals are retro-inferred from outcomes, such an approach holds little explanatory power. Moreover, it does not systematically consider the fundamental differences in exogenous conditions, especially the absence of an acute, severe, yet resolvable crisis in the Italian case – a crucial factor according to my theory.

CONCLUSION

The preceding analysis of European cases corroborates the main message of this book, namely that the populist strangulation of democracy is much less common than worried observers have warned in recent years (see also Bakke and Sitter 2022: 32–33). While personalistic plebiscitarian leadership undoubtedly poses inherent threats to liberal pluralism, it often runs into various obstacles and a great deal of resistance. Therefore, populist chief executives find it very difficult to dismantle institutional checks and balances, marginalize opposition forces in the electoral arena and civil society, establish their unchallenged political hegemony, and push toward authoritarian rule. Instead, as my theory highlights, stringent conditions have to coincide for serious democratic regression to occur, namely institutional weakness and a conjunctural opportunity for overriding the remaining constraints on populist power hunger.

Like the institutional debilities afflicting many presidential systems in Latin America, the easy changeability of parliamentarism prevailing in Europe does not give populist prime ministers free rein for enacting their illiberal projects. Instead, even comparatively weak checks and balances often obstruct the power hunger of personalistic plebiscitarian leaders and allow for the counter-mobilization of opposition parties and civil society. Accordingly, charismatic politicians ranging from Berlusconi in Italy to Babiš in the Czech Republic left democracy unscathed, and even autocratic Mečiar in Slovakia and Kaczyński in Poland have not managed to destroy liberal pluralism; it recovered quickly after Mečiar's electoral defeat in 1998 and has stayed afloat along the Vistula.

Because the attenuated institutional constraints of parliamentarism do not leave democracy defenseless against populist assaults, it falls only if personalistic plebiscitarian leaders benefit from the unusual conjunctural opportunity arising from a deep and pressing, yet resolvable economic crisis. This second necessary condition enables populist chief executives to bring dramatic relief, win widespread popular support and overwhelming political clout, and steamroll resistance to their hegemonic projects. This kind of crisis erupts infrequently, however, and its occurrence right before an election is even rarer. Moreover, some catastrophic problems are not easily resolvable, such as the massive economic downturn after the collapse of communism or the viral contagion driving the COVID-19 pandemic.

For these reasons, the two preconditions for the populist asphyxiation of democracy do not often coincide. Although personalistic plebiscitarian prime ministers operate in the favorable settings of parliamentarism, they frequently cannot take advantage of this relative institutional weakness because of the absence of politically exploitable crises. Thus, whereas the institutional configuration predominant in Europe in principle facilitates populists' undemocratic designs, the greater stability of economies – compared to those of commodity-dependent Latin America – offers an extra degree of protection (cf. Wibbels 2006).

Indeed, the EU has bolstered this economic resilience by integrating most of Eastern Europe into the common market. Admission to this zone of prosperity required a commitment to prudent economic policy-making, which the EU tries to enforce by imposing strict adjustment in case a crisis does erupt, as in Greece after 2008. Thus, the economic result of EU membership, namely a reduction of economic volatility, has further diminished the likelihood of crises that ambitious personalistic leaders could use for promoting their undemocratic goals. This salutary economic effect has counterbalanced the political downside of the completion of EU accession, which has made Brussels' political leverage less effective and has thus given illiberal populists such as Hungary's Orbán greater room of maneuver. In sum, whereas European integration gives the EU only limited political power over populist chief executives, it indirectly – by helping to forestall crises – limits those rulers' chances for gaining overwhelming domestic power.

6

Right-Wing Populism in the USA

Trump in Comparative Perspective

SUDDEN CONCERN ABOUT POPULISM'S THREATS
TO THE PROTOTYPE OF LIBERAL DEMOCRACY

As Chapter 5 mentions, regional specialists did not expect the asphyxiation of democracy in Hungary and the forceful attempt to emulate this strangulation in Poland; after all, liberal pluralism seemed consolidated in these Western-oriented countries, their economies and societies were fairly advanced, and Poland enjoyed sustained growth. But this surprise was nothing compared to the shock that befell scholars of all stripes when Donald Trump, against all odds, won the 2016 presidential contest in the USA. Not only was this crass outsider utterly unprepared for his demanding new job, but he had also revealed dangerously illiberal orientations and autocratic tendencies in his strident populist discourse and style.[1] Was democracy now endangered in the heartland of political liberalism as well?[2]

The new president indeed showed a disturbing eagerness to push through his arbitrary whims at all costs; and though living in ostentatious luxury, he had cultivated an intense charismatic affinity with his "deplorable" followers that gave him strong support and undergirded his unlikely electoral success. That such a typically personalistic plebiscitarian leader, who harbored obvious undemocratic inclinations, could capture the chief executive office in the country that had an institutional framework and constitution designed to forestall the rise of such a demagogue (see, e.g., Thomas 2016; Zuckert 2019)

---

[1] See the in-depth analysis of Trump's populist discourse in Rowland (2021) and the systematic measurement of this discourse in Hawkins and Littvay (2019: 12–19). On the ethno-nationalist strands of Trump's populism, see Bonikowski (2019).

[2] I thank my departmental colleagues Daron Shaw, Bartholomew Sparrow, and Christopher Wlezien for many important insights, explanations, and literature tips on the US case.

provoked enormous consternation among political scientists and broader circles of civil society. Whereas the USA had long served as the poster child of liberal pluralism and its main promoter across the world, it now looked like a serious problem case (Dionne, Ornstein, and Mann 2017; Ginsburg and Huq 2018b; Graber, Levinson, and Tushnet 2018; Levitsky and Ziblatt 2018; Sunstein 2018). These sudden fears were so acute, and the Trump phenomenon so unusual and hard to grasp, that quite a few commentators went so far as to depict the new president as a variant of (proto-)fascism (e.g., Connolly 2017; Stanley 2018; Rosenfeld 2019).

Thus, the political regime issue, which had long seemed settled and therefore irrelevant in the USA, unexpectedly arose with a red alert on the political – and academic – agenda: Would the institutional framework designed in the late eighteenth century have the resilience to constrain the domineering populist, or was it so rusty and corroded that it might cave under Trump's unconventional assault? Would the new president manage to follow in the footsteps of European and Latin American populists who had used their popular mandate and institutional prerogatives to smother democracy? A wide range of observers worried that the personalistic plebiscitarian occupant of the White House would march along the same path that Fujimori and Chávez, Orbán and Erdoğan, had already traced. Scholars therefore argued that liberal pluralism in the USA was now in serious peril (see especially Levitsky and Ziblatt 2018; Kaufman and Haggard 2019; see also Lieberman et al. 2019; Mettler and Lieberman 2020).

Not all academics shared these urgent concerns, however. Instead, advocates of different theoretical frameworks advanced divergent assessments and predictions. From a historical perspective, theorists of the cyclical installation, consolidation, and degeneration of partisan and policy regimes throughout American history had expected the emergence of an outsider who – after the exhaustion of Ronald Reagan's neoliberal policy regime – would test the boundaries and pursue new initiatives in distinctly transgressive ways. This recurring "politics of disjunction" had sometimes shaken but never destroyed American democracy (Skowronek 2020: 86–92, 203–11; see also 61–76). But even these authors saw some risks. After all, Trump's populism did not merely repeat a longstanding pattern but had genuinely new features (Skowronek 2020: 212–15). In particular, could the fervent mass following that the billionaire tycoon personally commanded turn his headstrong quest for dominance and strident rejection of democratic rules and liberal norms into a real threat to pluralist democracy?

Historical institutionalists also wondered whether the suddenly voiced worries, which sometimes bordered on panic, went too far. After all, the United States boasted the longest-standing democracy in the world. For more than two centuries, the constitution had successfully withstood the much-discussed "perils of presidentialism" (Linz 1990) and provided a persistent exception to the alleged "failure of presidential democracy" (Linz and Valenzuela 1994;

see recently Lieberman et al. 2019: 473). The liberal framework established in 1787 had survived mass incorporation and democratization, civil war and the abolition of slavery, world war and economic depression, the titanic struggles against fascism and communism, and many other problems and challenges along the way. Would these sturdy checks and balances not constrain and block Trump's autocratic leanings as well?

Besides a deeply rooted institutional framework, American democracy rested on other crucial sources of strength. Modernization theory pointed to a particularly important safeguard: According to one of the best-supported generalizations in political science, a highly developed economy made the established system "impregnable" against downfall (Przeworski 2019: 33–34). After all, innumerable statistical investigations showed that risks to liberal pluralism were concentrated at lower levels of development; in no country that was nearly as rich as the USA had democracy ever broken down. Advanced development protected liberal pluralism through a variety of mechanisms, such as mass education, the irresistible advance of individualistic, progressive values (Inglehart and Welzel 2005), and the resourcefulness and mobilizational energy of a vibrant civil society.[3] Even during the interwar years in crisis-racked Europe, these factors had given established democracies immunity against the unprecedented challenges of communism, fascism, and authoritarianism (Cornell, Møller, and Skaaning 2017, 2020). Thus, would these same strengths not enable US democracy to avert the less dramatic threat of populism?

Certainly, however, US democracy in the 2010s also suffered from serious problems and potential risk factors, as socioeconomic structuralism and class approaches highlighted. Since Ronald Reagan's enactment of neoliberalism, social inequality had increased substantially, to levels significantly higher than in the remainder of the Western world. Would the rich, now led by billionaire Trump, take effective control and turn democracy into a plutocracy?[4] Would socioeconomic deprivation and restrictive voting laws hinder the participation of poorer sectors? The growing income and wealth gap also aggravated long-standing racial disparities; after all, the USA had never overcome the socioeconomic legacies of slavery and Jim Crow. With the seductive tactics of populism, would Trump fortify class rule and cement white supremacy, hollowing out democracy (Belew 2022; Jardina and Mickey 2022; see also Mason, Wronski, and Kane 2021)?

Theorists of electoral competition, in turn, emphasized the risks arising from deepening partisan polarization. After all, the major effort to combat

---

[3] Even among Republican elites, there was a good deal of active opposition and passive resistance against Trump, throughout his term in office (Saldin and Teles 2020; Herbert 2021: 105–9; Kriner 2022: 136), including the turbulent final months (Woodward and Costa 2021: 197, 213–14, 226–32, 243, 342–43; Lee 2023).

[4] See Pierson 2017; Mettler and Lieberman 2020: 22–24, 197–98, 228–33; see also Gilens and Page 2014; for a strong contrast, see Branham, Soroka, and Wlezien 2017.

racial discrimination through the civil rights legislation of the 1960s had prompted a basic realignment of the two-party system. With the massive move of Southern conservatives from the Democratic to the Republican Party, political, ideological, and cultural sorting had turned the two main formations ever more homogeneous in their internal complexion, and ever more distinct and distant from each other. As partisan divergence bred a lack of empathy, as intense electoral competition fueled polarization and conflict, and as this rising hostility, in turn, made party competition ever fiercer and nastier, both sides were increasingly tempted to bend the rules or exploit temporary majorities to alter institutions opportunistically to their own advantage.[5] Because mutual trust and "forbearance" (Levitsky and Ziblatt 2018) had faded and institutional manipulation had proliferated, the checks-and-balances system was slowly eroding. Consequently, the room for nefarious political agency, including the power hunger of personalistic plebiscitarian leaders, seemed to grow. In 2016, therefore, the urgent question arose as to whether the ever more porous institutional framework would still have sufficient strength to contain the illiberal initiatives and autocratic machinations of the newly triumphant Trump (see among many others, Mettler and Lieberman 2020: 6–7, 212).

In sum, a variety of factors, invoked by divergent theoretical approaches, have been pushing and pulling US democracy in different directions. Given the threat posed by populism, there are strengths that predict resilience, but also weaknesses that suggest vulnerability. A focus on a single case, however, even a country as thoroughly researched as the USA, makes it difficult to sort out these contradictory tendencies, establish their relative weight, and arrive at an overall assessment. A historical perspective can certainly help (see especially Mettler and Lieberman 2020; Skowronek 2020), but it faces difficulty in gauging the danger of populism because the Trump phenomenon is so unprecedented in the modern USA. After all, the last personalistic plebiscitarian leader, Andrew Jackson,[6] left the White House in 1837.[7] Liberal democracy had been so successful in forestalling the rise of demagogues that the USA has had no recent experience with populist chief executives, the damage they can do, and the way to contain them. For this reason, it was not easy for specialists of American politics to weigh the counteracting tendencies that would shape the fate of democracy under Trump and arrive at a realistic appraisal of the danger posed by the pushy, illiberal president.

---

[5] Abramowitz 2018, 2021; Fiorina 2017; Graham and Svolik 2020; Lieberman, Mettler, and Roberts 2022; Sides, Tesler, and Vavreck 2018.

[6] Kazin 1998: 19–24; Skowronek 2020: 32–40. Trump indeed displayed a portrait of Jackson in the Oval Office – which Biden then removed (Woodward and Costa 2021: 292; see also Skowronek 2020: 198).

[7] Even if one follows Tulis (1987: 83, 87–93) and classifies Andrew Johnson (1865–69) as a populist, more than 150 years have gone by. This pre-history lies so far back that Lowndes' (2017: 232, 243) overview of US populism barely mentions these early leaders, and Savage (2019) not at all.

To help overcome the limitations of a single-country focus, this book includes the USA in its wide-ranging comparative investigation and draws insights from the global wave of populism (see earlier efforts in Weyland and Madrid 2019; Weyland 2020). The experiences of personalistic plebiscitarian chief executives in Europe and Latin America – regions with important similarities to the USA – can elucidate the real risks currently facing liberal pluralism. By identifying the principal institutional parameters and conjunctural developments that condition the populist asphyxiation of democracy, a comparative analysis can put the examination of the US case on firmer ground and facilitate a more reliable assessment of democracy's prospects.

Indeed, analyzing the USA in light of my wide-ranging theory is relevant not only for analytical purposes but also for practical reasons. After all, the 45th president has never accepted his electoral defeat in 2020 and is energetically running for reelection in 2024. Given that the charismatic populist is likely to confront a number of rivals in the primaries, which may well allow him to win the Republican candidacy again, and given that three important and salient issues – inflation, crime, and immigration – will probably favor the Republican opposition in the presidential contest, Trump's chances look good at this time (April 2023). Besides helping to understand the recent past, this chapter may therefore elucidate the near future as well.

Fortunately, the theory and empirical findings of the preceding chapters strongly suggest that US democracy remains quite safe from populist strangulation – as the experiences of Trump's (first?) term corroborate (see also Lee 2020: 381–82; Lee 2022: 97, 108–14). After all, despite his many attempted infringements and his unprecedented push for self-perpetuation in late 2020 and early 2021, the transgressive populist clearly failed with his illiberal and autocratic machinations. The overbearing president did not succeed in undermining or seriously weakening the myriad opposition forces he was facing, nor in mustering sufficient support for engineering a second consecutive term. Trump's incapacity to manipulate, obstruct, falsify, undermine, or reverse the vote count, and his inability to pass undemocratic institutional changes throughout his tenure, demonstrate the continuing strength of the USA's constitutional framework.

While an examination of the US case itself confirms the importance of this continuing institutional strength – one of the two principal factors of my theory – the role of the other crucial condition emerges only from a comparative perspective: As Trump's autocratic efforts were hindered by limited support and his mediocre and stagnant approval ratings (e.g., Binder 2021: 81; Smith 2021: 538; Sides, Tausanovitch, and Vavreck 2022: 59–66), he was hemmed in by the absence of the conjunctural opportunities that enabled leaders such as Fujimori and Chávez, Orbán and Erdoğan, to strangle democracy. As Chapters 3 to 5 showed, without such chances, provided by deep and acute, yet resolvable crises or by a huge hydrocarbon windfall, no personalistic plebiscitarian chief executive managed to cement his political hegemony and suffocate liberal pluralism. Because Trump lacked any of these unusual opportunities, he was unable to overwhelm American democracy.

After all, the US economy and its society are so complex, advanced, and prosperous that they are not very exposed to the risk of catastrophic crises. For instance, both of the disasters that Peru's Fujimori confronted in 1990, namely hyperinflation and a virtual civil war, are out of the question in the USA. Moreover, when drastic problems do afflict the USA, as in the COVID-19 pandemic, the government commands such resource abundance that it can quickly enact wide-ranging compensation measures, as the multitrillion dollar support distributed in 2020–21 demonstrates. The complexity and diversification of the US economy also preclude a massive revenue windfall. By contrast to Venezuela's enormous dependence on petroleum extraction, for instance, in America no sector is sufficiently important for a sudden price increase to exert a huge overall impact. For these reasons, a personalistic plebiscitarian leader such as Trump does not encounter propitious preconditions for winning overwhelming support and strangling democracy.

Thus, with its proven institutional strength and its socioeconomic solidity and avoidance of dramatic volatility, the USA fulfills neither one of the necessary prerequisites for the populist asphyxiation of liberal pluralism. American democracy therefore continues to be quite immune from the undeniable danger posed by transgressive charismatic leadership. Institutional resilience and limited socioeconomic fluctuations impede executive self-aggrandizement and guarantee the preservation of ample room for liberal pluralism. Even if Trump achieves reelection in 2024 and pushes his autocratic aspirations with redoubled energy, the regime founded in 1776–87 is unlikely to risk downfall.

THE CONTINUING INSTITUTIONAL STRENGTH OF US DEMOCRACY

Chapters 3 through 5 demonstrated that institutional weakness is a necessary precondition for the populist destruction of democracy. Even middling levels of institutional strength, however, seriously hinder power grabs by personalistic plebiscitarian leaders, as the cases of Colombia's Uribe (Chapter 3), Argentina's Fernández de Kirchner (Chapter 4), and Italy's Berlusconi (Chapter 5) show.

How much safer is US democracy with its high level of institutional strength! Through its constitutional structure, presidentialism with its dense web of checks and balances and federalism with its resourceful state and city governments enshrine a strict separation of power that precludes the president from imposing his will and establishing authoritarian preeminence (see in general Tsebelis 2002: 141–43, 153–57). Certainly, increasing ideological and affective polarization and the resulting fierce conflicts have started to corrode these protections, for instance through restrictions of filibuster use in the Senate (Ginsburg and Huq 2018b: 141–48; McCoy and Somer 2022: 75–79; Pierson and Schickler 2022: 51–54, 57–59). The stark partisan alignment at Trump's two impeachments, which precluded the president's conviction, showed this weakening of accountability and control mechanisms (Mettler and Lieberman 2020: 212, 240–43; Jacobs and Milkis 2021: 315–17; Skowronek, Dearborn, and King 2021: 165–89; Downs 2022: 365–66, 371–72; Kriner 2022: 137–40).[8]

But at the same time, pronounced polarization has also intensified the motivation for all sides to use their institutional attributions to the maximum. Because both parties "check and balance" their adversaries with great determination and energy, there has been worsening gridlock in this evenly divided polity.[9] The prevalence of "insecure" and "unstable majorities" (Lee 2016; Fiorina 2017), eager to employ any mechanism to gain some advantage, has exacerbated obstruction and conflict in the increasingly "dysfunctional Congress" (Binder 2015) and has aggravated "political stalemate" (Fiorina 2017), both inside the legislative branch and in its relations with the executive. As political scientists' insistent calls for strengthening the presidency suggest (Howell and Moe 2016, 2020), and as Trump's meager legislative record confirms (Nelson 2018: 82, 100, 148; Lee 2018, 2021; Smith 2021), the main problem plaguing US democracy is not excessive openness to change but "high-energy stasis" (Foley 2013: 354; see recently Binder 2021; Grossmann 2021). The great difficulty of passing reforms seriously hinders institutional alterations. This stickiness protects US democracy against populist projects of authoritarian transformation.

Interestingly, decades of partisan sorting, which have increased internal ideological cohesion (Fiorina 2017), and the deepening gulf between the GOP (Republican Party) and the Democrats have not enabled chief executives to take advantage of phases of unified government, resolutely concentrate power, and permanently skew political competitiveness. Instead, the institutional incentives driving presidentialism's different branches of government continue to induce pivotal congresspeople to check and balance even chief executives from their own party.[10] As the inability of President Trump to use temporary partisan majorities in Congress (2018–19) for approving hallmark projects shows, the separation of power remains firm and can block even high-profile initiatives, such as the promised repeal of "Obamacare." Senators, in particular, retain the independence and clout to pose insurmountable roadblocks (Lee 2018; Smith 2021).

---

[8] Ten Republican senators did publicly criticize and condemn Trump's actions that prompted the first impeachment, however (Woodward 2020: 239–41). Indeed, seven senators voted to convict Trump at the second impeachment. Note that before 2019, no senator from the governing party had ever cast such a vote against an incumbent (Downs 2022: 352–53, 371; see also Sides, Tausanovitch, and Vavreck 2022: 261).

[9] Abramowitz 2013; Howell and Moe 2016; for the Democrats under Trump, see Nelson 2018: 44–45, 67–68, 80–81, 145.

[10] Lee 2020: 381; Skowronek, Dearborn, and King 2021: 141, 163, 172, 187–88; Kriner 2022: 125–26, 134–37; Lee 2022: 109–11.

Thus, despite intense affective polarization, partisan loyalty does not give presidents the disciplining power to make their own party delegation uniformly fall in line; instead, they have difficulty pushing through controversial projects. Consequently, the checks-and-balances system continues to impose firm constraints on populist leadership. Above all, congresspeople's insistence on their autonomy impedes any serious institutional distortion that would boost presidential powers and undermine democracy.

A powerful judiciary constitutes another cornerstone of US democracy's high institutional strength. Drawing from the vast talent pool of an exceedingly well-trained and proud legal profession, the court system has jealously guarded its independence and frequently demonstrated its willingness to stop executive and legislative action at all levels.[11] Political forces from both parties have longstanding interests in sustaining this judicial autonomy (Whittington 2018). The courts are constantly called into action because a vibrant and hyperalert civil society, supported by "lawyers [operating] as activists" (Dorf and Chu 2018: 127), eagerly challenges all kinds of political and policy decisions. The judiciary therefore gets the last word in an ample gamut of political controversies. Wide-ranging venue shopping enables a multitude of groups and sectors to block executive action at least temporarily, until higher courts have the chance to overrule a lower-court decision. By using such a multiplicity of legal challenges, armies of Lilliputians can threaten to turn a seemingly powerful president, including a headstrong populist, into a rather hapless Gulliver.

With his illiberal projects and autocratic tendencies, President Trump provoked precisely such a legal guerrilla war (Dorf and Chu 2018; Nelson 2018: 71–74; Winer 2018; cf. Skowronek and Orren 2020: 360). Every single one of his problematic initiatives faced a variety of court challenges. Well-prepared and well-funded civil society groupings as well as state and city governments contested many of his decisions, from his controversial "Muslim bans" to his alterations of asylum rules. And whereas in many Latin American countries, populist presidents find ways to co-opt or pressure courts into doing their bidding, in the USA Trump often lost and suffered important, sometimes embarrassing setbacks (Cooley 2018: 34–35; Kalb and Bannon 2018: 1–3; Winer 2018: 910–21).

More remarkably even, the personalistic plebiscitarian occupant of the White House uniformly complied with negative rulings (Peabody 2018; see also Kalb and Bannon 2018: 3). While sometimes criticizing unfavorable decisions with uncivil language, Trump did not push his ostentatious penchant for transgression so far as to disrespect court orders, as populists elsewhere, ranging from Chávez in Venezuela to Mečiar in Slovakia, have frequently done. That the American populist refrained from defying adverse judicial decisions

---

[11] As Winer (2018: 922–34) emphasizes, courts, with many judges appointed by Democrats (Nelson 2018: 64, 73–74), often "went out of their way" to find legal reasons for striking down Trump's initial set of controversial executive orders.

demonstrates the strength of the rule of law, a fundamental liberal constraint on overbearing personalistic leaders.

The importance of judicial independence became even more obvious and crucial when Trump tried to overturn his defeat of November 2020 by contesting all aspects of the electoral process in six crucial battleground states. Yet in these high-stakes cases, which could have provoked a constitutional crisis, even Trump appointees consistently ruled against the pushy incumbent; the intensity of partisan loyalties in this era of polarization did not override professionalism and prompt deviations from the strict interpretation of the law. Despite a huge effort and massive expense, the personalistic plebiscitarian leader did not achieve any inroad; his team, which tried all angles and obsessively searched for any loopholes, uniformly lost eighty-six court cases (Busch and Pitney 2021: 182–89; Woodward and Costa 2021: 214; Jacobs and Choate 2022: 30).

In sum, the tripartite separation of power enshrined in the presidential system of government continues to impose firm constraints on the head of state that impede any serious power grab by a personalistic plebiscitarian leader. As a result, Trump ran into a host of checks and balances and was unable to undermine US democracy. By contrast to the openings created by para-legal change under Latin American presidentialism and by the comparatively easy changeability of European parliamentarism, the US populist found no path toward executive aggrandizement.

Federalism created additional obstacles against populist power concentration.[12] Many states and cities, especially those controlled by Democrats, tried hard to evade Trump's illiberal measures or challenged them directly in the courts. For instance, as the president sought to tighten the USA's immigration regime, "sanctuary cities" that prohibited the local police from enforcing federal provisions proliferated (Nelson 2018: 75; Zepeda-Millán and Wallace 2018: 91, 93, 98; Busch and Pitney 2021: 109). Moreover, presidential initiatives were blocked by large numbers of judicial cases brought by state and city governments (Nelson 2018: 76). Thus, different institutional constraints reinforced each other, forming a spiderweb of obstacles that hemmed in Trump's populist agency (e.g., see Woodward 2018: 206, 215, 317, 320–21).

All of these institutional limitations on the power hunger of a personalistic plebiscitarian ruler are anchored in an extraordinarily rigid, sacrosanct constitution inspired in the fundamental liberal goal of protecting individual freedom by dispersing political authority.[13] As the founding document of a nation of tremendous historical, cultural, religious, ethnic, and racial diversity that was held together primarily by a joint commitment to liberal-pluralist

---

[12] Hertel-Fernandez (2022), Rocco (2022), and Grofman (2022) highlight, however, that federalism can also create openings for populist machinations, as discussed later.

[13] Howell and Moe 2016. On gaps and omissions in the US constitution that create vulnerabilities to democratic backsliding, however, see Ginsburg and Huq (2018b: chap. 5).

principles (Hartz 1955; Huntington 1981: chaps. 2–3), the Philadelphia charter commands unassailable legitimacy and elicits profound normative "veneration" (Elkins, Ginsburg, and Melton 2009: 20–21, 29, 65).

Among written constitutions, the US charter is by far the oldest in the world (Ginsburg and Huq 2018b: 205), which makes its overhaul hard to imagine. Consequently, the effort spearheaded by populist leaders across the world to convoke a constituent assembly, use it to dismantle the liberal framework, and push toward competitive authoritarianism, is practically out of the question in the USA; even in his wildest dreams and uncontrolled tweet storms, President Trump did not advocate such a heretical move. Thus, the major avenue toward the strangulation of democracy that personalistic plebiscitarian chief executives of all stripes, ranging from Venezuela's Chávez to Hungary's Orbán, have employed, is foreclosed in the USA. The populist in the White House was unable to invoke popular sovereignty for starting the installation of autocratic hegemony.

Similarly, constitutional amendments, which are comparatively easy to pass in many countries (see, e.g., for Mexico, Rivera León 2017), are prohibitively difficult in the USA. Besides supermajorities in both houses of Congress, three-quarters of the states have to ratify changes; the great regional diversity of this far-flung country makes this requirement difficult to fulfill, and the increase in partisan polarization creates further barriers. Indeed, after the adoption of the first ten amendments via the Bill of Rights in 1791, the USA has in the subsequent 230-plus years passed a mere seventeen additional changes to the constitution; the 28th Amendment languished in the ratification process for decades. Consequently, American democracy leads the global ranking of constitutional stability and rigidity (Lutz 1994: 362–64; Lijphart 1999: 220–22; Elkins, Ginsburg, and Melton 2009: 101, 162; Tsebelis 2022: 290).

Moreover, the Philadelphia charter's susceptibility to reinterpretation is constrained by the inertial force of judicial precedent. The Supreme Court jealously guards its independence, is committed to professionalism, and commands great clout, despite the increasing politicization of its nomination process. Court-packing schemes that populists across the world have commonly used to subdue their judiciaries are politically inviable in the USA; the stigma of Roosevelt's failure helped to dissuade the Biden administration, for instance, from pursuing the proposals floated by left-wing sectors of the Democratic Party in 2020. Informal pressures by the chief executive, which can become overwhelming in Latin America, and acts of discriminatory legalism, such as politically targeted allegations of malfeasance and misconduct, are unheard of in the USA; whereas Mexico's AMLO, for instance, succeeded in forcing an oppositional Supreme Court justice off the bench through corruption accusations and then secured a government-aligned replacement, such a politicized purge remains unlikely in the USA.

Sustained in all these ways, the rigidity of the American constitution makes it practically impossible to dismantle democracy through formally legal mechanisms. After all, while populist attacks on democracy can start with ordinary legislation, they make real headway only through constitutional overhauls. But a package of illiberal amendments or the convocation of a constituent assembly that would promote an authoritarian involution is hard to imagine in the USA. Consequently, power-hungry Trump never had a chance to follow in the footsteps of Viktor Orbán, who exploited the relative flexibility of Hungary's charter (Lorenz 2005: 358–59) and asphyxiated liberal pluralism quickly and smoothly.

What if a populist in the White House, frustrated by this dense web of institutional obstacles, was tempted simply to override these formal-legal constraints, brashly arrogate power, and coercively impose illiberal and authoritarian transformations, as some personalistic plebiscitarian leaders in Latin America did (see Chapters 3 and 4)? The political cost and risk of such blatant rule-busting, which holds considerable danger even in weaker institutional settings (as the ignominious failure of Guatemala's Serrano and Peru's Castillo shows), would be prohibitive in the USA. A wide range of politicians in Congress, at the state level, and even some in the president's own party would resist such an abridgment of their own influence; courts would prohibit infringements of the law; and numerous groupings in the USA's resourceful, vibrant, and hyperlitigious civil society would defend their interests, needs, and causes. Thus, openly transgressive efforts to decree undemocratic change would provoke a huge backlash from liberal pluralism's many stakeholders, which would probably seal the fate of any attempted "end run" around the institutional framework.

A populist president is therefore hemmed in by a constitutional straightjacket. Determined regime change, which would require the constitution's overhaul, is infeasible in America. The worrisome Achilles Heel of modern democracy, namely the theoretical possibility for democratically elected rulers to abolish democracy, is firmly protected by the virtually impenetrable armor of a rigid constitution. In the USA, political liberalism with its congenital fear of a tyranny of the majority has successfully locked up popular sovereignty, the principle that personalistic plebiscitarian leaders opportunistically invoke to promote their power hunger. The charter of 1787 forecloses this sneaky line of attack, which the few populists who have managed to strangle democracy across the world have commonly used.

In sum, institutional strength continues to safeguard American democracy against the illiberal transformation spearheaded by populism (see also Lee 2020: 381–82; Lee 2022: 97, 108–14). In the firmly entrenched constitutional framework, US liberalism has enshrined an intense aversion to the concentration of political power, putting a host of obstacles before personalistic plebiscitarian leaders. As Chapters 3 through 5 showed, even institutions of middling restrictiveness and solidity are often sufficient for impeding the undemocratic designs of populist chief executives. Because the institutional scaffolding of US democracy is significantly more solid and effective than the presidential systems of Latin America and the parliamentary systems of Eastern Europe, Donald Trump faced practically insurmountable constraints during his term in the White House; and whoever tries to follow his illiberal playbook in the future is likely to confront similar difficulties.

THE IMPROBABILITY OF SEVERE CRISES AND HUGE WINDFALLS IN THE USA

Given the institutional strength of American democracy, only exceptional conjunctural opportunities could potentially enable a populist leader to obtain the massive, overwhelming support required for undermining, if not abolishing, liberal pluralism. Fortunately, however, such an eventuality is exceedingly unlikely. Advanced, highly developed economies tend to avoid drastic volatility, and they command abundant resources for cushioning any sudden shocks. The diversification of post-industrial knowledge economies, which diverges starkly from the oil dependency of Chávez's Venezuela, also precludes huge revenue windfalls. Moreover, a firmly institutionalized state maintains command over the national territory and can deploy ample coercive capacity to extinguish armed rebellions and contain an upsurge of common crime. Last but not least, the competence and reach of America's intelligence agencies and the fearsome firepower of its military forestall and deter major attacks by foreign terrorists. Consequently, 9/11 has remained a complete exception.

As regards the risk of deep economic crises, which played a crucial role for the strangulation of democracy by Fujimori in Peru, Orbán in Hungary, and Erdoğan in Turkey, America's advanced economy with its enormous variety of sectors offers a good deal of insurance. Comparative research shows that developed countries are subject to significantly less economic volatility than developing nations (Wibbels 2006), whose economies often depend on a few sectors and are therefore vulnerable to unexpected shocks. Moreover, the prosperity and fiscal capacity of advanced countries guarantees ample resources for compensatory programs that can mitigate the fallout of dramatic drops. Indeed, the USA's massive public spending during the COVID-19 pandemic *increased* average incomes (Sides, Tausanovitch, and Vavreck 2022: 199–200). As a result, neither the Great Recession of 2008 nor the health challenge of 2020–22 caused a drop in GDP that qualified as an economic crisis (−5 percent growth per year).

In the USA, a personalistic plebiscitarian president cannot benefit from an exorbitant revenue windfall either. Precisely because the American economy does not rest on a few sectors that could plunge it into a dreadful crisis, it also cannot be inundated by a sudden influx of surplus rents. Compared to the flood of petrodollars that fueled Hugo Chávez's undemocratic power concentration, the shale oil boom in the USA was of comparatively minor proportions and did not massively boost the public treasury. For these reasons, the

US economy is very unlikely to provide the conjunctural opportunities for the populist asphyxiation of liberal pluralism.

While political liberalism has prevented the American state from acquiring the coercive prowess and territorial penetration that its West European counterparts such as France command, the national and state governments certainly have the capacity to avert a public security crisis. Though clearly worrisome, armed militias remain confined to marginal areas, such as the trailer parks of Michigan and the Bitterroot Mountains of Idaho. The very proliferation of independent groupings and their lack of coordination, not to speak of a centralized command (see recently Lowndes 2022; Wendling 2022), suggest their aggregate weakness. Consequently, the specter of civil war raised by Walter (2022) is utterly implausible. The undeniable racial tensions plaguing this country are equally unlikely to explode into a "genocide" (contra Hinton 2021). In sum, the USA does not seem to be at risk of large-scale outbursts of violence that could allow a personalistic plebiscitarian leader to become a miraculous "savior" like Peru's Fujimori, and then use the resulting groundswell of support for smothering liberal pluralism.

The only potential threat arises from international terrorism, as the stunning surprise attacks of 9/11 shows. But such a well-planned, meticulously coordinated, and precisely executed assault on prominent symbols of American power would be difficult to repeat. Since that day, Fortress America has not suffered another serious strike by foreign terrorists – and not for lack of trying. Instead, the various intelligence agencies charged with protecting the homeland, and the military forces tasked with destroying threats brewing abroad, have demonstrated considerable competence and succeeded in foiling new strikes. Whereas European countries have continued to face major challenges in recent years, such as the Paris bloodbath of November 2015, the North American superpower has managed to safeguard its national territory and resident population.

For these reasons, a personalistic plebiscitarian leader in the USA has only a minimal chance of encountering the conjunctural opportunities provided by a severe and acute, yet resolvable crisis. Advanced developed countries are rarely subject to internal collapse or external shock. Moreover, the experiences of Argentina's Menem and Colombia's Uribe show that presidential democracies can survive one of these massive challenges, as explained in Chapter 3. Only when two deep crises hit a country at the same time did a populist president gain the opportunity to suffocate democracy; and even in contemporary Latin America, this unusual coincidence occurred only twice, namely in Peru under Fujimori and recently in El Salvador under Bukele. If even Latin America's presidential systems of middling institutional strength crack only under the enormous pressure arising from two simultaneous crises, then it would take an even more powerful shock for a populist leader to overwhelm and dismantle the solid institutional framework of the USA. Such an eventuality – a veritable catastrophe that a bold populist president can miraculously avert – is hard to imagine.

LIMITATIONS OF TRUMP'S POPULIST PROJECT

Because he lacked the two necessary preconditions specified in my theory and corroborated via the analysis of Latin American and European experiences, Donald Trump faced insurmountable constraints to his populist power hunger. The firm institutional framework of the USA hemmed in his quest for personalistic predominance, and the absence of conjunctural opportunities for boosting his plebiscitarian support prevented him from achieving his undemocratic aspirations. Consequently, the 45th president did not get very far with his illiberal machinations and made no serious dent in America's constitution. Moreover, he failed to perpetuate himself in power, the most basic populist goal, which he pursued so single-mindedly and unscrupulously in 2020–21 (see the thorough narrative in Woodward and Costa 2021: 133–288).

For a personalistic plebiscitarian leader, Trump suffered from a crippling weakness throughout his term in office: He never managed to win the backing of a majority of citizens. Though claiming to speak for *the* people, the billionaire in the White House failed to achieve popularity ratings above 50 percent; a majority of Americans consistently disapproved of his governance and political leadership (Busch and Pitney 2021: 24, 110, 134, 198). With this meager approval, his fervent appeals to popular sovereignty, designed to bolster his forceful quest for personal predominance, always rang hollow; even his ability to marshal support in Congress suffered (Binder 2021: 81; Smith 2021: 538). Whereas Peru's Fujimori, Venezuela's Chávez, and El Salvador's Bukele could steamroll liberal pluralism with lopsided popularity ratings approximating 70 to 90 percent, the US populist was mostly stuck in the low to mid-forties and clearly lacked the requisite clout.

The headstrong leader was painfully aware of this crucial deficit, which had already become obvious during his inauguration. With typically populist deceptiveness, he therefore lied that the crowd assembled on the Washington Mall was much larger than that celebrating his predecessor; photos proved the embarrassing truth, namely the exact opposite. The new president never enjoyed a honeymoon, and his approval ratings dropped in 2017 to little more than one-third of respondents. While the roaring economy brought some increase in 2018 and 2019, his popularity rarely, and only briefly, approached 50 percent (Sides, Tausanovitch, and Vavreck 2022: 59–66). Throughout his four years in office, this minoritarian support limited his power – and the damage he could do to democracy. After all, how can a populist with low popularity invoke plebiscitarian acclamation to bend or break liberal institutions?

In line with my theory, a crucial background reason for Trump's anemic approval ratings was the absence of conjunctural opportunities that could have allowed the daring president to perform magic and boost his charisma. As the preceding section established, the USA is not very vulnerable to drastic crises. When Trump took office, America was actually doing well on most fronts. Although the recovery from the Great Recession of 2008 had taken years, by the mid-2010s, economic growth was proceeding steadily and the job market had tightened, producing significant wage gains for ever broader segments of the workforce. Moreover, crime remained low, domestic political violence was merely sporadic, and foreign terrorism had not struck the homeland in years. By contrast to populist leaders such as Fujimori, Menem, and Uribe, the new president therefore found no occasion to perform a miracle by boldly and effectively averting a looming catastrophe and bringing great, clearly visible improvements.

Eventually, of course, Trump did have to confront a huge crisis, namely the COVID-19 pandemic. But to the consternation of populist chief executives across the world, this massive, potentially devastating problem cannot be eliminated and resolved through drastic countermeasures. The tiny virus therefore did not allow personalistic plebiscitarian leaders to turn into magic saviors, but revealed their claims as hollow and deflated their standing (Bayerlein et al. 2021; Meyer 2021; Foa et al. 2022). By contrast to resolvable crises such as hyperinflation, COVID-19 thus did not constitute an opportunity for populist politicians; instead, the pandemic put a big stumbling block in their path toward executive aggrandizement and competitive authoritarianism. The irruption of this health emergency therefore depressed Trump's political fortunes further.

The important role of crises for the extraordinary politics of populism, and the divergent political impact of different types of crises, is easy to miss in the study of American politics. A single-country focus has difficulty capturing non-events, such as the absence of acute problems at Trump's assumption of office and his resulting incapacity to broaden his plebiscitarian support. The comparative perspective of this book helps to reveal the contrast with presidents who encountered severe yet resolvable crises that enabled them to boost their personalistic plebiscitarian leadership, especially Fujimori and Bukele.

Due to America's longstanding success in forestalling the rise of demagogues, country specialists lack experience with the analysis of populism in the White House. Extant theories therefore focus on the normal choices and actions of mainstream politicians who operate by the established rules. Accordingly, they tend to regard crises merely as problems and challenges for presidents, not as opportunities for proving charisma.[14] In this vein, presidency expert Michael Nelson (2018: 1, 31) stressed how "fortunate" Trump was in not facing an economic or political crisis upon taking office. But from the political-strategic logic of populism, these seemingly favorable conditions deprived Trump of a potential opportunity. Because he did not have the chance miraculously to resolve a crisis, he was unable to win the overwhelming backing that allowed "savior" Fujimori to dismantle democracy (Madrid and Weyland 2019: 171–74; Weyland 2020: 401). Because populist leaders are by nature

---

[14] For an exception, see the perceptive discussion by Tulis (1987: 174–81).

transgressive and seek to bend, transform, or overturn the existing institutional order, they operate and succeed in very different ways than regular politicians in normal times, who confine themselves to functioning inside the established order (for a similar distinction of types of political leadership, see Burns 1978).

Trump's distinctly limited popularity and its virtually unmovable ceiling also reflect another facet of American politics on which this populist experience shines new light; again, a comparative perspective is instructive. Whereas in collapsing party systems with their crumbling political alignments and fluid popular preferences, leaders such as Fujimori, Chávez, and now Bukele can achieve lopsided majority support, the deep partisan and affective polarization that has increasingly plagued US democracy created virtually insurmountable barriers to the 45th president's approval ratings. A vast majority of Democrats were unconditional, unshakable opponents; they refused to acknowledge even Trump's obvious accomplishments, such as his contributions to the economic expansion of 2018–19 (Tinted Glasses 2019; see also Sides, Tesler, and Vavreck 2018: 23–24, and in general Achen and Bartels 2016). Even if the US populist had successfully faced and resolved a severe crisis, these automatic nay-sayers would probably have disputed such a "miracle" and refused to give him credit. After all, profound polarization induces opposition party affiliates reflexively to discount the incumbent's achievements; good performance simply cannot win them over.

While the underlying polarization has many problematic repercussions for political liberalism and democracy in the USA,[15] as in numerous other countries (Svolik 2019; McCoy and Somer 2022), it does have the unexpected benefit of serving as a dike against a potential upsurge of support for a personalistic plebiscitarian leader. Even a bold feat of charisma may no longer overcome the profound fault line cleaving contemporary American politics; it may therefore fail to unleash a groundswell of gratitude and enthusiasm that could give a populist president hegemonic predominance. What is a growing problem for the functioning of US democracy thus seems – paradoxically but logically – to constitute a safeguard against the specific threats posed by the expansive, transgressive tendencies inherent in populism (Weyland 2020: 399, 404 n. 13; see recently Lowande and Rogowski 2021: 1407, 1418–21).

In sum, general factors, namely the absence of conjunctural opportunities for demonstrating charismatic prowess, as well as US-specific factors, namely deep polarization and the resulting compartmentalization and "calcification" of partisan support bases (see recently Sides, Tausanovitch, and Vavreck 2022), confined Trump's popular backing to a minority of the citizenry. These obstacles prevented the headstrong president from employing the main power capability of personalistic plebiscitarian leaders, namely the mobilization of

---

[15] Abramowitz 2018; Graham and Svolik 2020; Mettler and Lieberman 2020; McCarty 2021; Lieberman, Mettler, and Roberts 2022; for a much less dire analysis, see Carey et al. 2022: 236–39.

overwhelming numbers of fervent admirers (Weyland 2001: 12–14). Without a massive following, Trump was unable to overcome the firm institutional constraints imposed by liberal checks and balances and cemented by a practically inalterable constitution.

PROBLEMS OF TRUMP'S POLITICAL AGENCY

By documenting the importance of institutional frameworks and of conjunctural opportunities that depend on structural developments such as global economic cycles, this study highlights the incentives and constraints arising from objective conditions, rather than the creative capacities of political agency. Chapter 3, for instance, demonstrated that crises are largely given, exogenous challenges; they are not simply "constructed" and performed (contra Moffitt 2016: 121–32). Populist leaders can highlight and exaggerate problems and frame them as symptoms of major decline, but they cannot conjure them up without a clear basis in objective facts (for the USA, see recently Lowande and Rogowski 2021: 1421).

Inside these institutions and structures, however, political agency does play a significant role. After all, although given constraints, challenges, and opportunities shape the probability distribution for actors' success, they do not determine specific outcomes. Some politicians are clearly more apt than others in responding to problems or in exploiting chances. In particular, acute crises only redound to the political benefit of populist leaders if they manage to resolve the costly problem and bring much-needed relief. If a leader fails with rescue efforts, as President Collor did in Brazil, the price can be high, namely an early eviction from the presidency (see Chapter 3).

As Chapter 2 explained, personalistic plebiscitarian politicians have some strengths, but also important weaknesses in trying to cope with problems and trace a path toward success. On the positive side, their penchant for bold initiatives can overcome longstanding obstacles and open up promising new horizons, as Latin America's neoliberal populists did with their enactment of market reforms, which permanently cured several countries of endemic inflation. But while concentrated decision-making can force beneficial breakthroughs, headstrong leaders' reliance on intuition and their corresponding reluctance to use expertise, advice, and deliberation can lead into a cul-de-sac and entail striking deterioration. In this vein, Hugo Chávez's headlong march into "twenty-first-century socialism" ruined the Venezuelan economy and produced a human catastrophe rarely seen in a nation not ravaged by war. Thus, populist leadership opens up an extraordinarily wide range of potential outcomes.

How did Donald Trump use his populist agency, and with what impact on US democracy? This political novice made strategic decisions that brought early advantages, but later reined in his political clout, thus limiting his capacity to undermine and destroy liberal pluralism. First of all, the ambitious celebrity decided to seek the presidential candidacy of an established party, rather than running as a true outsider like Ross Perot did in his third-party bid of 1992. Trump's decision added large numbers of loyal GOP voters to his populist core support, which had guaranteed him an unexpected triumph in the primaries. By enlisting Republican Party identification, his takeover of the GOP was crucial for his exceedingly narrow victory in the general election of November 2016 (Sides, Tesler, and Vavreck 2018: 157–61; Gibson and Shaw 2019: 459–63; see also Abramowitz 2018: 121–73).

But Trump's embrace of one pole in the two-party system also drew him into the trenches of fierce polarization, which then hindered his ability to extend his support across party lines, as just explained. By running and governing for the Republican Party, he greatly lowered his chances to make major inroads among Democrats. Therefore, he could never achieve the massive plebiscitarian backing that supremely successful populists such as Fujimori and Chávez enjoyed. Trump won the biggest prize in US politics, but paid a big price by seriously limiting his chances to win political hegemony and transform the institutional framework, the ultimate goal of personalistic leaders.

Trump's alignment with the GOP also restricted his maneuvering room in coalition formation. In the two-dimensional ideological space that structures much of US politics, the Republican Party has mostly combined economic liberalism with cultural conservatism, whereas the Democrats have combined economic protectionism with cultural liberalism (Miller and Schofield 2003, 2008). This distinctive clustering has left two other options largely open. With his pronounced nationalism, Trump seemed well positioned to occupy one of these empty cells, namely the combination of economic protectionism and cultural conservatism. If with this innovative move, he had filled the ideological space that the authors of this two-dimensional scheme label as "populism" (Miller and Schofield 2003: 248, 252–53; see also Ostiguy and Roberts 2016: 28, 32–35), the outsider president could – in principle – have appealed to a good portion of the Democratic base, such as working-class people from the Midwestern rust belt, who saw themselves as losers of economic globalization and who were averse to their party's high-profile embrace of ultra-liberal cultural values.

If Trump had pushed through Congress the massive program of infrastructure investments that he had announced in 2016–17 (Smith 2022: 162, 164, 167), and if he had in this way created millions of jobs in depressed regions, he may have managed to attract much larger numbers of poor white Democrats than the fraction that had already voted for him in November 2016 (cf. Busch and Pitney 2021: 5; Rutledge and Rackaway 2021: 368; Sides, Tausanovitch, and Vavreck 2022: 31, 35–36; Smith 2022: 167–68). Thus, such a bold move – in many ways a tempting ploy for a political novice and ambitious populist – could have transformed party politics in the USA.[16] But the new president's

---

[16] In the run-up to the 2020 election, when the irruption of the COVID-19 pandemic put Trump on the defensive and threatened his chances for reelection, his closest friend in the Senate,

alliance with congressional Republicans pulled him away from a major program of government spending. Instead, he followed his recently adopted party and pushed in the opposite direction, backing the GOP's proposal of tax cuts and other neoliberal initiatives.[17] With this high-profile decision, Trump forewent the chance to forge a true realignment in US politics and skew the electoral constellation by constructing a clear-cut majority for his populist project.[18] This self-limitation in turn safeguarded democracy by precluding efforts at profound institutional transformation that could have abridged liberal pluralism.

Trump's decisions to channel insurgent populist energy into the long-established tracks of two-party politics may have been driven by strategic calculations, especially the continuing strength of partisan identification and the depth of affective polarization in the contemporary USA; thus, the chances of overturning these longstanding coordinates of US politics may have been low to begin with. But the new president also missed many opportunities for improving his political standing because he committed innumerable unforced errors with his arbitrary and haphazard decision-making and his reliance on an ever-changing welter of unimpressive advisers. As explained in Chapter 2, these problems are rooted in populism's very core, which revolves around unaccountable personalistic leadership. Lacking solid organizational structures and firm programmatic commitments, charismatic politicians commonly privilege loyalty over competence; they surround themselves with friends, cronies, and family members, rather than drafting "the best and brightest" as their top aides (on Trump, see Nelson 2018: 32–37, 44–45; Skowronek, Dearborn, and King 2021: 128–37). In their supreme self-confidence, they shun expert advice, avoid systematic deliberation, and trust in their own intuition, which is seen as a reflection of divine inspiration.

Averse to rational procedures, this personalistic and charismatic approach to decision-making is prone to disorganization, flimsy preparation, and the resulting errors (Weber 1976: 141–42, 655–58). The hypercomplex machinery of a modern state and a global superpower is exceedingly difficult to run well from a narrow command center, with the help of a hodgepodge of inexperienced temporary advisers, old sidekicks, and relatives, such as son-in-law Jared

---

Lindsey Graham, urged the incumbent to propose and enact a massive infrastructure package – but to no avail (Woodward 2020: 348–51, 389).

[17] Howell and Moe 2020: 89–94; Busch and Pitney 2021: 8–9, 23; Hawley 2021: 262–64; Herbert 2021: 106–8, 112–13; Sides, Tausanovitch, and Vavreck 2022: 24, 31, 35–36, 45–46.

[18] Interesting reflections in Pierson 2017. Thus, Trump defied his adopted party less in his congressional policy-making than Jimmy Carter, the preceding "disjunctive" president, had done (Skowronek 2020: 74–76, 91–92 vs. 213–14). But in terms of politics, Trump was much more domineering, even antagonistic (see, e.g., Nelson 2018: 140), by imposing his personalistic will, employing a plebiscitarian strategy, and resolutely taking control of his party (Skowronek 2020: 212–15), which is the fundamental goal of (fully) populist leaders who rise in and through an established party.

Kushner. Every account of decision-making in Trump's White House paints a picture of virtual chaos (Nelson 2018: 36–38, 45, 58–59; Howell and Moe 2020: 86–89; Skowronek, Dearborn, and King 2021: 128–37). For instance, Woodward (2018: xviii–xxii, 141–43, 147, 158, 163) documents several instances in which presidential aides brazenly sabotaged the initiatives of other counselors that they regarded as deleterious, if not illegal; taking advantage of Trump's notoriously limited attention span, they simply removed proposals that were waiting for the president's signature from his desk and made them disappear (see also Anonymous 2018). In general, the unprecedented turnover among Trump's close aides impeded any systematic approach; decision-making proceeded in uncoordinated fits and starts, including many false starts.

These typical downsides of populist leadership came to haunt Trump with the irruption of the COVID-19 pandemic and probably sealed his electoral defeat in 2020. Despite this tremendous exogenous shock, the headstrong president mostly refused to listen to the expert knowledge that is so abundant in the USA. Even when the dangerous disease vector reached North America, he stubbornly downplayed the threat and quickly tried to soften or lift the protective measures urged by medical specialists.[19] After all, politicians who claim extraordinary gifts for "saving the people" are at a loss when confronted with a crisis that cannot be quickly resolved. The hypercontagious virus persistently falsified their central promise; rather than looking supremely powerful, they proved incapable of defeating the dramatic challenge.

Because charismatic leaders could not make this insurmountable problem disappear with bold countermeasures, their magical "solution" was simply to deny the problem's severity; like ostriches, they reflexively stuck their heads underground (Foa et al. 2022: 24–25). Besides this desperate effort to "perform non-crisis" (cf. Moffitt 2016: 121–32), populist chief executives across the world have offered the suffering population snake oil, ranging from the anti-malaria drug chloroquine to the injection of disinfectants (on Trump, see Woodward 2020: 286–87, 300, 305).[20] But as emphasized throughout this book, crises are real; just as they cannot simply be constructed, they cannot be deconstructed and wished away, either. Even a masterful performer such as Donald Trump was unable to perform this truly magic trick.

Trump's typically populist mishandling of the COVID-19 pandemic may have cost him reelection. While Joe Biden handily beat him in the countrywide vote count, the result in the Electoral College came down to a mere 43,000 votes distributed over three battleground states (Trende 2021: 239–40). Although party loyalty and intense polarization limited the incumbent's accountability

---

[19] Woodward 2020: xvii–xviii, 223, 233, 244, 251–52, 271, 275, 286, 296, 311–13, 318–25, 352–53, 376–77; Skowronek, Dearborn, and King 2021: 116–26; Chowkwanyun 2022: 315–17, 323, 330–32.

[20] Trump deserves credit for pushing forward COVID-19 vaccine development, however (Chowkwanyun 2022: 322; Roberts 2022: 8; Sides, Tausanovitch, and Vavreck 2022: 137–38).

for his deficient performance (Roberts 2022: 14–15; Sides, Tausanovitch, and Vavreck 2022: 133), his failures perhaps made the crucial difference in this very narrow race.[21]

Thus, in the beginning of his term, Trump did not benefit from conjunctural opportunities that an acute and severe yet resolvable crisis could have provided; and at the end of his turbulent tenure, he stumbled over a dramatic yet unresolvable crisis, which cast doubt on his grandiloquent claims of charismatic prowess. When the personalistic plebiscitarian president faced these given situations, his dysfunctional agency undermined his political prospects: He missed opportunities that he had, and failed in his response to challenges that appeared.

Interestingly, however, despite these inherent problems of populist leadership and their grave costs, Trump's pronounced personalism, his reliance on intuition rather than rationality, and his impulsive transgressions produced important political benefits as well, which may yet enable the vengeful loser of 2020 to make an electoral comeback in 2024. Above all, although his privileged personal background differs diametrically from his "deplorable" core following, this outsider has displayed an uncanny connection and affinity to his most fervent base, which came as a surprise to virtually all observers (Fracanzani 2021: 129–39, especially 138–39). How could a billionaire tycoon with an Ivy League education not only claim to speak for a disproportionately low-educated, partly working-class constituency, but in fact be seen by many of these people as their authentic voice?[22]

Similarly, how could a strange campaign slogan such as "Make America Great Again," which incumbent Obama derided in 2016, turn into a magnetic trademark proudly worn by millions of citizens all across this diverse country?[23] How could "the big lie" of the stolen election and the subsequent assault on the Capitol on January 6, 2021, which was initially seen as the final implosion of the incumbent's political fortunes (Abramowitz 2021: 75–77; Trende 2021: 226, 240; Woodward and Costa 2021: 261, 411, 413), soon become the foundation of his continued hold over good parts of the Republican Party, and the base for his probable reelection in 2024? Time and again, Trump's political moves looked hare-brained, ill-considered, and counterproductive, if not self-destructive – but soon turned out to embody sure-footed intuitions that strengthened and extended his unlikely success as a prototypical populist.

---

[21] Neundorf and Pardos-Prado 2022; Sides, Tausanovitch, and Vavreck 2022: 211, 215, 219–20; see also Busch and Pitney 2021: 70–78, 95, 134–35. Note also that Trump suffered significant losses among older voters (Trende 2021: 229), among whom death rates and therefore concerns about the pandemic ran particularly high.

[22] Oliver and Rahn 2016: 194–96; Ostiguy and Roberts 2016: 41–46; Lamont, Park, and Ayala-Hurtado 2017; Pierson 2017; Sides, Tesler, and Vavreck 2018: 35, 70–76, 80–96; background in Cramer 2016; Hochschild 2016.

[23] Rowland 2021: 23, 26, 28, 37–38, 54, 59, 130–32, 142, 147–48; Parker and Barreto 2022: 196–201.

Thus, in his charismatic connection to his mass following, the shady billionaire, a veritable disaster as a policy-maker, has demonstrated a strange and dark political brilliance,[24] which has allowed him to pose unprecedented threats to US democracy.

In sum, populist agency constitutes a bundle of counteracting tendencies, if not contradictions. Striking irrationality, which entails chaotic decision-making and deficient policy performance, coexists with surprisingly accurate political intuition. Personalistic predominance and insatiable power hunger coexist with the incapacity to effect lasting institutional transformations. Unexpected political success, such as Trump's triumph in 2016, is followed by unlikely failure, namely his defeat in 2020, one of the few instances of a US incumbent's loss in a reelection bid since Herbert Hoover in 1932 (Busch and Pitney 2021: 109). This combination of noteworthy strengths and weaknesses has enabled the American populist to put unusual pressure on liberal pluralism – but it has also prevented him from effectively strangling democracy.

TRUMP'S DAMAGE TO US DEMOCRACY: DEGRADATION OF NORMS, ROBUSTNESS OF INSTITUTIONS

The weaknesses and limitations of populist agency made it impossible for Donald Trump to overcome the obstacles that any quest for populist power concentration and autocratic transformation has to face in the USA. The solidity of institutional checks and balances, anchored in a rock-solid constitution, and the absence of conjunctural opportunities for winning an upsurge of support protected US democracy. In particular, his minoritarian approval ratings deprived the transgressive president of a realistic chance for cementing his political supremacy and dismantling liberal institutions, for instance through a constitutional transformation, a favorite mechanism of authoritarian populists. Rather than following in the footsteps of Fujimori and Chávez, Orbán and Erdoğan – a possibility that prominent observers initially feared (Levitsky and Ziblatt 2018; Kaufman and Haggard 2019) – Trump's political trajectory and the resulting regime impact had many parallels with the leader who shared the greatest similarities in background, namely Italy's Berlusconi (Fracanzani 2021). Like the populist in Rome,[25] his counterpart in Washington did not smother democracy by disfiguring or undermining the institutions of liberal pluralism. Moreover, while Trump degraded democratic quality by blatantly disrespecting crucial norms of political civility (Foa and Mounk 2021), these very aggressions also provoked a mobilizational backlash from a wide range of opposition forces, which infused the USA's exhausted democracy with new participatory energy.

Whereas personalistic plebiscitarian leaders need ample and intense political support to abridge and distort political institutions, they can undermine

---

[24] Stephen Skowronek employs the same term, in Kreitner (2020: 3).
[25] Taggart and Rovira 2016: 351–52; Newell 2019: 191–92, 199.

liberal norms unilaterally through flagrant disrespect in their statements and actions (as long as their own supporters acquiesce, maintain their backing, and protect the transgressors from political fallout and sanctions). Like Berlusconi, Trump indeed unleashed a flood of lies, insults, under-the-belt attacks, and other violations of well-established rules of democratic discourse. In fact, this ostentatious defiance is a central part of populist strategy, which seeks to whip up mass support by assaulting and provoking adversaries and elites with egregious slights that no major politician has dared to use before. For this purpose, personalistic plebiscitarian leaders commonly "flaunt the low" in order to reaffirm and supercharge their own identification and connection with "the little man," and to make well-spoken, circumspect establishment groupings seem out of touch (cf. Ostiguy 2017; on Trump, see Ostiguy and Roberts 2016). For Trump, breaking the stranglehold of "political correctness" and denouncing the cultural vanguard that has spearheaded progressive value change was an essential way of creating and constantly reinforcing his affinity with his "deplorable" base. By bluntly voicing grievances and openly expressing resentments, he managed to wrest the Republican candidacy away from the party barons and to defeat the Democratic Party with its embrace of identity politics.

After occupying the White House, the new president delighted in maintaining his crude, hyperaggressive, and ostentatiously illiberal style. Through constant provocations, he dragged every real or potential opponent into the mud; moreover, he launched vile attacks against any aides who showed signs of not practicing unconditional loyalty. Even more shockingly, Trump "got away with" the nastiest offenses; even the worst episodes depressed his already-low popularity ratings only temporarily. Out of party loyalty and charisma-based identification, his base tolerated, excused, or even approved and supported his transgressions. While the broad gamut of his opponents was appalled and many denounced his norm violations, they had always withheld their support and therefore lacked the leverage to exact an effective political and electoral price.

Since his appearance on the political scene, Trump has disrespected every entry in the liberal-democratic book of etiquette and has violated major norms, such as prohibitions on conflict of interest and important mandates of transparency and accountability, for instance, through the destruction of presidential records. In these ways, the brash populist has set a problematic precedent, which has tempted a number of GOP politicians to adopt a similarly injurious style. As a result, democratic quality in the USA has suffered; through Trump, the land of liberty turned "from 'clean' to 'dirty' democracy" (Foa and Mounk 2021). Proper behavior facilitates the smooth operation of a pluralist system with firm checks and balances and decentralized federalism, which provides many access points for shenanigans and obstruction; it therefore benefits from politicians' norm-compliant behavior, which Trump flagrantly undermined.

But despite all of these problematic repercussions, Trump's populism clearly did not suffocate US democracy. The autocratic president did not manage to overturn the institutional framework, as Fujimori and Chávez, Orbán and Erdoğan, so strikingly did. Instead, like Berlusconi, he did not transform the institutional configuration and left political competitiveness, the core of democracy, intact. Whereas personalistic plebiscitarian leaders who push toward competitive authoritarianism try to smother liberal pluralism and disadvantage the opposition through a host of electoral reforms and constitutional amendments, if not a new charter, Trump did not pass important measures of this type. While trying to corrode checks and balances and brazenly challenging electoral rules, he mostly failed; indeed, he did not even propose a major overhaul of the institutional order, the main project of every strangler of democracy.

Proof of the survival of US democracy lies in one evident fact: Like Berlusconi, Trump lost power via an election. By contrast, Fujimori, Chávez, Orbán, and Erdoğan ensured with all means that they never suffered this fate – by intimidating opposition supporters, banning their candidates, muzzling the media, etc. The US populist took none of these steps. Instead, elections remained free, fair, and clean. Despite his threatening campaign slogan of 2016, for instance, Trump never "locked up" any opponent – a measure that Chávez and especially Erdoğan did take. Despite his rhetorical assault on social movements and protestors, the US populist never passed institutional restrictions on civil society activism, as so many undemocratic populists have done. And despite nasty attacks on journalists and "fake media" (see, e.g., Mettler and Lieberman 2020: 248–49), he never imposed serious restrictions or censorship; the media certainly practiced no self-censorship, but eagerly concentrated on exposing Trump's outrages and failings.

In sum, the headstrong president did not distort and skew elections (contra Mettler and Lieberman 2020: 244). The resilience and vibrancy of US democracy limited his room of maneuver. His defeat in November 2020 is noteworthy because it is rare for populist presidents to lose in their bid for reelection (Corrales 2020). Trump's failure in achieving the most fundamental goal of every personalistic plebiscitarian leader, namely self-perpetuation in power, reveals the unusual strength and continued integrity of liberal pluralism in the USA.

After the November 2020 contest, however, the unsuccessful populist became even more transgressive. Facing electoral defeat, he pursued his avid power hunger by trying with all means to avert his exit and engineer inauguration to a second term. These unprecedented machinations, chronicled with great thoroughness by Woodward and Costa (2021: 133–288), exposed US democracy to a real stress test. With several dozen court challenges, massive pressure on election officials, and, finally, incitement of mob action and violence, the wounded incumbent used any weapon at his disposal in trying to overturn the vote result and stay in the White House (see the comprehensive overview in Busch and Pitney 2021: 182–95). This shockingly undemocratic rampage, which propelled the crowd assault on the Capitol on January 6, 2021 (McCauley 2021; Gellman 2022), shows how far personalistic plebiscitarian leaders are willing to go in their obsessive effort to maintain predominant power.

Yet while Trump's desperate attempts glaringly demonstrate the inherent danger of populism, their uniform failure shows the robustness of US democracy. In institutional terms, the incumbent clearly proved unsuccessful; the liberal framework held firm. Even Trump-appointed judges rejected his baseless challenges to election procedures and results, even Republican office holders faithfully counted the votes and certified the outcomes, sometimes resisting heavy pressure from the pushy incumbent (Bowden and Teague 2022), and even Trump's own vice-president strictly followed protocol and thus sealed his apoplectic boss's fate (Woodward and Costa 2021: 197–201, 226–30, 237–41). Certainly, a distressing number of Republican politicians went along with Trump's shenanigans, for instance by challenging two states' vote count in Congress (Woodward and Costa 2021: 255–58). But, as was obvious to all sides involved, this undemocratic behavior had no chance of affecting the outcome and probably constituted "cheap talk" and signaling to their partisan base (Lee 2023: 5). By contrast, virtually all Republican officeholders who were in a position to make a real difference fulfilled their institutional obligations and refused to give in to Trump's pleas, demands, and threats. Consequently, US democracy passed this unprecedented test (Busch and Pitney 2021: 184–95; Jacobs and Choate 2022: 23, 26–30; Issacharoff 2023: 167–70).

Moreover, while it was disturbing how far Trump was willing and able to go in trying to undo his loss in the voting booths, it is also noteworthy what the incumbent could *not* do, and did not even try. As commander in chief, a president has control over the state's forces of organized coercion. In political and constitutional crises, the chief executives of many countries have called out the military and police to demonstrate their preponderant clout, intimidate other branches of government, or repress their opponents in the streets (e.g., Levitsky and Murillo 2020). By contrast, President Trump did not take this route, although his aide Michael Flynn proposed it; even the unhinged US populist saw the legal risk as too high (Woodward and Costa 2021: 195, 287; Draper 2022: 34–35). Moreover, precisely because military leaders were concerned about their boss's wild shenanigans, they were determined to refuse providing the necessary muscle (Brooks 2021; Woodward and Costa 2021: xx–xxiv, xxviii, 274).[26] The fact that the defeated president could not count on the US military to push through his political goals imposed a fundamental limitation on his self-perpetuation project.

In sum, Trump's tumultuous passage through the presidency left US democracy largely intact. While suffering some reduction in quality (Foa and Mounk 2021; EIU 2023: 14, 33), it clearly survived in its institutional configuration. Checks and balances held firm, and political competitiveness did not suffer any compression, distortion, or skew (Lee 2020: 381–83). Certainly, however, the

[26] Even Pion-Berlin, Bruneau, and Goetze (2022: 12–14), who misclassify the mob assault on the Capitol as a self-coup attempt by President Trump (a label rejected, e.g., by Issacharoff 2023: 164), highlight the lack of military participation.

impact of the US populist on the constellation of political forces is more ambivalent. On the one hand, his leadership has had profoundly deleterious repercussions for the Republican Party, pushing important sectors, especially of the mass base, in a dangerously illiberal direction. Yet on the other hand, Trump's populist challenges to US democracy have had the salutary effect of shaking up political fatigue and mobilizing participatory energies among the Democratic Party and in civil society at large, which have helped to rejuvenate the polity.

Trump's hostile takeover of the GOP, which started with his stunning victory in the primary campaign of 2015–16 and was cemented during and after his presidency, has led this traditional mainstay of US democracy away from a firm commitment to liberal pluralism (Roberts 2019: 132–37, 144–49). In typically populist fashion, the domineering president has established a hold over part of the party. His charismatic grip over the most fervent segment of the party base, whose "politically incorrect" attitudes he has boldly expressed and further reinforced,[27] has enabled him to threaten intraparty opponents with loyal primary challengers;[28] and the GOP's control over large numbers of "safe" electoral districts often turns primaries decisive for eventual election. By mobilizing and strategically deploying his plebiscitarian base,[29] the personalistic leader can thus intimidate many of his party's ambitious politicians, push them to fall in line behind his self-serving project, and induce them to back or at least tolerate illiberal initiatives, especially his insatiable quest for power (Parton 2022; Lee 2023: 13–14). While pervasive passive resistance from many GOP leaders creates viscous outer bounds to this opportunistic acquiescence (see recently Lee 2023), good parts of the party have gone along with undemocratic moves that would have been unthinkable before the sudden appearance of the transgressive populist, such as the defense of the January 2021 assault on the Capitol as an expression of "legitimate political discourse" (Weisman and Epstein 2022).

It is a major problem for democracy when one of the two principal parties is beholden to an illiberal populist (Roberts 2019; In His Image 2022).[30]

---

[27] Abramowitz 2018: 121–73; Sides, Tesler, and Vavreck 2018: 82–90, 95–96, 209–15; Howell and Moe 2020: 73–81; Rowland 2021: 87–117.

[28] Nelson 2018: 49; Skowronek 2020: 212–15; Busch and Pitney 2021: 192; Jacobs and Milkis 2021: 291, 305–15; King and Milkis 2022: 282. Herbert (2021: 103–8, 112–13), however, highlights that the frequent alignment between Trump and GOP politicians does not only result from the populist leader's overbearing influence, but also from genuine programmatic and ideological affinities.

[29] The – typically populist – lack of serious organizational efforts limits the effectiveness and impact of Trump's charismatic mobilization, however (Hawley 2021: 265–68).

[30] Off and on, however, there have been indications that Trump's hold over the GOP base may be weakening (Signs of Less Trumpy Times 2022). Indeed, the vengeful ex-president has failed to defeat important GOP officials who resisted his post-electoral pressures in 2020–21; for instance, primary challengers he endorsed lost in two particularly high-profile races in Georgia (Corasaniti 2022). Moreover, the fissures and rifts between more mainstream conservatives and the most unconditional Trump followers, which have been longstanding (e.g., Lee 2021: 87–88, 91–95), may be increasing (Epstein 2022).

Trump's continuing control over a good part of GOP voters creates a serious risk that the party will use its clout to help its charismatic leader pursue his quest for political hegemony.[31] For such an attempt, the federal system of the USA provides innumerable access points,[32] increasing the danger of undemocratic penetration (Grofman 2022; Hertel-Fernandez 2022; Rocco 2022). In fact, a multitude of Republican activists have responded to Trump's narrow defeat in 2020, which they stubbornly refuse to recognize, by trying to occupy a variety of positions in the USA's surprisingly partisan electoral administration. This attempted invasion of single-minded Trump loyalists, who could use their operational discretion to favor their hero, could jeopardize the fairness of future vote counts (Razing Arizona 2021; Sides, Tausanovitch, and Vavreck 2022: 264–66).

Remarkably, however, many of the most high-profile and problematic Trump disciples lost in the state and congressional elections of November 2022, protecting the electoral administration from danger (EIU 2023: 33–34). These frequent defeats of potential election manipulators demonstrated that a small but pivotal segment of the Republican vote base puts the defense of democracy ahead of partisan interests (Homans, Ulloa, and Hounshell 2022; cf. Graham and Svolik 2020). These striking election outcomes, together with the significant vote penalty that Trump cronies suffered overall (Wallach 2022; Malzahn and Hall 2023), may send a powerful message to the GOP, namely that Trump-style "election denialism" is not a promising strategy (Lee 2023: 15–16). To what extent this important lesson will affect the primary campaigns and vote results in 2024 remains to be seen.

The defeat of strident partisans and potential manipulators, together with the longstanding tradition of professionalism and civic spirit among the politicians who do serve as election officials (Jacobs and Choate 2022), bode well for the upcoming presidential contest of 2024, in which Trump is trying hard to make a triumphant comeback. His populist transgressions will also face a

---

[31] It is important to highlight, however, that Trump's GOP is not alone in pushing the limits of liberal pluralism; from top to bottom, Democrats have engaged in many questionable actions as well. For example, Democratic presidents decreed unilateral changes in constitutionally problematic ways (Kriner 2022: 134–35). Democratic politicians have flagrantly gerrymandered states they control (Another Round of Election Rigging 2022: 17). And the fringes of the Democratic mass base hold attitudes that are as strikingly illiberal, and as widespread, as those of their Republican counterparts (Mason and Kalmoe 2022: 182–85). Thus, polarization and its deleterious effects involve both sides of the political-ideological spectrum.

[32] Certainly, however, the political fragmentation facilitated by federalism, especially the control by both parties over different states, limits the aggregate, national-level impact of political manipulation such as gerrymandering (Bateman 2022: 345–47, 360). Because both parties engage in such practices, their overall effect partially cancels out; in net terms, the national-level pro-GOP bias has diminished in recent years (Another Round of Election Rigging 2022: 18; Corasaniti and Epstein 2022; Graphic Detail: Gerrymandering 2022). That electoral administration is primarily a state-level responsibility thus provides an important safeguard against presidential efforts to skew the electoral arena.

vigilant opposition and alert civil society, which stand ready to denounce unfair tricks. Moreover, judging from the uniform failure of Trump's legal challenges in late 2020, the courts are likely to prohibit real procedural infringements. Indeed, even Republican members of Congress helped to close loopholes that the power-hungry populist had sought to exploit in early 2021: They cooperated with Democrats in a noteworthy bipartisan initiative, the Electoral Count Reform Act of 2022, which "largely succeeded in ensuring the supremacy of the rule of law in presidential elections" – a "phenomenal achievement" (Sunstein 2022: 1).[33] For these reasons, US democracy, though no longer completely immune, continues to command enormous resilience against populist power hunger. Most likely, it would survive a second term under the personalistic plebiscitarian leader as well.

Furthermore, while Trump's plebiscitarian hold over considerable segments of the Republican Party poses undeniable threats to liberal pluralism, this unprecedented populist challenge has also had unintended countervailing effects, especially by energizing a wide gamut of liberal-democratic forces (Madrid and Weyland 2019: 181–82; Weyland 2020: 402). The domineering leader's appearance on the main stage of presidential politics has provoked a notable upsurge in participation, leading to extraordinarily high turnout in the 2018 midterm elections and the presidential contest of 2020.[34] In fact, besides galvanizing the broader citizenry, Trump's provocations have prompted a significant increase in the number and diversity of electoral candidates (Hughes and Becker 2021: 95–96; Skocpol, Tervo, and Walters 2022: 390; Zarnow 2022: 137–38). Intense concern induced many people to set their private pursuits aside and enter the electoral arena. Moreover, a multitude of movements and associations in civil society have been fired up to oppose the US populist, especially through mass demonstrations and more or less contentious protests during his term in office (Meyer and Tarrow 2018; Kazin 2022: 336–38; King and Milkis 2022: 288–89; Skocpol, Tervo, and Walters 2022).

In all of these ways, Trump has inadvertently provoked a certain rejuvenation that has "clearly invigorated American small-d democracy" (Skocpol, Tervo, and Walters 2022: 399; similarly Parker and Barreto 2022: 197, 205, 215–19). In the West's representative systems with their professional-electoral parties and their tendency toward technocratic policy-making (Mounk 2018: chap. 2), politics has often faded in salience and turned into an unessential, if not peripheral aspect of many people's lives, as secular trends toward lower electoral turnout show. In this context, populism can provide a stimulant that

---

[33] I thank Frances Lee for calling my attention to this important reform.

[34] Jacobson 2019: 31–33; Abramowitz 2021: 68–69, 74–75; Hughes and Becker 2021: 86–87, 91–96; Panetta 2021: 194–95; Kazin 2022: 337; Sides, Tausanovitch, and Vavreck 2022: 216; Zarnow 2022: 136–37; EIU 2023: 33. In 2018, deliberate anti-Trump mobilization seems to have given the Democrats a larger congressional majority than regular trends of midterm losses by the presidential party predicted (Jacobson 2019: 11–15; for baseline predictions, see Wlezien 2017; Bafumi, Erikson, and Wlezien 2018).

helps reverse part of this downturn. Indeed, the transgressive leader managed to expand his own electorate, most clearly in the presidential contest of 2020 (Sides, Tausanovitch, and Vavreck 2022: 216) – a participatory benefit that many scholars attribute to populism (e.g., Mudde and Rovira Kaltwasser 2017: 81–84). Moreover, Trump unintentionally set in motion a "blue wave" of Democratic support, which brought a record turnout in 2018 and gave Joe Biden an advantage in the countrywide tally of more than seven million votes in 2020. Thus, precisely by threatening US democracy, Trump has also strengthened its defenses and provoked a partial improvement in its inclusionary dimension: While Republican incivility depressed participation in quality, democratic energy, channeled primarily through the Democratic Party, boosted it in terms of quantity.

Students of American political development (APD), who among country specialists have paid most attention to the Trump phenomenon, have tended to overlook this salutary backlash. As adherents of historical institutionalism, which has traditionally highlighted self-reinforcing mechanisms such as "increasing returns," path dependency, and the corresponding political-institutional continuities (Pierson 2000), they tend to think predominantly in terms of linear trends. In this view, deterioration begets further deterioration; for instance, partisan polarization unleashes a deepening, worsening dynamic (e.g., Pierson and Schickler 2020: 38, 45, 49). In fact, however, political development follows cyclical patterns as well, as even some APD scholars highlight (e.g., Skowronek 2020): Problems and crises sooner or later create opportunities for turnarounds and "reconstruction"; they stimulate growing demands for remediation and thus provide politicians with chances for spearheading major transformations. Even polarization may start to recede because common citizens eventually get exhausted by phases of heightened conflict and come to embrace a return to normalcy, as embodied in the contemporary USA by President Biden (see in general Hirschman 1982).

For all of these reasons, Trump's populism has done only limited damage to US democracy and is unlikely to propel its downfall in the future. The liberal institutional framework has remained intact, and political competitiveness has not suffered any significant skew. The transgressor has through his own behavior degraded liberal norms, but at the same time provoked a great deal of active opposition and passive resistance, even inside his own party (Nelson 2018: 85–89, 140; Woodward 2018: 206, 215, 317, 320–21; Binder 2021: 80–82; Herbert 2021: 105–9; Epstein 2022; Lee 2023). Most politicians continue to respect basic rules of civility. Although parts of the Republican mass base have converted to fervent populism and have given the personalistic leader a powerful instrument for pressuring GOP leaders, he cannot command unconditional compliance (Signs of Less Trumpy Times 2022; Lee 2023). Moreover, Trump's provocations have stimulated energetic responses from many other political and societal forces. In sum, while US democracy now suffers from some new vulnerabilities, liberal pluralism continues to enjoy great resilience and enormous strength.

CONCLUSION

To assess the threat posed by Trump's unprecedented populism, which is difficult to grasp from a single-country perspective, this chapter has applied the lessons that Chapters 3 to 5 derived from democracy's fate under personalistic plebiscitarian leadership in Latin America and Europe, the two world regions most similar to the USA. This wide-ranging investigation demonstrated that populism asphyxiates liberal pluralism only under restrictive conditions, namely the infrequent coincidence of institutional weakness and special conjunctural opportunities. In light of this crucial finding, the widespread alarmism that Trump's shocking victory in 2016 aroused seems exaggerated. Instead, my study strongly suggests that US democracy will not "die" under populist assault.

After all, the USA has continued to have a firm institutional framework with fairly resilient checks and balances, enshrined in a rigid, sacrosanct constitution. While these institutional constraints have gradually eroded, while norms of constitutional civility have frayed, with deepening partisan and affective polarization and Trump's recent transgressions, and while the politicized usage of institutional mechanisms for narrow partisan and personal advantage has grown, the separation of power embodied in US presidentialism continues to pose pervasive hindrances to the imposition of executive hegemony. With two assertive houses of Congress, a proudly independent judiciary, and the dispersal of power guaranteed by decentralized federalism, even a president with considerable partisan powers encounters a great deal of active opposition, passive resistance, and simple inertia and friction. The "liberal tradition in the US" (Hartz 1955; Huntington 1981: chaps. 2–3) forged a deliberately cumbersome process of political decision-making, designed to forestall political mistakes and prevent the governmental abuse of power (Howell and Moe 2016). This long-entrenched system continues to create a host of safeguards against the power-concentrating designs of populist leaders.

Moreover, the enormous complexity and advanced development of the American economy, the pluralism, resource wealth, and vibrancy of civil society, and the relative strength and territorial penetration of the state, make it quite improbable that a populist chief executive will encounter the conjunctural opportunities for garnering the massive backing required for pushing aside liberal guardrails and establishing undemocratic supremacy. A diversified economy precludes any huge revenue windfall like the flood of petrodollars benefiting Venezuela's Chávez. Together with overall prosperity, it also limits the severity of economic crises, whose fallout generous compensatory spending can mitigate, as during the COVID-19 pandemic. Furthermore, as the quick reversal of initiatives to "defund the police" shows, popular commitment, resource availability, and institutional capacity for controlling crime are assured. And the emergence of a large-scale paramilitary challenge or guerrilla insurgency, comparable to Peru's Shining Path or Colombia's FARC, is out of the question (contra Walter 2022).

Consequently, American populists, whether a reelected Trump or one of his imitators, is exceedingly unlikely to find propitious circumstances for seriously abridging US democracy and marching toward authoritarianism. Indeed, during his first term, the personalistic plebiscitarian leader achieved very little institutional impact with his constant transgressions, which deliberately, even ostentatiously, challenged longstanding political customs and norms. While the US populist further exacerbated partisan polarization and moved policy-making in a less liberal direction, his truly autocratic initiatives ran into a welter of obstacles and advanced very little. Despite some additional blemishes, American democracy escaped fairly unscathed from Trump's four years in office and is likely to withstand the redoubled pressures of a potential second term as well.

What is noteworthy from the comparative perspective of this book is not that US democracy has on several occasions suffered from serious, regime-threatening crises (Mettler and Lieberman 2020: 4, 190, 205, 250); after all, representative systems across the world have experienced severe challenges. Instead, it is remarkable that liberal pluralism in this country has passed all of these stress tests – whereas at some point or other, and sometimes repeatedly, it has collapsed or suffered destruction in so many other nations. Due to its extraordinary institutional resilience and vibrant democratic spirit, the USA has achieved the longest record of liberal constitutionalism in human history. That is an enormous accomplishment.

Of course, past achievements never guarantee future success, especially in the fast-changing world of the twenty-first century. But the impressive track record of US democracy together with the comparative lessons derived in preceding chapters clearly yield a probabilistic inference: US democracy continues to enjoy a great deal of institutional strength, can probably avoid conjunctural shocks, and is therefore likely to survive a second round of Trumpian populism; indeed, political learning may avert this renewed challenge.

7

Conclusion

Theoretical and Comparative Implications

THE MAIN ARGUMENT AND FINDINGS

Conditions for the Populist Asphyxiation of Democracy in Europe and Latin America

The global wave of populism that has unfolded in the early third millennium and accelerated after the worldwide economic crisis of 2008 instilled a great deal of concern among a broad gamut of observers: Would personalistic plebiscitarian leaders undermine or even suffocate liberal democracy? The surprising election of Donald Trump in the USA, long regarded as a least likely case for the rise of demagogues, further exacerbated these fears and prompted an outpouring of alarm (e.g., Levitsky and Ziblatt 2018; Mounk 2018; Sunstein 2018). Indeed, several authors went so far as to invoke the specter of fascism (Connolly 2017; Snyder 2017; Stanley 2018), whose reliance on overpowering charisma and the energetic mobilization of plebeian masses seemed to have similarities with right-wing populism.

To assess these worries, my book has conducted a comprehensive analysis of populist governance and its regime effects in Latin America and Europe. Fortunately, this investigation shows that populism is not as dangerous as widely feared. Only in a distinct minority of cases did personalistic plebiscitarian leaders who gained government power strangle liberal pluralism; democracy survived the pushing and shoving of populist chief executives in about 80 percent of instances, as statistical analyses find as well (Kyle and Mounk 2018: 17; Ruth-Lovell, Lührmann, and Grahn 2019: 9–10). Thus, populism does not pose as grave a threat to liberal pluralism as studies that focus only on the few cases of democracy's "death" suggest (Levitsky and Ziblatt 2018; Kaufman and Haggard 2019).

Instead, liberal pluralism displays considerable strength. Citizens commonly enjoy political freedom and are committed to defending it from governmental efforts at restriction or suppression. Civil society provides resources and organizational capacity for sustaining these defensive efforts. Unless taken over by the government, the media are determined, if not eager, to reveal and denounce abuses of power. The partisan opposition benefits from all these efforts and uses the opportunities provided by electoral competition and institutional access to contest governmental encroachments vigorously. A strong institutional framework, especially checks and balances that empower various veto players, provides the bastions for upholding all of these protective measures.

Consequently, populist assaults on liberalism and democracy do not advance easily and irresistibly; on the contrary, they often encounter a great deal of passive resistance and active opposition. The resulting friction and conflict make it difficult for personalistic plebiscitarian leaders to satisfy their congenital power hunger, dismantle institutional restraints, cement their political hegemony, and perpetuate their tenure in office. Indeed, the obstacles and counter-pressures that populist leaders face, and their precarious reliance on quasi-direct, uninstitutionalized, and therefore fickle mass support, expose these chief executives themselves to substantial political risks. Therefore, quite a few of them fail and suffer premature evictions (Weyland 2022a). As their infringements cease, liberal pluralism avoids further attacks and can often achieve a quick recovery.

Because liberal pluralism is less vulnerable than often feared, the populist asphyxiation of democracy can run its course only under special conditions. As Chapter 2 argued and Chapters 3 to 5 documented, two types of factors are indispensable; only their infrequent coincidence proves lethal. First, personalistic plebiscitarian leaders can only concentrate power and dismantle liberal constraints if they encounter some kind of institutional weakness. Only if democracy's defenses are already debilitated do transgressive chief executives have any chance of achieving an authoritarian takeover. Interestingly, however, even weak institutions do not crumble under the first push, but still give liberal pluralism a good deal of resilience.

Consequently, a second factor is necessary for the populist destruction of democracy, namely an unusual conjunctural opportunity for an illiberal chief executive to win massive, overwhelming popular support and leverage it to push aside the remaining institutional constraints. These infrequent chances arise from "opposite" developments, namely either from exceptional revenue windfalls, which enable a populist chief executive to obtain, even buy, support through the widespread distribution of generous benefits; or from acute and grave, yet resolvable crises, which allow a populist leader to "save the people" from impending doom, bring urgently needed relief, and receive intense gratitude for this miraculous rescue. Whereas resource booms boost the fortunes of populist leaders via the political rewards emerging from the provision of gains, success in combating a looming catastrophe yields particularly powerful payoffs because of people's intense aversion to losses; whoever can perform magic by pulling a country away from the abyss will enjoy an outpouring of backing.

Interestingly, different types of institutional weakness and of conjunctural opportunities combine in distinctive ways that trace three paths toward the populist strangulation of democracy. Where a democracy has already been battered and ruptured and where high instability therefore prevails, a big revenue windfall suffices for giving a personalistic plebiscitarian leader the clout for resolutely concentrating power and smothering liberal pluralism, as the cases of Hugo Chávez in Venezuela, Rafael Correa in Ecuador, and Evo Morales in Bolivia show. These three instances of left-wing, Bolivarian populism in Latin America thus took advantage of pronounced institutional weakness and the huge commodities boom of the early twenty-first century to move to competitive authoritarianism, as Chapter 4 showed.

By contrast, middling levels of institutional robustness can only be overcome with the special political momentum arising from loss aversion, namely the enormous political rewards for the successful resolution of urgent, serious crises. In parliamentary systems, the attenuated separation of power facilitates change, including populist efforts at power concentration. In this institutional setting, economic crises that lead to reductions in the number of partisan veto players and give populist forces strong parliamentary majorities or supermajorities open the door for the destruction of democracy. This combination of factors allowed two right-wing, traditionalist populists in Europe, namely Viktor Orbán in Hungary and Recep Tayyip Erdoğan in Turkey, to install authoritarian regimes, as demonstrated in Chapter 5.

Compared to parliamentarism, presidential systems enshrine firmer checks and balances (as long as they avoid high instability). Even where incumbents can bend or corrode these constraints through para-legal arrogations, the exceptional coincidence of two severe crises – in the economy and in public security – is required for asphyxiating liberal pluralism. Thus, a personalistic plebiscitarian president must perform true magic by effectively combating two huge challenges in order to win sufficient clout for removing the obstacles to authoritarian involution posed by a relatively firm separation of powers. Such extraordinary feats were the main reason that neoliberal populist Alberto Fujimori in Peru managed to overthrow democracy and that his chameleonic counterpart Nayib Bukele in El Salvador has energetically advanced in the same direction, as Chapter 3 found.

By documenting these three distinctive yet strikingly narrow paths to the populist strangulation of democracy, my study presents a core argument that rests on multiple conjunctural causation à la Charles Ragin (1987: chap. 2; 2000: chap. 4). Two types of factors – institutional weaknesses and severely challenging or exceptionally beneficial circumstances – both constitute necessary conditions for the populist march toward authoritarianism. Specific types of institutional weakness combine with different (combinations of) conjunctural opportunities to form three passageways toward this deleterious outcome. Each of these paths rests on a distinctive coincidence of necessary conditions; and each path is, on its own, sufficient for enabling personalistic plebiscitarian leaders to smother democracy.

This equifinality is theoretically meaningful because the three paths correspond to subtypes of populism long distinguished in the literature, namely left-wing, Bolivarian populism in Latin America, which rose and eventually fell with the global commodities boom; conservative, traditionalist, and ever more ethno-nationalist populism in Europe, which has spread in the last three decades; and neoliberal populism in Latin America, which emerged mainly during the debt crisis of the late 1980s and early 1990s.

As the in-depth examinations of Chapters 3 to 5 show, my theory captures qualitative differences between these well-known subtypes of populism, their specific context of emergence, advance, and decline, and their strikingly variegated regime outcomes. At the same time, my book incorporates these three subtypes and paths into an overarching framework, which revolves around a selective set of theoretical factors and rests on the logic of necessary and sufficient conditions. In these ways, my theory provides a fairly general yet nuanced assessment of the effective threat that contemporary populism poses to liberalism and democracy across two important regions of the world.

The Resilience of Liberal Pluralism and the Special Strength of Western Democracies

The main conclusion arising from the theory and empirical results of this book is that populism does not endanger democracy as much as worried observers have feared. Personalistic plebiscitarian leaders eagerly pursue their illiberal and authoritarian project and employ opportunistic and often savvy ways and means. But they cannot simply engineer and automatically guarantee success for this reprehensible goal. Instead, the actual impact and outcome of populist agency depend on institutional and conjunctural conditions that are largely given and exogenous – and therefore outside charismatic politicians' control – namely the preceding degree of institutional strength and the antecedent conjunctural context.

My findings thus run counter to constructivist arguments, which overestimate populist agency, especially by claiming that leaders can simply "perform" crises and reap the political benefits of combating these strategically framed challenges (Moffitt 2016: 121–32). This book demonstrates, by contrast, that populist chief executives can destroy democracy only when given conditions coincide; they cannot conjure up or create these conditions. The room for populist agency is limited by exogenous conditions and cannot be stretched at will.

Therefore, personalistic plebiscitarian leadership is much less dangerous for liberal pluralism than performative approaches imply. The conjunctural preconditions for the populist strangulation of democracy do not appear frequently. Under many circumstances, democracy survives episodes of populist governance; and even when it suffers considerable pressure or temporary damage, it often recovers quickly. Thus, liberal pluralism commands considerable defensive capacity and often proves immune to populist assaults.

These reassuring findings reflect the experiences of Latin America and Eastern Europe, where polities vary in institutional strength and economies and societies are exposed to substantial risks of volatility. In these settings, populist chief executives can sometimes find openings for their undemocratic designs. The fact that even these comparatively vulnerable democracies often endure suggests sanguine conclusions for the consolidated democracies of Western Europe and North America. In these advanced post-industrial countries, economic prosperity, high education levels, and robust civil societies undergird elevated levels of institutional strength *and* low volatility, that is, considerable immunity to exogenous shocks; after all, massive windfalls are unimaginable in complex First World economies, and deep crises erupt rarely and can be alleviated with compensatory resources before reaching catastrophic depth.

For these reasons, it is highly unlikely that personalistic plebiscitarian leaders will encounter the necessary preconditions for dismantling a Western democracy, not to speak of installing competitive authoritarianism. First, institutional strength poses a virtually insurmountable obstacle to any undemocratic plans. After decades of habituation and fairly successful operation, which has guaranteed the citizenry ample freedom and world-historically unprecedented respect for human and civil rights, the institutional framework of liberal pluralism is well entrenched and firm, in both presidential and parliamentary systems (see in general Svolik 2015). Populist leaders face forbidding constraints on their power hunger that would be exceedingly difficult to strip away. Before they can seriously skew the electoral arena, for instance, their term is up and they must submit to citizens' verdict in a contest that is still free and fair; consequently, they often lose, as did Berlusconi in 2006 and Trump in 2020.

Second, personalistic plebiscitarian incumbents are utterly unlikely to encounter conjunctural opportunities of exceptional magnitude, which would be required for razing the protective walls of liberal pluralism. Because First World economies consist of innumerable different sectors, an exceptional windfall in one sector could only have a modest impact overall, which is very different from the hydrocarbon bonanza that quickly lifted the political fortunes of Hugo Chávez and enabled him to defeat dangerous opposition challenges. Furthermore, this economic complexity, the steering capacity of advanced societies, and their resources for alleviation measures largely preclude the outbreak of cataclysmic crises. In the absence of such apocalyptic challenges, populist chief executives cannot bring urgent relief, miraculously boost their charisma, and establish "transformational leadership" (Burns 1978) – a preeminence that could jeopardize liberal pluralism.

These implications of my wide-ranging comparative analysis are corroborated by the experiences of Silvio Berlusconi and Donald Trump. Berlusconi's political fate is especially instructive because the Italian populist won chief executive office in a more propitious setting than his American counterpart. After all, parliamentarism is institutionally more open to change than US presidentialism with its interlocking checks and balances; and in the early 1990s,

Italy's electoral arena suffered from unusual fluidity after the longstanding, deeply corrupt party system had imploded. This organizational wasteland provided a potential opening for a new populist formation to achieve a clean sweep and win a parliamentary majority. For a First World country, Italy with its special institutional debility thus offered a personalistic plebiscitarian leader such as Berlusconi a unique opportunity for establishing political hegemony and cementing his power.

Nevertheless, the *Cavaliere* never managed to eliminate partisan veto players and achieve unchallengeable dominance, as Erdoğan did in Turkey and especially Orbán in Hungary. Instead, the Italian populist had to rely on diverse coalition partners that pushed and pulled in different directions, limited his political clout, and thus precluded determined power concentration and institutional overhaul. In line with my theory, the root cause of Berlusconi's troubles was the absence of an antecedent economic crisis that would have discredited other parties and enabled this populist outsider to win a strong majority. Thus, while Berlusconi benefited from special weaknesses in Italy's institutional configuration, the necessary other factor, namely an unusual conjunctural opportunity, was missing – and no undemocratic project could succeed. Consequently, Berlusconi's many years as prime minister left democracy undamaged; all his typically populist infractions of liberal norms and democratic values were contained by strong pushback from the courts, opposition forces, and the media, as Chapter 5 showed.

Compared to Italy's personalistic plebiscitarian prime minister, whom he resembles in political background and style (Fracanzani 2021), Donald Trump faced much greater obstacles to his autocratic power hunger; therefore, he clearly failed with his stunning, utterly unprecedented, and strikingly unrealistic efforts at self-perpetuation, as Chapter 6 demonstrated. The checks and balances of US presidentialism and the dispersal of power in the federal system, all anchored in a rock-solid constitution, hemmed in this populist leader and facilitated incessant pushback by a multitude of opponents. As my theory postulates, this institutional resilience, which has undergirded US democracy's world record of persistence despite a history of challenges and crises (Mettler and Lieberman 2020), was sufficient, in and of itself, for protecting liberal pluralism from Trump's nefarious machinations.

The second obstacle to the populist strangulation of democracy arose from the absence of the other prerequisite, namely conjunctural opportunities for boosting mass support and achieving irresistible predominance. Upon taking office, Trump faced neither a huge windfall nor a pressing crisis. Therefore, the transgressive leader clearly lacked the overwhelming force that would be required for breaching the brick wall of American presidentialism. Instead, conjunctural developments put Trump in an especially unfavorable position. Rather than encountering the great opportunity provided by a resolvable crisis, the US populist eventually had to confront an insidious challenge not amenable to quick resolution, namely the COVID-19 pandemic. Because this ineliminable threat cast doubt on his claims of charismatic redemption and because Trump, in typically populist fashion, mismanaged the health emergency, this exogenous shock further depressed his political prospects. For all of these reasons, he failed to win reelection – a rare defeat for an incumbent populist president.

Contrary to the intense fears of numerous observers, Trump therefore did not manage to undo the firm institutional constraints of US democracy. Even if the resentful leader achieves a comeback in 2024 – a distinct possibility in light of the Biden administration's struggles – he will most likely be unable to follow in the footsteps of the few populist chief executives who have smothered democracy. Instead, liberal pluralism in the USA has a high probability of surviving Trump's personalistic plebiscitarian leadership again.

In sum, the two most outstanding cases of populist chief executives in Western democracies corroborate my theory. After all, even in the weaker institutional settings of Latin America and Eastern Europe, personalistic plebiscitarian leaders succeeded in strangling liberal pluralism only under unusual exogenous conditions. Because those conditions are exceedingly unlikely to prevail in advanced countries, democracy in those advanced economies and societies is virtually safe from populist assaults.

BROADER INSIGHTS AND THEORETICAL CONTRIBUTIONS

The Role of Institutions and Conjunctures

Like so much of contemporary political science, my theory highlights the role of institutions as one of its two crucial sets of explanatory factors. This emphasis arises from the political-strategic definition of populism, which revolves around personalistic (and plebiscitarian) leadership. Accordingly, populist chief executives have greater room for their corrosive, undemocratic agency where the existing institutional framework suffers from weaknesses; by contrast, firm, sticky institutions impose constraints on their opportunistic machinations, hem in headstrong leadership, and thus protect liberal pluralism from severe damage.

Recent scholars have questioned the importance of institutions, especially their capacity to constrain political actors; these skeptics argue that institutions themselves need to be sustained by political actors, whose commitment to the underlying norms and values is therefore decisive (see especially Levitsky and Ziblatt 2018 and in general Mahoney and Thelen 2010). But these concerns underestimate the incentives created by institutions themselves: The existing structures shape the interests of actors and induce them to defend and extend the attributions and resources that their institutional positions provide. As a striking example, even GOP congresspeople, who were impressed and intimidated by President Trump's fervent mass support, offered a great deal of passive resistance to his distinctively populist initiatives and defended the independence of their chambers; their primary motivation was not principled commitment to constitutional norms and values but the opportunistic self-interest of electoral politicians (Lee 2018, 2022, 2023).

Thus, through their systematic feedback effects on political actors, institutions generate their own mechanisms of protection and perpetuation. In particular, the stronger that institutions have been, the more the very expectation of their continued persistence helps to guarantee this persistence; extrapolation thus inspires a self-fulfilling prophecy. At high levels of institutional stickiness, these mechanisms give rise to a great deal of path dependency (Pierson 2000; Hall 2016).

How about institutions that suffer from varying degrees of weakness? One of the unexpected findings of my wide-ranging analysis is that even institutions of middling strength, such as the parliamentary systems of Eastern Europe and many presidential systems in Latin America, pose substantial obstacles to populist power grabs. While instances of para-legal machinations and constitutional conflicts easily come to mind, these signs of vulnerability cannot hide the fact that personalistic plebiscitarian leaders have often faced considerable difficulty in pursuing their illiberal and undemocratic goals. Even weak institutions create friction that can dilute the push of headstrong populists and gradually sap the advance of power concentration projects. And the forceful efforts of charismatic politicians to steamroll these roadblocks can provoke contentious opposition and a growing backlash, which have felled a number of populist incumbents (Weyland 2022a: 30–31).

Interestingly, thus, even the weaker institutions prevailing in much of Eastern Europe and Latin America are not easy to overturn; only unusual conjunctural conditions allow personalistic plebiscitarian leaders to get their way. My comprehensive comparative analysis thus documents the significance of political institutions as constraints on political agency, including the power hunger of personalistic plebiscitarian leaders. This important result can allay recent observers' doubts and concerns about the impact of institutions: Their protective shield limits the danger facing liberal pluralism in the contemporary era.

Institutional structures are, however, only one crucial factor in my interactive theory. Critical conjunctures matter a great deal as well; and how these two types of factors intersect decisively shapes populism's repercussions for democracy. With this double-sided approach and its emphasis on multiple conjunctural causation, the book avoids the common problem of historical institutionalism, which traditionally overestimated the persistence of linear trajectories. Instead, depending on the preexisting strength of the institutional framework, unusual conjunctural developments can puncture longstanding trends and prompt striking turnarounds, which can occasionally produce a major change of direction – for better or for worse. These drastic inflections can occur in weaker institutional settings, where the plasticity of constraints provides greater room for political agency, including the pushing and shoving of populist leaders – but also the defensive and restorative moves of their opponents.

Such an inversion of trajectory can arise from crises, one of the two main types of conjunctural developments specified in my theory. After all, crises do not only pose serious challenges that risk perpetuating and aggravating ongoing deterioration. Instead, these very challenges can also offer opportunities for recovery and reform and thus prompt an inflection in a country's path. The looming threat of massive losses makes the suffering population long for a savior. If a new populist incumbent can forestall the impending catastrophe, citizens reward this hero with an outpouring of support. Backing by a supermajority in turn enables the charismatic leader to interrupt democratic development and push toward authoritarian rule. This dramatic descent has disrupted the seeming consolidation of post-communist democracy in Hungary, suppressed initially encouraging moves toward greater liberalism in Turkey, and pulverized the remnants of Venezuela's long-institutionalized party system.

Fortunately, my study has identified more salutary turnarounds as well. Indeed, populism's very threat to democracy, and the high-profile precedent of cases such as Hungary, Turkey, and Venezuela in which this threat has actually turned lethal (cf. Levitsky and Ziblatt 2018), have awakened the supporters of democracy and thus served as stimuli for countermobilization. Personalistic plebiscitarian leadership often exerts strong deterrent effects, as evident in the revulsion that untested outsiders with their illiberal rhetoric, undignified discourse, and "low" style (cf. Ostiguy 2017) arouse, especially among educated middle-class people.

While this antipathy is near-universal, from Menem's Argentina to Erdoğan's Turkey, from Chávez's Venezuela to Berlusconi's Italy, and from Fujimori's Peru to Le Pen's France, the social structure and institutional framework of different countries shape its specific political ramifications, including its differential impact on democracy. First, where lower economic development and starker social inequality prevail, the middle class comprises only a privileged minority of the population, which limits its political clout, especially in the electoral arena; with their plebeian mass support, charismatic incumbents can simply outvote their opponents. By contrast, in advanced countries such as the USA, the middle class constitutes a majority, especially among actual voters. Consequently, in Western democracies, populist leaders have difficulty winning chief executive office in the first place, as Jean-Marie and Marine Le Pen's repeated failures in France show; and where they do succeed, they face multifaceted resistance, which hinders their illiberal initiatives.

Second, strong institutions induce anti-populist forces to channel their pro-democratic energy into conventional forms of political involvement, especially electoral activities, ranging from simple turnout to the time-consuming tasks of campaigning or running as a candidate. This injection of participatory dynamism has a salutary impact by rejuvenating representative democracy. And where the opposition triumphs, as it happened in the USA in 2020, in Italy in 2006, and even in the weaker institutional settings of Slovakia in 1998 and Brazil in 2022, democracy can achieve reequilibration (Linz 1978: chap. 5).

By contrast, pronounced institutional debility enables populist incumbents to "take over" electoral and judicial bodies, manipulate their operation, and seriously skew the outcomes. Squeezed out in these ways, opposition forces may see no other option than resorting to extrainstitutional contention and street protest. But these desperate means of resistance carry high risks of backfiring. If anti-populist forces do not rely on formal-institutional mechanisms, but engage in irregular challenges, autocratic populist incumbents can opportunistically denounce them as undemocratic and try to justify their suppression. In the worst case, unconventional mobilization against personalistic plebiscitarian power hunger can prove counterproductive and inadvertently accelerate the march into authoritarianism, as happened in Venezuela (Gamboa 2017; Cleary and Öztürk 2022: 211–15).

In conclusion, both institutional frameworks and conjunctural developments play a crucial role in shaping the politics of populism, especially its regime effects. Institutions tend to have substantial constraining force; even institutions of middling strength create considerable friction and hinder the populist strangulation of democracy. Personalistic plebiscitarian leaders can overcome these constraints only under special circumstances, which depend on exogenous conjunctural developments. For these reasons, populist agency faces important obstacles to its incessant efforts to smother liberal pluralism.

The Analytical Value of the Political-Strategic Approach to Populism

Through its broad, cross-regional analysis of populism's differential impact on democracy, this book has demonstrated the inferential payoffs of the political-strategic definition of populism (Weyland 2001, 2017, 2021b). With its emphasis on personalistic plebiscitarian leadership, this approach draws attention to the crucial actor, whose machinations are decisive for populism's inherent threat to democracy. Because these charismatic leaders incessantly push for augmenting their autonomy and power, they – not their constituents – take the initiative and try to batter and breach the fortress of liberal pluralism.[1]

Ideational approaches miss this crucial core of populism by defining it via the Manichean contrast and conflict pitting the supposedly pure people against selfish, corrupt elites. But this conceptualization overlooks the main "mover and shaker" – namely, the leader. After all, "the people" are far too amorphous and heterogeneous, fragmented and disorganized, to command effective agency. On their own, the people simply *cannot* act. Instead, populist agency inevitably emanates from the leader, who simply claims to embody "the will of the people." This idea of organic representation and virtual incarnation allows the leader to act as he sees fit – and to engineer plebiscitarian acclamation for his undemocratic initiatives, while distorting or disabling effective

---

[1] While employing a different definitional approach, Bartels' brand-new study (2023) reaches the same substantive conclusion.

accountability. Contrary to its rhetorical claims, therefore, populism does not empower the people; instead, it effectively vests all agency in the leader and thus *dis*empowers the people – one of the fundamental reasons for its innate tendency toward authoritarianism.

Whereas ideational definitions fail to emphasize the central role of charismatic leadership, the political-strategic approach highlights this principal axis of populism; correspondingly, it focuses primarily on what personalistic plebiscitarian leaders do, rather than what they say. After all, a wide variety of politicians occasionally sound like populists, especially on the campaign trail. Because modern democracy rests on popular sovereignty, actors of all stripes have incentives for rhetorically invoking "the people." A focus on discourse and the underlying ideas is therefore not the best way of distinguishing populists from other types of political forces and leaders.

Indeed, words can amount to little more than "cheap talk." Politicians commonly deviate from their pronouncements and promises in their actual deeds. Political actions, by contrast, "speak louder" because they require a clearer choice between various options. A deed is harder to reverse and therefore has more impact than words. And in their political repercussions and consequences, actions tend to be much more important than discourse and rhetoric.

For political analysis, therefore, the political-strategic definition is more productive and fruitful than ideational approaches. This advantage prevails especially now, when many personalistic plebiscitarian leaders occupy chief executive offices across the world and when populism's threat to democracy therefore holds acute salience and high relevance. During these worrisome times, political science needs to analyze how these charismatic incumbents wield power, outmaneuver or attack opposition forces, put pressure on institutional checks and balances, and try hard to undermine and eventually suppress liberal pluralism. Accordingly, it matters primarily what populist leaders do, not what they say.

Whereas ideational definitions neglect the decisive role of charismatic leadership, constructivist and performative approaches risk the opposite problem, namely overestimating the power of populist agency. Their emphasis on framing and performance depicts leaders as demiurges who can shape their own environment; inversely, structures and institutions look flexible and transformable, lacking the capacity to impose constraints. But this plasticity assumption is problematic. As this study demonstrated, both preexisting institutions and shifting conjunctures are largely exogenous to populist agency and cannot simply be "constructed"; instead, they create fairly clear and often hard constraints even on politicians who boast a great deal of charismatic prowess. Consequently, the opportunities and limitations that personalistic plebiscitarian incumbents face and that shape their chances of success are mostly given.

By contrast to these one-sided approaches, which either neglect or overestimate the role and impact of populist leadership, the political-strategic definition paints a more realistic picture. It is particularly useful in focusing on the persistent efforts of personalistic plebiscitarian politicians to pursue their most fundamental goal of power concentration in settings of varying institutional strength and under fluctuating exogenous conjunctures. In advancing their self-proclaimed charismatic mission, populist politicians are fundamentally opportunistic: They try to evade or corrode obstacles and to exploit any opening they encounter. They eagerly seek to push through change, but are constrained by the starting conditions that they find upon assuming power. Studies resting on the political-strategic definition examine this interplay of agency and of structural conditions, arising from institutional configurations and conjunctural developments.

An additional benefit of the political-strategic approach is that it is ideologically neutral and unbiased; in particular, it recognizes that right-wing and left-wing populism pose equally serious threats to liberal pluralism. By contrast, some discourse approaches, especially the disciples of Argentine theorist Ernesto Laclau, depict left-wing populism as a rejuvenating force that advances the interests and needs of the popular masses and breaks the stifling hegemony of established elites. In this view, progressive charismatic leaders are the necessary ram for dislodging entrenched oligarchies and installing radical, participatory democracy.

In political reality, however, left-wing populism has proven as detrimental to democracy as have right-wing versions. Overall, Chávez, Correa, and Morales have not been significantly less autocratic and repressive than Fujimori and Bukele, Orbán and Erdoğan.[2] Regardless of their ideological leanings, which are usually vague and shifty, charismatic leaders have uniformly tried to chart an undemocratic course by relentlessly seeking political hegemony and unchallengeable predominance; even inside Spain's PODEMOS, held up by left-wing advocates as a great hope for participatory innovation, Pablo Iglesias soon engineered his domineering leadership and expelled his principal rival (De Nadal 2021; see also Villacañas 2017: 158–64, 253–57, 265, 273). Moreover, to realize their illiberal and authoritarian goals, both right-wing and left-wing populists have depended on a similar coincidence of necessary conditions, namely institutional weakness and unusual conjunctural opportunity. Contrary to the claims of Laclauian discourse analysts, right-wing and left-wing populists therefore pose essentially similar threats to liberal pluralism (Cohen 2019).

The political-strategic approach captures this equivalence of risks. Compared to left-wing populism, right-wing variants are not inherently more dangerous to democracy – and they will definitely not bring a revival of fascism, a special

---

[2] After the bloody coup attempt of mid-2016, Erdoğan turned into a partial exception with his large-scale purges. However, under his non-populist successor, Nicolás Maduro, the regime installed by Chávez has also descended into open autocracy, which has not only engaged in numerous human rights violations but has also turned mass destitution, even hunger, into a political control mechanism.

concern voiced recently.[3] As regards the inherent threat to liberal pluralism, the ideological leanings of charismatic leaders are not decisive; instead, what is crucial is their fundamentally similar political strategy. That is the central focus of the political-strategic approach – and its major advantage over ideational definitions and discursive theories. The comparative investigations of my book have demonstrated the heuristic value and analytical payoffs of this approach.

THE COMPLEXITY OF POPULIST POLITICS: INFLUENCES ACROSS CASES

To unearth the conditions for the populist strangulation of democracy, this study has employed systematic comparison and contrast. For this purpose, it has followed the traditional approach of comparative politics and treated each instance of populist incumbency as an independent case. This analytical strategy implicitly assumes that internal causal factors operate uniformly across all of these variegated cases, with the same strength and the same effect. The case studies have, however, invoked one type of international influence in several instances, namely external pressures exerted by the EU over East European countries (Chapter 5) and the constraints imposed by the USA, especially on several neoliberal populists (Chapter 3).

As a result of these powerful push factors, populist politics in contemporary Latin America and Europe unfolds under a fundamental exogenous context condition: The democracy protection regime erected and enforced primarily by the USA, yet also the EU, has largely ruled out military coups, which used to be the biggest terminator of populist governance in prior eras, especially in Latin America. On many occasions, the armed forces coercively stopped the suffocation of liberal pluralism by personalistic plebiscitarian incumbents, yet at the tragic cost of destroying democracy outright. Except for the case of Honduras' Zelaya in 2009, the vigilance of First World countries has ruled out these disastrous military interventions since the third wave of democratization and the end of the Cold War. Thus, external pressures have played a crucial role, firmly limiting the repertoire of available political means and mechanisms.

This basic historical development sets temporal and regional scope conditions for my theory, which reflects primarily the experiences of contemporary Europe and Latin America. Conversely, where Western influence is significantly weaker, namely in Africa, Asia, and the Middle East, personalistic plebiscitarian leaders live more dangerously because the armed forces may command independent veto power. As the political fate of Thailand's Thaksin Shinawatra shows (see section on "Populism in Southeast and South Asia" later in this chapter), populists have even lower chances of installing competitive authoritarianism. Unfortunately, however, democracy is not any safer as a result; instead, forceful military intervention creates especially grave risks.

---

[3] I have analyzed this question of a revival of fascism in Weyland (2021a: 328–32).

The foundation of the West's coup-prohibition regime, namely the external pressures that powerful countries such as the USA exert over weaker countries in "developing" regions, constitute vertical push factors. In addition, there have also been horizontal influences among episodes of populism in countries that are equally placed in the international hierarchy. The following subsections examine two types. First, diffusion effects unfold where an outstanding precedent of personalistic plebiscitarian leadership inspires ambitious politicians in other nations to emulate this role model and employ a similar political strategy. In Latin American history, classical populist Juan Perón in Argentina (1946–55) was the prime exemplar that stimulated such imitation efforts. In the third millennium, Venezuela's Hugo Chávez held similar appeal, as discussed shortly.

Second, there can be sequential developments in which a personalistic plebiscitarian leader in one country pushes open the door for a series of subsequent populists. By destructuring the party system, this path-breaker makes it more likely that, after his own exit from power, other populists will succeed him sooner or later. Interestingly, although this "serial populism" (Roberts 2014: 58–63) can perpetuate haphazard decision-making and cause manifold problems for governance, the very ease with which latter-day populists win office tends to prevent them from strangling democracy, as explained later.

Diffusion Effects: How International Precedents Can Affect Populism's Risks

In the regions under investigation, processes of cross-national diffusion have occasionally affected populism's regime outcomes in significant ways. As suggested by Huntington (1991: 104–6), inspiration and contagion have served as supplementary causal forces that have sometimes pushed domestic actors to follow a foreign precedent further than the constellation of internal factors alone would have allowed. In the language of necessary conditions, this added outside impulse lowered the domestic requirements for an outcome and thus made it more likely. Where internal preconditions were already close to the threshold for permitting this outcome, the supplementary impetus provided by learning from a foreign model ensured that this outcome would come to pass.

Interestingly, however, where the domestic constellation of factors was unfavorable for an outcome traced by an external precedent, the inspiration that domestic admirers took from this foreign example tended to backfire. In this situation, efforts to imitate the external precedent ran afoul of strong deterrent effects, which the foreign experience unleashed as well. Accordingly, opponents of the foreign model energetically and forcefully tried to block its emulation, and the unpropitious configuration of factors gave them the upper hand. Under these circumstances, the inspirational impulse coming from the outside was too weak to overpower the backlash that the foreign experience stimulated among its adversaries.

How these contagion vs. deterrent effects operated, and why contagion prevailed in some cases yet deterrent effects in others, becomes most evident in the waves that Chávez's Bolivarian populism made in Latin America at the height of the global commodities boom (see especially De la Torre 2017a). After all, Venezuela's charismatic leader served as a role model and, indeed, an active and energetic supporter for other left-wing populists across the region. But the precedent that Chávez set by quickly convoking a constituent assembly, using it to concentrate power, and then relentlessly dismantling democracy and pushing toward competitive authoritarianism had strikingly different effects. In countries where the constellation of causal factors – institutional instability and large revenue inflows – resembled Venezuela, Bolivarian populists eagerly replicated the *chavista* script. Yet in settings where the institutional framework was stronger or where windfall rents were much lower than in Venezuela, similar efforts failed, in various ways.

On the one hand, Ecuador and Bolivia were also suffering from high instability and benefiting from an upsurge in hydrocarbon revenues, though to a lower degree than Venezuela with its massive and almost exclusive reliance on oil exports. Under these propitious circumstances, inspiration (and support) from the Bolivarian chieftain provided the added impulse for Correa and Morales to follow Chávez's regime-transforming blueprint step by step and to succeed with their suffocation of democracy. The two Bolivarian disciples knew how to proceed and guided their supporters toward a clear goal. Accordingly, immediately upon taking office, Correa and Morales convoked constituent assemblies as well and used them for a profound institutional overhaul that augmented their power and allowed for its extension via reelection. At the same time, they forcefully marginalized the opposition and put heavy pressure on independent media, employing discriminatory legalism and persistent harassment. In these ways, they resolutely emulated Venezuela's descent into competitive authoritarianism (see especially De la Torre 2017a: 1275–78; for Correa, see Freidenberg 2015: 122–23; on the regime outcome, see Sánchez-Sibony 2017, 2018, 2021; Levitsky and Loxton 2019: 344–47).

On the other hand, where crucial causal factors differed significantly from Chávez's Venezuela, similar imitation efforts spearheaded by ambitious members of the Bolivarian fraternity failed. The most far-reaching effort was initiated and eventually aborted in Honduras. Precisely because Zelaya's stubborn push for a constituent assembly seemed to follow Chávez's script, it provoked grave concern and intransigent opposition from the democratically elected Congress and the courts. When the headstrong convert to left-wing populism confirmed these fears by persisting in his unconstitutional and illegal machinations, the military, as a last resort, evicted him with armed coercion, interrupting the newly polarized democracy in the process.

Zelaya lost this confrontation for two underlying reasons. First, despite Chávez's subsidies, he did not dispose of huge windfall rents and therefore did not manage to boost his meager popularity and win overwhelming support. Second, because Honduras did not suffer from high instability, opposition forces commanded fairly firm institutional bastions. Under these unfavorable conditions, the stubborn populist could not push aside his adversaries, as his Venezuelan role model had done. Consequently, the backlash caused by the specter of Chávez proved stronger than the inspirational effect of Bolivarianism. To prevent the populist suffocation of democracy à la Venezuela, the ample anti-populist forces pulled the emergency break and enlisted the traditional terminator of Latin American populism: The military evicted Zelaya, yet forcefully interrupted democracy in the process.

The precedent of Chávez also backfired in other Latin American countries, most clearly in Peru and Mexico in 2006, where fears of Bolivarian populism contributed to the narrow electoral defeat of left-wing outsiders who looked like disciples of the Bolivarian leader. Even at the height of the commodities boom, Mexico's diversified economy with its huge (semi-)manufactured exports did not enjoy a huge resource windfall; and Peru's voluminous mineral and hydrocarbon extraction was largely in private and foreign hands, limiting the state's extra income from tax revenues. Because neither country suffered from high instability either, they lacked the necessary conditions for replicating Chávez's ambitious project of populist transformation.

No wonder that left-wing populists who resembled the Bolivarian leader lost presidential elections in 2006. In Peru, Chávez actually interfered in the contest, insulting old populist Alan García and promoting radical nationalist and former military rebel Ollanta Humala, with whom he shared important similarities in background and ideology. Yet the Venezuelan chieftain's blatant involvement backfired; it may well have sealed García's victory by allowing him to claim the mantle of Peruvian nationalism. In Mexico's new democracy, overbearing, fairly radical AMLO also suffered from comparisons with the Venezuelan strangler of liberal pluralism and defiant enemy of "neoliberalism," the basis of Mexico's trade integration with the USA. Thus, in cases where conditions differed substantially from Venezuela, aversion to Chávez contributed to the electoral defeat of pushy populists and thus helped protect democracy from trouble.[4]

A similar divergence in the strength of populist contagion vs. deterrent effects has appeared in Europe; indeed, geographic differences in the crucial causal factors have made these divergent trends especially visible. After all, institutional strength is higher in the continent's West, as is the organizational solidity of the party system and the vibrancy of civil society; by contrast, all of these pillars of liberal pluralism are weaker in Eastern Europe. Consequently,

---

[4] Interestingly, these defeats induced both Humala and AMLO to moderate their stance on crucial political and socioeconomic issues, including the question of a constituent assembly. Thus, when both leaders finally achieved electoral victories, they posed significantly lower threats to democracy than if they had won in 2006.

populist precedents primarily provoke a backlash in the West, while finding much more imitation in the East.

Accordingly, the UK's Brexit referendum and the election of Donald Trump aroused widespread alarm and hurt the electoral chances of personalistic plebiscitarian leaders in the similar settings of Western Europe. In early 2017, for instance, soon after these shocking events, ethno-nationalist right-winger Geert Wilders in the Netherlands garnered a lower vote share than expected, and France's Marine Le Pen suffered a decisive defeat at the hands of Emmanuel Macron. Thus, high-profile populist leaders with their incendiary rhetoric and constant confrontation can inadvertently produce antibodies that inoculate other countries and limit contagion by this problematic political strategy.

By contrast, inspiration and contagion have prevailed in the weaker institutional, organizational, and societal settings of Eastern Europe. In particular, the easy success of Hungary's Orbán in smoothly and quickly undermining liberal pluralism and cementing his hegemony has increasingly served as a model for other right-wing populists in the region.[5] This precedent provided a road map and an added impulse for the Polish PiS to make a resolute push toward illiberalism. In fact, the Magyar leader visited Warsaw on several occasions to provide guidance, especially advice on how to subdue domestic opposition and evade international pressures.[6] As Jarosław Kaczyński learned from the authoritarian populist in Budapest, he has put relentless pressure on the judiciary and has long managed to avoid EU sanctions. Consequently, the deterioration of liberal pluralism along the Vistula has been more severe (Sadurski 2019) than domestic factors alone would predict, given the institutional checks and balances of Poland's semi-presidential system and the absence of any trace of crisis.

In sum, mechanisms of diffusion, ranging from inspirational influences to deterrent effects, affected the political fate of personalistic plebiscitarian leadership and its regime outcomes in several cases, both in Europe and in Latin America, and among right-wing and left-wing versions of populism. Interestingly, however, this additional factor did not produce major deviations from the predictions of my theory. The most noticeable impact has been that Kaczyński's PiS governments have subjected Polish democracy to unusual stress and strain, and that Zelaya's power concentration effort in Honduras failed in an extraordinary, disastrous way through a military coup, an exceedingly rare occurrence in contemporary Latin America. Attention to diffusion effects thus improves the accuracy of the analysis, yet diminishes its generality and parsimony – the fundamental trade-off faced by political science (Przeworski and Teune [1970] 1982: 17–22).

---

[5] Especially during his third term as prime minister (2020–22), Slovenia's Janez Janša also took a great deal of inspiration from Orbán – as well as from Trump.

[6] Ben Stanley, SWPS University of Social Sciences and Humanities, Warsaw, personal communication, April 25, 2022.

Serial Populism: How a Domestic Precedent Affects Populism's Risks

As there are cross-national influences among cases of populist leadership, there are also temporal effects that arise from the sequencing of populist episodes inside one country. In particular, the machinations of an early personalistic plebiscitarian incumbent tend to lower the remaining barriers to the rise of future political outsiders, and thus make renewed populism more likely – yet also less impactful, and therefore less dangerous for liberal pluralism. How do these sequential developments unfold?

The initial breakthrough of charismatic leadership often depends on crisis conditions (cf. Weber 1976: 142, 657), which can enable the new chief executive to smother democracy, as Chapters 3 and 5 showed. Yet because this populist front-runner with his anti-organizational tendencies further weakens the established party system (Haughton and Deegan-Krause 2015; Hollyer, Klašnja, and Titiunik 2022; see also Tanaka 2011: 76–82), after his eventual downfall other personalistic plebiscitarian leaders find it relatively easy to achieve electoral victories. But precisely because these outsider politicians manage to triumph in fairly normal circumstances, they do not face the conjunctural opportunities for obtaining massive support and erecting their unchallengeable hegemony. Therefore, these subsequent populists do not command the requisite clout for suppressing liberal pluralism – which the front-runner had. As a result, democracy has high chances of surviving these iterations of populism.

The most striking case of this "serial populism" is contemporary Peru (see Roberts 2014: 58–63, 126–28, 276).[7] As Chapter 3 highlighted, novice Alberto Fujimori emerged in an exceptionally dire situation, when raging hyperinflation and a wide-ranging terrorist insurrection had pushed his country to the brink of catastrophe. Because the Andean Samurai managed to spearhead a stunning turnaround, he achieved total predominance and used it to assault democracy. In his pronounced personalism, Fujimori also eviscerated the remnants of Peru's party system. His downfall in 2000 therefore left behind an organizational wasteland. In the virtual absence of political parties (Levitsky and Cameron 2003), only a personalistic plebiscitarian leader could win the next presidential election in 2001, namely "neopopulist" Alejandro Toledo (Barr 2003). Then Alan García, who had governed as a left-wing populist from 1985 to 1990 and who had facilitated Fujimori's rise in 1990, won a second term in 2006. He was followed by Ollanta Humala, yet another populist, whom Chapter 4 examined. And after a brief interregnum driven by a backlash to the revival of Fujimori-style populism, a new personalistic plebiscitarian leader won the 2021 election, Pedro Castillo (2021–22).

Another case of serial populism is Slovakia with its string of personalistic plebiscitarian prime ministers, discussed in Chapter 5. Right after the collapse of communism with its devastating socioeconomic hardship, headstrong

---

[7] The following paragraphs draw heavily on Weyland (2022a: 36–39).

Vladimír Mečiar achieved considerable electoral prowess and headed the government three times, putting increasing pressure on liberal pluralism with his autocratic machinations. Soon after a newly formed coalition of democratic forces defeated him in 1998, another populist, Robert Fico, started to rise and came to lead the government for two long periods. And after Fico tripped over a scandal prompted by widespread collusion and corruption in 2018, a new personalistic plebiscitarian politician – Igor Matovič – won the subsequent election in 2020.

Serial populism has also taken hold in Italy. The party collapse of the early 1990s was crucial for the rise of Silvio Berlusconi, who dominated Italian politics for nearly two decades. The decline and eventual demise of this personalistic leader then facilitated the emergence of further populist groupings, especially the ideologically and organizationally amorphous Five Star Movement founded by Beppe Grillo. And on the right side of the spectrum, Berlusconi's fading leadership opened space for the Northern League, led in recent years by Italy's most visible and controversial populist, Matteo Salvini (Verbeek and Zaslove 2019: 90–98).

Thus, early experiences with populism can pave the way for the further emergence of personalistic plebiscitarian leadership. By corroding the remainder of the party system, the front-runner lowers the barriers for later political outsiders to achieve electoral success. Through this type of path dependency, serial populism takes hold; it can turn into the political default option for countries that lack even halfway-organized and program-oriented parties.

Interestingly, while serial populism extends and prolongs the threat that personalistic plebiscitarian leadership poses to democracy, it tends to diminish the intensity and severity of this danger. On the one hand, the downfall of an autocratic populist and the subsequent restoration or reequilibration of democracy – as in Peru after Fujimori and in Slovakia after Mečiar – do not reliably immunize countries against the resurgence of personalistic plebiscitarian leadership. Instead, crucial preconditions for the rise of populism, especially an uninstitutionalized or collapsed party system, often persist. Indeed, populist incumbents deliberately dismantle remaining party organizations, creating even more room for the recurrence of populism. Once a country falls under populist leadership, therefore, it may well have difficulty emerging from this problematic equilibrium by constructing or rebuilding its party system.

Yet on the other hand, whereas serial populism depresses democratic quality, it does not tend to threaten the survival of democracy itself. Latter-day populists, such as Toledo, García, Humala, and Castillo in Peru, or Fico and Matovič in Slovakia, do not squeeze liberal pluralism nearly as hard as front-runners Fujimori and Mečiar had done (on Slovakia, see Walter 2017: 176). Perhaps these subsequent leaders learn from the eventual failure of their forebears and therefore embrace greater risk aversion (on Fico, see Nemčok and Spáč 2020: 249, 256); most do indeed refrain from aggressive confrontation and resolute attempts to extinguish democracy. For instance, Peru's Humala in 2011 backed away from his initial plan to convoke a constituent assembly à la Hugo Chávez, which could have started a determined push for undemocratic power concentration, but which also risked provoking fierce controversy and all-out conflict (Arnson and de la Torre 2013: 370–72); instead, Humala pledged commitment to the full maintenance of liberal democracy (Levitsky 2011: 89–90; McClintock 2013: 231–36), a promise that he was too weak to break later.

More basically, the very ease with which successive populists win power limits their capacity to endanger democracy. After all, the devastation of the party system aggravated by the initial populist turns populism into the principal option for electoral victory. Precisely because the door is wide open for personalistic plebiscitarian leadership (Roberts 2014: 58–59, 276), politicians employing this political strategy can win elections under normal circumstances, in the absence of acute, severe crises. Yet without such a dramatic challenge, politicians cannot perform miraculous feats, boost their charismatic prowess, and win overwhelming mass support – as indicated by the dramatic drop in popularity ratings that all of Peru's serial populists – Toledo, García, Humala, and Castillo – suffered soon after taking office. The very absence of crisis thus limits the clout that these easy winners can achieve, restricting their ability to do serious damage to democracy.

Serial populists therefore cannot be as undemocratic as the initial outsiders, who took office under crisis conditions and therefore had the opportunity to suffocate democracy.[8] Whereas the first populist was a savior who could abuse his heroic accomplishments, subsequent leaders are default options who lack the chances for garnering massive clout. Precisely because the initial leader with his corrosive impact on the party system greatly facilitated the recurrent success of the populist strategy, serial populists tend to be more self-contained and limited in their destructive agency. For these reasons, although the election of one personalistic leader after another hinders efforts to make democracy great again, it usually does not endanger the very persistence of liberal pluralism.

In sum, the political failure and dramatic downfall of a populist leader does not automatically vaccinate a country against the return of populism. On the contrary, an initial experience makes the recurrence of populism more likely. But it is exactly this easy accession to power that diminishes the subversive and destructive capacity of later personalistic leaders. As a result, the democracies that are quickly resurrected after the first populist's demise tend to persist, albeit in an enfeebled condition and at low levels of quality.

---

[8] Where serial populism plunges a country into high instability, however, and where a subsequent personalistic plebiscitarian leader happens to benefit from a huge hydrocarbon boom, as in Ecuador in the mid-2000s, the new president exceptionally encounters a golden opportunity for cementing his hegemony and smothering democracy – as Rafael Correa promptly did.

BROADER COMPARATIVE PERSPECTIVES

This book has been motivated by recent observers' intense fears about the insidious ways in which populism jeopardizes liberal pluralism: Democratically elected chief executives can dismantle democracy from the inside, and populists with their opportunistic efforts to win over large swaths of the citizenry and achieve overwhelming popular support are especially well positioned to achieve this sneaky feat. Because this gradual strangulation need not violate formal rules, even advanced industrialized countries with their firm rule of law may be subject to this risk. Therefore, Trump's triumph in the USA provoked such acute alarm.

Because First World nations have hitherto had little experience with populism in power, this study has assessed the effective danger of personalistic plebiscitarian leadership by conducting a comprehensive investigation of its regime impact in the two regions most similar to the USA and other First World countries, namely Europe and Latin America. Do my findings also apply to other continents, where populist governments have been more sporadic, emerging only recently in larger numbers? The present section offers some observations about the repercussions of personalistic plebiscitarian leadership in Asia, where several high-profile cases have arisen in the twenty-first century.[9] Because these politicians, especially Joseph Estrada (1998–2001) and Rodrigo Duterte (2016–22) in the Philippines, Thaksin Shinawatra in Thailand (2001–6), and Narendra Modi in India (2014–present), have drawn a good deal of attention, there is sufficient scholarly literature for such an examination from afar. By contrast, populism, as well as its study, is incipient in Africa and the Middle East.

Populism in Asia and Its Moderate Version in Northeast Asia

According to the first book published about "Populism in Asia," the global wave started to reach the continent after the deep economic crisis erupting in 1997 (Mizuno and Phongpaichit 2009: 5, 14).[10] The abrupt end of long stretches of rapid economic development caused widespread material hardship and social discontent and discredited the established political-economic elite. Typically, these crisis conditions made large parts of the citizenry receptive to, even clamor for, charismatic saviors who would revert recent losses and put their country back on the path toward greater prosperity. Moreover, people hoped that these heroes would effect political reform by opening up entrenched oligarchical regimes steeped in collusion and corruption, and in this way enhance democratic accountability and popular participation. These grievances and

---

[9] In his overview, Hellmann (2017) emphasizes the infrequency of populism in Asia, however.
[10] For an exceptionally early case of populism in Asia, namely Indira Gandhi in the 1970s, see Kenny (2017: chap. 6) and Varshney (2019: 332–33, 343).

expectations created fertile ground for the rise of personalistic plebiscitarian leaders across the region and drove their electoral victories in some countries.

In Northeast Asia's democracies of Japan, South Korea, and Taiwan, however, the economic downturn was not nearly as severe as in much of Southeast Asia. Moreover, comparatively strong institutions constrained charismatic politicians, who also faced fairly vibrant civil societies. While marking their differences from "the establishment" through innovative policy initiatives and an unconventional, popularity-seeking style, these populist chief executives therefore acted with moderation (Mizuno and Phongpaichit 2009: 6–8). In particular, they did not whip up confrontation, infringe on existing rules, and forcefully try to concentrate power. Japan's Junichiro Koizumi (2001–6) never even quit the long-ruling, heavily patronage-based Liberal Democratic Party, but rose inside this mainstay of the establishment (Kabashima and Steel 2007);[11] for a populist, he therefore proceeded with considerable moderation (Otake 2009: 212–14).

Consequently, personalistic plebiscitarian leaders in Northeast Asia "did not challenge the political systems in their countries in any fundamental sense" (Mizuno and Phongpaichit 2009: 8), nor did they seriously jeopardize democracy. In line with my theory, institutional strength and the absence of acute, profound crises precluded the suffocation of liberal pluralism in this subregion. The setting that personalistic plebiscitarian leaders encountered in these nations was similar to the Western democracies examined in Chapters 5 (Italy) and 6 (United States). Facing firm constraints and very limited opportunities for overcoming these barriers to power concentration, populist leaders proceeded in a self-contained fashion and left political liberalism unscathed.

Populism in Southeast and South Asia: Transgressive Leaders and Their Regime Impact

By contrast to Northeast Asia, weaker institutions and greater socioeconomic volatility, including susceptibility to severe crises, have turned populism into a substantial threat to democracy in Southeast and South Asia, where development levels significantly lag behind the Northeast. Charismatic politicians find more room for their ambitious machinations, and more opportunities for boosting their clout. For these reasons, the political impact of personalistic plebiscitarian leadership is more uncertain and contested. Can my theory elucidate the effective risk that populism poses in these settings?

A tentative assessment requires an examination of individual countries and cases that is different from the analyses of Chapters 3 to 5, which covered whole world regions and broader subtypes of populism. After all, due to the

---

[11] South Korea's Roh Moo-hyun also won as the candidate of the then-ruling party, but that party had earlier had an oppositional trajectory (Kimura 2009: 169, 172–75).

cross-national commonalities prevailing in Latin America and Europe, particularly Eastern Europe, there have been important similarities among populist leaders, who have often appeared in region-wide groupings, especially neoliberal, Bolivarian, and conservative-traditionalist populism. By contrast, Asia's pronounced ethnic, cultural, religious, political, and historical heterogeneity has given each case its own peculiar characteristics. My brief analysis therefore proceeds in a disaggregated way.

Thailand: The Dramatic Rise and Drastic Fall of Thaksin Shinawatra's Hegemonic Populism

Democracy suffered the gravest threat and biggest damage in Thailand, where the massive economic crisis afflicting the country from 1997 onward allowed for the emergence of Thaksin Shinawatra (2001–6),[12] who won a clear victory in the 2001 elections and governed with a parliamentary majority thereafter (Phongpaichit and Baker 2009: 16–17, 62, 96, 226; McCargo and Pathmanand [2005] 2010: 5, 13–15, 35, 217). As a superrich businessman, Thaksin had sought to boost his electoral chances by promising extensive social programs for the broader population, especially the vast rural groupings, which felt neglected by the old Bangkok-based elite. When and because his quick and effective implementation of these benefit schemes raised his popularity to sky-high levels, the new prime minister belatedly embraced populism, adopted a folksy style, and tried hard to appeal directly to his surprisingly fervent followers (Phongpaichit and Baker 2008: 63–70; Treerat 2009: 117–20; Hawkins and Selway 2017: 383–89).[13]

As a new convert to personalistic plebiscitarian leadership, Thaksin drew enormous clout from his unprecedented popular support, which seemed to make him unbeatable in the electoral arena and indeed ensured him a lopsided victory and corresponding supermajority in the parliamentary contest of 2005 (Phongpaichit and Baker 2009: 237; Tamada 2009: 101–5; Treerat 2009: 121). Given this political-electoral hegemony, the prime minister did not see the need to promote institutional reforms to cement his predominance, skew the playing field, and firmly install an authoritarian regime. After all, Thailand's parliamentary system of government with its fairly limited checks and balances left broad latitude for the prime minister, whose institutional position the 1997 constitution had already fortified.[14] Moreover, parliamentarism by design allowed

---

[12] The scholarly literature commonly uses his first name (e.g., Phongpaichit and Baker 2009), which also helps distinguish him from his sister and eventual successor, Yingluck Shinawatra.

[13] Phongpaichit and Baker (2009: 231–34) claim that Thaksin turned even more populist in 2004, when he started to face challenges, yet also prepared for the 2005 election. Indeed, Hellmann (2017: 168) dates Thaksin's turn to populism in 2005 only. By contrast, Kenny (2018: 56–60) classifies Thaksin as a populist since the beginning of his political career.

[14] Phongpaichit and Baker 2009: 94–96; McCargo and Pathmanand [2005] 2010: 215; Tamada 2009: 105–6.

for reelection, a crucial goal of personalistic plebiscitarian leaders with their insatiable quest for self-perpetuation. Conversely, formal-institutional changes would have been limited in their impact because it would have been politically impossible to cut the effective clout of the most decisive veto players, namely the military and the king (see Chambers 2013: 67–71).

Instead of suffocating democracy through institutional means, Thaksin simply sought incessantly to concentrate political power and increase his personalistic latitude by using strategic appointments and various informal inducements, especially widespread, massive payoffs. He literally bought support from other political parties, nudging several of them to merge with his own ever-growing formation; he even drew individual politicians away from the biggest remaining opposition party.[15] With these tricks, the personalistic prime minister quickly advanced toward his apparent goal of creating an unchallengeable hegemonic party regime, a form of electoral authoritarianism. He effectively eliminated political competitiveness, the core principle of democracy (Schmitter 1983: 887–91) – not by distorting institutional rules and procedures, but by manipulating their outcomes and results through the takeover and buyout of most of the competition.

In this way, Thaksin formed "the most authoritarian government Thailand ha[d] seen for more than 30 years" (McCargo and Pathmanand [2005] 2010: 253; see also Pongsudhirak 2003: 278; Phongpaichit and Baker 2008: 70). To silence critics, he systematically intimidated journalists and had his cronies take over the main media outlets, asphyxiating liberal pluralism.[16] To secure his nascent autocracy against a military veto, the ambitious premier even built a bridgehead of support in the armed forces through targeted nominations and juicy patronage (Pongsudhirak 2003: 283–84, 288; Phongpaichit and Baker 2009: 176, 181–84, 248–50; Chambers 2013: 72–73).

Thus, in line with my theory, the coincidence of institutional weakness and a deep economic crisis enabled the Thai populist to asphyxiate democracy. The parliamentary system of government with its strong prime-ministerial position provided a propitious constitutional setting for energetic power concentration, and the severe downturn of 1997 enabled Thaksin to win overwhelming mass support, which then induced the tycoon to adopt a populist strategy. With this combination of underlying causal factors, Thailand's march to authoritarianism resembles the cases of Hungary's Orbán and Turkey's Erdoğan examined in Chapter 5.

But due to one of Asia's regional specificities, namely the weakness of the democracy protection regime promoted and enforced by Western democracies, Thaksin did not manage to complete and consolidate his strangulation effort.

---

[15] Pongsudhirak 2003: 279; Phongpaichit and Baker 2009: 95, 227, 235, 239–40; McCargo and Pathmanand [2005] 2010: 83–86, 106–8, 126, 248–49; Tamada 2009: 104.

[16] Pongsudhirak 2003: 285–86; Phongpaichit and Baker 2009: 134, 144–57; McCargo and Pathmanand [2005] 2010: 189–96; Treerat 2009: 115–17, 121–22.

After all, his massive plebiscitarian backing from rural sectors and the resulting political supremacy did not only disturb urban middle-class groupings, but also important generals and the king, who feared being pushed aside. The military resented total subordination to a civilian politician, and the monarch did not want to turn into a mere figurehead of his overbearing prime minister.[17] These essential veto players therefore removed Thaksin through a coup in 2006, replaced him with a military junta, and banned him and his party from politics (Phongpaichit and Baker 2009: 283–88).

Thus, whereas military coups have become exceedingly rare in Latin America and in Europe,[18] they are still part of the political repertoire in Thailand, used especially by the king as an emergency brake on civilian politics. Because the monarchy rests on a traditionalist foundation that starkly diverges from popular sovereignty, it can legitimate such fundamentally undemocratic moves. Indeed, soon after Thaksin's eviction, history came close to repeating itself. A few years later, the ousted leader's sister, Yingluck Shinawatra, resumed populist mobilization, won an impressive electoral victory in 2011, and governed with a parliamentary majority thereafter – only to be toppled by a forced judicial ruling and subsequent military coup as well, in 2014 (Prasirtsuk 2015).

In sum, populism in Thailand arose and unfolded under broadly similar conditions as in Europe, but due to regional particularities, it faced additional obstacles and therefore suffered a different fate. In line with my theory, the institutional openness of parliamentarism and the shake-up produced by a profound economic crisis allowed Thaksin's personalistic plebiscitarian leadership to grow and expand for years, enabling the domineering prime minister to smother liberal pluralism from the inside. But then, veto players that have been contained and marginalized in contemporary Europe and Latin America coercively intervened, destroying democracy on their own. Interestingly, the outcome of the Thai case resembles the fate of Latin American populism in earlier decades, when military coups frequently overthrew personalistic plebiscitarian leaders, most prominently Juan Perón in Argentina in 1955; the forced ouster of Honduras' pushy populist Zelaya in 2009 was the sole, exceptional recurrence of such a drastic extraconstitutional veto in the contemporary era.[19]

[17] Phongpaichit and Baker 2008: 77–79; Phongpaichit and Baker 2009: 241–43, 249–50, 260, 266–67, 358–60; Tamada 2009: 106–7; Hewison and Kitirianglarp 2010: 179–83, 192–96; Barany 2012: 194–96; Chambers 2013: 67–73; Kenny 2018: 61.
[18] The Thaksin case provides an interesting contrast to contemporary Turkey. In this country suspended between Europe and Asia, forceful military intervention continues to pose a realistic threat to populist governance, but faces increasing difficulties in achieving "success" by ousting the chief executive. Therefore, as Chapter 5 demonstrated, Erdoğan initially managed to push the overbearing generals aside by allying with domestic and foreign advocates of liberal democracy; and then, after the new Sultan had turned toward Islamist authoritarianism, he survived the dangerous coup attempt of 2016 through populist counter-mobilization.
[19] Interestingly, however, the Honduran coup differed in important ways from the "classical" military coups that toppled Perón and Thaksin. Above all, the available evidence suggests that in

The Philippines: The Quick Failure of Joseph Estrada's Haphazard Populism

By contrast to Thailand's Thaksin, Joseph Estrada (1998–2001) in the Philippines faced distinctly unfavorable conditions for authoritarian power concentration. Moreover, he squandered any potential opportunity through incompetence, irresolution, and distractedness. Democracy therefore survived this strikingly haphazard, aimless episode of populist governance.

As a well-known movie actor, Estrada won a clear victory in the presidential contest of 1998. In the wake of the Asian financial crisis, which caused a short-term recession in the Philippines, his Robin Hood–like persona of taking from the rich to give to the poor endeared him to the popular masses (Bautista 2002: 2–4; David 2002: 148–49; Rocamora 2009: 44–48; Webb and Curato 2019: 56–57). But the new chief executive lacked the necessary preconditions for undermining liberal pluralism. Philippine presidentialism, which features a bicameral legislature, created firmer institutional constraints than did Thai parliamentarism. Moreover, the economic downturn was much less severe and persistent in the island archipelago. Therefore, Estrada lacked the unusual conjunctural opportunity for demonstrating charismatic prowess that allowed Thaksin to establish unprecedented political-electoral hegemony.

As my theory predicts, the Philippine president in fact did not inflict serious damage on democracy. Yet the direct reason for this outcome was not the absence of the necessary conditions highlighted in Chapter 2 but the haphazardness of populist agency. Because most personalistic plebiscitarian leaders are untested outsiders, their performance in office is highly unpredictable. While some of the new chief executives display striking surefootedness and dedication, and while a few of them manage to avert or combat crises and thus turn into their countries' saviors (e.g., Peru's Fujimori), others reveal their lack of experience, superficial grasp of politics and the economy, limited attention span, or other serious flaws.

The Philippine populist fell squarely into the latter category. Whereas he had successfully played the hero in movies, he proved completely out of his depth in the presidential palace (Hellmann 2017: 165–66). Instead of designing and executing a coherent political strategy – not to speak of a systematic policy project – Estrada devoted much of his time to nightlong drinking sessions with his personal friends, gambling, and other hedonistic pursuits (Abueva 2002: 91–94; Constantino-David 2002: 214–17, 222–26; Rocamora 2009: 48–55). To the despair of his aides, the government was left adrift (Constantino-David 2002; David 2002). But of course, Estrada's inaction also meant that democracy was not at risk.

the Central American country, civilian opponents, not the military – or a king – took the main initiative (see Chapter 4). Accordingly, the generals never grabbed power, but let constitutional succession rules unfold, which led to the installation of the civilian head of Congress as interim president.

Thus, the immediate reason that liberal pluralism persisted in the Philippines was not its institutional robustness nor the absence of a conjunctural opportunity for its strangulation; instead, Estrada never tested its strength. Indeed, the outsider's presidential performance was so suboptimal and his tenure so scandal-ridden that he even failed to serve out his full term. Evidence of corruption in his entourage prompted an impeachment trial in the Senate;[20] and when Estrada's allies tried to cover up and exculpate his misdeeds, these shenanigans provoked an outburst of mass demonstrations that forced out the utterly discredited people's hero in early 2001 (Abueva 2002: 80, 95; David 2002: 168–71; Lim 2002: 136; Palabrica 2002: 235; Rocamora 2009: 48–49). Accordingly, Philippine democracy survived this first episode of personalistic plebiscitarian leadership due to the dysfunctional agency of its potential strangler – an experience quite similar to the case of Bucaram in Ecuador, as examined in Chapter 3.

The Philippines: The Illiberal Reign but Limited Duration of Rodrigo Duterte's Punitive Populism

Philippine democracy faced much greater pressure and suffered considerable damage under Rodrigo Duterte (2016–22), who won office with a tough law-and-order message and then unleashed a bloody, cruel war on drug traffickers. But despite his deeply autocratic tendencies, which he ostentatiously flaunted, this punitive populist did not impose an authoritarian regime. While his government brought large-scale human rights violations, "elections largely remain[ed] robust" (Garrido 2022: 686); accordingly, full competitiveness prevailed, the core principle of democracy. Moreover, the strong-willed incumbent forewent any serious effort to pursue the typically populist goal of self-perpetuation in power and stepped down right on schedule at the end of his single constitutional term, which was strikingly different from the incessant efforts to abolish or evade term limits that so many personalistic plebiscitarian presidents have undertaken in contemporary Latin America.[21]

The two principal types of factors emphasized by my theory can account for the ultimate survival of Philippine democracy. As regards institutional strength, the presidential system of government with its checks and balances hindered the concentration of power and impeded a serious deformation of the constitutional framework. Indeed, the democratic constitution of 1987 firmly prohibited presidential reelection (as discussed later). And as regards conjunctural opportunities, the island archipelago was enjoying a phase of robust economic growth when Duterte assumed the presidency in 2016. Thus, the Philippine populist lacked

---

[20] Abueva 2002: 92–93; Bautista 2002: 4–6; David 2002: 154–57, 162–66; De Dios 2002: 43–56; Lim 2002: 126–29; Palabrica 2002: 229, 233–34.
[21] I thank Marco Garrido, Bonn Juego, and Mark Thompson for many very interesting comments, observations, and reflections on the case of Duterte.

one of the situational preconditions for the strangulation of democracy that has played such a crucial role in Latin America and Europe.

The only potential chance that Duterte had for pushing his illiberal goals arose from the scourge of crime and drug trafficking that this personalistic plebiscitarian leader highlighted and seized upon. Murders in the Philippines had jumped by approximately 50 percent in 2009 and continued at these higher levels thereafter. The populist promise to enforce public safety with whatever means necessary therefore found great resonance and gave Duterte a clear electoral victory in 2016 (Curato 2017: 148–52; Curato and Yonaha 2022: 392–94; Garrido 2022). Indeed, when the new president declared a full-scale assault on the narcotics trade that provoked thousands of extrajudicial killings, his popularity soared. While corpses piled up in the streets, the reported murder rate quickly fell by almost half. The resulting sky-high approval levels throughout his six-year term, which hovered around 75–85 percent and sometimes rose beyond 90 percent, allowed the punitive populist to ignore sustained criticism from domestic and international human rights advocates.[22]

In Latin America, equivalent popularity ratings empowered personalistic plebiscitarian presidents such as Fujimori and Chávez to expand and cement their overwhelming clout and move toward competitive authoritarianism via constitutional changes, especially by eliminating the ban on reelection. Yet although populist leaders are generally eager to extend their tenure in office, Duterte saw this path foreclosed. The new constitution adopted after the long reign of Ferdinand Marcos (1965–86), who had prepared his installation of a dictatorship (1972) by engineering his reelection in 1969, imposed a strict single-term limit. Due to the traumatic memory of Marcos, the no reelection rule constituted "a political taboo," whose violation elites uniformly opposed and mobilized swaths of the citizenry were committed to contest.[23]

Duterte tentatively explored various ways of bending or breaking this prohibition, such as a "revolutionary government" installed through constitutional change.[24] But the populist president anticipated "considerable elite and ... societal pushback" and lacked the clout or will to combat this resistance.[25] Thus, as Mexico's sacrosanct no reelection rule has posed an insurmountable obstacle to the power hunger of current populist AMLO (see Chapter 4), Duterte faced a similarly firm political-institutional constraint in the Philippines, which protected democracy from his autocratic aspirations. While he pushed populist agency to the extreme with his flagrant assault on human rights, he lacked the

---

[22] Juego 2017: 132–35, 142–44; Webb and Curato 2019: 49; Kenny and Holmes 2020: 189, 199–200; Garrido 2022: 678–85; Teehankee 2022: 129–30; Thompson 2022: 413–15.

[23] Mark Thompson, City University of Hong Kong, personal communication, April 26, 2022.

[24] Heydarian 2022: 72; Bonn Juego, University of Helsinki, personal communication, June 5, 2022.

[25] Marco Garrido, University of Chicago, personal communication, April 20, 2022; the inserted quote is from Mark Thompson (April 26, 2022). When Duterte announced the plan to "run for vice-president – a constitutionally dubious move – so disapproving was the popular reaction that he quickly withdrew" (Forgettable Populist 2022).

capacity to overcome the ultimately decisive restriction on this agency, namely the Philippines' unmovable term limit.

For these reasons, although the rule of law suffered grave damage during Duterte's brutal reign, the Philippines did not descend into authoritarian rule. In line with my theory, institutional strength, especially the impregnability of the no-election rule, circumscribed the effective danger that populism posed to democracy. The personalistic plebiscitarian president did not transform the constitutional system nor systematically skew the electoral arena. Because he based his popularity and political support on the unrestrained drug war, he actually relied less on vote buying, clientelism, patronage, and similar informal mechanisms of distorting the popular vote that Filipino politicians have commonly used (Thompson 2022: 411, 415, 420). Indeed, the election of Duterte's successor in 2022 was "the first time an incumbent administration did not field a candidate for president" (Teehankee 2022: 133; see also Heydarian 2022: 63, 72).

Yet while my theory can explain why Duterte's punitive populism did not destroy Philippine democracy, the severity of the threat that this personalistic plebiscitarian leader posed is exceptional and reflects specific context factors. Different from the Latin American presidents who are theoretically most similar, namely Peru's Fujimori and El Salvador's Bukele,[26] Duterte did not need an acute double crisis to achieve sky-high approval ratings. Indeed, it was years before his election that crime increased; while murders continued at these high levels, they did not surge further, and thus did not create a pressing crisis (Thompson 2022: 403–4, 411–14).[27] Consequently, the conjunctural opportunity that boosted Duterte's political fortunes was much less pronounced and unusual than in the cases of Fujimori and Bukele.

The enormous political payoff that Duterte reaped from his all-out war on drugs, which is noteworthy from the comparative perspective of this book, probably resulted from cultural specificities highlighted by country experts. With sparser linkages to the West and a good deal of nationalist resentment against the USA as the former colonial power, the human rights norms and values promoted by advanced industrialized democracies held less sway, allowing for higher rewards for cracking down hard (Curato 2017; Curato and Yonaha 2022).[28] Relatedly, regional specialists commonly emphasize the popular

---

[26] Similar to Fujimori, Duterte also charted a predominantly neoliberal course in his economic policy (Juego 2017: 147–50).

[27] Also, by contrast to El Salvador, where the murder rate reached a very high 51 per 100,000 in the year before Bukele's election, it ran at a much lower 9 per 100,000 in the Philippines.

[28] A comparison with Brazil's Bolsonaro provides further evidence of the differential sway of human rights norms in the Philippines vs. Latin America: Whereas both Duterte and the Brazilian right-winger won office with promises of a resolute crackdown on crime, only Duterte actually unleashed a war on drugs with innumerable extrajudicial killings, whereas Bolsonaro – despite much higher crime rates – refrained from charting this cruel course, as he indicated from the beginning by appointing as his justice minister high-profile judge Sergio Moro, then widely seen as a symbol of the rule of law.

veneration for strongman rule, which Duterte with his ostentatious toughness and domineering behavior evoked (Kenny and Holmes 2020: 197–201; Garrido 2022: 678–85; see also Rocamora 2009: 43, 57–58).[29]

Thus, whereas in contemporary Latin America, urgent, massive public security crises constitute necessary conditions for vast numbers of citizens to disregard human rights concerns and strongly approve of tough punitive populists, in the Philippines a lesser threat was sufficient. And as another contrast to Fujimori and Bukele, Duterte did not need the simultaneous eruption of a second, economic crisis to achieve stratospheric popularity. Due to these contextual differences, Philippine democracy was more exposed to the overbearing force of personalistic plebiscitarian leadership than liberal-pluralist regimes in Latin America.

But institutional strength, the other crucial condition postulated by my theory, contained the danger arising from Duterte's high levels of popular support and sustained the Philippines' battered democracy. What ultimately proved decisive was the strict prohibition on presidential reelection enshrined in the constitution. Whereas in many Latin American countries, term limits have softened and have frequently fallen to constitutional amendments or various para-legal tricks, in the Asian archipelago this crucial impediment to the inherent populist drive toward self-perpetuation stands firm. After all, "one lasting legacy of the Marcos dictatorship has been an aversion to *continuismo*,"[30] that is, presidents' urge to extend their own rule. Consequently, liberal pluralism survived Duterte's bloody reign and has a chance of recovery under the successor government.

India: Systematic yet Contested Backsliding under Narendra Modi's Ethno-Nationalist Populism

As an emblematic instance of the global wave of populism (McDonnell and Cabrera 2019; Varshney 2019), the world's largest democracy is currently suffering from a gradual strangulation effort as well. Since his election in 2014, Narendra Modi has relentlessly pursued the typical project of power concentration by overusing decrees, putting pressure on the judiciary, harassing the political opposition, interfering in civil society, and intimidating the media. Yet because this personalistic plebiscitarian leader has faced substantial institutional constraints, has lacked a constitution-changing supermajority, and has provoked a great deal of contestation and pushback, the basic framework of Indian democracy has so far withstood this grave threat (Democracy in India 2022; Varshney 2022: 62–64).

From the comparative perspective of this book, the Indian case resembles contemporary Poland, where the fate of liberal pluralism hangs in the balance as well (see Chapter 5). The main variables of my theory – the level of institutional

---

[29] For India, see Jaffrelot (2021: 461, 464).
[30] Thompson, personal communication, April 26, 2022.

strength and conjunctural opportunity – can elucidate these struggles. In institutional terms, the South Asian country features a fairly similar number of veto players as the East European nation. Both India and Poland have bicameral legislatures, which hinder populist power grabs (for India, see Jaffrelot 2021: 355, 360). India's parliamentarism creates more openness to change than Poland's semi-presidential system. But by contrast to unitary Poland, Indian federalism disperses power across the vast subcontinent and gives the larger states considerable clout (Aiyar 2020: 18; Mitra 2020: 38, 41; Varshney 2022: 67). Considering these similarities and compensating differences, Modi overall faces the middling degree of checks and balances that Kaczyński has confronted.

As regards conjunctural factors, both personalistic plebiscitarian leaders have been limited by the lack of potential opportunities arising from acute crises. Indeed, when Modi and Kaczyński made their bids for power and achieved electoral success, their countries were in the midst of substantial stretches of robust economic growth. There were no major public security challenges nor massive hydrocarbon windfalls either. Thus, factors that my theory specifies as necessary conditions for the populist asphyxiation of democracy were conspicuous by their absence.

Due to this dearth of opportunities, the Indian populist, like his Polish counterpart, did not manage to garner overwhelming support and win a parliamentary supermajority that would have enabled him to change the constitution – as Viktor Orbán so quickly and easily did in Hungary. Nor could Modi follow the Magyar leader by changing the institutional rules and structures of India's electoral system to engineer a bias for his own party (Jaffrelot 2021: 446; see also Aiyar 2020: 16–17; Mitra 2020: 38, 40; Varshney 2022: 62–63).[31] Instead, the new premier was compelled to cope with the constraints posed by the middling levels of institutional strength that Indian democracy commanded. As in Poland, however, these hindrances did not contain Modi's power hunger.

Instead, like Kaczyński, the Indian populist immediately used his political clout to put pressure on liberal pluralism. Just as in Poland, the judiciary constituted the single most important target of this energetic assault. Through a variety of tactics, ranging from juicy offers of plum positions after the end of judges' terms to tricks of discriminatory legalism, the government persistently sought to undermine judicial autonomy. But because independent-minded judges offered resistance and blocked attempts to manipulate the appointment process, the pushy prime minister achieved only limited success in his efforts to subdue this essential veto player.[32] Modi also sought to weaken the partisan opposition,

---

[31] Chhibber and Verma (2019) analyze the 2019 election without any reference to new institutional biases or other forms of political manipulation, and thus implicitly depict this contest as free and fair.

[32] Aiyar 2020: 15, 17–18, 20; Mitra 2020: 39; Jaffrelot 2021: 276–98; Khosla and Vaishnav 2021: 116–17; Ashutosh Varshney, Brown University, personal communication, November 14, 2022.

control the media, and rein in civil society in this vast pluralistic country.[33] All these illiberal machinations and para-legal tricks have slowly made headway.

But as in Poland, the absence of a constitutional supermajority prevented the populist power grab from advancing smoothly via formal-legal changes as in Orbán's Hungary. Instead, Modi pursued his undemocratic project with pushiness and trickery. Like Kaczyński, he therefore provoked a great deal of passive resistance and open opposition, from a variety of domestic groupings and international actors. The prime minister's forceful promotion of Hindu nationalism, which abridged the rights of religious minorities, especially India's numerous Muslims, proved especially controversial. The resulting protests and conflicts, which have erupted across the far-flung country on many occasions (Aiyar 2020: 12, 15, 20; Mitra 2020: 36, 38, 40–41), have slowed down India's march to populist illiberalism and have so far prevented a descent into authoritarianism.[34] In particular, elections at the national and state levels have remained largely free and fair, though turbulent and marred by some violence (Varshney 2022: 62–64).[35] With a reduction in civil liberties, yet a compensating increase in political participation, India's overall democracy score has deteriorated only slightly under Modi's tenure (Democracy in India 2022: 29; see also Aiyar 2020: 19–20).[36]

In sum, Modi's personalistic plebiscitarian leadership has propelled worrisome democratic backsliding but has not managed to suppress liberal pluralism – just as in Poland. My theory can account for this admittedly precarious and fiercely contested outcome. Commanding middling strength, India's institutional constraints have not crumbled under sustained pressure. Above all, the absence of special conjunctural opportunities has limited the incumbent populist's clout and has foreclosed a constitutional transformation that could pave the way toward authoritarian rule. While stressed and strained, the largest democracy on the globe has retained a chance of survival and recovery.

---

[33] Chacko 2018: 557–59; Mate 2018: 389–94; Aiyar 2020: 13–14; Jaffrelot 2021: 175–85, 236–47, 298–306, 332–41, 351–55; Democracy in India 2022; Hall 2022: 199–200.

[34] While providing a systematic, comprehensive analysis and assessment of Modi's efforts to strangle India's democracy, Jaffrelot (2021: passim, including 455–60) is unclear in his overall verdict, constantly shifting between various labels of diminished democracy and authoritarian rule.

[35] With the recent eviction of opposition leader Rahul Gandhi from parliament, however – a striking instance of discriminatory legalism – the government may start to skew the electoral arena more decisively (Indian Democracy 2023).

[36] While systematically documenting the increasing ethnic bias of India's political system, Adeney (2021: 405–7) concludes that India clearly remains democratic. Hall (2022: 191) calls Modi authoritarian, but provides no evidence to sustain this label. Khosla and Vaishnav (2021), in turn, place the Modi governments in a useful historical perspective by highlighting how many blemishes on India's democracy preceded the populist's election in 2014; his rule has not brought a downward inflection of this problematic trajectory. Similarly, Aiyar (2020: 13–14) emphasizes that the harassment of political opponents and civil society forces is nothing new in India's persistently imperfect democracy – a point also made by Varshney (2022: 62–64), who highlights the persistence of free and fair elections and therefore concludes that India remains democratic.

Conclusion: Asian Populism in Comparative Perspective

Democracy's fate under populist governance in Asia is profoundly shaped by the two main factors highlighted in my theory, namely institutional strength and unusual conjunctural opportunities for personalistic plebiscitarian leaders to boost their mass support and political clout. In many aspects and ways, the four high-profile experiences examined here followed similar trajectories as the Latin American and European cases that featured the most similar constellation of factors. The parallels between contemporary India and Poland, between Estrada in the Philippines and Bucaram in Ecuador, and – for years – between Thailand and both Turkey and Hungary are particularly noteworthy.

But regional specificities also played a role. In Thailand, the quest for populist supremacy faced additional veto players that coercively aborted Thaksin's assault on democracy – a fate that Orbán and, more narrowly, Erdoğan managed to avoid. And under Duterte in the Philippines, punitive populism went much farther than under Brazil's Bolsonaro, and its political payoff was unusually high, but personalistic power hunger faced an outer limit in a firm prohibition on presidential reelection as in Mexico. In sum, my theory seems to have a good deal of broader applicability, but here and there, regional particularities do make a difference.

THE MAIN LESSON: THE LIMITS OF POPULISM'S THREAT TO DEMOCRACY

This book can help allay the grave concerns about democracy's fate that many scholars and observers have expressed in recent years. My wide-ranging comparative analysis shows that populism is not as dangerous for liberal pluralism as is often feared. These worries are mainly derived from the few outstanding cases in which personalistic plebiscitarian leaders, especially Fujimori and Chávez, Erdoğan and Orbán, did succeed in dismantling democracy and installing competitive authoritarianism. But this deleterious outcome prevailed only infrequently; in a much larger number of cases, populist chief executives did not inflict lethal damage.

Recent alarm reflects the distortions of the availability heuristic, a common cognitive shortcut with logically problematic results (Kahneman, Slovic, and Tversky 1982: chaps. 11, 13; Gilovich, Griffin, and Kahneman 2002: chaps. 4–5, 28; Kahneman 2011: chaps. 12–13): Dramatic, vivid phenomena that grab people's attention exert a disproportionate impact on their inferences and probability assessments, while undramatic, everyday events of equal objective significance are discounted. As an example, after the shocking terrorism of 9/11, many Americans feared plane travel and drove by car instead – an ill-advised decision that exposed them to significantly higher risk of accidents. By scholarly estimates, the resulting excess toll amounted to approximately 1,500 extra deaths (Gigerenzer 2006).

In a similar vein, the striking strangulation of democracy by Fujimori and Chávez, Erdoğan and Orbán, gained enormous notoriety. The availability heuristic gave these high-profile fatalities extraordinary weight and impressed them on observers' judgments. By contrast, the inability of many populist chief executives to overturn liberal pluralism, which is of equal importance, has attracted far less attention. Indeed, the numerous personalistic plebiscitarian leaders who failed and lost power prematurely are largely forgotten, and sometimes erased from their countries' collective memory. Who, for instance, remembers Brazil's Collor, Ecuador's Bucaram, and Guatemala's Serrano (Chapter 3), Ecuador's Gutiérrez and Peru's Castillo (Chapter 4), and Slovakia's Matovič, Slovenia's Janša, and Slovakia's Mečiar (Chapter 5)?

Through its skewed impact, the availability heuristic has led observers to overestimate populism's dangers while making them underrate democratic resilience. In methodological terms, this cognitive bias has inspired "selection on the dependent variable": Important studies focus on cases of populist suffocation of democracy and do not consider instances of liberal pluralism's survival (e.g., Levitsky and Ziblatt 2018; Kaufman and Haggard 2019). Yet while this one-sided focus can elucidate "*how* democracy dies" (Levitsky and Ziblatt 2018), it hinders an analysis of how common this lethal outcome is, and under what specific conditions personalistic plebiscitarian leaders manage to commit such suffocation (see King, Keohane, and Verba 1994: 129–37, 141–49). For those tasks of probability assessment and causal risk analysis, it is decisive to investigate the contrast cases of democratic survival as well – which are much more numerous.

With its comprehensive examination of populist experiences across Europe and Latin America, supplemented with a brief glimpse at Asia, the present book seeks to overcome this methodological deficit and correct the distorted focus arising from the availability heuristic. My investigation of populism's varied regime effects has the broad scope required for arriving at valid conclusions. Indeed, this book has drawn its main inferences precisely from the contrast between instances of populist strangulation vs. democratic survival. For this purpose, it has paid special attention to cases that share many background similarities, yet differ in this crucial regime outcome (cf. Przeworski and Teune [1970] 1982: 32–34).

This in-depth investigation clearly demonstrates that populism's threat to democracy faces distinct limits. The prospects of liberal pluralism are not as dire as many recent authors have feared. Many personalistic plebiscitarian leaders do not succeed with their persistent efforts to smother democracy; liberal pluralism "dies" only under specific combinations of exogenous conditions that appear infrequently. Even institutions that suffer from weaknesses offer a good deal of protection; they can be overturned or broken only under special conjunctural circumstances, which do not often prevail.

Thus, democracy is far from defenseless against the inherent danger posed by populism. The recent outpouring of alarmism is exaggerated. Instead, my book yields an encouraging message for democracy's advocates and adherents.

References

Aboy Carlés, Gerardo. 2009. Nacionalismo e indigenismo en el gobierno de Evo Morales. In Julio Aibar and Daniel Vázquez, eds. *"Autoritarismo o democracia" Hugo Chávez y Evo Morales*, 259–86. Tlalpan, Mexico: FLACSO.

Abrahám, Samuel. 2000. The Rise and Fall of Illiberal Democracy in Slovakia: 1989–1998. Ph.D. dissertation, Carleton University, Ottawa, Canada.

Abramowitz, Alan. 2021. The Politics of Good versus Evil. In Larry Sabato, Kyle Kondik, and Miles Coleman, eds. *A Return to Normalcy? The 2020 Elections That (Almost) Broke America*, 63–80. Lanham, MD: Rowman & Littlefield.

2018. *The Great Alignment: Race, Party Transformation, and the Rise of Donald Trump*. New Haven, CT: Yale University Press.

2013. The Electoral Roots of America's Dysfunctional Government. *Presidential Studies Quarterly* 43:4 (December): 709–31.

Abueva, Jose. 2002. A Crisis of Political Leadership. In Amando Doronila, ed. *Between Fires: Fifteen Perspectives on the Estrada Crisis*, 78–97. Pasig City: Anvil Publishing.

Achen, Christopher, and Larry Bartels. 2016. *Democracy for Realists*. Princeton, NJ: Princeton University Press.

Acosta, Alberto. 2005. Ecuador: Ecos de la rebelión de los forajidos. *Nueva Sociedad* 198 (July): 42–54.

Ádám, Zoltán. 2019. Explaining Orbán: A Political Transaction Cost Theory of Populism. *Problems of Post-Communism* 66:6 (November/December): 385–401.

Adeney, Katharine. 2021. How Can We Model Ethnic Democracy? An Application to Contemporary India. *Nations and Nationalism* 27:2 (April): 393–411.

Aguilar Rivera, José. 2022. Dinámicas de la Autocratización: México 2021. *Revista de Ciencia Política* 42:2 (August): 355–82.

Aiyar, Swaminathan. 2020. *Despite Modi, India Has Not Yet Become a Hindu Authoritarian State*. Washington, DC: CATO Institute. Policy Analysis # 903 (24 November).

Akkerman, Tjitske. 2017. Populist Parties in Power and Their Impact on Liberal Democracies in Western Europe. In Reinhard Heinisch, Christina Holtz-Bacha, and Oscar Mazzoleni, eds. *Political Populism: A Handbook*, 169–80. Baden-Baden: Nomos.

Akkerman, Tjitske, Sarah de Lange, and Matthijs Rooduijn, eds. 2016. *Radical Right-Wing Populist Parties in Western Europe: Into the Mainstream?* London: Routledge.

Albertazzi, Daniele, and Duncan McDonnell. 2005. The Lega Nord in the Second Berlusconi Government. *West European Politics* 28:5 (November): 952–72.

Albertazzi, Daniele, and James Newell. 2015. Introduction: A Mountain Giving Birth to a Mouse? On the Impact and Legacy of Silvio Berlusconi in Italy. *Modern Italy* 20:1 (February): 3–10.

Aldaz Peña, Raúl. 2021. Oiling Congress: Windfall Revenues, Institutions, and Policy Change in the Long Run. *Journal of Politics in Latin America* 13:2 (August): 141–65.

Alsogaray, Álvaro. 1993. *Experiencias de cincuenta años de política y economía argentina*. Buenos Aires: Planeta.

Alston, Lee, Marcus Melo, Bernardo Mueller, and Carlos Pereira. 2008. On the Road to Good Governance: Recovering from Economic and Political Shocks in Brazil. In Eduardo Stein and Mariano Tommasi, eds. *Policymaking in Latin America*, 111–53. Washington, DC: Inter-American Development Bank.

Althoff, Andrea. 2019. Right-Wing Populism and Evangelicalism in Guatemala: The Presidency of Jimmy Morales. *International Journal of Latin American Religions* 3:2 (December): 294–324.

Alvarado, Jimmy. 2021. El gobierno de El Salvador incluye un gabinete a la sombra con pupilos de Leopoldo López. *El Faro* (7 June). armando.info/el-gobierno-de-el-salvador-incluye-un-gabinete-a-la-sombra-con-pupilos-de-leopoldo-lopez/, accessed 29 October 2021.

Amaral, Oswaldo. 2021. Partidos políticos e o Governo Bolsonaro. In Leonardo Avritzer, Fábio Kerche, and Marjorie Marona, eds. *Governo Bolsonaro*, 111–20. Belo Horizonte: Autêntica.

Ames, Barry. 2001. *The Deadlock of Democracy in Brazil*. Ann Arbor: University of Michigan Press.

Amézquita Quintana, Constanza. 2008. Fuerzas políticas movilizadas ante el referendo de 2003 en Colombia. *Análisis Político* 63 (May–August): 78–102.

Amorim, Ana. 2021. A imprensa no Governo Bolsonaro sob os ataques à liberdade de expressão. In Leonardo Avritzer, Fábio Kerche, and Marjorie Marona, eds. *Governo Bolsonaro*, 467–80. Belo Horizonte: Autêntica.

Andersen, Jørgen, and Michael Ross. 2014. The Big Oil Change. *Comparative Political Studies* 47:7 (June): 993–1021.

Andrews-Lee, Caitlin. 2021. *The Emergence and Revival of Charismatic Movements*. Cambridge: Cambridge University Press.

Anonymous. 2018. I Am Part of the Resistance Inside the Trump Administration. *New York Times* (5 September): A23.

Another Round of Election Rigging: Congressional Redistricting. 2022. *Economist* (February 12): 17–18.

Anria, Santiago. 2018. *When Movements Become Parties*. Cambridge: Cambridge University Press.

Arce, Moisés, and Julio Carrión. 2010. Presidential Support in a Context of Crisis and Recovery in Peru, 1985–2008. *Journal of Politics in Latin America* 2:1 (April): 31–51.

Arceneaux, Craig, and David Pion-Berlin. 2007. Issues, Threats, and Institutions. *Latin American Politics and Society* 49:2 (Summer): 1–31.

Archondo, Rafael. 2020. "Fue golpe" Pulsando el debate sobre la supuesta fascistización de Bolivia. *Revista Euro Latinoamericana de Análisis Social y Político* 1:1 (June): 245–60.

Arenas, Nelly. 2009. El gobierno de Hugo Chávez. In Julio Aibar and Daniel Vázquez, eds. *"Autoritarismo o democracia" Hugo Chávez y Evo Morales*, 59–111. Tlalpan, Mexico: FLACSO.

Arnson, Cynthia, and Carlos de la Torre. 2013. Conclusion: The Meaning and Future of Latin American Populism. In Carlos de la Torre and Cynthia Arnson, eds. *Latin American Populism in the Twenty-First Century*, 351–76. Washington, DC: Woodrow Wilson Center Press.

Arrow, Kenneth. (1951) 1963. *Social Choice and Individual Values*, 2nd ed. New Haven, CT: Yale University Press.

Aslanidis, Paris. 2021. Coalition-Making under Conditions of Ideological Mismatch: The Populist Solution. *International Political Science Review* 42:5 (November): 631–48.

Assies, Willem. 2011. Bolivia's New Constitution and Its Implications. In Adrian Pearce, ed. *Evo Morales and the Movimiento al Socialismo in Bolivia*, 93–116. London: Institute for the Study of the Americas, University of London.

Avritzer, Leonardo, and Lucio Rennó. 2021. The Pandemic and the Crisis of Democracy in Brazil. *Journal of Politics in Latin America* 13:3: 442–57.

Aytaç, Erdem, and Ezgi Elçi. 2019. Populism in Turkey. In Daniel Stockemer, ed. *Populism around the World*, 89–108. Cham: Springer.

Aytaç, Erdem, and Ziya Öniş. 2014. Varieties of Populism in a Changing Global Context. *Comparative Politics* 47:1 (October): 41–59.

Bafumi, Joseph, Robert Erikson, and Christopher Wlezien. 2018. Forecasting the 2018 Midterm Elections using National Polls and District Information. *PS – Political Science and Politics* 51:S1 (October): 7–11.

Bakke, Elisabeth, and Nick Sitter. 2022. The EU's Enfants Terribles: Democratic Backsliding in Central Europe since 2010. *Perspectives on Politics* 20:1 (March): 22–37.

Baldini, Gianfranco, and Matteo Nels Giglioli. 2020. Italy 2018: The Perfect Populist Storm? *Parliamentary Affairs* 73:2 (April): 363–84.

Ballesteros, Cecilia. 2021. La gente mandó al carajo todo y le dio a Bukele todo el poder. *El País* (25 October).

Bankov, Petar. 2020. The Fireman's Ball in Bulgaria? A Comparison between Sergey Stanishev and Boyko Borisov. In Sergiu Gherghina, ed. *Party Leaders in Eastern Europe*, 44–66. Cham: Palgrave Macmillan.

Bánkuti, Miklós, Gábor Halmai, and Kim Lane Scheppele. 2015. Hungary's Illiberal Turn. In Péter Krasztev and Jon Van Til, eds. *The Hungarian Patient*, 37–46. Budapest: Central European University Press.

Barany, Zoltan. 2012. *The Soldier and the Changing State: Building Democratic Armies in Africa, Asia, Europe, and the Americas*. Princeton, NJ: Princeton University Press.

   2002. Bulgaria's Royal Elections. *Journal of Democracy* 13:2 (April): 141–55.

Barr, Robert. 2003. The Persistence of Neopopulism in Peru? From Fujimori to Toledo. *Third World Quarterly* 24:6 (December): 1161–78.

Barrenechea, Rodrigo, and Daniel Encinas. 2022. Perú 2021: Democracia por defecto. *Revista de Ciencia Política* 42:2 (July): 407–38.

Bartels, Larry. 2023. *Democracy Erodes from the Top: Leaders, Citizens, and the Challenge of Populism in Europe*. Princeton, NJ: Princeton University Press.

Bartlett, David. 1997. *The Political Economy of Dual Transformations: Market Reform and Democratization in Hungary*. Ann Arbor: University of Michigan Press.

Bateman, David. 2022. Elections, Polarization, and Democratic Resilience. In Robert Lieberman, Suzanne Mettler, and Kenneth Roberts, eds. *Democratic Resilience: Can the United States Withstand Rising Polarization?* 343–68. Cambridge: Cambridge University Press.

Baturo, Alexander, and Jakob Tolstrup. 2022. Incumbent Takeovers. *Journal of Peace Research*, forthcoming.

Bautista, Maria. 2002. People Power 2: 'The Revenge of the Elite on the Masses'? In Amando Doronila, ed. *Between Fires: Fifteen Perspectives on the Estrada Crisis*, 1–42. Pasig City: Anvil Publishing.

Bayerlein, Michael, Vanessa Boese, Scott Gates, Katrin Kamin, and Syed Mansoob Murshed. 2021. *Populism and COVID-19: How Populist Governments (Mis) Handle the Pandemic*. Kiel: Institute for the World Economy. Working paper No. 2192 (July).

Baykan, Toygar Sinan. 2018. *The Justice and Development Party in Turkey: Populism, Personalism, Organization*. Cambridge: Cambridge University Press.

Becker, Marc. 2014. Rafael Correa and Social Movements in Ecuador. In Steve Ellner, ed. *Latin America's Radical Left*, 127–48. Lanham, MD: Rowman & Littlefield.

Bejarano, Ana María. 2013. Politicizing Insecurity. In Carlos de la Torre and Cynthia Arnson, eds. *Latin American Populism in the Twenty-First Century*, 323–49. Washington, DC: Woodrow Wilson Center Press.

2011. *Precarious Democracies: Understanding Regime Stability and Change in Colombia and Venezuela*. Notre Dame, IN: University of Notre Dame Press.

Belew, Kathleen. 2022. Militant Whiteness in the Age of Trump. In Julian Zelizer, ed. *The Presidency of Donald J. Trump*, 83–102. Princeton, NJ: Princeton University Press.

Bermeo, Nancy. 2016. On Democratic Backsliding. *Journal of Democracy* 27:1 (January): 5–19.

Bermúdez, Jaime. 2010. *La audacia del poder: Momentos clave del primer gobierno de Uribe contados por uno de sus protagonistas*. Bogotá: Planeta.

Bernhard, Michael. 2021. Democratic Backsliding in Poland and Hungary. *Slavic Review* 80:3 (Fall): 585–607.

2020. What Do We Know about Civil Society and Regime Change Thirty Years after 1989? *East European Politics* 36:3 (July): 341–62.

1993. *The Origins of Democratization in Poland: Workers, Intellectuals, and Oppositional Politics, 1976–1980*. New York: Columbia University Press.

Bilgin, Hasret Dikici, and Emre Erdoğan. 2018. Obscurities of a Referendum Foretold: The 2017 Constitutional Amendments in Turkey. *Review of Middle East Studies* 52:1 (April): 29–42.

Bill, Stanley, and Ben Stanley. 2020. Whose Poland Is It To Be? *East European Politics* 36:3 (September): 378–94.

Binder, Sarah. 2021. Legislative Stalemate in Postwar America, 1947–2018. In Eric Patashnik and Wendy Schiller, eds. *Dynamics of American Democracy*, 65–86. Lawrence: University Press of Kansas.

2015. The Dysfunctional Congress. *Annual Review of Political Science* 18: 85–101.

Blokker, Paul. 2020. Populism and Constitutional Reform: The Case of Italy. In Giacomo Delledonne, Giuseppe Martinico, Matteo Monti, and Fabio Pacini, eds. *Italian Populism and Constitutional Law*, 11–38. London: Palgrave Macmillan.

Bodnar, Adam. 2021. "Für meine Feinde das Gesetz:" Das Rechtsverständnis der PiS-Regierung in Polen. *Osteuropa* 71:3 (July): 99–114.

2018. Protection of Human Rights after the Constitutional Crisis in Poland. *Jahrbuch des öffentlichen Rechts der Gegenwart* 66: 639–62.

Böhmelt, Tobias, Lawrence Ezrow, and Roni Lehrer. 2022. Populism and Intra-Party Democracy. *European Journal of Political Research* 61:4 (November): 1143–54.

Bogaards, Matthijs. 2018. De-democratization in Hungary. *Democratization* 25:8 (December): 1481–99.

Bolívar Meza, Rosendo. 2017. Liderazgo político: El caso de Andrés Manuel López Obrador en MORENA. *Estudios Políticos* 42 (November-December): 99–118.

2014. El Partido de la Revolución Democrática en crisis. *Estudios Políticos* 33 (September–December): 27–50.

Bologna, Alfredo. 1996. Los autogolpes en América Latina: El caso de Guatemala (1993). *Estudios Internacionales* 29:113 (January–March): 3–18.

Boloña, Carlos. 1993. *Cambio de rumbo*. Lima: Instituto de Economía de Libre Mercado.

Bonikowski, Bart. 2019. Trump's Populism. In Kurt Weyland and Raúl Madrid, eds. *When Democracy Trumps Populism*, 110–31. Cambridge: Cambridge University Press.

Bornhausen, Roberto. 1991. *Reflexões sobre o Brasil*. Cadernos do Instituto Roberto Simonsen no. 18. São Paulo: Federação das Indústrias do Estado de São Paulo.

Bowden, Mark, and Matthew Teague. 2022. *The Steal: The Attempt to Overturn the 2020 Election and the People Who Stopped It*. New York: Atlantic Monthly Press.

Bozóki, András. 2015. Broken Democracy, Predatory State, and Nationalist Populism. In Péter Krasztev and Jon Van Til, eds. *The Hungarian Patient*, 3–36. Budapest: Central European University Press.

Branham, Alexander, Stuart Soroka, and Christopher Wlezien. 2017. When Do the Rich Win? *Political Science Quarterly* 132:1 (March): 43–62.

Brazil's Democratic Institutions under Attack. 2023. *Latin American Weekly Report* WR-23-02 (12 January): 1–3

Bresser Pereira, Luiz Carlos. 1991. *Os Tempos Heróicos de Collor e Zélia*. São Paulo: Nobel.

Brewer-Carías, Allan. 2010. *Dismantling Democracy in Venezuela*. Cambridge: Cambridge University Press.

Brinks, Daniel, Steven Levitsky, and Victoria Murillo. 2019. *Understanding Institutional Weakness: Power and Design in Latin American Institutions*. Cambridge: Cambridge University Press.

Brockmann Quiroga, Erika. 2020. Tentativa de toma gradual del poder: Prorroguismo fallido y transiciones. In Fernando Mayorga, ed. *Crisis y cambio político en Bolivia*, 29–60. La Paz: CESU-UMSS (Centro de Estudios Superiores Universitarios de la Universidad Mayor de San Simón).

Broder, Pablo. 2005. *Dos años en la era K: La economía en la postconvertibilidad*. Buenos Aires: Planeta.

Brooks, Risa. 2021. Through the Looking Glass: Trump-Era Civil-Military Relations. *Strategic Studies Quarterly* 15:2 (Summer): 69–98.

Bruhn, Kathleen. 2021. AMLO y su Partido. *Política y Gobierno* 28:2 (Second Semester): 19–26.

2012. "To Hell with Your Corrupt Institutions!": AMLO and Populism in Mexico. In Cas Mudde and Cristóbal Rovira Kaltwasser, eds. *Populism in Europe and the Americas*, 88–112. Cambridge: Cambridge University Press.

Buendía and Márquez. 2021. *Encuesta nacional de opinión pública: Agosto 2021.* Mexico City: B & M.

Bukele Gears up for 2024. 2023. *Latin American Weekly Report* WR-23-11 (16 March): 15.

Bull, Benedicte, and Francisco Sánchez. 2020. Élites y populistas: Los casos de Venezuela y Ecuador. *Ibero-Americana – Nordic Journal of Latin American Studies* 49:1 (December): 96–106.

Bull, Martin. 2007. Constitutional Referendum of June 2006. *Italian Politics* 22: 99–118.

Burni, Aline, and Eduardo Tamaki. 2021. Populist Communication during the Covid-19 Pandemic: The Case of Brazil's President Bolsonaro. *Partecipazione e Conflitto* 14:1 (March): 113–31.

Burns, James MacGregor. 1978. *Leadership*. New York: Harper & Row.

Busch, Andrew, and John Pitney. 2021. *Divided We Stand: The 2020 Elections and American Politics*. Lanham, MD: Rowman & Littlefield.

Bútora, Martin and Zora Bútorová. 1999. Slovakia's Democratic Awakening. *Journal of Democracy* 10:1 (January): 80–95.

Bútorová, Zora, and Martin Bútora. 2019. The Pendulum Swing of Slovakia's Democracy. *Social Research* 86:1 (Spring): 83–112.

Buzogány, Aron. 2017. Illiberal Democracy in Hungary. *Democratization* 24:7 (December): 1307–25.

Buzogány, Aron, and Mihai Varga. 2021. Illiberal Thought Collectives and Policy Networks in Hungary and Poland. *European Politics and Society*, forthcoming: 1–19.

Cabada, Ladislav, and Matevž Tomšič. 2016. The Rise of Person-Based Politics in the New Democracies: The Czech Republic and Slovenia. *Politics in Central Europe* 12:2 (December): 29–50.

Cagaptay, Soner. 2017. *The New Sultan: Erdogan and the Crisis of Modern Turkey.* London: I.B. Tauris.

Calvo, Ernesto, and María Victoria Murillo. 2012. Argentina: The Persistence of Peronism. *Journal of Democracy* 23:2 (April): 148–61.

Cameron, Maxwell. 2018. Making Sense of Competitive Authoritarianism. *Latin American Politics and Society* 60:2 (May): 1–22.

2011. Peru: The Left Turn that Wasn't. In Steven Levitsky and Kenneth Roberts, eds. *The Resurgence of the Latin American Left*, 375–98. Baltimore, MD: Johns Hopkins University Press.

2006. Endogenous Regime Breakdown. In Julio Carrión, ed. *The Fujimori Legacy*, 268–93. University Park: Pennsylvania State University Press.

1998a. Latin American autogolpes. *Third World Quarterly* 19:2 (May): 219–39.

1998b. Self-Coups: Peru, Guatemala, Russia. *Journal of Democracy* 9:1 (January): 125–39.

Campello, Daniela. 2022. When Incompetence Meets Bad Luck: Bolsonaro's Third Year in the Brazilian Presidency. *Revista de Ciencia Política* 42:2 (July): 203–23.

Carey, John, Katherine Clayton, et al. 2022. Who Will Defend Democracy? *Journal of Elections, Public Opinion and Parties* 32:1 (February): 230–45.

Carpenter, Michael. 1997. Slovakia and the Triumph of Nationalist Populism. *Communist and Post-Communist Studies* 30:2 (June): 205–20.

Carrera, Jorge. 1994. La política económica de la delegación. In *Anales de la Asociación Argentina de Economía Política. XXIX Reunión Annual*, vol. 2, 339–63. La Plata: Universidad Nacional de La Plata.

Carrillo Nieto, Juan. 2020. El segundo año de gobierno de López Obrador en México. *Revista de Estudios Internacionales* 2:2 (July–December): 298–315.

Carrión, Julio. 2022. *A Dynamic Theory of Populism in Power: The Andes in Comparative Perspective*. Oxford: Oxford University Press.

2006b. Public Opinion, Market Reforms, and Democracy in Fujimori's Peru. In Julio Carrión, ed. *The Fujimori Legacy*, 126–49. University Park: Pennsylvania State University Press.

Carrión, Julio, ed. 2006a. *The Fujimori Legacy*. University Park: Pennsylvania State University Press.

Castillo Impeached and Arrested after Attempted Self-Coup Backfires. 2022. *Latin American Weekly Report* WR-22-49 (8 December): 1–3.

Castle, Marjorie, and Ray Taras. 2002. *Democracy in Poland*, 2nd ed. Boulder, CO: Westview.

Casullo, María, and Flavia Freidenberg. 2017. Populist Parties of Latin America. In Reinhard Heinisch, Christina Holtz-Bacha, and Oscar Mazzoleni, eds. *Political Populism: A Handbook*, 293–306. Baden-Baden: Nomos.

Cavallo, Domingo. 1997. *El Peso de la Verdad*. Buenos Aires: Planeta.

CEC (Centro de Estudios Ciudadanos, Universidad Francisco Gavidia). 2021. Los Salvadoreños evalúan dos años de gobierno del presidente Nayib Bukele. San Salvador: CEC.

CEDATOS. 2012. *Opinión CEDATOS: Aprobación Presidentes del Ecuador, 1979–2011*. Quito: CEDATOS.

Ceresole, Norberto. 2000. *Caudillo, Ejército, Pueblo*. Madrid: Estudios Hispano-árabes.

Chacko, Priya. 2018. The Right Turn in India: Authoritarianism, Populism, and Neoliberalisation. *Journal of Contemporary Asia* 48:4 (August): 541–65.

Chambers, Paul. 2013. Military "Shadows" in Thailand since the 2006 Coup. *Asian Affairs: An American Review* 40:2 (April): 67–82.

Charlemagne: Return to Centre. 2023. *Economist* (4 February): 49.

Cheibub, José. 2007. *Presidentialism, Parliamentarism, and Democracy*. Cambridge: Cambridge University Press.

Cheresky, Isidoro. 2006. In the Name of the People: The Possibilities and Limits of a Government Relying on Public Opinion. In Edward Epstein and David Pion-Berlin, eds. *Broken Promises? The Argentine Crisis and Argentine Democracy*, 205–27. Lanham, MD: Lexington.

Cherny, Nicolás. 2014. La relación presidente – partido de gobierno en el Kirchnerismo. In Marcos Novaro, ed. *Peronismo y democracia*, 143–59. Buenos Aires: Edhasa.

Chiaramonte, Alessandro, Lorenzo De Sio, and Vincenzo Emanuele. 2020. Salvini's Success and the Collapse of the Five-Star Movement. *Contemporary Italian Politics* 12:2 (June): 140–54.

Chhibber, Pradeep, and Rahul Verma. 2019. The Rise of the Second Dominant Party System in India: BJP's New Social Coalition in 2019. *Studies in Indian Politics* 7:2 (December): 131–48.

Cholova, Blagovesta, and Jean-Michel De Waele. 2011. Bulgaria: A Fertile Ground for Populism? *Slovak Journal of Political Science* 11:1 (January): 25–54.

Chowkwanyun, Merlin. 2022. The 60/40 Problem: Trump, Culpability, and COVID-19. In Julian Zelizer, ed. *The Presidency of Donald J. Trump*, 315–34. Princeton, NJ: Princeton University Press.

Christofis, Nikos. 2020. Introduction: Accelerating Political Crisis in Erdoğan's Turkey. In Nikos Christofis, ed. *Erdoğan's 'New' Turkey*, 1–28. London: Routledge.

Chumacero, Rómulo. 2019. *El camaleón, el mutante y Houdini: Resultados de las elecciones en Bolivia.* Santiago: Universidad de Chile, Departamento de Economía.

Cirhan, Tomáš, and Petr Kopecký. 2020. From Ideology to Interest-Driven Politics: Václav Klaus, Andrej Babiš and Two Eras of Party Leadership in the Czech Republic. In Sergiu Gherghina, ed. *Party Leaders in Eastern Europe*, 93–119. Cham: Palgrave Macmillan.

Cleary, Matthew, and Aykut Öztürk. 2022. When Does Backsliding Lead to Breakdown? *Perspectives on Politics* 20:1 (March): 205–21.

Cohen, Jean. 2019. What's Wrong with the Normative Theory (and the Actual Practice) of Left Populism. *Constellations* 26:3 (September): 391–407.

Cole, Wade, and Evan Schofer. 2023. Destroying Democracy for the People: The Economic, Social, and Political Consequences of Populist Rule, 1990–2017. *Social Problems*, forthcoming.

Colectivo de Abogados José Alvear Restrepo. 2003. Hacia un Estado autoritario. In Plataforma Colombiana de Derechos Humanos, Democracia y Desarrollo, ed. *El embrujo autoritario*, 15–24. Bogotá: Plataforma Colombiana.

Collor de Mello, Fernando. 1995. Author interview with Brazilian ex-president (1990–92), Brasília: 9 June.

Colombia: Still Armed, Still Dangerous. 2021. *Economist* (27 November): 35–37.

Coman, Ramona, and Clara Volintiru. 2021. Anti-Liberal Ideas and Institutional Change in Central and Eastern Europe. *European Politics and Society*, forthcoming.

Conaghan, Catherine. 2016. Delegative Democracy Revisited. *Journal of Democracy* 27:3 (July): 109–118.

2011. Ecuador: Rafael Correa and the Citizens' Revolution. In Steven Levitsky and Kenneth Roberts, eds. *The Resurgence of the Latin American Left*, 261–82. Baltimore, MD: Johns Hopkins University Press.

2005. *Fujimori's Peru.* Pittsburgh, PA: University of Pittsburgh Press.

1995. Polls, Political Discourse, and the Public Sphere. In Peter Smith, ed. *Latin America in Comparative Perspective*, 227–55. Boulder, CO: Westview.

Connelly, John. 2020. *From Peoples into Nations: A History of Eastern Europe.* Princeton, NJ: Princeton University Press.

Connolly, William. 2017. *Aspirational Fascism.* Minneapolis: University of Minnesota Press.

Constantino-David, Karina. 2002. Surviving Erap. In Amando Doronila, ed. *Between Fires: Fifteen Perspectives on the Estrada Crisis*, 212–26. Pasig City: Anvil Publishing.

Cooley, Jason. 2018. American Exceptionalism during the Populist Wave. *Fletcher Forum of World Affairs* 42:1 (Winter): 27–38.

Corasaniti, Nick. 2022. Raffensperger Fends Off a 2020 Election Denier to Win Georgia's G.O.P. Secretary of State Primary. *New York Times* (25 May).

Corasaniti, Nick, and Reid Epstein. 2022. State Courts Emerge as Firewall Against Gerrymandering by Both Parties. *New York Times* (3 April): 25.

Cornell, Agnes, Jørgen Møller, and Svend-Erik Skaaning. 2020. *Democratic Stability in an Age of Crisis: Reassessing the Interwar Period.* Oxford: Oxford University Press.

2017. The Real Lessons of the Interwar Years. *Journal of Democracy* 28:3 (July): 14–28.

Coronil, Fernando. 2011. State Reflections: The 2002 Coup against Hugo Chávez. In Thomas Ponniah and Jonathan Eastwood, eds. *The Revolution in Venezuela: Social and Political Change under Chávez,* 37–65. Cambridge, MA: Harvard University Press.

Corrales, Javier. 2022. *Autocracy Rising: Venezuela's Transition to Authoritarianism.* Washington, DC: Brookings Institution Press.

2020. Trump's Defeat Was World Historic. *Foreign Policy* (November 17) <https:// foreignpolicy.com/2020/11/17/trump-populist-authoritarian-defeat-biden/, accessed 22 February 2022>.

2018. *Fixing Democracy: Why Constitutional Change Often Fails to Enhance Democracy in Latin America.* Oxford: Oxford University Press.

2015. The Authoritarian Resurgence: Autocratic Legalism in Venezuela. *Journal of Democracy* 26:2 (April): 37–51.

2011. Why Polarize? Advantages and Disadvantages of a Rational-Choice Analysis of Government-Opposition Relations under Hugo Chávez. In Thomas Ponniah and Jonathan Eastwood, eds. *The Revolution in Venezuela: Social and Political Change under Chávez,* 67–97. Cambridge, MA: Harvard University Press.

2010. The Repeating Revolution. In Kurt Weyland, Raúl Madrid, and Wendy Hunter, eds. *Leftist Governments in Latin America,* 28–56. Cambridge: Cambridge University Press.

2002. *Presidents without Parties: The Politics of Economic Reform in Argentina and Venezuela in the 1990s.* University Park: Pennsylvania State University Press.

1997. Why Argentines Followed Cavallo. In Jorge Domínguez, ed. *Technopols: Freeing Politics and Markets in Latin America in the 1990s,* 49–93. University Park: Pennsylvania State University Press.

Corrales, Javier, Gonzalo Hernández, and Juan Salgado. 2020. Oil and Regime Type in Latin America. *Energy Policy* 142 (July).

Corrales, Javier, and Michael Penfold. 2011. *Dragon in the Tropics.* Washington, DC: Brookings.

Correa, Rafael. 2003. La política económica del gobierno de Lucio Gutiérrez. *Íconos* 16 (May): 6–10.

Couto, Cláudio Gonçalves. 2021. Do governo-movimento ao pacto militar-fisiológico. In Leonardo Avritzer, Fábio Kerche, and Marjorie Marona, eds. *Governo Bolsonaro,* 35–49. Belo Horizonte: Autêntica.

Cox, Gary, and Scott Morgenstern. 2001. Latin America's Reactive Assemblies and Proactive Presidents. *Comparative Politics* 33:2 (January): 171–89.

Cramer, Katherine. 2016. *The Politics of Resentment: Rural Consciousness in Wisconsin and the Rise of Scott Walker.* Chicago, IL: University of Chicago Press.

Cristova, Christiana. 2010. Populism: The Bulgarian Case. *Sociedade e Cultura* 13:2 (July–December): 221–32.

Csehi, Robert. 2019. Neither Episodic, nor Destined to Failure? The Endurance of Hungarian Populism after 2010. *Democratization* 26:6 (September): 1011–27.

Csehi, Robert, and Edit Zgut. 2021. 'We Won't Let Brussels Dictate Us': Eurosceptic Populism in Hungary and Poland. *European Politics and Society* 22:1 (February): 53–68.

Cunha Filho, Clayton, André Coelho, and Fidel Pérez Flores. 2013. A Right-to-Left Policy Switch? An Analysis of the Honduran Case under Manuel Zelaya. *International Political Science Review* 34:5 (November): 519–42.

Curato, Nicole. 2017. Flirting with Authoritarian Fantasies? Rodrigo Duterte and the New Terms of Philippine Populism. *Journal of Contemporary Asia* 47:1 (March): 142–53.

Curato, Nicole, and Yvan Yonaha. 2022. Rodrigo Duterte: Macho Populism and Authoritarian Practice. In Klaus Larres, ed. *Dictators and Autocrats*, 384–98. London: Routledge.

Çarkoğlu, Ali, and Melvin Hinich. 2006. A Spatial Analysis of Turkish Party Preferences. *Electoral Studies* 25:2 (June): 369–92.

Dahl, Robert. 1971. *Polyarchy*. New Haven, CT: Yale University Press.

Dallara, Cristina. 2015. Powerful Resistance against a Long-Running Personal Crusade: The Impact of Silvio Berlusconi on the Italian Judicial System. *Modern Italy* 20:1 (February): 59–76.

Dargent, Eduardo. 2021. Perú, entre la crispación y la mediocridad. *New York Times* (23 September) <www.nytimes.com/es/2021/09/23/espanol/opinion/pedro-castillo-peru .html, accessed 24 September 2021>.

2009. *Demócratas precarios: Élites y debilidad democrática en el Perú y América Latina*. Lima: Instituto de Estudios Peruanos.

Dargent, Eduardo, and Stéphanie Rousseau. 2021. Perú 2020: ¿El quiebre de la continuidad? *Revista de Ciencia Política* 41:2 (August): 377–400.

David, Randolf. 2002. Erap: A Diary of Disenchantment. In Amando Doronila, ed. *Between Fires: Fifteen Perspectives on the Estrada Crisis*, 148–79. Pasig City: Anvil Publishing.

Davies, Norman. 2005. *God's Playground: History of Poland*, vol. 2: 1795 to the Present, revised ed. New York: Columbia University Press.

De Dios, Emmanuel. 2002. Corruption and the Fall. In Amando Doronila, ed. *Between Fires: Fifteen Perspectives on the Estrada Crisis*, 43–61. Pasig City: Anvil Publishing.

Deegan-Krause, Kevin. 2019. Donald Trump and the Lessons of East-Central European Populism. In Kurt Weyland and Raúl Madrid, eds. *When Democracy Trumps Populism*, 60–83. Cambridge: Cambridge University Press.

2012. Populism, Democracy, and Nationalism in Slovakia. In Cas Mudde and Cristóbal Rovira Kaltwasser, eds. *Populism in Europe and the Americas*, 182–204. Cambridge: Cambridge University Press.

De Faro, Clovis, ed. 1991. *A Economia pós Plano Collor II*. Rio de Janeiro: LTC.

1990. *Plano Collor: Avaliações e Perspectivas*. Rio de Janeiro: LTC.

Degregori, Carlos, and Romeo Grompone. 1991. *Elecciones 1990: Demonios y redentores en el nuevo Perú*. Lima: Instituto de Estudios Peruanos.

De la Torre, Carlos, ed. 2019. *Routledge Handbook of Global Populism*. London: Routledge.

De la Torre, Carlos. 2018. Ecuador after Correa. *Journal of Democracy* 29:4 (October): 77–88.

2017a. Hugo Chávez and the Diffusion of Bolivarianism. *Democratization* 24:7 (December): 1271–88.

2017b. Populism in Latin America. In Cristóbal Rovira Kaltwasser, Paul Taggart, et al., eds. *Oxford Handbook of Populism*, 195–213. Oxford: Oxford University Press.

2015. *De Velasco a Correa*. Quito: Universidad Andina Simón Bolívar.

De la Torre, Carlos, and Treethep Srisa-nga. 2022. *Global Populisms*. London: Routledge.

Delić, Anuška. 2020. Europe's New Orban. *Index on Censorship* 49:4 (December): 39–41.

Deloy, Corinne. 2012. *The Future of Romania, the Focus of the Referendum on the Impeachment of the President of the Republic Traian Basescu*. Paris: Fondation Robert Schuman. Analysis D-15 (29 July).

Democracy in India. 2022. *Economist* (12 February): 29–30.

De Nadal, Lluis. 2021. On Populism and Social Movements: From the Indignados to Podemos. *Social Movement Studies* 20:1 (January): 36–56.

Diamint, Rut. 2006. Crisis, Democracy, and the Military in Argentina. In Edward Epstein and David Pion-Berlin, eds. *Broken Promises? The Argentine Crisis and Argentine Democracy*, 163–79. Lanham, MD: Lexington.

Dinçşahin, Şakir. 2012. A Symptomatic Analysis of the Justice and Development Party's Populism in Turkey. *Government and Opposition* 47:4 (Autumn): 618–40.

Dionne, Eugene, Norman Ornstein, and Thomas Mann. 2017. *One Nation after Trump*. New York: St. Martin's Press.

Dorf, Michael, and Michael Chu. 2018. Lawyers as Activists. In David Meyer and Sidney Tarrow, eds. *The Resistance: The Dawn of the Anti-Trump Opposition Movement*, 127–42. Oxford: Oxford University Press.

Dornbusch, Rüdiger, and Sebastian Edwards, eds. 1991. *The Macroeconomics of Populism in Latin America*. Chicago, IL: University of Chicago Press.

Downs, Gregory. 2022. Impeachment after Trump. In Julian Zelizer, ed. *The Presidency of Donald J. Trump*, 351–72. Princeton, NJ: Princeton University Press.

Dragoman, Dragoş. 2013. Post-Accession Backsliding in Romania. *South-East European Journal of Political Science* 1:3 (July–September): 27–46.

Draper, Robert. 2022. The Mystery of Michael Flynn. *New York Times Magazine* (February 13): 32–39, 45.

Dresser, Denise. 2022. Mexico's Dying Democracy. *Foreign Affairs* 101:6 (November–December): 74–90.

Dweck, Esther. 2021. A agenda neoliberal em marcha forçada. In Leonardo Avritzer, Fábio Kerche, and Marjorie Marona, eds. *Governo Bolsonaro*, 241–54. Belo Horizonte: Autêntica.

Echegaray, Fabián, and Carlos Elordi. 2001. Public Opinion, Presidential Popularity, and Economic Reform in Argentina, 1989–1996. In Susan Stokes, ed. *Public Support for Market Reforms in New Democracies*, 187–214. Cambridge: Cambridge University Press.

EIU (Economist Intelligence Unit). 2023. *Democracy Index 2022: Frontline Democracy and the Battle for Ukraine*. London: EIU.

El Salvador: Bukele's Bulldozer. 2021. *Economist* (8 May): 34–35.

Elff, Martin, and Sebastian Ziaja. 2018. Methods Factors in Democracy Indicators. *Politics and Governance* 6:1 (March): 92–102.

Elizondo, Carlos. 2021. *Y mi palabra es la ley: AMLO en Palacio Nacional*. Mexico City: Debate.

Elkins, Zachary, Tom Ginsburg, and James Melton. 2009. *The Endurance of National Constitutions*. Cambridge: Cambridge University Press.

Ellner, Steve. 2008. *Rethinking Venezuelan Politics: Class, Conflict, and the Chávez Phenomenon*. Boulder, CO: Lynne Rienner.

Encarnación, Omar. 2002. Venezuela's "Civil Society Coup." *World Policy Journal* 19:2 (July): 38–48.

Enyedi, Zsolt. 2020. Right-Wing Authoritarian Innovations in Central and Eastern Europe. *East European Politics* 36:3 (September): 363–77.

Epstein, Edward, and David Pion-Berlin. 2006. The Crisis of 2001 and Argentine Democracy. In Edward Epstein and David Pion-Berlin, eds. *Broken Promises? The Argentine Crisis and Argentine Democracy*, 3–26. Lanham, MD: Lexington.

Epstein, Reid. 2022. Scheme to Reinstall Trump Opens a Schism in Wisconsin G.O.P. *New York Times* (February 20): 1, 17.

Erdogan's Empire. 2023. *Economist. Special Report: Turkey* (January 21): 1–12.

Escobari, Diego, and Gary Hoover. 2020. *Evo Morales and Electoral Fraud in Bolivia: A Natural Experiment and Discontinuity Evidence.* Edinburg: University of Texas Rio Grande Valley, Department of Economics and Finance.

Esen, Berk, and Sebnem Gumuscu. 2018. The Perils of "Turkish Presidentialism." *Review of Middle East Studies* 52:1 (April): 43–53.

2016. Rising Competitive Authoritarianism in Turkey. *Third World Quarterly* 37:9 (September): 1581–606.

Espino, Luis Antonio. 2021. *López Obrador: El poder del discurso populista.* Mexico City: Turner.

Etchemendy, Sebastián, and Candelaria Garay. 2011. Argentina: Left Populism in Comparative Perspective, 2003–2009. In Steven Levitsky and Kenneth Roberts, eds. *The Resurgence of the Latin American Left*, 283–305. Baltimore, MD: Johns Hopkins University Press.

EU eröffnet Verfahren gegen Ungarn. 2022. *Deutsche Welle* (27 April).

EU (European Union). EEM (Election Expert Mission). 2020. *Bolivia 2019: Final Report.* Brussels: EU.

Ezquerro-Cañete, Arturo, and Ramón Fogel. 2017. A Coup Foretold: Fernando Lugo in Paraguay. *Journal of Agrarian Change* 17:2 (April): 279–95.

Feinberg, Richard, and Daniel Kurtz-Phelan. 2006. Nicaragua between "Caudillismo" and Modernity. *World Policy Journal* 23:2 (July): 76–84.

Fella, Stefano, and Carlo Ruzza. 2013. Populism and the Fall of the Centre-Right in Italy. *Journal of Contemporary European Studies* 21:1 (May): 38–52.

Fernández, Cristina, and Leonardo Villar. 2014. *Bonanzas temporales de recursos.* Bogotá: Fedesarrollo.

Fernández Camacho, Carmen. 2004. La oposición al autogolpe de Serrano Elías. *Ámbitos* 11–12 (1st and 2nd Semester): 237–59.

Ferreira Rubio, Delia, and Matteo Goretti 1998. When the President Governs Alone: The Decretazo in Argentina, 1989–93. In John Carey and Matthew Shugart, eds. *Executive Decree Authority*, 33–61. Cambridge: Cambridge University Press.

FES (Friedrich Ebert Stiftung). n.d. Innenpolitische Entwicklung seit der Selbstständigkeit. Bonn-Bad Godesberg: FES.

Fierro, Marta. 2014. Álvaro Uribe Vélez: Populismo y neopopulismo. *Análisis Político* 27:81 (May–August): 127–47.

Fiorina, Morris. 2017. *Unstable Majorities: Polarization, Party Sorting, and Political Stalemate.* Stanford, CA: Hoover Institution Press.

Fish, Steven. 1999. The End of Meciarism. *East European Constitutional Review* 8: 1–2 (Winter-Spring): 47–55.

Flannery, Nathaniel. 2013. Calderón's War. *Journal of International Affairs* 66:2 (Spring–Summer): 181–96.

Flores-Macías, Gustavo. 2022. *Contemporary State Building: Elite Taxation and Public Safety in Latin America*. Cambridge: Cambridge University Press.

Foa, Roberto, and Yascha Mounk. 2021. America after Trump: From "Clean" to "Dirty" Democracy? *Policy Studies* 42: 5–6 (September): 455–72.

Foa, Roberto, Xavier Romero-Vidal, et al. 2022. *The Great Reset: Public Opinion, Populism, and the Pandemic*. Cambridge: Centre for the Future of Democracy, Cambridge University.

Foley, Michael. 2013. Barack Obama and the Calculus of Presidential Ambiguity. *Political Studies Review* 11:3 (September): 345–57.

Forgettable Populist. 2022. *Economist* (January 8): 35.

Fracanzani, Edoardo. 2021. *Norms under Siege: The Parallel Political Lives of Donald Trump and Silvio Berlusconi*. Winchester, UK: Zero Books.

Frantz, Erica, Andrea Kendall-Taylor, Jia Li, and Joseph Wright. 2022. Personalist Ruling Parties in Democracies. *Democratization* 29:5 (July): 918–38.

Freedom House (FH). 2022a. *Freedom in the World 2022*. Washington, DC: FH.

2022b. *Freedom in the World 2022. Country Report: Hungary*. Washington, DC: FH.

2022c. *Freedom in the World 2022. Country Report: Poland*. Washington, DC: FH.

Freidenberg, Flavia. 2015. ¡En tierra de caciques! *Revista Opera* 16 (January–June): 99–130.

Fujimori, Alberto. 1992. *Hacia la reconstrucción nacional. Mensaje a la Nación y Memoria Anual, 2° año de gobierno*. Lima: Secretaría General de la Presidencia.

Furlong, Paul. 2015. Silvio Berlusconi and the Italian Presidency. *Modern Italy* 20:1 (February): 77–90.

Galarraga Cortázar, Naiara. 2021. La caótica gestión de la pandemia impulsa las peticiones de 'impeachment' contra Bolsonaro. *El País* (27 January).

Galindo Hernández, Carolina. 2007. Neopopulismo en Colombia. *Íconos* 27 (January): 147–62.

Gálvez Borrell, Víctor. 2011. El golpe de Estado de 1993 en Guatemala. *Espacios Políticos* 4:5 (September): 47–80.

Gamboa, Laura. 2017. Opposition at the Margins. *Comparative Politics* 49:4 (July): 457–77.

Ganev, Venelin. 2018. "Soft Decisionism" in Bulgaria. *Journal of Democracy* 29:3 (July): 91–103.

1999. Bulgaria. In Robert Elgie, ed. *Semi-Presidentialism in Europe*, 124–49. Oxford: Oxford University Press.

García-Sánchez, Miguel, and Juan Rodríguez-Raga. 2019. Personality and an Internal Enemy: Understanding the Popularity of Álvaro Uribe, 2002–2010. *Revista Latinoamericana de Opinión Pública* 8:2 (Second semester): 99–123.

Garrido, Marco. 2022. The Ground for the Illiberal Turn in the Philippines. *Democratization* 29:4 (July): 673–91.

Gavarrete, Julia. 2021. In El Salvador, Bukele Reigns Supreme. *NACLA – Report on the Americas* 53:2 (Summer): 115–17.

Gellman, Barton. 2022. January 6 Was Practice. *The Atlantic* 329:1 (January–February): 24–44.

Germani, Gino. 1978. *Authoritarianism, Fascism, and National Populism*. New Brunswick, NJ: Transaction.

Gerring, John. 2012. Concepts. Chap. in *Social Science Methodology*, 2nd ed., 107–40. Cambridge: Cambridge University Press.

Gerring, John, and Daniel Weitzel. 2023. Measuring Electoral Democracy with Observables. Ms. University of Texas at Austin, Department of Government.

Gervasoni, Carlos. 2015. Libertades y derechos políticos, 2003–2014: El Kirchnerismo evaluado desde siete modelos de democracia. In Carlos Gervasoni and Enrique Peruzzotti, eds. *"Década Ganada" Evaluando el legado del Kirchnerismo*, 19–60. Buenos Aires: Debate.

Gherghina, Sergiu, and Sorina Soare. 2021. Electoral Performance Beyond Leaders? The Organization of Populist Parties in Postcommunist Europe. *Party Politics* 27:1 (January): 58–68.

Ghodsee, Kristen. 2008. Left Wing, Right Wing, Everything. *Problems of Post-Communism* 55:3 (May–June): 26–39.

Gibson, Nadine, and Daron Shaw. 2019. Politics as Usual? Exploring Issues and the 2016 Presidential Vote. *Social Science Quarterly* 100:2 (April): 447–65.

Gigerenzer, Gerd. 2006. Out of the Frying Pan into the Fire: Behavioral Reactions to Terrorist Attacks. *Risk Analysis* 26:2 (April): 347–51.

Gilens, Martin, and Benjamin Page. 2014. Testing Theories of American Politics: Elites, Interest Groups, and Average Citizens. *Perspectives on Politics* 12:3 (September): 564–81.

Gilovich, Thomas, Dale Griffin, and Daniel Kahneman, eds. 2002. *Heuristics and Biases*. Cambridge: Cambridge University Press.

Ginsburg, Tom, and Aziz Huq. 2018a. Democracy's Near Misses. *Journal of Democracy* 29:4 (October): 16–30.

2018b. *How to Save a Constitutional Democracy*. Chicago, IL: University of Chicago Press.

Gliszczyńska-Grabias, Aleksandra, and Wojciech Sadurski. 2021. The Judgment that Wasn't (But which Nearly Brought Poland to a Standstill). *European Constitutional Law Review* 17:1 (March): 130–53.

Goodman, Peter. 2018. The West Saw a Democracy; Turkey Embraced an Autocrat. *New York Times* (19 August): A1, A10.

Gomez, Gabriel, and Sven Leunig. 2022. Fidesz, Liberal Democracy and the Fundamental Law in Hungary. *Zeitschrift für Politikwissenschaft* 32:3 (September): 655–82.

Graber, Mark, Sanford Levinson, and Mark Tushnet, eds. 2018. *Constitutional Democracy in Crisis?* Oxford: Oxford University Press.

Graham, Carol, and Cheikh Kane. 1998. Opportunistic Government or Sustaining Reform? *Latin American Research Review* 33:1: 67–104.

Graham, Matthew, and Milan Svolik. 2020. Democracy in America? Partisanship, Polarization, and the Robustness of Support for Democracy in the United States. *American Political Science Review* 114:2 (May): 392–409.

Granovetter, Mark. 1973. The Strength of Weak Ties. *American Journal of Sociology* 78:6 (May): 1360–80.

Graphic Detail: Gerrymandering. 2022. *Economist* (4 June): 81.

Gray Molina, George. 2010. The Challenge of Progressive Change under Evo Morales. In Kurt Weyland, Raúl Madrid, and Wendy Hunter, eds. 2010. *Leftist Governments in Latin America: Successes and Shortcomings*, 57–76. Cambridge: Cambridge University Press.

Grofman, Bernard. 2022. Prospects for Democratic Breakdown in the United States. *Perspectives on Politics* 20:3 (September): 1040–47.

Grossmann, Matt. 2021. Incremental Liberalism or Prolonged Partisan Warfare. In Eric Patashnik and Wendy Schiller, eds. *Dynamics of American Democracy*, 40–62. Lawrence: University Press of Kansas.

Grzymala-Busse, Anna. 2019. How Populists Rule: The Consequences for Democratic Governance. *Polity* 51:4 (October): 707–17.

2018. Poland Path's to Illiberalism. *Current History* 117:797 (March): 96–101.

2017. Global Populisms and Their Impact. *Slavic Review* 76:S1 (August): S3–S8.

2002. *Redeeming the Communist Past: The Regeneration of Communist Parties in East Central Europe*. Cambridge: Cambridge University Press.

Guasti, Petra. 2020. Populism in Power and Democracy in the Czech Republic. *Politics and Governance* 8:4 (December): 473–84.

Guasti, Petra, and Lenka Buštiková. 2022. Pandemic Power Grabs. Paper for conference on "Still the Age of Populism?" University of Florida, Gainesville, April 22–23.

Guiler, Kimberly. 2021. From Prison to Parliament: Victimhood, Identity, and Electoral Support. *Mediterranean Politics* 26:2 (April): 168–97.

Gurov, Boris, and Emilia Zankina. 2013. Populism and the Construction of Political Charisma: Post-Transition Politics in Bulgaria. *Problems of Post-Communism* 60:1 (January–February): 3–17.

Gutiérrez, Raquel, Luis Tapia, Raúl Prada, and Álvaro García Linera. 2002. *Democratizaciones Plebeyas*. La Paz: Muela del Diablo.

Gwiazda, Anna. 2016. *Democracy in Poland*. London: Routledge.

Gyárfášová, Ol'ga, and Peter Učeň. 2020. Radical Party Politics and Mobilization Against It in the Slovak Parliamentary Elections 2020. *Politologický Časopis – Czech Journal of Political Science* 27:3 (October): 323–52.

Hadiz, Vedi. 2014. A New Islamic Populism and the Contradictions of Development. *Journal of Contemporary Asia* 44:1 (January): 125–43.

Haggard, Stephan, and Robert Kaufman. 2021. *Backsliding*. Cambridge: Cambridge University Press.

Hall, Ian. 2022. Narendra Modi: Elected Authoritarian. In Klaus Larres, ed. *Dictators and Autocrats*, 191–203. London: Routledge.

Hall, Peter. 2016. Politics as a Process Structured in Space and Time. In Orfeo Fioretos, Tulia Falleti, and Adam Sheingate, eds., *Oxford Handbook of Historical Institutionalism*, 31–50. Oxford: Oxford University Press.

Hallock, Jeffrey, and Charles Call. 2021. The Biopolitical President? Sovereign Power and Democratic Erosion in El Salvador. *Democratization* 28:8 (December): 1583–601.

Hanley, Seán, and Milada Vachudova. 2018. Understanding the Illiberal Turn in the Czech Republic. *East European Politics* 34:3 (September): 276–96.

Harper, Jo. 2021. *Our Man in Warszawa: How the West Misread Poland*. Budapest: Central European University Press.

Harten, Sven. 2011. Towards a 'Traditional Party'? Internal Organisation and Change in the MAS in Bolivia. In Adrian Pearce, ed. *Evo Morales and the Movimiento al Socialismo in Bolivia*, 63–91. London: Institute for the Study of the Americas, University of London.

Hartz, Louis. 1955. *The Liberal Tradition in America*. New York: Harcourt, Brace.

Haughton, Tim. 2003. Facilitator and Impeder: The Institutional Framework of Slovak Politics during the Premiership of Vladimír Mečiar. *Slavonic and East European Review* 81:2 (April): 267–90.

2002. Vladimír Mečiar and his Role in the 1994–1998 Slovak Coalition Government. *Europe-Asia Studies* 54:8 (December): 1319–38.

2001. HZDS: The Ideology, Organisation and Support Base of Slovakia's Most Successful Party. *Europe-Asia Studies* 53:5 (July): 745–69.

Haughton, Tim, and Kevin Deegan-Krause. 2015. Hurricane Season: Systems of Instability in Central and East European Party Politics. *East European Politics and Societies and Cultures* 29:1 (February): 61–80.

Haughton, Tim, and Marek Rybář. 2008. A Change of Direction: The 2006 Parliamentary Elections and Party Politics in Slovakia. *Journal of Communist Studies and Transition Politics* 24:2 (June): 232–55.

Havler-Barrett, Chris. 2020. Ganging Up against the Truth: El Salvador's Government Do Not Want You to Hear about a Potential Deal They've Made with the Country's Biggest Gang. *Index on Censorship* 49:4 (December): 32–34.

Havlík, Vlastimil. 2019. Technocratic Populism and Political Illiberalism in Central Europe. *Problems of Post-Communism* 66:6 (November): 369–84.

Hawkins, Kirk. 2010. *Venezuela's Chavismo and Populism in Comparative Perspective.* Cambridge: Cambridge University Press.

Hawkins, Kirk, Ryan Carlin, Levente Littvay, and Cristóbal Rovira Kaltwasser, eds. 2019. *The Ideational Approach to Populism.* London: Routledge.

Hawkins, Kirk, and Levente Littvay. 2019. *Contemporary US Populism in Comparative Perspective.* Cambridge: Cambridge University Press.

Hawkins, Kirk, and Cristóbal Rovira Kaltwasser. 2017a. The Ideational Approach to Populism. *Latin American Research Review* 52:4: 513–28.

2017b. What the (Ideational) Study of Populism Can Teach Us, and What It Can't. *Swiss Political Science Review* 23:4 (December): 526–42.

Hawkins, Kirk, and Joel Selway. 2017. Thaksin the Populist? *Chinese Political Science Review* 2:3 (September): 372–94.

Hawley, George. 2021. The Stillborn Revolution: The Failure of Right-Wing Populism in the United States. In Gisela Pereyra Doval and Gastón Souroujon, eds. *Global Resurgence of the Right,* 255–69. London: Routledge.

Haydanka, Yevheniy. 2021. Authoritization or Democratization: Directions of Electoral Processes in Present-Day Slovakia. *Journal of Comparative Politics* 14:2: 4–15.

Hein, Michael. 2015. The Fight against Government Corruption in Romania. *Europe-Asia Studies* 67:5 (July): 747–76.

Held, David. 2006. *Models of Democracy,* 3rd ed. Stanford, CA: Stanford University Press.

Hellinger, Daniel. 2007. When "No" Means "Yes to Revolution:" Electoral Politics in Bolivarian Venezuela. In Steve Ellner and Miguel Tinker Salas, eds. *Venezuela: Hugo Chávez and the Decline of an "Exceptional Democracy,"* 157–84. Lanham, MD: Rowman & Littlefield.

Hellmann, Olli. 2017. Populism in East Asia. In Cristóbal Rovira Kaltwasser, Paul Taggart et al., eds. *Oxford Handbook of Populism,* 161–78. Oxford: Oxford University Press.

Helmke, Gretchen. 2017. *Institutions on the Edge: The Origins and Consequences of Inter-Branch Crises in Latin America.* Cambridge: Cambridge University Press.

Herbert, Jon. 2021. Governing in Conflict or Cooperation? Trump's Populism and the Republican Party. *Taiwan Journal of Democracy* 17:1 (July): 89–117.

Hertel-Fernandez, Alexander. 2022. Conservative Extra-Party Coalitions and State-House Democracy. In Robert Lieberman, Suzanne Mettler, and Kenneth Roberts, eds. *Democratic Resilience: Can the United States Withstand Rising Polarization?* 320–40. Cambridge: Cambridge University Press.

Hewison, Kevin, and Kengkij Kitirianglarp. 2010. 'Thai-Style Democracy': The Royalist Struggle for Thailand's Politics. In Søren Ivarsson and Lotte Isager, eds. *Saying the Unsayable: Monarchy and Democracy in Thailand*, 179–202. Copenhagen: Nordic Institute of Asian Studies Press.

Heydarian, Richard. 2022. The Return of the Marcos Dynasty. *Journal of Democracy* 33:3 (July): 62–76.

Higgins, Andrew. 2021. Populist Leader of Czech Republic Narrowly Defeated in Election. *New York Times* (9 October) <www.nytimes.com/2021/10/09/world/europe/andrej-babis-defeated-czech-republic.html, accessed 14 October 2021>.

Hinton, Alexander. 2021. *It Can Happen Here: White Power and the Rising Threat of Genocide in the US*. New York: New York University Press.

Hirschman, Albert. 1982. *Shifting Involvements: Private Interest and Public Action*. Princeton, NJ: Princeton University Press.

Hochschild, Arlie. 2016. *Strangers in Their Own Land: Anger and Mourning on the American Right*. New York: Free Press.

Hochstetler, Kathryn. 2006. Rethinking Presidentialism. *Comparative Politics* 38:4 (July): 401–18.

Hofbauer, Hannes, and David Noack. 2012. *Slowakei: Der mühsame Weg nach Westen*. Vienna: Promedia.

Hollyer, James, Marko Klašnja, and Rocío Titiunik. 2022. Parties as Disciplinarians: Charisma and Commitment Problems in Programmatic Campaigning. *American Journal of Political Science* 66:1 (January): 75–92.

Homans, Charles, Jazmine Ulloa, and Blake Hounshell. 2022. Slice of Voters Averted Threat to Fair Elections. *New York Times* (25 December): 1, 16.

Howell, William, and Terry Moe. 2020. *Presidents, Populism, and the Crisis of Democracy*. Chicago: University of Chicago Press.

2016. *Relic: How Our Constitution Undermines Effective Government*. New York: Basic Books.

Huber, Robert, and Christian Schimpf. 2017. Populism and Democracy. In Reinhard Heinisch, Christina Holtz-Bacha, and Oscar Mazzoleni, eds. *Political Populism: A Handbook*, 329–44. Baden-Baden: Nomos.

Hughes, Tyler, and Lawrence Becker. 2021. Trump and the 2018 Midterms. In Paul Rutledge and Chapman Rackaway, eds. *The Unorthodox Presidency of Donald J. Trump*, 86–106. Lawrence: University Press of Kansas.

Hunter, Wendy. 1997. *Eroding Military Influence in Brazil*. Chapel Hill: University of North Carolina Press.

Hunter, Wendy, and Timothy Power. 2023. Lula's Second Act. *Journal of Democracy* 34:1 (January): 126–40.

2019. Bolsonaro and Brazil's Illiberal Backlash. *Journal of Democracy* 30:1 (January): 68–82.

Hunter, Wendy, and Diego Vega. 2022. Populism and the Military: Symbiosis and Tension in Bolsonaro's Brazil. *Democratization* 29:2 (February): 337–59.

Huntington, Samuel. 1991. *The Third Wave*. Norman: University of Oklahoma Press.

1981. *American Politics: Promise of Disharmony.* Cambridge, MA: Harvard University Press.

1968. *Political Order in Changing Societies.* New Haven, CT: Yale University Press.

Hurtado Miller, Juan. 1992. *201 días de gestión.* Lima: N.p.

Ibarra, Hernán. 1997. La caída de Bucaram. *Ecuador Debate* 40 (April): 21–33.

Idrobo, Nicolás, Dorothy Kronick, and Francisco Rodríguez. 2022. Do Shifts in Late-Counted Votes Signal Fraud? Evidence from Bolivia. *Journal of Politics* 84:4 (October): 2202–15.

Iguíñiz, Javier. 1991. Perú: Ajuste e inflación en el Plan Fujimori. In Guillermo Rozenwurcel, ed. *Elecciones y política en América Latina*, 387–432. Buenos Aires: Tesis.

Impact of Gang Crackdown Acknowledged. 2023. *Latin American Weekly Report* WR-23-06 (9 February): 14.

In His Image: The Republican Party. 2022. *Economist* (1 January): 16–18.

Indian Democracy: Nobbling Rahul Gandhi. 2023. *Economist* (1 April): 29.

Inglehart, Ronald, and Christian Welzel. 2005. *Modernization, Cultural Change, and Democracy.* Cambridge: Cambridge University Press.

Issacharoff, Samuel. 2023. *Democracy Unmoored: Populism and the Corruption of Popular Sovereignty.* Oxford: Oxford University Press.

IUDOP (Instituto Universitario de Opinión Pública, Universidad Centroamericana José Simeón Cañas – UCA). 2022. Evaluación ciudadana del tercer año del presidente Nayib Bukele. *Boletín de Prensa* 36:3 (June): 1–46.

2020. Sondeo de opinión sobre el primer año del Gobierno del presidente Nayib Bukele y el manejo de la pandemia COVID-19. *Boletín de Prensa* 34:4 (July): 1–22.

2019. *Encuesta poselectoral de las elecciones presidenciales de 2019.* San Salvador: IUDOP. UCA.

Jacobs, Lawrence, and Judd Choate. 2022. Democratic Capacity: Election Administration as Bulwark and Target. *Annals of the American Academy for Political and Social Science* 699 (January): 22–35.

Jacobs, Nicholas, and Sidney Milkis. 2021. Our "Undivided Support:" Donald Trump, the Republican Party, and Executive-Centered Partisanship. In Eric Patashnik and Wendy Schiller, eds. *Dynamics of American Democracy*, 291–322. Lawrence: University Press of Kansas.

Jacobson, Gary. 2019. Extreme Referendums: Donald Trump and the 2018 Midterm Elections. *Political Science Quarterly* 134:1 (Spring): 9–38.

Jaffrelot, Christophe. 2021. *Modi's India.* Princeton, NJ: Princeton University Press.

Jardina, Ashley, and Robert Mickey. 2022. White Racial Solidarity and Opposition to American Democracy. *Annals of the American Academy for Political and Social Science* 699 (January): 79–89.

Johnston, Jake, and David Rosnick. 2020. *Observing the Observers: The OAS in the 2019 Bolivian Elections.* Washington, DC: Center for Economic and Policy Research.

Jonas, Susanne. 1995. Electoral Problems and the Democratic Project in Guatemala. In Mitchell Seligson and John Booth, eds. *Elections and Democracy in Central America, Revisited*, enlarged ed., 25–44. Chapel Hill: University of North Carolina Press.

Jones, Erik. 2023. Italy's Hard Truths. *Journal of Democracy* 34:1 (January): 21–35.

Jornal do Brasil. 2020. "E daí?", diz Bolsonaro sobre número recorde de mortes por Covid-19 no Brasil. April 29. <www.jb.com.br/pais/politica/2020/04/1023526--e-dai----diz-bolsonaro-sobre-numero-recorde-de-mortes-por-covid-19-no-brasil.html>.

Judicial Independence Stressed as SCJN Enters New Era. 2023. *Latin American Weekly Report* WR-23-06 (9 February): 13.

Juego, Bonn. 2017. The Philippines 2017: Duterte-Led Authoritarian Populism and Its Liberal-Democratic Roots. *Asia Maior* 28: 129–63.

Jungkunz, Sebastian, Robert Fahey, and Airo Hino. 2021. How Populist Attitudes Scales Fail to Capture Support for Populists in Power. *PLOS One* 16:12 (December): 1–20.

Kabashima, Ikuo, and Gill Steel. 2007. How Junichiro Koizumi Seized the Leadership of Japan's Liberal Democratic Party. *Japanese Journal of Political Science* 8:1 (April): 95–114.

Kada, Naoko. 2003. Impeachment as a Punishment for Corruption? The Cases of Brazil and Venezuela. In Jody Baumgartner and Naoko Kada, eds. *Checking Executive Power: Presidential Impeachment in Comparative Perspective*, 113–35. Westport, CT: Praeger.

Kahneman, Daniel. 2011. *Thinking, Fast and Slow*. New York: Farrar, Straus, and Giroux.

Kahneman, Daniel, Paul Slovic, and Amos Tversky, eds. 1982. *Judgment under Uncertainty*. Cambridge: Cambridge University Press.

Kalb, Johanna, and Alicia Bannon. 2018. Courts under Pressure. *New York University Law Review* 93: 1–6.

Kanev, Dobrin. 2013. Parliamentary Elections in Bulgaria 2013. *SEER: Journal for Labour and Social Affairs in Eastern Europe* 16:1: 21–35.

Kaufman, Robert, and Stephan Haggard. 2019. Democratic Decline in the United States. *Perspectives on Politics* 17:2 (June): 417–32.

Kazin, Michael. 2022. The Path of Most Resistance: How Democrats Battled Trump and Moved Left. In Julian Zelizer, ed. *The Presidency of Donald J. Trump*, 335–50. Princeton, NJ: Princeton University Press.

1998. *The Populist Persuasion: An American History*, revised ed. Ithaca, NY: Cornell University Press.

Kenney, Charles. 2004. *Fujimori's Coup and the Breakdown of Democracy in Latin America*. Notre Dame, IN: University of Notre Dame Press.

Kenny, Paul. Forthcoming. The Strategic Approach to Populism. In Dambaru Subedi, Alan Scott, et al. eds. *Routledge Handbook of Populism in the Asia Pacific*. London: Routledge.

2023. *Why Populism: The Economics of Winning and Keeping Power from Antiquity to the Present*. Cambridge: Cambridge University Press.

2020. "The Enemy of the People:" Populists and Press Freedom. *Political Research Quarterly* 73:2 (June): 261–75.

2018. *Populism in Southeast Asia*. Cambridge: Cambridge University Press.

2017. *Populism and Patronage*. Oxford: Oxford University Press.

Kenny, Paul, and Ronald Holmes. 2020. A New Penal Populism? Rodrigo Duterte, Public Opinion, and the War on Drugs in the Philippines. *Journal of East Asian Studies* 20:2 (July): 187–205.

Kestler, Thomas. 2022. Radical, Nativist, Authoritarian – Or All of These? Assessing Recent Cases of Right-Wing Populism in Latin America. *Journal of Politics in Latin America* 14:3 (December): 289–310.

Khosla, Madhav, and Milan Vaishnav. 2021. The Three Faces of the Indian State. *Journal of Democracy* 32:1 (January): 111–25.

Kimura, Kan. 2009. A Populist with Obsolete Ideas: The Failure of Roh Moo-hyun. In Kosuke Mizuno and Pasuk Phongpaichit, eds., *Populism in Asia*, 167–80. Singapore: National University of Singapore Press.

King, Desmond, and Sidney Milkis. 2022. Polarization, the Administrative State, and Executive-Centered Partisanship. In Robert Lieberman, Suzanne Mettler, and Kenneth Roberts, eds. *Democratic Resilience: Can the United States Withstand Rising Polarization?* 267–96. Cambridge: Cambridge University Press.

King, Gary, Robert Keohane, and Sidney Verba. 1994. *Designing Social Inquiry.* Princeton, NJ: Princeton University Press.

(The) Kirchners v the Farmers. 2008. *Economist* (March 27).

Kitschelt, Herbert. 2000. Linkages between Citizens and Politicians in Democratic Politics. *Comparative Political Studies* 33:6–7 (August-September): 845–79.

Kitroeff, Natalie. 2023. At a Price, El Salvador Stamps Out Its Gangs. *New York Times* (10 April): A1, A10.

Klašnja, Marko, and Grigore Pop-Eleches. 2022. Anticorruption Efforts and Electoral Manipulation in Democracies. *Journal of Politics* 84:2 (April): 739–52.

Kline, Harvey. 2015. *Fighting Monsters in the Abyss.* Tuscaloosa: University of Alabama Press.

2009. *Showing Teeth to the Dragons.* Tuscaloosa: University of Alabama Press.

Körösényi, András, Gábor Illés, and Attila Gyulai. 2020. *The Orbán Regime.* London: Routledge.

Körösényi, András, and Veronika Patkós. 2017. Liberal and Illiberal Populism: Berlusconi and Orbán. *Corvinus Journal of Sociology and Social Policy* 8 (special issue): 315–37.

Kostadinova, Petia, and Magda Giurcanu. 2015. Political Blackmail, Institutional Infighting, and Electoral Politics: The Fate of Governing Parties during the Great Recession (2008–12) in Romania and Bulgaria. *Politics and Policy* 43:6 (December): 789–821.

Kostadinova, Tatiana, and Barry Levitt. 2014. Toward a Theory of Personalist Parties. *Politics and Policy* 42:4 (August): 490–512.

Kotwas, Marta, and Jan Kubik. 2019. Symbolic Thickening of Public Culture and the Rise of Right-Wing Populism in Poland. *East European Politics and Societies and Cultures* 33:2 (May): 435–71.

Krastev, Ivan, and Stephen Holmes. 2019. *The Light that Failed: Why the West Is Losing the Fight for Democracy.* New York: Pegasus.

Krasztev, Péter, and Jon Van Til, eds. 2015. *The Hungarian Patient.* Budapest: Central European University Press.

Kreitner, Richard. 2020. What History Tells Us about Trump's Implosion and Biden's Opportunity: Interview with Stephen Skowronek. *The Nation* (October 12) <www.thenation.com/article/politics/interview-stephen-skowronek/, accessed 21 February 2022>.

Krekó, Péter, and Zsolt Enyedi. 2018. Orbán's Laboratory of Illiberalism. *Journal of Democracy* 29:3 (July): 39–51.

Kriner, Douglas. 2022. Unilateralism Unleashed? Polarization and the Politics of Executive Action. In Robert Lieberman, Suzanne Mettler, and Kenneth Roberts, eds. *Democratic Resilience: Can the United States Withstand Rising Polarization?* 118–40. Cambridge: Cambridge University Press.

Kuehn, David, and Harold Trinkunas. 2017. Conditions of Military Contestation in Populist Latin America. *Democratization* 24:5 (October): 859–80.

Kulakevich, Tatsiana, and Aaron Augsburger. 2021. Contested Elections, Protest, and Regime Stability: Comparing Belarus and Bolivia. *Canadian Slavonic Papers* 63:3–4 (December): 316–37.

Kyle, Jordan, and Yascha Mounk. 2018. *The Populist Harm to Democracy*. Washington, DC: Tony Blair Institute for Global Change.

Lamont, Michèle, Bo Park, and Elena Ayala-Hurtado. 2017. Trump's Electoral Speeches and his Appeal to the American White Working Class. *British Journal of Sociology* 68:S1 (November): S153–80.

Lamounier, Bolivar. 1993. Institutional Structure and Governability in the 1990s. In Maria D'Alva Kinzo, ed. *Brazil: The Challenges of the 1990s*, 117–37. London: University of London, Institute of Latin American Studies.

Landau, David. 2018. Constitution-Making and Authoritarianism in Venezuela. In Mark Graber, Sanford Levinson, and Mark Tushnet, eds. *Constitutional Democracy in Crisis?* 161–75. Oxford: Oxford University Press.

Landeros, Edgar. 2021. El populismo de Nayib Bukele. In Juliana Gil Ortiz, ed. *Bicentenario de Centroamérica*, 77–108. Buenos Aires: CLACSO.

Lee, Frances. 2023. Populism, Democracy, and the Post-2020 Republican Party in Congress. *Presidential Studies Quarterly*, forthcoming.

  2022. Crosscutting Cleavages, Political Institutions, and Democratic Resilience in the United States. In Robert Lieberman, Suzanne Mettler, and Kenneth Roberts, eds. *Democratic Resilience: Can the United States Withstand Rising Polarization?* 95–117. Cambridge: Cambridge University Press.

  2021. Challenges of Measuring Party Unity in a Polarized Era. In Eric Patashnik and Wendy Schiller, eds. *Dynamics of American Democracy*, 87–111. Lawrence: University Press of Kansas.

  2020. Populism and the American Party System. *Perspectives on Politics* 18:2 (June): 370–88.

  2018. The 115th Congress and Questions of Party Unity in a Polarized Era. *Journal of Politics* 80:4 (October): 1464–73.

  2016. *Insecure Majorities: Congress and the Perpetual Campaign*. Chicago, IL: University of Chicago Press.

Leff, Carol Skalnik. 1997. *The Czech and Slovak Republics*. Boulder, CO: Westview.

Legutko, Ryszard. 2018. *The Demon in Democracy*. New York: Encounter Books.

Lehoucq, Fabrice. 2020. Bolivia's Citizen Revolt. *Journal of Democracy* 31:3 (July): 130–44.

  2012. *The Politics of Modern Central America*. Cambridge: Cambridge University Press.

  2008. Bolivia's Constitutional Breakdown. *Journal of Democracy* 19:4 (October): 110–24.

Lendvai, Paul. 2017. *Orbán: Europe's New Strongman*. Oxford: Oxford University Press.

Levitsky, Steven. 2011. Peru's 2011 Elections. *Journal of Democracy* 22:4 (October): 84–94.

  2003. *Transforming Labor-Based Parties in Latin America: Argentine Peronism in Comparative Perspective*. Cambridge: Cambridge University Press.

Levitsky, Steven, and Maxwell Cameron. 2003. Democracy without Parties? *Latin American Politics and Society* 45:3 (September): 1–33.

Levitsky, Steven, and James Loxton. 2019. Populism and Competitive Authoritarianism in Latin America. In Carlos de la Torre, ed. *Routledge Handbook of Global Populism*, 334–50. London: Routledge.

2013. Populism and Competitive Authoritarianism in the Andes. *Democratization* 20:1 (January): 107–36.

Levitsky, Steven, and María Victoria Murillo. 2020. La tentación militar en América Latina. *Nueva Sociedad* 285 (January–February): 4–11.

2013. Lessons from Latin America: Building Institutions on Weak Foundations. *Journal of Democracy* 24:2 (April): 93–107.

2009. Variation in Institutional Strength. *Annual Review of Political Science* 12: 115–33.

2006. Building Castles in the Sand? The Politics of Institutional Weakness in Argentina. In Steven Levitsky and María Victoria Murillo, eds. *Argentine Democracy: The Politics of Institutional Weakness*, 21–44. University Park: Pennsylvania State University Press.

Levitsky, Steven, and Kenneth Roberts, eds. 2011. *The Resurgence of the Latin American Left*. Baltimore, MD: Johns Hopkins University Press.

Levitsky, Steven, and Lucan Way. 2010. *Competitive Authoritarianism*. Cambridge: Cambridge University Press.

Levitsky, Steven, and Daniel Ziblatt. 2018. *How Democracies Die*. New York: Crown Publishers.

Lieberman, Robert, Suzanne Mettler, Thomas Pepinsky, Kenneth Roberts, and Richard Valelly. 2019. The Trump Presidency and American Democracy. *Perspectives on Politics* 17:2 (June): 470–79.

Lieberman, Robert, Suzanne Mettler, and Kenneth Roberts, eds. 2022. *Democratic Resilience: Can the United States Withstand Rising Polarization?* Cambridge: Cambridge University Press.

Lijphart, Arend. 1999. *Patterns of Democracy*. New Haven, CT: Yale University Press.

Lim, Joseph. 2002. The Detrimental Role of Biased Policies. In Amando Doronila, ed. *Between Fires: Fifteen Perspectives on the Estrada Crisis*, 113–47. Pasig City: Anvil Publishing.

Linz, Juan. 1990. The Perils of Presidentialism. *Journal of Democracy* 1:1 (Winter): 51–69.

1978. *Breakdown of Democratic Regimes: Crisis, Breakdown and Reequilibration*. Baltimore, MD: Johns Hopkins University Press.

Linz, Juan, and Arturo Valenzuela, eds. 1994. *The Failure of Presidential Democracy*. Baltimore, MD: Johns Hopkins University Press.

Llach, Juan. 1997. *Otro siglo, otra Argentina*. Buenos Aires: Ariel.

Llanos, Mariana, and Leiv Marsteintredet. 2010. Ruptura y continuidad: La caída de "Mel" Zelaya en perspectiva comparada. *America Latina Hoy: Revista de Ciencias Sociales* 55: 173–97.

López Bayona, Álvaro. 2016. El Uribismo y su carácter populista. *Virajes: Revista de Sociología y Antropología* 18:1 (January-June): 87–107.

López-Maya, Margarita. 2011. Venezuela: Hugo Chávez and the Populist Left. In Steven Levitsky and Kenneth Roberts, eds. *The Resurgence of the Latin American Left*, 213–38. Baltimore, MD: Johns Hopkins University Press.

2009. Venezuela: Ascenso y gobierno de Hugo Chávez y sus fuerzas bolivarianas. In Julio Aibar and Daniel Vázquez, eds. *¿Autoritarismo o democracia? Hugo Chávez y Evo Morales*, 19–58. Tlalpan, Mexico: FLACSO.

López-Maya, Margarita, and Alexandra Panzarelli. 2013. Populism, Rentierism, and Socialism in the Twenty-First Century: The Case of Venezuela. In Carlos de la

Torre and Cynthia Arnson, eds. *Latin American Populism in the Twenty-First Century*, 239–68. Washington, DC: Woodrow Wilson Center Press.

Lorenz, Astrid. 2005. How to Measure Constitutional Rigidity. *Journal of Theoretical Politics* 17:3 (July): 339–61.

Los ultra K quieren reformar la Constitución para tener una "Cristina eterna." 2011. *Clarín* (28 February).

Lowande, Kenneth, and Jon Rogowski. 2021. Executive Power in Crisis. *American Political Science Review* 115:4 (November): 1406–23.

Lowndes, Joseph. 2022. The Political Creativity of the Populist Right. Paper for conference on "Still the Age of Populism?" University of Florida, April 22–23.

  2017. Populism in the United States. In Cristóbal Rovira Kaltwasser, Paul Taggart, et al., eds. *Oxford Handbook of Populism*, 232–47. Oxford: Oxford University Press.

Lust, Jan. 2016. Social Struggle and the Political Economy of Natural Resource Extraction in Peru. *Critical Sociology* 42:2 (March): 195–210.

Lutz, Donald. 1994. Toward a Theory of Constitutional Amendment. *American Political Science Review* 88:2 (June): 355–70.

Madrid, Raúl. 2012. *The Rise of Ethnic Politics in Latin America*. Cambridge: Cambridge University Press.

Madrid, Raúl, and Kurt Weyland. 2019. Conclusion. In Kurt Weyland and Raúl Madrid, eds. *When Democracy Trumps Populism*, 154–86. Cambridge: Cambridge University Press.

Mahoney, James, and Kathleen Thelen. 2010. A Theory of Gradual Institutional Change. In James Mahoney and Kathleen Thelen, eds. *Explaining Institutional Change*, 1–37. Cambridge: Cambridge University Press.

Mainwaring, Scott. 2018. Party System Institutionalization in Contemporary Latin America. In Scott Mainwaring, ed. *Party Systems in Latin America*, 34–70. Cambridge: Cambridge University Press.

  1999. *Rethinking Party Systems in the Third Wave of Democratization: The Case of Brazil*. Stanford, CA: Stanford University Press.

Mainwaring, Scott, and Timothy Scully. 1995. Introduction: Party Systems in Latin America. In Mainwaring and Scully, eds. *Building Democratic Institutions*, 1–34. Stanford, CA: Stanford University Press.

Mainwaring, Scott, and Matthew Shugart, eds. 1997. *Presidentialism and Democracy in Latin America*. Cambridge: Cambridge University Press.

Malzahn, Janet, and Andrew Hall. 2023. Election-Denying Republican Candidates Underperformed in the 2022 Midterms. Ms. Stanford University.

Marona, Marjorie, and Lucas Magalhães. 2021. Guerra e Paz? O Supremo Tribunal Federal nos dois primeiros anos do Governo Bolsonaro. In Leonardo Avritzer, Fábio Kerche, and Marjorie Marona, eds. *Governo Bolsonaro*, 121–33. Belo Horizonte: Autêntica.

Marsteintredet, Leiv, Mariana Llanos, and Detlef Nolte. 2013. Paraguay and the Politics of Impeachment. *Journal of Democracy* 24:4 (October): 110–23.

Masek, Vaclav, and Luis Aguasvivas. 2021. Consolidando el poder en El Salvador: El caso de Nayib Bukele. *Ecuador Debate* 112 (April): 157–73.

Mason, Lilliana, and Nathan Kalmoe. 2022. The Social Roots, Risks, and Rewards of Mass Polarization. In Robert Lieberman, Suzanne Mettler, and Kenneth Roberts, eds. *Democratic Resilience: Can the United States Withstand Rising Polarization?* 171–94. Cambridge: Cambridge University Press.

Mason, Lilliana, Julie Wronski, and John Kane. 2021. Activating Animus: The Unique Social Roots of Trump Support. *American Political Science Review* 115:4 (November): 1508–16.

Mate, Manoj. 2018. Constitutional Erosion and the Challenge to Secular Democracy in India. In Mark Graber, Sanford Levinson, and Mark Tushnet, eds. *Constitutional Democracy in Crisis?* 377–94. Oxford: Oxford University Press.

Matovski, Aleksandar. 2021. *Popular Dictatorships: Crises, Mass Opinion, and the Rise of Electoral Authoritarianism.* Cambridge: Cambridge University Press.

Matthes, Claudia. 2021. Safeguarding Democracy and the Rule of Law by Civil Society Actors? The Case of Poland. In Astrid Lorenz and Lisa Anders, eds. *Illiberal Trends and Anti-EU Politics in East Central Europe,* 263–80. Cham: Palgrave Macmillan.

Mauceri, Philip. 2006. An Authoritarian Presidency. In Julio Carrión, ed. *The Fujimori Legacy,* 39–60. University Park: Pennsylvania State University Press.

  1995. State Reform, Coalitions, and the Neoliberal *Autogolpe* in Peru. *Latin American Research Review* 30:1: 7–37.

  1991. Military Politics and Counter-Insurgency in Peru. *Journal of Interamerican Studies and World Affairs* 33:4 (Winter): 83–109.

Mayka, Lindsay. 2016. Delegative Democracy Revisited. *Journal of Democracy* 27:3 (July): 139–47.

Mayorga, Fernando. 2009. El proyecto político del MAS. In Julio Aibar and Daniel Vázquez, eds. *"Autoritarismo o democracia" Hugo Chávez y Evo Morales,* 171–218. Tlalpan, Mexico: FLACSO.

Mayorga, René. 1997. Bolivia's Silent Revolution. *Journal of Democracy* 8:1 (January): 142–56.

Mazzolini, Samuele, and Arthur Borriello. 2022. The Normalization of Left Populism? The Paradigmatic Case of Podemos. *European Politics and Society* 23:3 (May): 285–300.

McAdams, James. 2017. *Vanguard of the Revolution: The Global Idea of the Communist Party.* Princeton, NJ: Princeton University Press.

McCargo, Duncan, and Ukrist Pathmanand. (2005) 2010. *The Thaksinization of Thailand.* Copenhagen: Nordic Institute of Asian Studies Press.

McCarty, Nolan. 2021. Polarization and the Changing American Constitutional System. In Eric Patashnik and Wendy Schiller, eds. *Dynamics of American Democracy,* 112–38. Lawrence: University Press of Kansas.

McCauley, Clark. 2021. Putting the Capitol Breach in Context. *Dynamics of Asymmetric Conflict* 14:2 (June): 94–109.

McClintock, Cynthia. 2013. Populism in Peru. In Carlos de la Torre and Cynthia Arnson, eds. *Latin American Populism in the Twenty-First Century,* 203–37. Washington, DC: Woodrow Wilson Center Press.

  1989. The Prospects for Democratic Consolidation in a "Least Likely" Case: Peru. *Comparative Politics* 21:2 (January): 127–48.

McCoy, Jennifer, and Murat Somer. 2022. Pernicious Polarization and Democratic Resilience. In Robert Lieberman, Suzanne Mettler, and Kenneth Roberts, eds. *Democratic Resilience: Can the United States Withstand Rising Polarization?* 61–92. Cambridge: Cambridge University Press.

  2019. Toward a Theory of Pernicious Polarization and How It Harms Democracies. *Annals of the American Academy for Political and Social Science* 681 (January): 234–71.

McDermott, Rose. 2004. *Political Psychology in International Relations*. Ann Arbor: University of Michigan Press.

McDonnell, Duncan, and Luis Cabrera. 2019. The Right-Wing Populism of India's Bharatiya Janata Party (and Why Comparativists Should Care). *Democratization* 26:3 (April): 484–501.

McGuire, James. 1997. *Peronism without Perón*. Stanford, CA: Stanford University Press.

McKay, Ben, and Gonzalo Colque. 2021. Populism and Its Authoritarian Tendencies: The Politics of Division in Bolivia. *Latin American Perspectives*, forthcoming.

McNelly, Angus. 2021. The Uncertain Future of Bolivia's Movement toward Socialism. *New Labor Forum* 30:2 (May): 81–89.

Mebane, Walter. 2019. *Evidence against Fraudulent Votes Being Decisive in the Bolivia 2019 Election*. Ann Arbor: University of Michigan, Department of Political Science.

Mehlum, Halvor, Karl Moene, and Ragnar Torvik. 2006. Institutions and the Resource Curse. *Economic Journal* 116:508 (January): 1–20.

Mejía Acosta, Andrés, María Araujo, Aníbal Pérez-Liñán, and Sebastián Saiegh. 2008. Veto Players, Fickle Institutions, and Low-Quality Policies: The Policymaking Process in Ecuador. In Eduardo Stein and Mariano Tommasi, eds. *Policymaking in Latin America*, 243–85. Washington, DC: Inter-American Development Bank.

Mejía Acosta, Andrés, and John Polga-Hecimovich. 2011. Coalition Erosion and Presidential Instability in Ecuador. *Latin American Politics and Society* 53:2 (Summer): 87–111.

Meléndez-Sánchez, Manuel. 2021a. Millennial Authoritarianism in El Salvador. *Journal of Democracy* 32:3 (July): 19–32.

2021b. *Political Institutions in El Salvador, 2014-Present*. Harvard University, Department of Government.

Meléndez-Sánchez, Manuel, and Steven Levitsky. 2021. El Salvador's President Launched a "Self-Coup." *Washington Post* (20 May). <www.washingtonpost.com/politics/2021/05/20/el-salvadors-president-launched-self-coup-watch-creeping-corruption-authoritarianism/, accessed 23 June 2022>.

Melo, Carlos. 2021. A Câmara dos Deputados pós-2018. In Leonardo Avritzer, Fábio Kerche, and Marjorie Marona, eds. *Governo Bolsonaro*, 95–109. Belo Horizonte: Autêntica.

Méndez Ortiz, Heinz. 2017. La presidencia de Abdalá Bucaram y su incidencia en la inestabilidad política del Ecuador. Quito: Universidad Central del Ecuador. Tesis de Licenciatura en Ciencias de la Educación.

Meneguello, Rachel. 2021. Opinião pública em um governo de risco e contrassenso. In Leonardo Avritzer, Fábio Kerche, and Marjorie Marona, eds. *Governo Bolsonaro*, 495–506. Belo Horizonte: Autêntica.

Mesežnikov, Grigorij, and Ol'ga Gyárfášová. 2018. Slovakia's Conflicting Camps. *Journal of Democracy* 29:3 (July): 78–90.

Metcalf, Lee. 1998. The Evolution of Presidential Power in Estonia. *Journal of Baltic Studies* 29:4 (Winter): 333–52.

Mettler, Suzanne, and Robert Lieberman. 2020. *Four Threats: The Recurring Crises of American Democracy*. New York: St. Martin's.

Metz, Rudolf, and Réka Várnagy. 2021. "Mass," "Movement," "Personal," or "Cartel" Party? Fidesz's Hybrid Organisational Strategy. *Politics and Governance* 9:4 (December): 317–28.

Mexico: Power Struggles in Judiciary. 2021. *Latin American Weekly Report* WR-21-32 (12 August): 11–12.

Mexico Election Outcome Forces Recall Referendum Rethink – Analyst. 2021. *BNAmericas* (9 June) <www.bnamericas.com/en/news/mexico-election-outcome-forces-recall-referendum-rethink--analyst, accessed 29 October 2021>.

Mexico's Populist President: The Puritan from Tepetitán. 2021. *Economist* (29 May): 18–20.

Meyer, Brett. 2021. *A Playbook against Populism? Populist Leadership in Decline in 2021.* Washington, DC: Tony Blair Institute for Global Change.

Meyer, David, and Sidney Tarrow, eds. 2018. *The Resistance: The Dawn of the Anti-Trump Opposition Movement.* Oxford: Oxford University Press.

Miller, Gary, and Norman Schofield. 2008. The Transformation of the Republican and Democratic Party Coalitions in the U.S. *Perspectives on Politics* 6:3 (September): 433–50.

2003. Activists and Partisan Realignment in the United States. *American Political Science Review* 97:2 (May): 245–60.

Miranda, Danilo. 2021. Nayib Bukele: "El Estado soy yo". *Envío* 40:468 (March): 1–11.

Mitra, Subrata. 2020. For India, "Middle" Democracy Works. *Global Asia* 15:1 (March): 36–41.

Mizuno, Kosuke, and Pasuk Phongpaichit. 2009. Introduction. In Kosuke Mizuno and Pasuk Phongpaichit, eds., *Populism in Asia*, 1–17. Singapore: National University of Singapore Press.

Moallic, Benjamin. 2022. État d'exception: Que se passe-t-il au Salvador? *Amérique Latine* 1:1 (November): 143–57.

2020. El Salvador: La Révolution Introuvable. *Problèmes d'Amérique Latine* 116:1 (January): 103–25.

Moffitt, Benjamin. 2016. *The Global Rise of Populism.* Stanford: Stanford University Press.

Montúfar, César. 2013. Rafael Correa and his Plebiscitary Citizens' Revolution. In Carlos de la Torre and Cynthia Arnson, eds. *Latin American Populism in the Twenty-First Century*, 295–321. Washington, DC: Woodrow Wilson Center Press.

2006. *Lucio Gutiérrez y el fracaso de un proyecto autoritario.* Quito: Universidad Andina Simón Bolívar.

1997. Las contradicciones de la convertibilidad. *Íconos* 1 (February): 20–32.

Mora y Araujo, Manuel. 2011. *La Argentina bipolar: Los vaivenes de la opinión pública (1983–2011).* Buenos Aires: Sudamericana.

Morales Solá, Joaquín. 2007. La decision se tomó: Cristina Kirchner será la candidata. *La Nación* (9 May).

Morgan, Jana. 2018. Deterioration and Polarization of Party Politics in Venezuela. In Scott Mainwaring, ed. *Party Systems in Latin America*, 291–325. Cambridge: Cambridge University Press.

Mounk, Yascha. 2018. *The People vs. Democracy.* Cambridge, MA: Harvard University Press.

Mouzelis, Nicos. 1985. On the Concept of Populism. *Politics & Society* 14:3 (September): 329–48.

Mudde, Cas. 2017. Populism: An Ideational Approach. In Cristóbal Rovira Kaltwasser, Paul Taggart, et al., eds. 2017. *Oxford Handbook of Populism*, 27–47. Oxford: Oxford University Press.

Mudde, Cas, and Cristóbal Rovira Kaltwasser. 2017. *Populism: A Very Short Introduction.* Oxford: Oxford University Press.

———. 2013. Exclusionary vs. Inclusionary Populism: Comparing Contemporary Europe and Latin America. *Government and Opposition* 48:2 (April): 147–74.

Müller, Jan-Werner. 2016. *What Is Populism?* Philadelphia: University of Pennsylvania Press.

Mungiu-Pippidi, Alina. 2018. Romania's Italian-Style Anticorruption Populism. *Journal of Democracy* 29:3 (July): 104–16.

Muñoz, Paula. 2021. Peru Goes Populist. *Journal of Democracy* 32:3 (July): 48–62.

Muñoz, Paula, and Yamilé Guibert. 2016. Perú: El fin del optimismo. *Revista de Ciencia Política* 36:1 (April): 313–38.

Murakami, Yusuke. 2012. *Perú en la era del Chino*, 2nd ed. Lima: Instituto de Estudios Peruanos.

Murillo, María Victoria, and Rodrigo Zarazaga. 2020. Argentina: Peronism Returns. *Journal of Democracy* 31:2 (April): 125–36.

Murillo Ramírez, Óscar. 2012. "Oro y agua:" Dilemas y giros políticos de Ollanta Humala. *Nueva Sociedad* 240 (July–August): 4–15.

Murphy, Matt. 2022. Janez Jansa: Slovenia Votes Out Pro-Trump Populist. *BBC News* (25 April).

Navarrete Vela, Juan Pablo, Omar Camacho Sánchez, and Manuel Ceja García. 2017. Formación, liderazgo y desempeño electoral de MORENA. *Revista Mexicana de Estudios Electorales* 18 (July–December): 11–60.

Nayib Bukele consolida su poder con una victoria sin precedentes en El Salvador. 2021. *El País* (1 March).

Negretto, Gabriel. 2013. *Making Constitutions: Presidents, Parties, and Institutional Choice in Latin America.* Cambridge: Cambridge University Press.

Nelson, Michael. 2018. *Trump's First Year.* Charlottesville: University of Virginia Press.

Nemčok, Miroslav, and Peter Spáč. 2020. The Rise and Sustainability of Party Leaders in Slovakia: Robert Fico and Mikuláš Dzurinda. In Sergiu Gherghina, ed. *Party Leaders in Eastern Europe*, 241–64. Cham: Palgrave Macmillan.

Nesbet-Montesinos, Felipe. 2011. Humala antes de Ollanta: Evolución política del nuevo presidente peruano. *European Review of Latin American and Caribbean Studies* 91 (October): 81–90.

Neundorf, Anja, and Sergi Pardos-Prado. 2022. The Impact of COVID-19 on Trump's Electoral Demise. *Perspectives on Politics* 20:1 (March): 170–86.

Neuwahl, Nanette, and Charles Kovcs. 2021. Hungary and the EU's Rule of Law Protection. *Journal of European Integration* 43:1 (January): 17–32.

Newell, James. 2019. *Silvio Berlusconi: A Study in Failure.* Manchester, UK: Manchester University Press.

Newman, John. 2020. The OAS Conclusions about the Election Integrity of the Bolivian Election are Correct. Annapolis, MD: Kenact LLC.

Nič, Milan. 2020. Slovakia's 2020 Elections. DGAP Commentary 6 (February). Berlin: Forschungsinstitut der Deutschen Gesellschaft für Auswärtige Politik.

Nicas, Jack. 2023. Is Brazil's Ombudsman of Democracy Actually Good for Democracy? *New York Times* (January 22): 7.

Nilsson, Martin. 2022. Nayib Bukele: Populism and Autocratization? *Journal of Geography, Politics and Society* 12:2 (June): 16–26.

Nooruddin, Irfan. 2020. *Comment on the 2019 Bolivia Presidential Election and OAS Statistical Analysis*. Washington, DC: Georgetown University, School of Foreign Service.

Novaro, Marcos. 2009. *Argentina en el fin del siglo: Democracia, mercado y nación*. Buenos Aires: Paidós.

1998. Populismo y gobierno: Las transformaciones en el Peronismo y la consolidación democrática en Argentina. In Felipe Burbano de Lara, ed. *El fantasma del populismo*, 25–48. Caracas: Nueva Sociedad.

OAS (Organization of American States). 2019a. *Electoral Integrity Analysis: General Elections in the Plurinational State of Bolivia, October 20, 2019. Final Report*. Washington, DC: OAS.

2019b. *Electoral Integrity Analysis: General Elections in the Plurinational State of Bolivia, October 20, 2019. Preliminary Findings: Report to the General Secretariat*. Washington, DC: OAS.

O'Donnell, Guillermo, and Philippe Schmitter. 1986. *Tentative Conclusions about Uncertain Democracies*. Baltimore: Johns Hopkins University Press.

Öniş, Ziya. 2016. Turkey's Two Elections. *Journal of Democracy* 27:2 (April): 141–54.

2015. Monopolising the Centre: The AKP and the Uncertain Path of Turkish Democracy. *International Spectator* 50:2 (June): 22–41.

Özel, Soli. 2003. Turkey at the Polls. *Journal of Democracy* 14:2 (April): 80–94.

Offe, Claus. 1991. Capitalism by Democratic Design? Democratic Theory Facing the Triple Transition in East Central Europe. *Social Research* 58:4 (Winter): 865–92.

Oliver, Eric, and Wendy Rahn. 2016. Rise of the *Trumpenvolk*: Populism in the 2016 Election. *Annals of the American Academy for Political and Social Science* 667 (September): 189–206.

Ollier, María. 2015. El ciclo de las presidencias dominantes: Néstor y Cristina Kirchner (2003–2013). In Carlos Gervasoni and Enrique Peruzzotti, eds. *"Década Ganada" Evaluando el legado del Kirchnerismo*, 61–87. Buenos Aires: Debate.

Olsen, Orjan. 2022. Tendência dos Votos para Presidente no Brasil desde 1998. Ms. São Paulo: Analítica Consultoria (November).

Ortuño Yáñez, Armando. 2020. Movilizados, satisfechos e indiferentes: Maneras de vivir la crisis. In Fernando Mayorga, ed. *Crisis y cambio político en Bolivia*, 61–77. La Paz: CESU-UMSS (Centro de Estudios Superiores Universitarios de la Universidad Mayor de San Simón).

Osorio, María. 2012. *Primer mandato presidencial de Uribe Vélez*. Quito: Universidad Andina Simón Bolívar.

Ospina Peralta, Pablo. 2021. The Right Turn as a Process, not an Assault: The Ecuadorian Case, 2007–2019. In Gisela Pereyra Doval and Gastón Souroujon, eds. *Global Resurgence of the Right*, 235–54. London: Routledge.

Ostiguy, Pierre. 2017. Populism: A Socio-Cultural Approach. In Cristóbal Rovira Kaltwasser, Paul Taggart, et al., eds. *Oxford Handbook of Populism*, 73–97. Oxford: Oxford University Press.

Ostiguy, Pierre, and Kenneth Roberts. 2016. Putting Trump in Comparative Perspective: Populism and the Politicization of the Sociocultural Low. *Brown Journal of World Affairs* 23:1 (Fall–Winter): 25–50.

Otake, Hideo. 2009. Neoliberal Populism in Japanese Politics. In Kosuke Mizuno and Pasuk Phongpaichit, eds., *Populism in Asia*, 202–16. Singapore: National University of Singapore Press.

Pachano, Simón. 2005. Ecuador: Cuando la inestabilidad se yuelve estable. *Íconos* 23 (September): 39–46.

1997. Democracia a la medida. *Íconos* 1 (February): 7–13.

Pakulski, Jan. 2016. Crumbling Elite Consensus and the Illiberal Turn in Poland. In Jan Pakulski, ed. *The Visegrad Countries in Crisis*, 51–86. Warsaw: Collegium Civitas.

Palabrica, Raul. 2002. The Road to Impeachment and Ouster Was Short and Bumpy. In Amando Doronila, ed. *Between Fires: Fifteen Perspectives on the Estrada Crisis*, 227–35. Pasig City: Anvil Publishing.

Palata, Luboš. 2023. Tschechische Präsidentschaftswahl: Aufwind für den "tschechischen Orban"? *Deutsche Welle* (10 January).

Paldam, Martin. 2021. Measuring Democracy – Eight Indices. Aarhus: Aarhus University, Department of Economics. Working Paper 2021-10.

Palermo, Vicente, and Marcos Novaro. 1996. *Política y poder en la Argentina de Menem*. Buenos Aires: Norma.

Panetta, Grace. 2021. Defending Democracy during a Pandemic. In Larry Sabato, Kyle Kondik, and Miles Coleman, eds. *A Return to Normalcy? The 2020 Elections that (Almost) Broke America*, 185–202. Lanham, MD: Rowman & Littlefield.

Pappas, Takis. 2020. The Pushback Against Populism: The Rise and Fall of Greece's New Illiberalism. *Journal of Democracy* 31:2 (April): 54–68.

2019. *Populism and Liberal Democracy*. Oxford: Oxford University Press.

Parker, Christopher, and Matt Barreto. 2022. The Great White Hope: Threat and Racial Resilience in Trump's America. In Robert Lieberman, Suzanne Mettler, and Kenneth Roberts, eds. *Democratic Resilience: Can the United States Withstand Rising Polarization?* 195–225. Cambridge: Cambridge University Press.

Parton, Heather. 2022. GOP Leaders: Trapped between "Legitimate Political Discourse" and the Trumpian Abyss. *Salon* (February 9). <www.salon.com/2022/02/09/leaders-trapped-between-legitimate-political-discourse-and-the-trumpian-abyss/, accessed 9 February 2022>.

Pasquino, Gianfranco. 2021. The Right in Italy. In Gisela Pereyra Doval and Gastón Souroujon, eds. *Global Resurgence of the Right*, 161–72. London: Routledge.

2007. The Five Faces of Silvio Berlusconi. *Modern Italy* 12:1 (February): 39–54.

Paul, Max. 2022. Who Desires Authoritarian Leadership in the Latin America and Caribbean Region? Nashville, TN: Vanderbilt University. LAPOP. Insights Series # 155 (November).

Peabody, Bruce. 2018. The Curious Incident of Trump and the Courts. *British Journal of American Legal Studies* 7:2 (Fall): 237–56.

Pearson, Andy, Andrea Prado, and Forrest Colburn. 2021. The Puzzle of COVID-19 in Central America and Panama. *Journal of Global Health* 11:03077 (June): 1–7.

Pécaut, Daniel. 2003. *Midiendo fuerzas: Balance del primer año del gobierno de Álvaro Uribe Vélez*. Bogotá: Planeta.

Pehe, Jiri. 1991. Political Conflict in Slovakia. *Radio Free Europe Radio Liberty – Report on Eastern Europe* 10 (10 May): 1–6.

Pelke, Lars, and Aurel Croissant. 2021. Conceptualizing and Measuring Autocratization Episodes. *Swiss Political Science Review* 27:2 (June): 434–48.

Penski, Victoria. 2018. Why Are Violent Non-State Actors Able to Persist in the Context of the Modern State? The Case of the Maras in the Northern Triangle. *Journal of Intelligence, Conflict and Warfare* 1:1 (June): 1–23.

Perelló, Lucas, and Patricio Navia. 2022. The Disruption of an Institutionalised and Polarised Party System: Discontent with Democracy and the Rise of Nayib Bukele in El Salvador. *Politics* 42:3 (August): 267–88.

Pereyra Doval, Gisela. 2021. Bolsonaro in Brazil. In Gisela Pereyra Doval and Gastón Souroujon, eds. *Global Resurgence of the Right*, 214–34. London: Routledge.

Pérez-Liñán, Aníbal. 2007. *Presidential Impeachment and the New Political Instability in Latin America*. Cambridge: Cambridge University Press.

Peru: A Country Tearing Itself Apart. 2023. *Economist* (4 February): 27–28.

Peru: Jobs for the Comrades. 2021. *Economist* (23 October): 34–35.

Petersen, German, and Fernanda Somuano. 2021. Mexican De-Democratization? *Revista de Ciencia Política* 41:2 (August): 353–76.

Petőcz, György. 2015. Milla: A Suspended Experiment. In Péter Krasztev and Jon Van Til, eds. *The Hungarian Patient*, 207–29. Budapest: Central European University Press.

Petrović, Miloš, and Zlatan Jeremić. 2021. Damaging Effects of Vaccine Geopolitics and the EU's Distorted Soft Power. *Medjunarodni problemi* 73:4 (December): 709–35.

Petrović, Valentina. 2020. Threats to Democracy: Measures Taken by Right–Wing Populist Regimes during the Covid-19 Crisis in Eastern Europe. *Političe Perspektive* 10:2–3: 51–67.

Philips, David. 2017. *An Uncertain Ally: Turkey under Erdogan's Dictatorship*. London: Routledge.

Phongpaichit, Pasuk, and Chris Baker. 2009. *Thaksin*, 2nd ed. Chiang Mai: Silkworm Books.

2008. Thaksin's Populism. *Journal of Contemporary Asia* 38:1 (February): 62–83.

Pierson, Paul. 2017. American Hybrid: Donald Trump and the Strange Merger of Populism and Plutocracy. *British Journal of Sociology* 68:S1 (November): S105–19.

2000. Increasing Returns, Path Dependence, and the Study of Politics. *American Political Science Review* 94:2 (June): 251–67.

Pierson, Paul, and Eric Schickler. 2022. Polarization and the Durability of Madisonian Checks and Balances. In Robert Lieberman, Suzanne Mettler, and Kenneth Roberts, eds. *Democratic Resilience: Can the United States Withstand Rising Polarization?* 35–60. Cambridge: Cambridge University Press.

2020. Madison's Constitution Under Stress: A Developmental Approach to Political Polarization. *Annual Review of Political Science* 23: 37–58.

Pion-Berlin, David, Thomas Bruneau, and Richard Goetze Jr. 2022. The Trump Self-Coup Attempt. *Government and Opposition*, forthcoming.

Pirro, Andrea, and Ben Stanley. 2022. Forging, Bending, and Breaking: Enacting the "Illiberal Playbook" in Hungary and Poland. *Perspectives on Politics* 20:1 (March): 86–101.

PNP (Partido Nacionalista Peruano). 2011. Propuesta Nacionalista: "Afirmar la Nación, Transformar el Estado." Lima: PNP.

Polga-Hecimovich, John. 2020. *Ecuadorian Military Culture 2019*. Miami: Florida International University, Steven J. Green School of International & Public Affairs.

2013. Ecuador: Estabilidad institucional y la consolidación de poder de Rafael Correa. *Revista de Ciencia Política* 33:1 (April): 135–60.

Polga-Hecimovich, John, and Francisco Sánchez. 2021. Ecuador's Return to the Past. *Journal of Democracy* 32:3 (July): 5–18.

Pongsudhirak, Thitinan. 2003. Democratic Authoritarianism. *Southeast Asian Affairs* 6:1: 277–290.

Prasirtsuk, Kitti. 2015. Thailand in 2014: Another Coup, a Different Coup? *Asian Survey* 55:1 (January-February): 200–06.

Protests in Hungary. 2019. *Economist* (22 November): 46–47.

Przeworski, Adam. 2019. *Crises of Democracy.* Cambridge: Cambridge University Press.

1991. *Democracy and the Market.* Cambridge: Cambridge University Press.

Przeworski, Adam, and Henry Teune. (1970) 1982. *The Logic of Comparative Social Inquiry.* Malabar, FL: Krieger.

Putnam, Lara, and Theda Skocpol. 2018. Middle America Reboots Democracy. *Democracy: A Journal of Ideas* (20 February). <https://democracyjournal.org/arguments/middle-america-reboots-democracy/>

Pytlas, Bartek. 2021. Party Organisation of PiS in Poland. *Politics and Governance* 9:4 (November): 340–53.

Ragin, Charles. 2000. *Fuzzy-Set Social Science.* Chicago, IL: University of Chicago Press.

1987. *The Comparative Method.* Berkeley: University of California Press.

Ranis, Peter. 1995. *Class, Democracy, and Labor in Argentina.* New Brunswick: Transaction.

Rathbone, John. 2011. Mood of Cautious Optimism Takes Hold. *Financial Times, Special Report: Investing in Peru* (September 21): 1.

Razing Arizona. 2021. *Economist* (July 3): 29–34.

Reading into Mexico's Recall Result. 2022. *Latin American Weekly Report* WR-22–15 (14 April): 1–3.

Rebossio, Alejandro. 2010. Kirchner toma con la policía el control del Banco Central. *El País* (January 26) <https://elpais.com/diario/2010/01/26/economia/126446 0408_850215.html, accessed 28 February 2022>.

Reyna, José, and Richard Weinert, eds. 1977. *Authoritarianism in Mexico.* Philadelphia, PA: Institute for the Study of Human Issues.

Rhodes-Purdy, Matthew, and Raúl L. Madrid. 2020. The Perils of Personalism. *Democratization* 27:2 (February): 321–39.

Ribeiro, Guilherme. 2020. A ilusão de Paschoal ou: Cinco efeitos negativos do impeachment de Jair Bolsonaro para a esquerda e para a democracia no Brasil. *Espaço e Economia* 9:18 (May): 1–13.

Ribeiro, Ludmila, and Valeria Oliveira. 2021. "Eu quero que o povo se arme:" A política de segurança pública de Bolsonaro. In Leonardo Avritzer, Fábio Kerche, and Marjorie Marona, eds. *Governo Bolsonaro*, 327–41. Belo Horizonte: Autêntica.

Riegert, Bernd. 2022. Die EU hält zwölf Milliarden im Streit mit Ungarn zurück. *Deutsche Welle* (13 December).

Rivas Molina, Federico. 2023. Javier Milei, el candidato libertario que capitaliza el descontento en Argentina. *El País* (20 March).

Rivera León, Mauro. 2017. Understanding Constitutional Amendments in Mexico. *Mexican Law Review* 9:2 (January–June): 3–27.

Roberts, Kenneth. 2022. Performing Crisis? Trump, Populism and the GOP in the Age of COVID-19. *Government and Opposition,* forthcoming.

2019. Parties, Populism, and Democratic Decay: A Comparative Perspective on Political Polarization in the United States. In Kurt Weyland and Raúl Madrid, eds. *When Democracy Trumps Populism*, 132–53. Cambridge: Cambridge University Press.

2014. *Changing Course in Latin America*. Cambridge: Cambridge University Press.

2006. Populism, Political Conflict, and Grass-Roots Organization in Latin America. *Comparative Politics* 38:2 (January): 127–48.

1995. Neoliberalism and the Transformation of Populism in Latin America: The Peruvian Case. *World Politics* 48:1 (October): 82–116.

Rocamora, Joel. 2009. Estrada and the Populist Temptation in the Philippines. In Kosuke Mizuno and Pasuk Phongpaichit, eds., *Populism in Asia*, 41–65. Singapore: National University of Singapore Press.

Rocco, Philip. 2022. Laboratories of What? American Federalism and the Politics of Democratic Subversion. In Robert Lieberman, Suzanne Mettler, and Kenneth Roberts, eds. *Democratic Resilience: Can the United States Withstand Rising Polarization?* 297–319. Cambridge: Cambridge University Press.

Rodríguez, Francisco. 2008. An Empty Revolution: The Unfulfilled Promises of Hugo Chávez. *Foreign Affairs* 87:2 (March–April): 49–62.

Rojas Ortuste, Gonzalo. 2009. Trayectoria del proceso político boliviano. In Julio Aibar and Daniel Vázquez, eds. *"Autoritarismo o democracia" Hugo Chávez y Evo Morales*, 219–55. Tlalpan, Mexico: FLACSO.

Roque Baldovinos, Ricardo. 2021. Nayib Bukele: Populismo e implosión democrática en El Salvador. *Andamios: Revista de Investigación Social* 18:46 (May–August): 231–53.

Rori, Lamprini. 2020. The 2019 Greek Parliamentary Election. *West European Politics* 43:4 (June): 1023–37.

Rosanvallon, Pierre. 2020. *Le Siècle du Populisme*. Paris: Seuil.

Rosen, Jonathan. 2021. Understanding Support for Tough-on-Crime Policies in Latin America. *Latin American Policy* 12: 116–31.

Rosen, Jonathan, Sebastián Cutrona, and Katy Lindquist. 2022. Gangs, Violence, and Fear: Punitive Darwinism in El Salvador. *Crime, Law and Social Change*, forthcoming.

Rosenfeld, Gavriel. 2019. An American Führer? *Central European History* 52:4 (December): 554–87.

Rospigliosi, Fernando. 1992. Las elecciones peruanas de 1990. In Instituto Interamericano de Derechos Humanos (IIDH), ed. *Una tarea inconclusa*, 345–88. San José, Costa Rica: IIDH.

Ross, Michael. 2015. What Have We Learned about the Resource Curse? *Annual Review of Political Science* 18: 239–259.

2012. *The Oil Curse*. Princeton, NJ: Princeton University Press.

Rossi, Michael. 2020. Slovakia after Fico. *Politologický Časopis – Czech Journal of Political Science* 27:3 (October): 235–58.

Rovira Kaltwasser, Cristóbal. 2019. Dealing with Populism in Latin America. In Kurt Weyland and Raúl Madrid, eds. *When Democracy Trumps Populism: European and Latin American Lessons for the U.S.*, 35–59. Cambridge: Cambridge University Press.

Rovira Kaltwasser, Cristóbal, Paul Taggart, et al., eds. 2017. *Oxford Handbook of Populism*. Oxford: Oxford University Press.

Rowland, Robert. 2021. *The Rhetoric of Donald Trump*. Lawrence: University Press of Kansas.

Ruhl, Mark. 2010. Honduras Unravels. *Journal of Democracy* 21:2 (April): 93–107.

Rule of Law in Poland: Judgment Call. 2023. *Economist* (18 February): 48–49.

Ruth, Saskia, and Kirk Hawkins. 2017. Populism and Democratic Representation in Latin America. In Reinhard Heinisch, Christina Holtz-Bacha, and Oscar Mazzoleni, eds. *Political Populism: A Handbook*, 255–73. Baden-Baden: Nomos.

Ruth-Lovell, Saskia, Anna Lührmann, and Sandra Grahn. 2019. *Democracy and Populism*. Gothenburg: Varieties of Democracy Institute. Working paper 2019:91.

Rutledge, Paul, and Chapman Rackaway. 2021. Conclusion: The Unorthodox Presidency. In Paul Rutledge and Chapman Rackaway, eds. *The Unorthodox Presidency of Donald J. Trump*, 365–83. Lawrence: University Press of Kansas.

Rybář, Marek, and Peter Spáč. 2017. The March 2016 Parliamentary Elections in Slovakia. *Electoral Studies* 45 (February): 153–56.

Sabino, Fernando. 1991. *Zélia, uma Paixão*. Rio de Janeiro: Record.

Sachs, Jeffrey. 1989. *Social Conflict and Populist Policies in Latin America*. Cambridge, MA: National Bureau of Economic Research.

Sadurski, Wojciech. 2023. A Pandemic of Populists. Webinar, University of Texas at Austin, Polish Club (1 April).

2022. *A Pandemic of Populists*. Cambridge: Cambridge University Press.

2019. *Poland's Constitutional Breakdown*. Oxford: Oxford University Press.

2018. How Democracy Dies (in Poland). *Revista Forumul Judecătorilor* 10:1 (First Semester): 104–78.

Saldin, Robert, and Steven Teles. 2020. *Never Trump: The Revolt of the Conservative Elites*. Oxford: Oxford University Press.

Sánchez-Sibony, Omar. 2021. Competitive Authoritarianism in Morales's Bolivia. *Latin American Politics and Society* 63:1 (February): 118–44.

2018. Competitive Authoritarianism in Ecuador under Correa. *Taiwan Journal of Democracy* 14:2 (December): 97–120.

2017. Classifying Ecuador's Regime Under Correa. *Journal of Politics in Latin America* 9:3 (December): 121–40.

Sánchez-Talanquer, Mariano, and Kenneth Greene. 2021. Is Mexico Falling into the Authoritarian Trap? *Journal of Democracy* 32:4 (October): 56–71.

Santander, Carlos. 2021. Pedro Castillo se aleja de los radicales. *Página Siete* (24 October).

Santoro, Daniel. 1994. *El hacedor: Una biografía política de Domingo Cavallo*. Buenos Aires: Planeta.

Sato, Yuko, and Moisés Arce. 2022. Resistance to Populism. *Democratization* 29:6 (August): 1137–56.

Savage, Ritchie. 2019. Populism in the U.S. In Carlos de la Torre, ed. *Routledge Handbook of Global Populism*, 402–15. London: Routledge.

Schady, Norbert. 2000. The Political Economy of Expenditures by the Peruvian Social Fund (FONCODES), 1991–1995. *American Political Science Review* 94:2 (June): 289–304.

Schamis, Hector. 2013. From the Peróns to the Kirchners. In Carlos de la Torre and Cynthia Arnson, eds. *Latin American Populism in the Twenty-First Century*, 145–78. Washington, DC: Woodrow Wilson Center Press.

Scheppele, Kim. 2022. How Viktor Orbán Wins. *Journal of Democracy* 33:3 (July): 45–61.

2018. Autocratic Legalism. *University of Chicago Law Review* 85:2 (March): 545–83.

Schmidt, Gregory. 1998. Presidential Usurpation or Congressional Preference? In John Carey and Matthew Shugart, eds. *Executive Decree Authority*, 104–41. Cambridge: Cambridge University Press.

1996. Fujimori's 1990 Upset Victory in Peru. *Comparative Politics* 28:3 (April): 321–54.

Schmitter, Philippe. 1983. Democratic Theory and Neocorporatist Practice. *Social Research* 50:4 (Winter): 885–928.

Schmitter, Philippe, and Terry Karl. 1991. What Democracy Is... and Is Not. *Journal of Democracy* 2:3 (July): 75–88.

Schneider, Ben. 1991. Brazil under Collor. *World Policy Journal* 8:2 (Spring): 321–47.

Serra, Gilles. 2018. The Electoral Strategies of a Populist Candidate: Does Charisma Discourage Experience and Encourage Extremism? *Journal of Theoretical Politics* 30:1 (January): 45–73.

Serrano Mancilla, Alfredo. 2021. *Evo: Operación Rescate*. Buenos Aires: Sudamericana.

Shin, Michael, and John Agnew. 2008. *Berlusconi's Italy*. Philadelphia, PA: Temple University Press.

Sides, John, Chris Tausanovitch, and Lynn Vavreck. 2022. *The Bitter End: The 2020 Presidential Campaign and the Challenge to American Democracy*. Princeton, NJ: Princeton University Press.

Sides, John, Michael Tesler, and Lynn Vavreck. 2018. *Identity Crisis: The 2016 Presidential Campaign and the Battle for the Meaning of America*. Princeton, NJ: Princeton University Press.

Signs of Less Trumpy Times: Voters' Allegiance. 2022. *Economist* (February 12): 22.

Siles, Ignacio, Erica Guevara, et al. 2023. Populism, Religion, and Social Media in Central America. *International Journal of Press/Politics* 28:1 (January): 138–59.

Silva, Cláudio Humberto Rosa e. 1993. *Mil Dias de Solidão: Collor Bateu e Levou*. São Paulo: Geração.

Silva-Herzog Márquez, Jesús. 2020. *La casa de la contradicción*. Mexico City: Taurus.

Sin maras y sin democracia. 2023. *El Faro* (3 February).

Skocpol, Theda, Caroline Tervo, and Kirsten Walters. 2022. Citizen Organizing and Party Polarization from the Tea Party to the Anti-Trump Resistance. In Robert Lieberman, Suzanne Mettler, and Kenneth Roberts, eds. *Democratic Resilience: Can the United States Withstand Rising Polarization?* 369–400. Cambridge: Cambridge University Press.

Skowronek, Stephen. 2020. *Presidential Leadership in Political Time*, 3rd ed., revised and expanded. Lawrence: University Press of Kansas.

Skowronek, Stephen, John A. Dearborn, and Desmond King. 2021. *Phantoms of a Beleaguered Republic: The Deep State and the Unitary Executive*. Oxford: Oxford University Press.

Skowronek, Stephen, and Karen Orren. 2020. The Adaptability Paradox: Constitutional Resilience and Principles of Good Government in Twenty-First Century America. *Perspectives on Politics* 18:2 (June): 354–69.

Slowakei: Ungewöhnlicher Rücktritt des Ministerpräsidenten. 2021. *Deutsche Welle* (March 29).

Smith, Jason. 2022. The Rhetoric and Reality of Infrastructure during the Trump Presidency. In Julian Zelizer, ed. *The Presidency of Donald J. Trump*, 162–80. Princeton, NJ: Princeton University Press.

Smith, Laura. 2021. Trump and Congress. *Policy Studies* 42: 5–6 (September): 528–43.

Smith, William. 1991. State, Market, and Neoliberalism in Post-Transition Argentina. *Journal of Interamerican Studies and World Affairs* 33:4 (Winter): 45–82.

Smolecová, Alexandra, and Daniel Šárovec. 2021. Heading Towards Collapse? Assessment of the Slovak Party System after the 2020 General Elections. *Slovak Journal of Political Sciences* 21:1 (January): 27–50.

Snyder, Timothy. 2017. *On Tyranny: Twenty Lessons from the Twentieth Century.* New York: Crown.

Somer, Murat. 2019. Turkey: The Slippery Slope from Reformist to Revolutionary Polarization and Democratic Breakdown. *Annals of the American Academy for Political and Social Science* 681 (January): 42–61.

Souroujon, Gastón, and Cecilia Lesgart. 2021. Populism: Uses, Abuses, and Travels of an Uncomfortable Concept. In Gisela Pereyra Doval and Gastón Souroujon, eds. *Global Resurgence of the Right*, 54–76. London: Routledge.

Spirova, Maria, and Radostina Sharenkova-Toshkova. 2021. Juggling Friends and Foes: Prime Minister Borissov's Surprise Survival in Bulgaria. *East European Politics* 37:3 (September): 432–47.

Staniszkis, Jadwiga. 1984. *Poland's Self-Limiting Revolution.* Princeton, NJ: Princeton University Press.

Stanley, Ben. 2020. A Comparison of Two Polish Party Leaders: Jarosław Kaczyński and Donald Tusk. In Sergiu Gherghina, ed. *Party Leaders in Eastern Europe*, 171–95. Cham: Palgrave Macmillan.

2017. Populism in Central and Eastern Europe. In Cristóbal Rovira Kaltwasser, Paul Taggart, et al., eds. *Oxford Handbook of Populism*, 140–60. Oxford: Oxford University Press.

2016. Confrontation by Default and Confrontation by Design: Strategic and Institutional Responses to Poland's Populist Coalition Government. *Democratization* 23:2 (March): 263–82.

Stanley, Ben, and Mikołaj Cześnik. 2019. Populism in Poland. In Daniel Stockemer, ed. *Populism around the World*, 67–87. Cham: Springer Nature Switzerland.

Stanley, Jason. 2018. *How Fascism Works.* New York: Random House.

Ştefan, Laurenţiu. 2021. Puppets of the President? Prime Ministers in Post-Communist Romania. *East European Politics* 37:3 (September): 481–95.

Stefanoni, Pablo, and Hervé do Alto. 2006. *Evo Morales, de la coca al Palacio.* La Paz: Malatesta.

Stelmach, Michał. 2021. Public Security Policy in El Salvador during the Presidency of Nayib Bukele (2017–2019). *Anuario Latinoamericano de Ciencias Políticas y Relaciones Internacionales* 12: 65–85.

Stokes, Susan. 2001. *Mandates and Democracy.* Cambridge: Cambridge University Press.

Sunstein, Cass. 2022. The Rule of Law vs. "Party Nature:" Presidential Elections, the U.S. Constitution, the Electoral Count Act of 1887, the Horror of January 6, and the Electoral Count Reform Act of 2022. *Boston University Law Review*, forthcoming.

Sunstein, Cass, ed. 2018. *Can It Happen Here? Authoritarianism in America.* New York: Dey St.

Svolik, Milan. 2019. Polarization versus Democracy. *Journal of Democracy* 30:3 (July): 20–32.

2015. Which Democracies Will Last? *British Journal of Political Science* 45(4): 715–38.

2012. *The Politics of Authoritarian Rule.* Cambridge: Cambridge University Press.

Sydorchuk, Oleksii. 2014. The Impact of Semi-Presidentialism on Democratic Consolidation in Poland and Ukraine. *Demokratizatsiya* 22:1(Winter): 117–44.

Szomolányi, Soňa. 2016. Slovakia's Elite. In Jan Pakulski, ed. *The Visegrad Countries in Crisis*, 67–86. Warsaw: Collegium Civitas.

Taggart, Paul, and Cristóbal Rovira Kaltwasser. 2016. Dealing with Populists in Government: Conclusions. *Democratization* 23:2 (June): 304–23.

Tamada, Yoshifumi. 2009. Democracy and Populism in Thailand. In Kosuke Mizuno and Pasuk Phongpaichit, eds., *Populism in Asia*, 94–111. Singapore: National University of Singapore Press.

Tanaka, Martín. 2011. Peru's 2011 Elections. *Journal of Democracy* 22:4 (October): 75–83.

Teehankee, Julio. 2022. The Philippines in 2021: Twilight of the Duterte Presidency. *Asian Survey* 62:1 (January–February): 126–36.

Teichman, Judith. 2001. *The Politics of Freeing Markets in Latin America*. Chapel Hill: University of North Carolina Press.

    1997. Mexico and Argentina: Economic Reform and Technocratic Decision Making. *Studies in Comparative International Development* 32:1 (Spring): 31–55.

Thaler, Richard. 1992. *The Winner's Curse: Paradoxes and Anomalies of Economic Life*. Princeton, NJ: Princeton University Press.

Theuns, Tom. 2022. The Need for an EU Expulsion Mechanism. *Res Publica*, forthcoming.

Thomas, George. 2016. Madison and the Perils of Populism. *National Review* 29 (Fall): 142–56.

Thompson, Mark. 2022. Duterte's Violent Populism. *Journal of Contemporary Asia* 52:3 (May): 403–28.

Tinted Glasses: Presidential Approval. 2019. *Economist* (May 25): 28.

Tismaneanu, Vladimir. 2013. Democracy on the Brink: A Coup Attempt Fails in Romania. *World Affairs* 175:5 (January): 83–87.

Tobar, Mónica. 2020. Gobernabilidad en tiempos de crisis: La relación entre el Ejecutivo y el Legislativo en la gestión del presidente Nayib Bukele en El Salvador. *Reflexión Política* 22:45 (August): 70–78.

Topcu, Elmas. 2022. Ekrem Imamoglu: Was steckt hinter dem Politikverbot für Istanbuls Bürgermeister? *Deutsche Welle* (15 December).

Torres y Torres Lara, Carlos. 1992. *Los nudos del poder*. Lima: Desarrollo y Paz.

Treerat, Nualnoi. 2009. Thaksin Shinawatra and Mass Media. In Kosuke Mizuno and Pasuk Phongpaichit, eds., *Populism in Asia*, 112–26. Singapore: National University of Singapore Press.

Treisman, Daniel. 2020. Democracy by Mistake. *American Political Science Review* 114:3 (August): 792–810.

Trejo, Guillermo, and Sandra Ley. 2020. *Votes, Drugs, and Violence: The Political Logic of Criminal Wars in Mexico*. Cambridge: Cambridge University Press.

Trende, Sean. 2021. Was Trump Worth It for Republicans? In Larry Sabato, Kyle Kondik, and Miles Coleman, eds. *A Return to Normalcy? The 2020 Elections that (Almost) Broke America*, 225–43. Lanham, MD: Rowman & Littlefield.

Tsai, Jung-Hsiang. 2019. Populism and Democratic Crisis in Semi-Presidential Countries. *Democratization* 26:8 (December): 1458–74.

Tsatsanis, Emmanouil, Eftichia Teperoglou, and Angelos Seriatos. 2020. Two-Partyism Reloaded: Polarisation, Negative Partisanship, and the Return of the Left-Right Divide in the Greek Elections of 2019. *South European Society and Politics* 25:3–4 (October): 503–32.

Tsebelis, George. 2022. Constitutional Rigidity Matters. *British Journal of Political Science* 52:1 (January): 280–99.

2002. *Veto Players: How Political Institutions Work*. Princeton, NJ: Princeton University Press.

1995. Decision Making in Political Systems. *British Journal of Political Science* 25:3 (July): 289–325.

Tulis, Jeffrey. 1987. *The Rhetorical Presidency*. Princeton, NJ: Princeton University Press.

Turan, İlter. 2015. *Turkey's Difficult Journey to Democracy*. Oxford: Oxford University Press.

Tworzecki, Hubert. 2019. Poland: A Case of Top-Down Polarization. *Annals of the American Academy for Political and Social Science* 681 (January): 97–119.

Urbinati, Nadia. 2019. *Me the People*. Cambridge, MA: Harvard University Press.

Uribe, Álvaro. 2012. *No Hay Causa Perdida: Memorias*. New York: Celebra.

2002. Manifiesto democrático del presidente de los colombianos Dr. Álvaro Uribe Vélez. Reprinted in María Osorio. 2012. *Primer mandato presidencial de Uribe Vélez*, 91–104. Quito: Universidad Andina Simón Bolívar.

Vachudova, Milada. 2005. *Europe Undivided: Democracy, Leverage, and Integration after Communism*. Oxford: Oxford University Press.

Van Cott, Donna. 2005. *From Movements to Parties in Latin America*. Cambridge: Cambridge University Press.

Van Gunten, Tod. 2015. Cohesion, Consensus, and Conflict: Technocratic Elites and Financial Crisis in Mexico and Argentina. *International Journal of Comparative Sociology* 56:5 (October): 366–90.

Van Til, Jon. 2015. Democratic Resurgence in Hungary. In Péter Krasztev and Jon Van Til, eds. *The Hungarian Patient*, 367–83. Budapest: Central European University Press.

Varshney, Ashutosh. 2022. India's Democratic Longevity and its Troubled Trajectory. In Scott Mainwaring and Tarek Masoud, eds. *Democracy in Hard Places*, 34–72. Oxford: Oxford University Press.

2019. The Emergence of Right-Wing Populism in India. In Niraja Gopal Jayal, ed. *Re-Forming India*, 327–45. New Delhi: Penguin India.

Velarde, Julio, and Martha Rodríguez. 1994. *El programa de estabilización peruano: Evaluación del período 1991–1993*. Documento de Trabajo no. 18. Lima: Centro de Investigación, Universidad del Pacífico (CIUP).

1992. *El programa económico de Agosto de 1990*. Documento de Trabajo no. 2. Lima: CIUP.

Vélez, Cristina, Juan Ossa, and Paula Montes. 2006. Y se hizo la reforma... In Gary Hoskin and Miguel García Sánchez, eds. *La reforma política de 2003*, 1–31. Bogotá: Universidad de los Andes and Fundación Konrad Adenauer.

Verbeek, Bertjan, and Andrej Zaslove. 2019. Has Populism Eroded the Quality of European Democracy? In Kurt Weyland and Raúl Madrid, eds. *When Democracy Trumps Populism*, 84–109. Cambridge: Cambridge University Press.

2016. Italy: A Case of Mutating Populism? *Democratization* 23:2 (June): 304–23.

Vergara, Alberto. 2013. Alternancia sin alternativa: "Un año de Humala o veinte años de un sistema" Chap. in *Ciudadanos sin República*, 233–54. Lima: Planeta.

2007. *Ni amnésicos ni irracionales: Las elecciones peruanas de 2006 en perspectiva histórica*. Lima: Solar.

Villacañas, José. 2017. *El lento aprendizaje de Podemos*. Madrid: Catarata.

Villagrán de León, Francisco. 1993. Thwarting the Guatemalan Coup. *Journal of Democracy* 4:4 (October): 117–24.

Villegas Aldas, Juan. 2010. *Lucio Gutiérrez entra la antipolítica y el neopopulismo*. M.A. thesis, FLACSO-Ecuador.

Vittori, Davide. 2018. Party Change in "Populist" Parties in Government: The Case of the Five Star Movement and SYRIZA. *Italian Political Science* 13:2 (October): 78–91.

Vivas, Fernando. 2022. Golpe a sí mismo: ¿Por qué Pedro Castillo intentó dissolver el Congreso sin tener un plan? *El Comercio* (Lima) (7 December).

Von Bülow, Marisa, and Rebecca Abers. 2022. Denialism and Populism: Two Sides of a Coin in Jair Bolsonaro's Brazil. *Government and Opposition*, forthcoming.

Waldmann, Peter. 1974. *Der Peronismus 1943–1955*. Hamburg: Hoffmann und Campe.

Waldner, David, and Ellen Lust. 2018. Unwelcome Change: Coming to Terms with Democratic Backsliding. *Annual Review of Political Science* 21: 93–113.

Wallach, Philip. 2022. We Can Now Quantify Trump's Sabotage of the GOP's House Dreams. *Washington Post* (15 November).

Walter, Aaron. 2017. The Good, Bad, and Ugly of Populism: A Comparative Analysis of the U.S. and Slovakia. *Slovak Journal of Political Sciences* 17:2 (July): 166–83.

Walter, Barbara. 2022. *How Civil Wars Start*. New York: Crown.

Webb, Adele, and Nicole Curato. 2019. Populism in the Philippines. In Daniel Stockemer, ed. *Populism around the World*, 49–65. Cham: Springer Nature Switzerland.

Weber, Max. 1976. *Wirtschaft und Gesellschaft*, 5th ed. Johannes Winckelmann. Tübingen: J.C.B. Mohr.

Weisman, Jonathan, and Reid Epstein. 2022. G.O.P. Declares Jan. 6 Attack "Legitimate Political Discourse." *New York Times* (4 February).

Welcome to Normal Politics: Italy's Populists. 2020. *Economist* (August 22): 43.

Wendling, Mike. 2022. Far-Right Groups had Racism Rift before Capitol Riot. *BBC News* (December 22).

Werz, Nikolaus. 2007. Hugo Chávez und der "Sozialismus des 21. Jahrhunderts." *Ibero-Analysen* 21 (December): 3–26.

Weyland, Kurt. 2022a. How Populism Dies: Political Weaknesses of Personalistic Plebiscitarian Leadership. *Political Science Quarterly* 137:1 (Spring): 9–42.

2022b. Why US Democracy Trumps Populism: Comparative Lessons Reconsidered. *PS: Political Science and Politics* 55:3 (July): 478–83.

2021a. *Assault on Democracy: Communism, Fascism, and Authoritarianism During the Interwar Years*. Cambridge: Cambridge University Press.

2021b. Populism as a Political Strategy: An Approach's Enduring – and Increasing – Advantages. *Political Studies* 69:2 (May): 185–89.

2020. Populism's Threat to Democracy. *Perspectives on Populism* 18:2 (June): 389–406.

2019. Populism and Authoritarianism. In Carlos de la Torre, ed. *Routledge Handbook of Global Populism*, 319–33. London: Routledge.

2017. Populism: A Political-Strategic Approach. In Cristóbal Rovira Kaltwasser, Paul Taggart, et al., eds. *Oxford Handbook of Populism*, 48–72. Oxford: Oxford University Press.

2013. Latin America's Authoritarian Drift: The Threat from the Populist Left. *Journal of Democracy* 24:3 (July): 18–32.

2009. The Rise of Latin America's Two Lefts: Insights from Rentier State Theory. *Comparative Politics* 41:2 (January): 145–64.

2002. *The Politics of Market Reform in Fragile Democracies: Argentina, Brazil, Peru, and Venezuela.* Princeton, NJ: Princeton University Press.

2001. Clarifying a Contested Concept: "Populism" in the Study of Latin American Politics. *Comparative Politics* 34:1 (October): 1–22.

2000. A Paradox of Success? Determinants of Political Support for President Fujimori. *International Studies Quarterly* 44:3 (September): 481–502.

1999. Neoliberal Populism in Latin America and Eastern Europe. *Comparative Politics* 31:4 (July): 379–401.

1996. Neo-Populism and Neo-Liberalism in Latin America: Unexpected Affinities. *Studies in Comparative International Development* 32:3 (Fall 1996): 3–31.

1993. The Rise and Fall of President Collor. *Journal of Interamerican Studies* 35:1 (Summer): 1–37.

Weyland, Kurt, and Raúl Madrid, eds. 2019. *When Democracy Trumps Populism: European and Latin American Lessons for the United States.* Cambridge: Cambridge University Press.

Weyland, Kurt, Raúl Madrid, and Wendy Hunter, eds. 2010. *Leftist Governments in Latin America: Successes and Shortcomings.* Cambridge: Cambridge University Press.

Whittington, Keith. 2018. The Bounded Independence of the American Courts. *New York University Law Review* 93: 70–74.

Wibbels, Erik. 2006. Dependency Revisited. *International Organization* 60:2 (Spring): 433–68.

Williams, Jack, and John Curiel. 2020. *Analysis of the Quick Count in the 2019 Bolivia Elections.* Commissioned by Center for Economic and Policy Research, Washington, DC.

Wills-Otero, Laura. 2014. Colombia: Analyzing the Strategies for Political Action of Álvaro Uribe's Government, 2002–10. In Juan Pablo Luna and Cristóbal Rovira Kaltwasser, eds. *The Resilience of the Latin American Right*, 194–215. Baltimore, MD: Johns Hopkins University Press.

Wilpert, Gregory. 2007. *Changing Venezuela by Taking Power: The History and Policies of the Chávez Government.* London: Verso.

Winer, Anthony. 2018. Action and Reaction: The Trump Executive Orders and their Reception by the Federal Courts. *Mitchell Hamline Law Review* 44:3 (October): 907–34.

Wlezien, Christopher. 2017. Policy (Mis) Representation and the Cost of Ruling. *Comparative Political Studies* 50:6 (May): 711–38.

Wlezien, Christopher, and Stuart Soroka. 2012. Political Institutions and the Opinion-Policy Link. *West European Politics* 35:6 (November): 1407–32.

Wolf, Sonja. 2021. A Populist President Tests El Salvador's Democracy. *Current History* 120: 823: 64–70.

Wolff, Jonas. 2020. The Turbulent End of an Era in Bolivia. *Revista de Ciencia Política* 40:2 (August): 163–86.

2018. Ecuador after Correa. *Revista de Ciencia Política* 38:2 (August): 281–302.

Woodward, Bob. 2020. *Rage.* New York: Simon & Schuster.

2018. *Fear: Trump in the White House.* New York: Simon & Schuster.

Woodward, Bob, and Robert Costa. 2021. *Peril.* New York: Simon & Schuster.

Wuthrich, Michael, and Melvyn Ingleby. 2020. The Pushback against Populism in Turkey. *Journal of Democracy* 31:2 (April 2020): 24–40.

Wylde, Christopher. 2016. Post-Neoliberal Developmental Regimes in Latin America: Argentina under Cristina Fernández de Kirchner. *New Political Economy* 21:3 (May): 322–41.

2011. State, Society, and Markets in Argentina: The Political Economy of *Neodesarrollismo* under Néstor Kirchner. *Bulletin of Latin American Research* 30:4 (October): 436–52.

Yavuz, Hakan. 2021. *Erdoğan: The Making of an Autocrat.* Edinburgh: Edinburgh University Press.

Yegen, Oya. 2017. Constitutional Changes under the AKP Government of Turkey. *Tijdschrift voor Constutioneel Recht* 70:1 (January): 70–84.

Zamir, Eyal. 2014. Loss Aversion: An Overview. Chap. in *Law, Psychology, and Morality: The Role of Loss Aversion,* 3–52. Oxford: Oxford University Press.

Zankina, Emilia. 2016. Theorizing the New Populism in Eastern Europe. *Czech Journal of Political Science* 23:2 (June): 182–99.

Zarnow, Leandra. 2022. "Send Her Back:" Trump's Feud with Feminists and Conservative Women's Triumph. In Julian Zelizer, ed. *The Presidency of Donald J. Trump,* 121–43. Princeton, NJ: Princeton University Press.

Zemmouche, Florent. 2021. Elecciones legislativas y muncipales en El Salvador. *Análisis Carolina* 8 (March): 1–15.

Zepeda-Millán, Chris, and Sophia Wallace. 2018. Mobilizing for Immigrant and Latino Rights under Trump. In David Meyer and Sidney Tarrow, eds. *The Resistance: The Dawn of the Anti-Trump Opposition Movement,* 90–108. Oxford: Oxford University Press.

Zifcak, Spencer. 1995. The Battle over Presidential Power in Slovakia. *East European Constitutional Review* 4:3 (Summer): 61–65.

Zuckert, Michael. 2019. Populism and Our Political Institutions. *National Review* 39 (Spring): 170–82.

Index

AKP. *See* Justice and Development Party
Alfonsín, Raúl, 84
Alianza Republicana Nacionalista (ARENA)
  (political party) (El Salvador), 109
AMLO. *See* López Obrador, Andrés Manuel
ARENA. *See* Alianza Republicana
  Nacionalista
Argentina. *See also* Fernández de Kirchner,
  Cristina; Kirchner, Néstor; Menem,
  Carlos; Perón, Juan
  abolishment of term limits in, 44, 150–51
  commodities boom in, 149–50
  hyperinflation in, 84–87
  institutional constraints in, 37
  institutional strength of, 149
  liberal pluralism in, 84–87
  Pacto de Olivos, 86
  Peronist Party, 84, 86–87
  windfall rents in, 148–51
    Fernández de Kirchner and, 148–51
    Kirchner and, 148–51
Asia, populism in, 247–59. *See also specific*
  people
  in India, 256–58
  in Northeast Asia, 248
  in the Philippines, 252–56
  in Southeast Asia, 248–49
  in Thailand, 249–51
Atatürk, Mustafa Kemal, 165
Austria, populism in, 2–3
authoritarianism, 33–35. *See also* competitive
  authoritarianism; self-coups
  of Bolsonaro, 105

in Eastern Europe, 185
in Hungary, 169
through institutional mechanisms, 86–87
institutional weaknesses as factor for, 53–58
in Latin America, 69
  competitive, 9–10
in Mexico, 154
personalism and, 33
personalistic plebiscitarian leadership and, 33
populist
  under Erdoğan, 164–68
  in Poland, 173
autocracy
  under Bukele, 113
  under Chávez, 119–20
  populism in, 177–83
  Trump and, 203, 232
autocratic legalism, 37
autocratic populism, in Slovakia, 177–83
availability heuristic, 259–60
aversion. *See* loss aversion

Babiš, Andrej, 10, 162, 185–89
Băsescu, Traian, 162, 185–89
  impeachment of, 187
  minority coalition government of, 187–88
  suspension from office, 187
Berlusconi, Silvio, 21, 41, 57, 69, 162–63,
    189–93, 231–32
  conjunctural opportunities for, 192–93
  Forza Italia Party, 191–92
  Orbán compared to, 192–93
  personalistic plebiscitarian leadership of, 190

Berlusconi, Silvio (cont.)
 political party fragmentation under, 41
 reelection of, 24
 serial populism of, 245
Biden, Joe, 215–16
Bolívar, Simón, 117
Bolivarian authoritarianism, 133–37
 Correa and, 133–35
 hydrocarbon booms and, 134
 Maduro and, 134
 Morales and, 135–37
 Moreno and, 135
Bolivarian populism, 9. *See also* Chávez,
  Hugo; Correa, Rafael; Morales, Evo
 analysis of, 157–58
 in Ecuador, 137–40
 Gutiérrez and, 137–40
 in Honduras, 140–43
 instability of institutional frameworks and, 45
 presidential systems and, 121–23
 under Zelaya, 140–43
Bolivia, 45. *See also* Morales, Evo
 constitutional reform in, 45–46
 hydrocarbon windfalls in, 59–60
 Movement toward Socialism Party, 130,
  131, 137
 strangulation of democracy in, 130–31
Bolsonaro, Jair, 2, 10, 36, 103–7
 authoritarianism of, 105
 COVID-19 pandemic and, 51, 77, 105–7
 cultural conservatism of, 102
 Duterte and, 255
 Guedes and, 103
 ideological marginality and, 11
 liberal pluralism and, 43
 loss of presidency for, 107
 neoliberal populism and, 103–7
 as "Tropical Trump," 77, 103, 106
Borisov, Boyko, 10, 21, 162, 185–89
 economic recession under, 186
 opposition challenges to, 188
 reelection of, 24
Bosnia, 160
Brazil, 10. *See also* Bolsonaro, Jair; Collor de
  Mello, Fernando
 COVID-19 pandemic in, 51, 77, 105–7
 democratic systems in, 97, 103–6
 hyperinflation in, 76, 94–95
 institutional constraints in, 36
 liberal pluralism in, 107
 public safety issues in, 104
 technocratic elite cohesion in, 95
Brexit, 243

Bucaram, Abdalá, 12, 76, 97–99, 132
 Cavallo and, 97–98
 economic adjustment plans, 98
 political downfall of, 97–99
 public protests against, 140
 removal from office, 123
Bukele, Nayib, 2, 10, 35, 36, 108–15
 autocratic powers of, 113
 competitive authoritarianism and, 10
 gang violence and, 112–14
 political crises for, 43
 political rise of, 109
 response to COVID-19 pandemic, 56,
  76–77, 108, 110–13
 as conjunctural opportunity, 114–15
Bulgaria, 10. *See also* Borisov, Boyko
 Great Recession in, 186
 personalistic plebiscitarian leadership in, 185
Bush, George W., 92

Calderón, Felipe, 52
Cárdenas, Lázaro, 154
Carter, Jimmy, 214
Castillo, Pedro, 10, 145–48, 244
 Chávez as political influence on, 147
 COVID-19 pandemic and, 146
 left-wing populism and, 145–48
Cavallo, Domingo, 84–85
 Bucaram and, 97–98
 hyperinflation and, 97–98
Central American Peace Accord (1987), 101
charisma
 personalistic plebiscitarian leadership and, 4
 in political-strategic approach to populism,
  21, 22
 of Trump, 216–17, 221
charismatic politicians. *See also specific people*
 follower outreach by, 34–35
 political polarization practiced by, 35
Chávez, Hugo, 2, 10, 22, 35, 117, 124–29,
  229, 245–46. *See also* Correa, Rafael;
  Morales, Evo; windfall rents
 autocratic goals of, 119–20
 as Bolivarian populist, 122–23
 Castillo influenced by, 147
 commodities boom under, 126
 competitive authoritarianism of, 124–29, 149
 coups and, 45
 defeat of recall referendum, 127
 economic crises as political opportunity
  for, 59
 hydrocarbon windfalls and, 59, 126–29
 government-control of, 128–29

illiberal project of, 128, 129
liberal democracy under, 124–27
media use by, 34
Peronism as influence on, 163
public demonstrations against, 126
purges under, 238
rejection of neoliberalism, 124
socialism for, 212
socioeconomic transformation under,
125–26
classical crisis argument, 50
Collor de Mello, Fernando, 76, 94–97
confrontation with power centers, 95
hyperinflation under, 94–95
impeachment of, 121–22
political coalitions for, 95–96
political downfall of, 94–97
Colombia, 44. *See also* Uribe, Álvaro
guerrilla insurgencies in, 87–92
institutional framework for, 91–92
liberal pluralism in, 87–92
Plan Colombia, 89, 91–92
presidential democracy in, 83–87
Colorado Party (Paraguay), 145
commodities boom, 58–60. *See also*
hydrocarbon windfalls
in Argentina, 149–50
under Chávez, 126
democracy influenced by, 121
under Gutiérrez, 137–40
in Mexico, 155–56
oil windfalls, 137–40
competitive authoritarianism
analysis of, 157–58
Bukele and, 10
Chávez and, 124–29, 149
Fujimori, A., and, 9–10, 15
hydrocarbon windfalls and, 129–33
in Latin America, 9–10
conjunctural opportunities, populism and,
233–36
aversion of catastrophic loss, 31
for Berlusconi, 192–93
conceptual approach to, 30–33
in Eastern Europe, 186
economic benefits of, 31–32
for López Obrador, 154–55
methodological approach to, 7–9
objectivist approaches to, 32
conservatism, cultural, in populist
movements, 2
Constitution, US, 205–6
constitutional reform

in Bolivia, 45–46
as transformation of frameworks and rules,
38–39
constitutions. *See also* constitutional reform
US Constitution, 205–6
in Venezuela, 45–46
Correa, Rafael, 10, 35, 99, 117, 132–35, 229
Bolivarian authoritarianism and, 133–35
hydrocarbon windfalls and, 59–60
lack of command of military, 134–35
liberal pluralism suffocated by, 118–19
political context for, 45
presidential decrees by, 133
strangulation of democracy under, 132–33
coups
civil-military, 45, 132
in Honduras, 251
by military, 45
in Venezuela, 45
COVID-19 pandemic
Bolsonaro's response to, 51, 77, 105–7
Bukele's response to, 56, 76–77, 108, 110–13
as conjunctural opportunity, 114–15
Castillo and, 146
as exogenous opportunity for populist
politicians, 51–52
in Slovakia, 184
Trump and, 210, 213, 215–16
cultural approach, to populism, 17–18
cultural conservative populism, 102
Czech Republic, 10. *See also* Babiš, Andrej
personalistic plebiscitarian leadership in, 185
Czechoslovakia. *See also* Czech Republic;
Slovakia
dissolution of, 177–78

decrees. *See* presidential decrees
democracies, advanced. *See also* United States
conjunctural solidity of, 66–70
consolidated, 70
institutional strength of, 66–70
public security threats and, 69
in parliamentary systems, 67–69
resilience against exogenous shocks, 69–70
democracy. *See also specific topics*
as anti-personalistic, 33–34
in Bolivia, 130–31
in Brazil, 97, 103–6
competitiveness in, 15–16
composition of, 13–14
definition of, 13–14
in Ecuador, 119
strangulation of democracy, 132–33

democracy (cont.)
in El Salvador, 113
global commodities boom as influence on, 121
instability of, 8
institutional approach to, 13–16
  popular sovereignty in, 13–15
majoritarian, 40
in Mexico, 153–54
personalistic plebiscitarian leadership and,
  15, 70–71
in Poland, 172–77
populism's threat to, 3–7, 60–66
  conditions for, 63–64
  institutional conditions, 7–9
  limits on, 259–60
  methodological organization of, 26–29
  research design for, 24–26
  severity of, 5–7
  unintended consequences of, 70–72
presidential, 83–87
procedural approach to, 13–16
  liberal safeguards in, 13–15
resilience of, 30–31
in Slovakia, 183–85
termination of, 15–16
third wave of, 44
in Venezuela, 124–27
democratic elections. *See* electoral rules;
  electoral systems
democratic neutralism, 1
Democratic Party (USA), 223–24
demonstrations and protests
  against Bucaram, 140
  against Chávez, 126
diffusion, 176
  of liberal principles, 43
  mechanisms of, 243
diffusion effects, 240–43
Duterte, Rodrigo, 21, 104, 253–56
  Bolsonaro and, 255

Eastern Europe. *See also* right-wing populism;
  specific countries
authoritarianism in, 185
conjunctural opportunities for populists in, 186
fragmented party systems in, 186–87
Great Recession in, 186
illiberal democracies in, 185–89
illiberal projects in, 189
institutional weakness in, 72–73
liberal pluralism in, 189
personalistic plebiscitarian leadership in, 185
populism in, 185–89

Ecuador, 15. *See also* Bucaram, Abdalá;
  Correa, Rafael; Gutiérrez, Lucio
Bolivarian populism in, 137–40
Bucaram in, 12, 76
civil-military coups in, 45, 132
democracy in, 119
  strangulation of, 132–33
economic crises in, 139
fragmented party system in, 138, 139
hydrocarbon windfalls in, 59–60
hyperinflation in, 76, 97–98
political instability in, 138
presidential instability in, 123
El Salvador, 36, 108–15. *See also* Bukele,
  Nayib
Alianza Republicana Nacionalista (political
  party), 109
democracy rating for, 113
Frente Farabundo Martí para la Liberación
  Nacional (political party), 109
institutional framework in, 108, 113
elections. *See* electoral systems; *specific people*
electoral competition theory, 198–99
Electoral Count Reform Act, US (2022), 223
electoral rules, as institutional constraint, 37
electoral systems, democratic, under
  Fujimori, A., 80
Erbakan, Necmettin, 165
Erdoğan, Recep Tayyip, 9, 21, 35, 161, 164–68
  economic crisis as exogenous opportunity
    for, 164–65
  liberal pluralism and, 165–66, 168
  parliamentary system under, 40
  personalistic leadership of, 165
  political hegemony of, 167
  populist authoritarianism under, 164–68
  strangulation of democracy, 168
Estrada, Joseph, 12, 252–53
ethno-nationalist populism, 256–58
European Union (EU). *See also* Eastern
  Europe; right-wing populism; *specific
  countries*
hydrocarbon windfalls in, 160
integration of Eastern Europe into, 195
left-wing populism in, 163–64
personalistic plebiscitarian leadership in, 2–3
populist movements in, 2–3
public security crises in, 160
response to Kaczyński, 176
strangulation of democracy in, 227–30
exogenous opportunities, for populist
  politicians, 48–60
  loss aversion and, 49–58

political instability and, 58–60
  commodities booms and, 58–60
  hydrocarbon windfalls and, 59–60
  societal crisis as, 49–58
    classical crisis argument, 50
    COVID-19 pandemic, 51–52
    hyperinflation, 51
    institutional weaknesses and, 53–58
    in parliamentary systems, 57–58
    with presidential systems, 55–56
    public security issues, 52

Farage, Nigel, 21
fascism, 5. *See also* authoritarianism
  paleo-fascism, 1
federalism, 204
Fernández de Kirchner, Cristina, 6, 20, 37, 44,
    119, 149–51
  abolishment of term limits and, 150–51
  hydrocarbon windfalls and, 148
  limited electoral mandate for, 150
Fico, Robert, 162, 183–84, 245
Five Star Movement, in Italy, 193
Flynn, Michael, 220
FMLN. *See* Frente Farabundo Martí para la
    Liberación Nacional
Fortuyn, Pim, 21
Forza Italia Party (Italy), 191–92
France, populism in, 2–3
Frente Farabundo Martí para la Liberación
    Nacional (FMLN) (El Salvador), 109
Fujimori, Alberto, 2, 15, 35, 36, 77–83
  competitive authoritarianism and, 9–10, 15
  democratic elections under, 80
  destruction of democracy under, 77–83
  economic market reforms under, 79
  guerrilla insurgency under, 78, 79
  hyperinflation under, 78
  as neoliberal populist, 75
  paradox of success for, 80
  political crises for, 43
  resignation of, 82
  self-coup of, 48, 77–78
  social programs under, 81
  societal crisis as opportunity for, 55
Fujimori, Keiko, 146
Fundación Mediterránea, 84–85

Gandhi, Rahul, 258
gang violence, Bukele and, 112–14
García, Alan, 144, 244
general will. *See volonté générale*
Graham, Lindsey, 213

Great Recession, in Eastern Europe, 186
Greece, left-wing populism in, 163–64
Grillo, Beppe, 245
Guatemala, 76. *See also* Serrano, Jorge
  Central American Peace Accord and, 101
  guerrilla insurgencies in, 101
  hyperinflation in, 101
  self-coups in, 99–102
Guedes, Paulo, 103
guerrilla insurgencies
  in Colombia, 87–92
  under Fujimori, A., 78, 79
  in Guatemala, 101
  Uribe's response to, 87–92
    through tax policies, 88–89
Gutiérrez, Lucio, 59, 118, 132, 137–40
  Bolivarian populism and, 137–40
  economic crises under, 139
  loss of political support, 139
  before oil windfalls, 137–40
  removal from office, 123

Haider, Jörg, 21
HDP. *See* People's Democratic Party
Honduras, 120
  Bolivarian populism in, 140–43
  coups in, 251
  institutional weaknesses in, 142
How Democracies Die (Levitsky and
    Ziblatt), 5
Humala, Ollanta, 144–45, 244–46
human rights norms, in the Philippines, 255
Hungary. *See also* Orbán, Viktor
  authoritarianism in, 169
  democracy in
    majoritarian, 40
    suppression of, 169–72
  global recession in, 161
  institutional flexibility in, 170–71
  parliamentary system in, 170
  populism in, 2–3
hydrocarbon windfalls
  in Argentina, 148
  Bolivarian authoritarianism and, 134
  Chávez and, 59, 126–29
    government control of, 128–29
  EU subsidies for, 60
  in Europe, 160
  as exogenous opportunity for populist
    politicians, 59–60
  in Bolivia, 59–60, 130–31
  in Ecuador, 59–60
  in Venezuela, 59, 126, 128–29

hydrocarbon windfalls (cont.)
  Morales and, 59–60, 130–31
  in Paraguay, 145
  in presidential systems, 61–62
  serial populism and, 246
hyperinflation
  adjustment programs for, 75
  in Argentina, 84–87
  in Brazil, 76, 94–95
  in Ecuador, 76, 97–98
  as exogenous opportunity for populist
    politicians, 51
  under Fujimori, A., 78
  in Guatemala, 101
  Menem and, 55–56, 75–76, 85

ideational approach, to populism, 17–18,
    20, 237
ideological marginality, 11
Iglesias, Pablo, 238
illiberal democracies, in Eastern Europe, 185–89
illiberal projects
  in Eastern Europe, 189
  of Trump, 203
  in Venezuela, 128, 129
India, populism in, 256–58
  personalistic plebiscitarian leadership in, 258
instability, political-institutional
  in Ecuador, 123, 138
  exogenous opportunities for populist
    politicians and, 58–60
  commodities boom and, 58–60
  hydrocarbon windfalls and, 59–60
  in Peru, 147
  of presidential systems, 61
  in Venezuela, 124–25, 127–28
instability of institutional frameworks, 44–47,
    233–36
  Bolivarian populists and, 45
institutional change, openness to
  analysis of, 47–48
  instability of institutional frameworks, 44–47
    Bolivarian populists and, 45
  paralegal imposition of, 42–44
    on presidential systems, 43–44
    rule of law traditions and, 42
  in parliamentary systems, 39–42
    political party fragmentation in, 41
    separation of powers in, 40
    stability of, 47–48
    veto players, 39–42
    Westminster model of, 39
  weak presidential systems and, 42–44

institutional constraints, populism and,
    233–36
  in Argentina, 37
  autocratic legalism and, 37
  in Brazil, 36
  conceptual approach to, 30–33
  in El Salvador, 36
  electoral rules as, 37
  Menem and, 44
  in Peru, 36
  political party strength, 36
  populist agency compared to, 36–39
  transformation of constitutional
    frameworks and rules, 38–39
  in US, 36
Institutional Revolutionary Party (PRI)
    (Mexico), 152
international terrorism, 208
interventionism, 62
Italy. *See also* Berlusconi, Silvio
  Five Star Movement in, 193
  Forza Italia Party, 191–92
  Northern League in, 191, 193
  personalistic plebiscitarian leadership in,
    190, 193
  populism in, 2–3
  serial populism in, 245

Janša, Janez, 10, 162, 185–89
  autocratic tendencies of, 188
  Orbán as influence on, 188
  reelection of, 24
  Trump as influence on, 188
Japan, 21, 248
Johnson, Boris, 192
Justice and Development Party (AKP)
    (Turkey), 165

Kaczyński, Jarosław, 21–22, 161–62
  EU response to, 176
  Law and Justice Party and, 172–77
    suppression of democracy by, 176–77
    propagation of conspiracy theories by, 172
Kirchner, Néstor, 20, 119, 148–50
  hydrocarbon windfalls and, 148
Koizumi, Junichiro, 21, 248
Kuczynski, Pedro Pablo, 146
Kushner, Jared, 214–15

Laclau, Ernesto, 19
Lasso, Guillermo, 102
Latin America. *See also specific countries;
    specific people; specific topics*

authoritarianism in, 69
competitive, 9–10
Central American Peace Accord, 101
institutional weakness in, 72–73
left-wing populism in, 2, 102
neoliberal populism in, 74–77, 102
Organization of American States and, 136–37
personalistic plebiscitarian leadership in, 1, 2
"pink tide" in, 117
populist movements in, 2, 9–10
Bolivarian populism, 9
competitive authoritarianism and, 9–10
democratic instability and, 10
failure of, 93–102
presidential systems in, 44–45
right-wing populism in, 74–77, 102–15, 157–58
strangulation of democracy in, 227–30
termination of democracy in, 15–16
third wave of democracy in, 44, 100
Law and Justice Party (PiS) (Poland), 161–62, 172–77
Le Pen, Jean Marie, 21, 235
Le Pen, Marine, 21, 235, 243
leadership, leaders and. *See also* personalistic plebiscitarian leadership
personalistic, 4
left-wing populism. *See also* Bolivarian populism
conceptual approach to, 117–23
in Europe, 163–64
in Latin America, 2, 102
conceptual approach to, 117–23
in Peru, 145–48
as "pink tide," 117
Levitsky, Steve, 5
liberal democracy. *See* democracy
liberal pluralism, 13. *See also* democracy
in Argentina, 84–87
Bolsonaro and, 43
in Colombia, 87–92
Correa and, 118–19
in Eastern Europe, 189
Morales and, 131
in Poland, 161–62, 174, 175
populism and, 5
resilience of, 227–28, 230–33
Trump and, 12, 196–201
in USA, 222
liberalism. *See also specific topics*
diffusion of, 43
institutional limitations under, 14
in Slovakia, 178

López Obrador, Andrés Manuel (AMLO), 10, 110, 120–21, 151–56, 242, 254–55
conjunctural opportunities for, 154–55
Movement of National Regeneration and, 152–53
Party of the Democratic Revolution and, 152
strangulation of democracy under, 153–54
loss aversion, 49–58
low style populism, 17
Lugo, Fernando, 20, 145

Macri, Mauricio, 102
Macron, Emmanuel, 243
Maduro, Nicolás, 22, 134, 238
Bolivarian authoritarianism and, 134
Magyars. *See* Hungary
majoritarian democracy, in Hungary, 40
Orbán's abuse of, 172, 172
Marcos, Ferdinand, 254
MAS. *See* Movement toward Socialism Party
Matovič, Igor, 10, 184, 245
Mečiar, Vladimír, 21, 41, 162, 177–83, 244–45
adjustment programs of, 179
as autocratic populist, 177–83
charisma of, 180
economic crisis in Slovakia and, 57
para-legal abuses of power by, 180
public opposition to, 181
reelection of, 24
media, use of, 34
Menem, Carlos, 20, 36, 37, 84–87, 149
authoritarianism through institutional mechanisms, 86–87
constitutional constraints for, 44
economic reforms under, 84
hyperinflation and, 55–56, 75–76, 85
as neoliberal populist, 149–50
presidential democracy under, 83–87
public approval ratings for, 85–86
Mexican Revolution, 154
Mexico. *See also* López Obrador, Andrés Manuel
authoritarian rule in, 154
commodities boom in, 155–56
constitution in, 151
institutional constraints in, 151–56
Institutional Revolutionary Party, 152
institutional strength in, 120–21, 154–55
Movement of National Regeneration Party and, 152–53
Party of the Democratic Revolution, 152
populism in, 151–56
Milei, Javier, 102

military, coups by, 45
military repression, 87–88, 123
modernization theory, for liberal
    institutions, 198
Modi, Narendra, 21, 256–58
    historical perspective on, 258
    Orbán compared to, 257
    personalistic plebiscitarian leadership of, 258
Moldova, 160
Moraes, Alexandre de, 43
Morales, Evo, 2, 10, 18, 22, 35, 117, 229
    Bolivarian authoritarianism and, 135–37
    electoral rejection of, 24
    hydrocarbon windfalls and, 59–60, 130–31
    liberal pluralism and, 131
    Movement toward Socialism Party and,
        130, 131
    opposition to, 131
    political context for, 45
    resignation from office, 137
    strangulation of democracy under, 130–31
MORENA. *See* Movement of National
    Regeneration Party
Moreno, Lenín, 119, 135
    Bolivarian authoritarianism and, 135
Movement of National Regeneration Party
    (MORENA) (Mexico), 152–53
Movement toward Socialism Party (MAS)
    (Bolivia), 130, 131, 137

NATO. *See* North Atlantic Treaty
    Organization
Nelson, Michael, 210
neoliberal populism, 2. *See also specific people*
    Bolsonaro and, 103–7
    comparative case studies for, 115–16
    in Latin America, 74–77, 102
        Fujimori, A., and, 75
        Menem and, 149–50
neoliberalism, 62
    Chávez rejection of, 124
neutralism. *See* democratic neutralism
North Atlantic Treaty Organization (NATO),
    181–82

OAS. *See* Organization of American States
objectivism, populism and, 32
Orbán, Viktor, 9, 21–22, 35, 161, 169–72
    Berlusconi compared to, 192–93
    economic crises as exogenous opportunity
        for, 57, 170
    Janša influenced by, 188
    majoritarian mechanisms abused by, 172

Modi compared to, 257
    parliamentary systems under, 40
        changeability of, 171–72
    suppression of democracy by, 169–72
    Trump and, 205–6
    windfall rents and, 170
Organization of American States (OAS),
    136–37
Ortega, Daniel, 22

Pacto de Olivos (Argentina), 86
paleo-fascism, populist movements and, 1
Paraguay, 145. *See also* Lugo, Fernando
parliamentary systems
    economic crises and, 61–62
    under Erdoğan, 40
    exogenous opportunities for populist
        politicians in, 57–58
    in Hungary, 170
        under Orbán, 40, 171–72
    institutional change in, 39–42
        political party fragmentation in, 41
        political stability of parliamentary
            systems, 47–48
        separation of powers and, 40
        veto players and, 39–42
        Westminster model of, 39
    presidential systems compared to, 229
    stability of, 47–48
Party of the Democratic Revolution (PRD)
    (Mexico), 152
Pastrana, Andrés, 88
Peña Nieto, Enrique, 152–53
People's Democratic Party (HDP)
    (Turkey), 167
Pérez, Carlos Andrés, 122
performative approach, to populism, 17–18
Perón, Juan Domingo, 2, 84
Peronist Party (Argentina), 84, 86–87.
    See also Fernández de Kirchner,
    Cristina; Kirchner, Néstor
Perot, Ross, 212–13
personalism
    of Fujimori, 244
    performative, 33–34
    political, 4, 20–22
    of Trump, 216
personalistic leaders, 4. *See also* personalistic
    plebiscitarian leadership
    Erdoğan, 165
    political-strategic approach to populism
        and, 20–21
    Uribe and, 90

personalistic plebiscitarian leadership, 1, 4,
11–13. *See also* charismatic politicians;
populism; *specific people*
authoritarianism and, 33
in Bulgaria, 185
charisma and, 4
in Czech Republic, 185
democracy and, 15, 70–71
in Eastern Europe, 185
in Europe, 2–3
in India, 258
in Italy, 190, 193
in Latin America, 2, 1
in Peru, 82, 83
plebiscitarianism and, 4–5
in Romania, 185
in Slovenia, 185
in USA, 208, 209, 243
weaknesses of, 11
Peru, 10, 15. *See also* Castillo, Pedro;
Fujimori, Alberto; Humala, Ollanta
dual crises in, 55–56, 77–83
institutional constraints in, 36
institutional resilience in, 78, 79
left-wing populism in, 145–48
neoliberal populism in, 75
personalistic plebiscitarian leadership in,
82, 83
political instability in, 147
populism
left-wing, 145–48
neoliberal, 75
populism in, serial, 244
Shining Path leadership in, 79, 81, 104
windfall rents in, 143–48
Castillo and, 145–48
Humala and, 144–45
primary exports and, 143–44
the Philippines, populism in, 252–56
human rights norms in, 255
punitive populism, 253–56
Piłsudski, Józef, 22
Plan Colombia, 89, 91–92
plebiscitarianism, 4–5, 34
pluralism. *See also* liberal pluralism
in Brazil, 107
Poland. *See also* Kaczyński, Jarosław
institutional structure in, 173
semi-presidential system in, 173–74
Law and Justice Party in, 161–62, 172–77
suppression of democracy by, 176–77
liberal democracy in, 172–77
liberal pluralism in, 161–62, 174, 175

populism in, 2–3
populist authoritarianism in, 173
Solidarity Movement in, 178
political parties
Alianza Republicana Nacionalista, 109
Colorado Party, 145
Democratic Party, 223–24
Forza Italia Party, 191–92
fragmentation of
under Berlusconi, 41
in Eastern Europe, 186–87
in Ecuador, 138, 139
in US, 222
Frente Farabundo Martí para la Liberación
Nacional, 109
Institutional Revolutionary Party, 152
Justice and Development Party, 165
Law and Justice Party, 161–62, 172–77
Movement of National Regeneration Party,
152–53
Movement toward Socialism Party, 130, 131
Party of the Democratic Revolution, 152
People's Democratic Party, 167
Peronist Party, 84
Republican Party, 220–22
strength of, 36
political personalism, 4, 20–22
political-strategic approach, to populism,
20–24
analytical value of, 236–39
charisma in, 21, 22
definition of, 4, 7–8, 16–24
personalistic leaders and, 20–21
Weber's influence on, 22
politics of disjunction, in US, 197
populism. *See also* Bolivarian populism;
exogenous opportunities; left-wing
populism; political-strategic approach;
populist movements; right-wing
populism; *specific topics*
agency of, 11–13
in Austria, 2–3
autocratic, 177–83
cultural conservative, 102
definition of
cultural approaches in, 17–18
ideational, 17–18, 20, 237
performative approaches in, 17–18
democracy threatened by, 3–7, 60–66
conditions for, 63–64
institutional conditions, 7–9
limits on, 259–60
methodological organization of, 26–29

populism (cont.)
   research design for, 24–26
   severity of, 5–7
   unintended consequences of, 70–72
  in Eastern Europe, 185–89
  ethno-nationalist, 256–58
  in France, 2–3
  global scope of, 1
  Laclau on, 19
  left-wing, 2, 102
   conceptual approach to, 117–23
   in Peru, 145–48
   as "pink tide," 117
  liberal pluralism and, 5
  low style, 17
  methodological approach to, 7–13
   conjunctural factors in, 7–9
  in Mexico, 151–56
  neoliberal, 2
   in Latin America, 74–77, 102
  in Peru
   left-wing populism, 145–48
   neoliberal populism, 75
   serial populism, 244
  in Poland, 2–3
  punitive, 253–56
  serial, 240, 244–46
   hydrocarbon booms and, 246
   in Italy, 245
   in Peru, 244
   in Slovakia, 244–45
  volonté générale, 18, 122
populist authoritarianism
  under Erdoğan, 164–68
  in Poland, 173
populist governments, 65. *See also* exogenous
   opportunities
  press freedom under, 6
populist movements. *See also specific topics*
  cultural conservatism in, 2
  in Europe, 2–3
  in Latin America, 2, 9–10
   Bolivarian populism, 9
   competitive authoritarianism and, 9–10
   democratic instability and, 10
   failure of, 93–102
  paleo-fascism and, 1
PRD. *See* Party of the Democratic Revolution
presidential decrees
  by Correa, 133
  by Serrano, 100
presidential democracy, in Argentina, 83–87
presidential systems

  Bolivarian populists and, 121–23
  dual crises in, 55–56
  economic crises in, 61–62
  exogenous opportunities for populist
   politicians and, 55–56
  hydrocarbon windfalls in, 61–62
  instability of, 61, 121–23
  institutional change and, 43–44
  in Latin America, 44–45
  parliamentary systems compared to, 229
  perils of, 47
  security crises in, 61–62
  weak, 42–44
press, freedom of, under populist
  governments, 6
PRI. *See* Institutional Revolutionary Party
protectionism, 62
protests. *See* demonstrations and protests
public protests. *See* demonstrations and
  protests
public safety issues, in Brazil, 104
public security
  in advanced democracies, 69
  as exogenous opportunity for populist
   politicians, 52
  presidential systems and, 61–62
  under Uribe, 87–88
punitive populism, 253–56
Putin, Vladimir, 69

Ragin, Charles, 229
Reagan, Ronald, 197
regimes, political, 197. *See also* parliamentary
  systems; presidential systems; *specific*
  topics
repression, 79, 80
  military, 87–88, 123
  in Venezuela, 126, 134
Republican Party (USA), 220–22
revolution. *See* demonstrations and protests
right-wing populism. *See also* Erdoğan, Recep
  Tayyip; Orbán, Viktor; *specific people*
  conceptual approach to, 159–63
  in Latin America, 74–77, 102–115,
   157–58
  parliamentary systems and, 159–61
  changeability of, 160
Roh Moo-hyun, 248
Romania. *See also* Băsescu, Traian
  Great Recession in, 186
  personalistic plebiscitarian leadership in, 185
  semi-presidential system in, 187
Rousseau, Jean-Jacques, 18

Rousseff, Dilma, 102
  impeachment of, 104
rule of law traditions, institutional change
  and, 42

Salvini, Matteo, 21, 245
Saxe-Coburg-Gotha, Simeon Borisov, 182
self-coups
  Fujimori, A., and, 48, 77–78
  Serrano and, 99–102
  Zelaya and, compared, 141
semi-presidential systems
  in Poland, 173–74
  in Romania, 187
  in Slovakia, 178
serial populism, 240, 244–46
  hydrocarbon booms and, 246
  in Italy, 245
  in Peru, 244
  in Slovakia, 244–45
Serrano, Jorge, 76, 99–102, 176
  government by decree under, 100
  hyperinflation under, 101
  messianic tendencies of, 100
  political influences on, 100
  self-coup attempt by, 99–102
  Zelaya and, 141
Serrano Mancilla, Alfredo, 137
Shining Path leadership, in Peru, 79, 81, 104
Slovakia (Slovak Republic), 10, 41. *See also*
    Mečiar, Vladimír
  autocratic populism in, 177–83
  collapse of communist development model
    in, 182
  COVID-19 pandemic in, 184
  democracy in, 183–85
  economic crises in, 57, 162
  inclusion in EU for, 181–82
  liberal pluralism in, 183–85
  NATO membership for, 181–82
  presidential elections in, 178
  rise of liberalism in, 178
Slovenia, 10
  personalistic plebiscitarian leadership in, 185
social protests. *See* demonstrations and
    protests
socialism, for Chávez, 212
Solidarity Movement, in Poland, 178
South Korea, 248

technocratic elite cohesion, in Brazil, 95
terrorism. *See* international terrorism
Thailand, populism in, 249–51

Thaksin Shinawatra, 21, 249–51
third wave of democracy, 44, 100
Toledo, Alejandro, 20, 244
traditionalist populism, conceptual approach
    to, 159–63
Trump, Donald, 5, 10, 36, 69, 227, 231–32
  autocratic tendencies of, 203, 232
  Bolsonaro compared to, 77, 103, 106
  COVID-19 pandemic and, 210, 213,
    215–16
  Democratic Party mobilized by, 223–24
  election denialism of, 222
  global counterparts for, 217
  illiberal projects of, 203
  impeachments of, 202
  Janša influenced by, 188
  liberal pluralism and, 12
    political challenges to, 196–201
  media use by, 34
  opposition to, 198
  Orbán and, 205–6
  personalistic plebiscitarian leadership of,
    209, 243
  political agency of, 212–17
    personal charisma as element in,
    216–17, 221
  political-regime issue and, 197
  as populist candidate, 3
    lack of conjunctural opportunities,
    209–12, 216
    limitations of, 209–12
  Republican Party and
    damage to democracy supported by,
    220–22
    opposition to Trump within, 221
  US democracy damaged by, 217–24
    attacks against electoral systems, 219
    degradation of political norms, 217–18
    Republican Party support of, 220–22
    within US liberal institutional framework,
    197–201
Tsipras, Alexis, 163–64
Turkey. *See also* Erdoğan, Recep Tayyip
  economic crises in, 57, 164–65
  Justice and Development Party, 165
  People's Democratic Party, 167
  populist authoritarianism in, 164–68
tyranny, 5

United States (USA). *See also* Trump, Donald;
    specific topics
  challenges to liberal pluralism in, 222
  economic stability of, 207–8

United States (USA) (cont.)
  Electoral Count Reform Act, 223
  institutional constraints in, 36
  institutional strength of democracy in,
      199–207
    constitution as backbone for, 205–6
    federalism and, 204
    judiciary branch and, 203, 204
    political partisanship and, 202–3
    separation of powers framework and, 204
  international terrorism and, 208
  liberal institutional framework, 197–201,
      225–26
    electoral competition theory and, 198–99
    modernization theory for, 198
  personalistic plebiscitarian leadership in,
      208, 209
  Plan Colombia, 89, 91–92
  political party fragmentation in, 222
  politics of disjunction in, 197
Uribe, Álvaro, 20, 44, 55–56, 83–84, 87–92
  centralization of executive power under,
      75–76
  as personalistic leader, 90
  Plan Colombia, 89, 91–92
  political turn to populism, 87–88
  popularity of, 91
  response to guerrilla insurgencies, 87–92
    through tax policies, 88–89
  security crises under, 87–88
USA. *See* United States

Vargas, Getúlio, 2
Venezuela, 71. *See also* Chávez, Hugo
  constitutions in, 45–46

coups in, 45
democratic instability in, 124–25, 127–28
hydrocarbon windfalls in, 59
  government control of, 128–29
  illiberal projects in, 128, 129
  repression in, 126, 134
  transformation of socioeconomic structures
      in, 125–26
Vizcarra, Martín, 146
volonté générale (general will), 18, 122

Wałęsa, Lech, 178–79
Weber, Max, 22, 33–34
  classical crisis argument, 50
Wilders, Geert, 21
windfall rents, weak populism with, 143–51
  in Argentina, 148–51
    Fernández de Kirchner and, 148–51
    Kirchner and, 148–51
    Orbán and, 170
  in Peru, 143–48
    Castillo and, 145–48
    Humala and, 144–45
    primary exports and, 143–44
windfalls. *See* hydrocarbon windfalls

Yingluck Shinawatra, 251
Yugoslavia, 160

Zelaya, Manuel, 120
  Bolivarian populism and, 140–43
  lack of political support for, 142–43
  self-perpetuation attempt by, 141
  Serrano and, 141
Ziblatt, Daniel, 5